SOURCES OF JAPANESE TRADITION

VOLUME II

INTRODUCTION TO

ORIENTAL CIVILIZATIONS

WM. THEODORE DE BARY, EDITOR

Sources of

Japanese Tradition

VOLUME II

COMPILED BY

Ryusaku Tsunoda
Wm. Theodore de Bary
Donald Keene

WITH SPECIAL CONTRIBUTIONS BY

Marius Jansen, Hyman Kublin, Arthur Tiedemann,
Herschel Webb, Masao Abe, John F. Howes,
George O. Totten

COLUMBIA UNIVERSITY PRESS New York

The addition to the "Records of Civilization: Sources and Studies" of a group of translations of Oriental historical materials in a clothbound edition, from which this volume is taken, was made possible by funds granted by Carnegie Corporation of New York. That Corporation is not, however, the author, owner, publisher, or proprietor of this publication, and is not to be understood as approving by virtue of its grant any of the statements made or views expressed therein.

UNESCO COLLECTION OF REPRESENTATIVE WORKS, JAPANESE SERIES
This work has been accepted in the Japanese Translation Series of the United Nations Educational, Scientific, and Cultural Organization (UNESCO).

Text edition in two volumes published 1964
ISBN 0-231-08605-9

PRINTED IN THE UNITED STATES OF AMERICA
15   14   13

FOREWORD

In this edition of *Sources of Japanese Tradition* the main focus of Volume I is on the development from earliest times to the eighteenth century of three major traditions of Japanese thought: Shinto, Buddhism, and Confucianism. Volume II deals with the legacy of these traditions in modern times, not as separate systems or schools of thought, but as they have interacted with recent trends from the West. We are dealing here with new movements of multiple origins and heterogeneous character, whose continuity with the past is not bound up with any single religion or teaching, and whose unifying element is most often a strengthened national consciousness.

Through these diverse movements run certain persistent themes: How can the Japanese people meet the challenge of the expanding West? How can they adapt and reorganize to preserve their own society and culture? What national identity can the Japanese hope to preserve in a rapidly changing world, and what role fulfill? What is worth preserving that is distinctively Japanese?

The Japanese were not alone among the peoples of Asia in confronting such questions, but their success in dealing with them—by such ordinary standards as economic development, political vitality, and cultural activity—has been almost unique. And in this effective response to the challenge of the modern world, the major factor, most observers agree, has been the remarkable capacity of the Japanese for cohesive action in the achievement of national goals. The massive national effort in which the lives and thoughts of most Japanese were caught up after 1868 thus becomes the center of attention in Volume II. The full story of Japanese thought in the past century, if space and time allowed it to be told, would of course be richer, more varied, and less dominated by politics than the very selective account given here.

Japan's rise as a modern nation, so rapid after Perry's dramatic "opening" of the country in 1853, was prepared for by developments preceding this fateful encounter. One of the most significant was the powerful reassertion of native religious traditions in the Shinto revival, of which the intellectual spearhead was the School of National Learning. After centuries of apparent allegiance to the ideals of Buddhism and Confucianism and of deference to Chinese culture, the Japanese had begun to find their own cultural identity. In this process Japanese thinkers were already formulating some conception of Japan's distinctive role in the world.

WM. THEODORE DE BARY

Columbia College
New York City
July, 1963

EXPLANATORY NOTE

In the pronunciation of Japanese words or names, the consonants are read as in English (with "g" always hard) and the vowels as in Italian. There are no silent letters. The name Abe, for instance, is pronounced "Ah-bay." The long vowels "ō" and "ū" are indicated except in the names of cities already well known in the West, such as Tokyo and Kyoto. All romanized terms have been standardized according to the Hepburn system for Japanese, the Wade-Giles for Chinese, and the McCune-Reischauer for Korean. Chinese philosophical terms used in Japanese texts are given in their Japanese readings (e.g., *ri* instead of *li* for "principle," "reason") except where attention is specifically drawn to the Chinese original. Sanskrit words appearing in italics, such as technical terms or titles, are rendered in accordance with the standard system of transliteration as found in Louis Renou's *Grammaire Sanskrite* (Paris, 1930), pp. xi–xiii. Other Sanskrit terms and names appearing in roman letters are rendered according to the usage of Webster's New International Dictionary, 2d edition Unabridged, except that here the macron is used to indicate long vowels and the Sanskrit symbols for ś (ç) and ṣ are uniformly transcribed "sh." Personal names have also been spelled in this manner except when they occur in the titles of works.

Japanese names are rendered here in their Japanese order, with the family name first and the personal name last. Dates given after personal names are those of birth and death except in the case of rulers whose reign dates are preceded by "r." Generally the name by which a person was most commonly known in Japanese tradition is the one used in the text. Since this book is intended for the general reader, rather than the specialist, we have not burdened the text with a list of the alternate names or titles which usually accompany biographical reference to a scholar in Chinese or Japanese historical works. For the same reason, the

[vii]

sources of translations, given at the beginning of each selection, are rendered as concisely as possible. In the reference at the head of each selection, unless otherwise indicated, the author of the book is the sources of translations, given at the beginning of each selection, are rendered as concisely as possible. Full bibliographical data can be obtained from the list of sources at the end of the book. In the reference at the head of each selection, unless otherwise indicated, the author of the book is the writer whose name precedes the selection. Where excerpts have been taken from existing translations, they have usually been adapted and edited to suit our purposes. In particular, unnecessary brackets and footnotes have been suppressed wherever possible, but if essential commentary could be inserted parenthetically in the text, we have preferred to do so rather than add a footnote. Those interested in the full text and annotations may, of course, refer to the original translation cited with each such excerpt. As sources for our own translations we have tried to use standard editions, if such exist, which would be available to other scholars.

W. T. DE B.

CONTENTS

[x]

[xi]

CHRONOLOGICAL TABLE

Tokugawa Shogunate

1769   Kamo Mabuchi (1697–1769), Neo-Shintoist.
1791–1792   American and Russian ships visit Japan. Thereafter, for the next half century, repeated attempts are made to open relations with Japan.
1801   Motoori Norinaga (1730–1817), Neo-Shintoist and philologist.
1821   Honda Toshiaki (1744–1821), economic and political thinker.
1825   *New Proposals* (*Shinron*), by Aizawā Seishisai (1782–1863).
1843   Hirata Atsutane (1776–1843), Neo-Shintoist.
1846   U.S. warships under Biddle at Uraga request opening of Japan to trade.
1850   Satō Nobuhiro (1769–1850), political thinker.
1853   Perry expedition.
1854   Perry returns and negotiates Treaty of Kanagawa. Yoshida Shōin, with Sakuma Shōzan's encouragement, tries to stowaway to America.
1856   Townsend Harris, first American minister to Japan, arrives. Ninomiya Sontoku (1787–1856), religious reformer.
1858   United States–Japanese commercial treaty.
1859   Yoshida Shōin executed.
1860   First Japanese mission to the United States.
1863   British bombardment of Kagoshima in retaliation for antiforeign outbursts.
1867   Keiki, last Tokugawa shogun, resigns.

Meiji Period

1868   Meiji Restoration. Charter Oath. Fukuzawa Yukichi's school given regular status as Keiō-gijuku.
1871   Feudal domains abolished by imperial decree.
1872   Conscription ordinance.
1873   Debate over forceful "opening" of Korea. Edict against Christianity removed.
1877   Satsuma Rebellion.
1881   Ōkuma memorializes the Throne, demanding a parliament. Parliament promised for 1890.
1882   Fukuzawa Yukichi founds *Jiji Shimpo*.

1885 First cabinet.
1889 Meiji Constitution adopted.
1890 First Diet convened. Imperial Rescript on Education.
1894–1895 Sino-Japanese War.
1900 Imperial Ordinance stipulating that war and navy ministers be generals or admirals on the active list. Boxer uprising.
1902 Anglo-Japanese Alliance.
1904–1905 Russo-Japanese War.
1910 Annexation of Korea. Kōtoku Shūsui's alleged plot to assassinate the emperor.

Taishō Period

1912 Death of Emperor Meiji.
1914–1918 First World War.
1915 Twenty-one Demands.
1918 Siberian Expedition. First Party Cabinet (Hara Takashi, premier).
1921 Hara Takashi assassinated.

Shōwa Period

1925 Universal manhood suffrage.
1930 London Naval Treaty.
1931 Manchurian "Incident."
1932 Formation of Manchukuo.
1936 Attempted rightist *coup d'état* (February 26).
1937 Commencement of China "Incident."
1940 Rome-Berlin-Tokyo Axis.
1941–1945 Pacific War.
1950 Commencement of Korean War.
1952 End of military occupation by Allied forces.

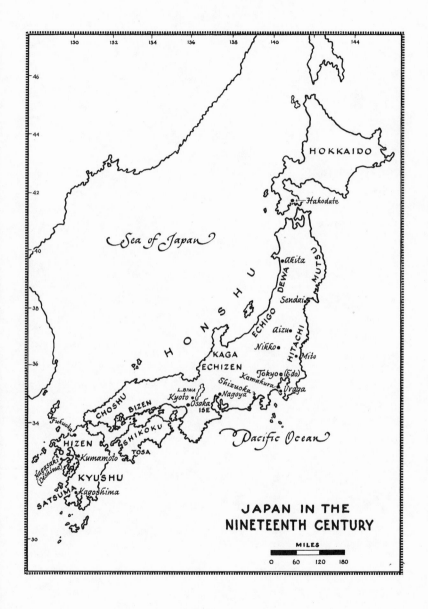

Sea of Japan

HOKKAIDO

•Hakodate

HONSHU

•Akita

DEWA

MUTSU

Sendai•

ECHIGO

Aizu•

Nikko•

HITACHI

•Mito

KAGA

ECHIZEN

Tokyo (Edo)

Kamakura•

•Uraga

L. BIWA

Shizuoka•

CHOSHU

BIZEN

Kyoto•

•Osaka

Nagoya•

ISE

Fukuoka•

SHIKOKU

Pacific Ocean

—B

HIZEN

TOSA

Nagasaki

(Deshima)

Kumamoto•

KYUSHU

SATSUMA

Kagoshima•

JAPAN IN THE
NINETEENTH CENTURY

MILES

0   60   120   180

CHAPTER XXII

THE SHINTO REVIVAL

The Shinto revival, which took place in the eighteenth century, was in no sense a resurrection of a religion which had almost died out. True, during the long centuries of Buddhist and Confucian dominance Shinto had shown little intellectual vitality, and even its most ardent defenders, in contending with these more highly articulated systems of thought, had been forced to draw heavily upon them for ideas. Nevertheless on a more basic level the native cult continued to make itself felt in the lives of the people. In almost every community life was organized around two Shinto shrines, one representing the ancestor of the most important family in each locality, and the other the creator or early owner of the land itself. There were also shrines at scenic spots, atop hills and on the banks of rivers or lakes, in almost every region. Often they were surrounded by groves of tall trees, with enough ground for recreation and tournaments at festival time. They had lay priests and more often priestesses to serve on the occasion of a festival. Under their guidance the shrines flourished when the community that supported them flourished. In fact the Shinto shrine, as the cynosure of each locality, was considered the measure of the community's prosperity, both economic and cultural. A spirited rivalry was carried on among the youths of the various communities, especially at festivals where they competed in demonstrations of strength and exhibits of skill—exhibits containing among other things poems by villagers which were hung on the walls of the shrine in painted frames. Thus without any articulated doctrine or creed, Shinto shrines were symbols of communal pride, exercising seasonal sway over the hearts of the people.

In the seventeenth century, as we have already seen, a renewed interest was taken in Shinto by some of the scholars most closely identified with the establishment of Neo-Confucian orthodoxy under the Tokugawa. Though taking a strong stand against Buddhism, these Neo-Confucianists were by no means completely hostile to religion, and saw in Shinto a traditional form of worship which did not directly challenge the social values of Confucianism. If eventually this revival led to an intensely nationalistic rejection of all things Chinese, as well as a powerful reaction against the rationalistic tendencies fostered by Neo-Confucianism, it nonetheless owed much to the latter. At its inception, especially, this movement was stimulated by the traditionalism, historicism, and reverence for high antiquity which was so characteristic of Neo-Confucianism, and the more Neo-Shintoism became a movement directed toward nationalistic goals, the more it unconsciously drew upon the ethical and political values which Confucianism had instilled in the Japanese. Thus, in the end, despite its vociferous repudiation of this foreign teaching, the Shinto revival contributed significantly to the naturalization of Confucian ethics in the land of its adoption.

Perhaps the most immediate need of Shinto, if it were to become a truly national religion rather than simply an assemblage of local cults, was less a fully developed philosophy than simply a set of basic scriptures. Having had in very early times no written language in which to express itself, Shinto lacked canonical texts comparable to the Chinese classics or the Buddhist *Tripiṭaka*. In medieval times, as a matter of fact, some Shintoists had felt this lack keenly enough to have canonized spurious texts in a set of Five Shinto Scriptures. Here, consequently, was a logical point of departure for a man like Kada Azumamaro (1669–1736), lay priest at the Inari Shrine in Kyoto, who had been much influenced by the example of Ogyū Sorai in calling for a re-examination of the Chinese classics. Kada was moved to petition a scion of the Tokugawa house for his support of a new study of Japan's own ancient literature, which he called the "National Learning." It was this that started the Shinto revival and led to such far-reaching results. By the middle of the nineteenth century, the National Learning movement had come to be regarded as the true expression of Japanese national feelings, unstained by alien culture. As scripture it claimed not only ancient Shinto hymns and prayers, but also the early collections of Japanese poetry, including the first anthology, known as the *Manyōshū*, and also the oldest annals of Japan, the *Kojiki*.

The National Learning movement emphasized the importance of Japan's own literature, but as the influence of Chinese culture, including Confucianism, had reached Japan very early by way of Korea, and as Buddhism in the sixth century had already swept over these islands after a transcontinental journey, the leaders of the movement had difficulty finding anything they could claim as wholly their own in the early literature. The best they could do was bewail the lack of historical study of their own literature. Kamo Mabuchi (1697–1769), the first scholar of national importance in this movement, insisted that the *Manyōshū* poetry of the eighth century and before had been free of foreign influences and represented a true expression of Japanese national sentiments in an unspoiled form. The poems of the first anthology, he asserted, were spontaneous, vigorous, masculine, and guileless. "They are the natural expression of our ancient heritage; they are the voice of our divine land." Mabuchi started composing his own poems in the *Manyōshū* style with remarkable success, and invited other poets (including the great number of amateur versifiers abounding in Japan) to follow his example. This appeal through poetry proved of immense value, for it went straight to the hearts of the Japanese audience, surmounting all intellectual or class barriers. And the creative participation of the people in this movement won it far more wholehearted acceptance than volumes of doctrine and history would have.

Nevertheless an enduring religious movement needed more scriptural authority than *Manyōshū* poetry could give. The first Japanese annals, the *Kojiki,* though compiled as early as 712, had long lain neglected owing to the greater importance assigned the official chronicle, the *Nihongi.* Another reason for the *Kojiki*'s neglect was the great difficulty of reading its text. It took Motoori Norinaga (1730–1801), the second great leader of the Shinto revival, more than thirty years of persistent effort to establish this work as the basic scripture of the movement. But as Chamberlain's English translation demonstrates, the *Kojiki* consists mainly of curious legends and genealogical records of the ruling family or others closely associated with it, interspersed with anecdotes some of which the translator discreetly rendered into Latin. There is little food for thought or inspiration for the soul in such a text. Yet Motoori, if he recognized this fact after all his labors, did not readily admit defeat. Instead he tried to circumvent the problem by arguing that, in any case, all things pertaining to gods and goddesses lay beyond the realm of human understanding. He nevertheless found in the *Kojiki* some primeval elements, such as strong indications of a sun worship expressed in the adoration of the Sun Goddess, and the sublimation of the life-impulse symbolized by installing

[3]

Takami-musubi (vitality) and Kami-musubi (fertility) in the early Shinto pantheon. For Motoori the primal acts of adoration, which he called pure and spontaneous sentiment, meant more in human life than philosophical systems or ethical injunctions. This shift in emphasis from the rational and moral to the emotional side of human nature is characteristic of Motoori's whole approach to the study of Japanese history and literature, wherein he attempts to show what is genuinely Japanese and what is adulterated. Thus he is especially known for his acclamation of the *Tale of Genji* as a masterpiece of human sensitivity and also of the *New Collection of Ancient and Modern Poetry (Shinkokinshū)*, compiled under imperial auspices in 1205, as the best of all such anthologies because of its depth of sentiment.

Until Motoori's time the *Tale of Genji,* because of its tremendous popularity, had been represented by Buddhists for propaganda purposes as a literary rendition of the *Lotus Sutra,* and by Confucianists as a series of female biographies which were fictional counterparts of the biographies in Ssu-ma Ch'ien's great history. Motoori disparaged the Buddhist and Confucian claims by pointing out that the *Tale of Genji* is neither doctrinal in implication nor historical in construction; instead it is a delineation of the emotional life of man, and an expression of that aspect of nature and life which moves men most deeply—what he called *mono no aware*. The term he thus used for the sensitive aspect of life was, as we have seen, a common expression in earlier literature and has since become a key word in the vocabulary of Japanese literary criticism. By calling the *Tale of Genji* a classic expression of the sensitive aspect of human life, Motoori not only defined a new classical tradition, independent of the Chinese and Indian, but he laid claim to this masterpiece as a scripture of the National Learning movement.

When he expressed his preference for the *New Collection* as the best in Japanese poetry, Motoori did not mean to belittle the *Manyōshū,* which his teacher Mabuchi had regarded so highly; nor did he say anything derogatory about the second anthology, the *Collection of Ancient and Modern Poetry* of 905, which had been the most popular of all official anthologies. He was only extending the domain of favored poetry to include that of later time, indicating thereby his breadth of appreciation. As a matter of simple justice it must be admitted that in style and especially in depth of sentiment, the *New Collection* surpasses the other anthologies, for it contains the poetry of those who witnessed the most stunning changes in Japanese history: the downfall of the imperial and Fujiwara aristocracy before the rise of the military clans.

Unfriendly critics of Motoori have insinuated that he took up the study of National Learning because it offered easier chances of recognition than the already overcrowded field of Confucian studies, but this seems clearly untrue. His work represented at once a continuation of the Shinto revival initiated by such men as Kamo Mabuchi, and a sharp reaction to the Confucian thought prevalent in Japan during the eighteenth century. The work of earlier scholars of National Learning led Motoori to devote years of his life to an intensive study of the Japanese classics, just as the very different activities of Confucianists (some of whom tried to explode on rational grounds the mythology of Shinto) led him to seek refuge in a kind of sublime irrationalism. He managed on both scores to touch upon certain aspects of the Japanese temperament, as revealed in the literature and in popular worship, which had never been satisfied by Confucianism. The preference of the Japanese for love poetry rather than didactic verse, and for gentle reflections on the evanescence of beauty rather than speculations on the nature of good and evil, was not only justified but exalted by Motoori, as demonstrating the inadequacy of rationalism. It remained, however, for later men with fewer scruples than Motoori to make of this combination of irrationality and National Learning the instrument of fanatical nationalism.

KADA AZUMAMARO
Petition for the Establishment of a School of National Learning

This memorial submitted to the Shogun Yoshimune in 1728, without contesting the position of the orthodox Neo-Confucian school, appeals for the creation of a school which would rescue traditional Japanese literature from oblivion. The unquestioned prestige of Chinese learning at the time is attested by the very form of the memorial itself: it is in an extremely ornate style of classical Chinese, surfeited with obscure allusions to the Chinese classics— the farthest thing from the native language and literature Kada wished to revive. Even more significant is his adaptation of Neo-Confucianism principles to his own purpose. Thus he uses the slogan of the Confucian revival in the Sung dynasty, "Restore the Ancient Order (or Way)" (Ch. *fu-ku,* Jap. *fukko*) to justify a kind of Japanese neo-classicism. In Kada's mind, however, it is

[5]

clear that these classical studies must be literary and philological in nature, for the Ancient Way can only be rediscovered through textual research.

It is important to note, incidentally, how this text reflects the prevailing view that loyalty to the shogun and to the emperor go hand-in-hand. There is no suggestion of a conflict of interests or authority such as arose in the nineteenth century.

[From *Kada zenshū*, I, 1–6]

Respectfully submitted, craving your bountiful favor in promoting the creation of a school of National Learning. I bow my head in awe and trepidation; vile and base as I am, I abjectly offer my words.

Tokugawa Ieyasu rose in Mikawa Province and soon succeeded in assuming command of the various daimyo to bring peace to the nation. All were as grass before the wind; who could surpass him? Changes brought about by his renewing of the country first led to the establishment of the Kōbunkan,[1] which has grown and prospered. What could be added to it?

Enlightened rulers have successively ascended to power, and the literary pursuits have grown increasingly splendid; their refulgence shines ever farther. The military arts are more perfected than ever; how noble and accomplished they are! Could the love of the Kamakura rulers for sobriety compare to this? Could the respect of the Muromachi family for literature be mentioned on the same day? In keeping with this age of great peace, Heaven has sent us a generous and benevolent ruler.[2] The country has witnessed the mild rule vouchsafed by his innate gifts. No talented men are without employ; the court is thronged with upright men. Above he respects the emperor and devotes himself to effecting a government without deceit. Below he cherishes the daimyo, who offer him tribute. Because his policies are perfected and he has leisure for other pursuits, he has turned his mind to ancient studies; when the teachings in them are not complete he gives profound study to the rule of the men of old. He buys rare books for a thousand pieces of gold. The celebrated scholars of the nation, following his example, search for rare and forgotten books. Visitors of unusual talent from all over the world flock to his court. . . .

Everywhere now Confucian studies are followed, and every day the

[1] The official Hayashi school of Neo-Confucianism founded in 1630 by a grant of land in Edo from the Shogun Iemitsu.

[2] The Shogun Yoshimune (1684–1751)

Buddhist teachings flourish more. "Humanity" and "righteousness" have become household words; even common soldiers and menials know what is meant by the *Book of Songs*. In every family they read the sūtras; porters and scullery-maids can discuss Emptiness (*shūnyatā*). The people's manner of living has benefited by great advances, but our National Learning is gradually falling into desuetude. Cultivated fields are being abandoned steadily and possessions are being exhausted by contributions to Buddhism. Most lamentably, however, the teachings of our Divine Emperors are steadily melting away, each year more conspicuously than the past. Japanese learning is falling into ruin and is a bare tenth of what it once was. The books of law are disappearing: who is there to ask about studies of the old learning? The way of the *waka* [poetry] is falling into oblivion; what can revive the great refinement of the old styles?

Those who now treat Shinto all follow theories of yin-yang or of the Five Elements.[3] Those who consider the *waka* tend to adopt the explanations of Tendai doctrines or of the Four Disciplines of Chinese poetry. If these scholars are not the dregs of T'ang and Sung Confucianists, they are exudations from the Womb and Diamond Mandalas. If their writings are not fabrications composed of vain theories and idle hair-splittings, they are eccentricities devoid of foundation or thought. They speak of "secrets" and "traditions," but of the true traditions of the wise men of old, what knowledge have they? They speak of "depths" and "recondite meanings," but how many are the forgeries of recent men!

From the time when I was young I went without sleep or food in order to combat such heterodox ideas. When I grew to maturity, I tried ceaselessly, with learning and with thought, to revive the Ancient Way. If now I do not bestir myself and strive to explain the rights and wrongs, it will certainly later come about that people will confound the true and the false, for their ears will be stopped and their hearts shut. If I try to keep aloof, the old writings will become vague and obscure. If I try to pursue the matter I will find how old and weary I am. In this state of doubt, I cannot make a decision. Uncertain, I fail to do what I should.

Prostrate, I here make my humble request: that I be given a quiet tract of land in Kyoto where I can open a school for studies of the Imperial Land. I have collected since my youth many secret and obscure writings, and have corrected since becoming aged numerous old records and ac-

[3] For example, the school of Yamazaki Ansai.

counts. I propose to store them at this school to provide for the researches of future days. There must be persons living in remote villages who experience great difficulty in getting hold of such books. There must also be many scholars in forsaken hamlets who cannot realize their ambitions to study the Japanese classics. We should lend the necessary texts throughout the country and enable scholars to read them. A familiarity with only a single volume permits one to know of the downfall of many kings; a careful study of antiquity can save the people from countless sufferings. If by great good fortune some extraordinary man of talent arises, the way of Prince Toneri [4] will not perish. If there are men who polish the gems of poetry, the teachings of Kakinomoto Hitomaro [5] will again flourish. If the Six Dynastic Histories are clear, it will be of no small aid to the officials in improving the people. If the laws of the three reigns [6] are given new life, this will also prove of great benefit to the prestige and permanence of the nation. The *Manyoshū* is [the *Shih Ching* of the East and] [7] the pure essence of our national temperament. He who studies it will not be slandered as an ignoramus. The *Kokinshū* is the finest flower of the anthologies. He who is unfamiliar with it will be admonished as being unfit to converse with.

The first school established in our country was at the Ōmi [8] court. The first teaching of the Way of Letters originated at the time of the Emperor Saga. The Sugawara and Ōe families [9] had academies of learning. The Minamoto, Fujiwara, Tachibana, and Wake families followed them. At the Dazaifu in Kyushu there was a school; in Ashikaga and Kanazawa education was furthered. However, they taught Chinese history and the Chinese classics in these schools, even in those for the imperial family. Offerings were made to the spirit of Confucius. Alas, how ignorant the Confucian scholars were of the past, not knowing a single thing about the imperial Japanese learning. How painful, the stupidity of later scholars—who cannot bewail the destruction of the ancient learning? This is

[4] Compiler of the *Nihongi* (*Chronicles of Japan*), died A.D. 735.

[5] Greatest of the poets of the *Manyōshū*.

[6] The codes of the Kōnin, Jōkan, and Engi eras. Used here, however, to balance the "six dynastic histories" in the preceding sentence, and meaning more generally the laws of the Heian times.

[7] The phrase in brackets is found in the rough draft of this petition, but was deleted by Kada in the final version. It is restored here because of its interest.

[8] Site of the court, near the modern city of Ōtsu, during the reign of Emperor Tenchi

[9] The following are all important families with literary traditions.

why foreign teachings have prevailed, and one meets them in street conversations and corner gossip. This is why too our teachings have so declined. False doctrines are rampant, taking advantage of our weakness. . . .

I am an exceedingly ignorant man. What can I claim to know? If, indeed, there is one thing I dare claim for myself some acquaintance, it is the explanation of words. There are many misconceptions about our national writings. The fact that there still seem to be some people aware of them today is probably because the books survive. There are few explanations for the old Japanese words. The fact that one does not hear of anyone who has been thoroughly versant in them must be because the documents and men are insufficient. It has indeed been several hundred years since the old learning was taught. There are only a bare three or four books which offer explanations for the words, and these books vie with one another in claiming to be the authority, advancing new and outlandish theories in support of their claims. Such books are exceedingly superficial; how can they hope to attain the true meanings? If the old words are not understood the old meanings will not be clear. If the old meanings are not clear, the old learning will not revive. The way of the former kings is disappearing; the ideas of the wise men of antiquity have almost been abandoned. The loss will not be a slight one if we fail now to teach philology. We must devote ourselves to this project. I have given my life's energies to the study of the old words. I humbly believe that the rise or fall of Japanese learning depends on whether or not my plan is accepted. I pray that Your Excellency will grant it your attention and consider it favorably.

Your servant Kada submits the above in awe and trepidation.

KAMO MABUCHI
A Study of the Idea of the Nation

Unlike Kada Azumamaro, who presented in ornamental Chinese his petition for the establishment of a school for national learning, Kamo Mabuchi wrote this work in almost pure Japanese. It was composed in 1765. Although this is an attack on Chinese thought, particularly Confucian, it is conceived largely in Taoist terms, and there are numerous direct or indirect references to Lao Tzu. The anti-intellectual, intuitive teachings of Taoism were to prove congenial to later Shinto scholars as well, and in many instances we find in this work of Kamo Mabuchi the arguments which Hirata Atsutane and other men were to voice with even greater intemperance.

[From *Sekai Daishisō Zenshū,* Vol. 54, pp. 2–10; cf. Dumoulin, *Monumenta Nipponica,* II, 165–92]

Someone remarked to me, "I pay no heed to such petty trifles as Japanese poetry; what interests me is the Chinese Way of governing a nation."

I smiled at this and did not answer. Later, when I met the same man he asked, "You seem to have an opinion on every subject—why did you merely keep smiling when I spoke to you?"

I answered, "You mean when you were talking about the Chinese Confucian teachings or whatever you call them? They are no more than a human invention which reduces the heart of Heaven and Earth to something trivial."

At these words he became enraged. "How dare you call our Great Way trivial?"

I answered, "I would be interested in hearing whether or not the Chinese Confucian learning has actually helped to govern a country successfully." He immediately cited the instances of Yao, Shun, Hsia, Yin, Chou, and so on. I asked if there were no later examples, but he informed me that there were not.

I pursued the matter, asking this time about how far back Chinese traditions went. He answered that thousands of years had passed from Yao's day to the present. I then asked, "Why then did the Way of Yao continue only until the Chou and afterwards cease? I am sure that it is because you restrict yourself to citing events which took place thousands of years ago that the Way seems so good. But those are merely ancient legends. It takes more than such specious ideas to run a country!"

When I said this he grew all the more furious, and ranted on about ancient matters. I said, "You are utterly prejudiced. You say that Yao yielded the throne to that rascal Shun? That sounds as if it must have been a good thing for the country, but that is the sort of thing we avoid in Japan as being 'too good.' [1] In China there were also ruffians who, far from yielding the throne, sprang up from nowhere to kill their sovereigns and seize control of the country. That is what we find 'too bad' and equally avoid. An excess of good can thus lead to excess of evil. [Kamo goes on to cite many other similar instances in Chinese history.]

[1] That is, something which though good in itself can lead to unfortunate consequences.

"Things in China grew more and more chaotic, although in the time of the Emperor Wen of the Han dynasty, there seems to have been a short interval of good government because the Emperor took to heart what Lao Tzu had said. As you can see, whenever some base-born individual appeared to slay his lord and proclaim himself emperor, everyone bowed his head and served this upstart obediently. That is not the worst of it. Although the Chinese despise all foreign countries as 'barbarian,' when someone from one of the 'barbarian' countries became emperor, they all prostrated themselves before him. Wouldn't you say, then, that to despise others as 'barbarian' was irresponsible? It is not a word to be applied indiscriminately.

"Thus, despite the fact that their country has been torn for centuries by disturbances and has never really been well administered, they think that they can explain with their Way of Confucius the principles governing the whole world. Indeed, when one has heard them through, there is nothing to be said: anyone can quickly grasp their doctrines because they consist of mere quibbling. What they value the most and insist on is the establishment and maintenance of good government. Everybody in China would seem to have been in agreement on this point, but belief in it did not in fact lie very deep. It is obvious that many gave superficial assent who did not assent in their hearts. Yet when these principles were introduced to this country it was stated that China had obtained good government through the adoption of them. This was a complete fabrication. I wish it were possible to send to China anyone who clung to such a belief! He would discover like Urashima Tarō [2] when he returned to his home, what an illusion he had been suffering from!

"Japan in ancient days was governed in accordance with the natural laws of Heaven and earth. There was never any indulgence in such petty rationalizing as marked China, but when suddenly these teachings were transmitted here from abroad, they quickly spread, for the men of old in their simplicity took them for the truth. In Japan there had been generation after generation, extending back to the remote past, which had known prosperity, but no sooner were these Confucian teachings propagated here than in the time of Temmu [3] a great rebellion occurred. Later,

[2] The hero of a Japanese fairy tale who returns to his village after extraordinary adventures in a dragon's palace to discover, like Rip Van Winkle, that many years have elapsed and he himself is an old man.

[3] The Emperor Temmu (631–686) ascended the throne only after a struggle with Prince Ōtomo, the appointed successor of Tenchi.

[11]

at Nara, the palace, dress, and ceremonies were Chinesified, and every-thing took on a superficial elegance; under the surface, however, con-tentiousness and dishonesty became more prevalent.

"Confucianism made men crafty, and led them to worship the ruler to such an excessive degree that the whole country acquired a servant's mentality. Later it even came about that an emperor was sacrilegiously driven to an island exile. This occurred because the country had become infected with Chinese ideas. Some people speak ill of Buddhism, but since it is a teaching which makes men stupid, it does not represent a grave evil; after all, rulers do not prosper unless the people are stupid.[4]

"Just as roads are naturally created when people live in uncultivated woodlands or fields, so the Way of the Age of the Gods spontaneously took hold in Japan. Because it was a Way indigenous to the country it caused our emperors to wax increasingly in prosperity. However, the Confucian teachings had not only repeatedly thrown China into disorder, but they now had the same effect in Japan. Yet there are those unwitting of these facts who reverence Confucianism and think that it is the Way to govern the country! This is a deplorable attitude.

"Japanese poetry has as its subject the human heart. It may seem to be of no practical use and just as well left uncomposed, but when one knows poetry well, one understands also without explanation the reasons gov-erning order and disorder in the world. They say that Confucius himself did not reject poetry, but placed the *Book of Songs* at the head of the classics. Things which are explained in terms of theories are as dead. Those which operate together with Heaven and earth spontaneously are alive and active. I do not mean to say that it is a bad idea to have a general knowledge of all things, but it is a common human failing to tend to lean excessively in that direction. It is advisable not to cling too tenaciously to things once one has learned them. Even though some Japa-nese poems have as their themes evil desires, the poems do not corrupt the reader's heart, but instead make it more gentle and more understanding of all things.

"When ruling the country a knowledge of Chinese things is of no help in the face of an emergency. In such a situation some man will spon-taneously come forth to propose things which are wise and true. In the same way, doctors often study and master Chinese texts, but very seldom

[4] On the Taoist principle that knowledge leads to greed and ambition, craftiness and contentiousness.

do they cure any sickness. On the other hand, medicines which have been transmitted naturally in this country with no reasons or theoretical knowledge behind them, infallibly cure all maladies. It is good when a man spontaneously devotes himself to these things. It is unwise to become obsessed with them. I would like to show people even once what is good in our Way. The fact that the Confucian scholars know very little about government is obvious from the frequent disorders which arise in China whenever the government is left to them. . . .

"It is another bad habit of the Chinese to distinguish men from beasts, by way of self-praise for being men and dispraise for the rest. It is like their custom of despising all other countries as 'barbarian,' a meaningless expression. Are not all creatures which live between Heaven and earth so many insects? Why should only man be considered precious? What is so exceptional about man? In China they venerate man as 'the soul of all things' or some such, but I wonder if man should not rather be called 'the most evil of all things'? By this I mean that, just as the sun and moon have not changed, birds, beasts, fish and plants are all exactly as they were in ancient days, but ever since man impetuously decided that knowledge would be of use to him, evil motives of every kind have sprung up among people, and have finally thrown the world into turmoil. Even when they enjoy peaceful rule men deceive one another. It might be desirable if just one or two men in the world had knowledge, but when everyone possesses it, what a dreadful chaos ensues, and in the end the knowledge itself is useless. If one looked through the eyes of a bird or a beast, one would say, 'Man is evil. His ways should not be followed.'"

. . . .

People also tell me, "We had no writing in this country and therefore had to use Chinese characters. From this one fact you can know everything about the relative importance of our countries." I answer, "I need not recite again how troublesome, evil, turbulent a country China is. To mention just one instance—there is the matter of their picture-writing. There are about 38,000 characters in common use,[5] as someone has determined. . . . Every place name and plant name has a separate character for it which has no other use but to designate that particular place or plant. Can any man, even one who devotes himself to the task earnestly,

[5] An extraordinary exaggeration. Even in Kamo's day not more than 2,500 characters could have been in common use.

[13]

learn all these many characters? Sometimes people miswrite characters, sometimes the characters themselves change from one generation to the next. What a nuisance, a waste of effort, and a bother! In India, on the other hand, fifty letters suffice for the writing of the more than 5,000 volumes of the Buddhist scriptures. A knowledge of a mere fifty letters permits one to know and transmit innumerable words of past and present alike. This is not simply a matter of writing—the fifty sounds are the sounds of Heaven and earth, and words conceived from them are naturally different from the Chinese characters. Whatever kind of writing we may originally have had, ever since Chinese writing was introduced we have mistakenly become enmeshed in it. Now only the old words, but not their writing are preserved. These words are not identical with the fifty Indian sounds . . . but the fifty sounds suffice to express all words without the nuisance of characters. In Holland, I understand, they use twenty-five letters. In this country there should be fifty. The appearance of letters used in all countries is in general the same, except for China where they invented their bothersome system. . . . The opinion that the characters are precious is not worth discussing further."

. . . .

What do we know of China in most ancient days? Because the Chinese of later generations invented things, does it follow that here in Japan we too must have invented history? There are bound to be many mistakes in what human minds invent. When we look at things recorded in China by the learned men, we see that the country never profited by any Way unless it was in accord with Heaven and earth. Therefore the sayings of Lao Tzu derived from the Will of Heaven and earth were in consonance with the proper Way of the country. In ancient days China was also a decent country. . . . In ancient times words and things were few. When things are few the heart is sincere, and there is no need for difficult teachings. All will go satisfactorily even without teachings because men are honest. It is true that since men's hearts are manifold there is always some evil in them, but evil itself cannot remain hidden in an honest heart. If it is not hidden, it will not develop into anything serious, but will remain no more than a moment's aberration. Thus, in ancient days though the land was not absolutely devoid of the teachings of good men, a few easy ones sufficed. However, since China is a country of wicked-heartedness, no amount of profound instruction could keep the innate evil from overwhelming the country, despite the surface appearance. Japan has always been a country where the people are honest. As long as a few teachings were carefully observed and we worked in accordance with the Will of Heaven and earth, the country would be well off without any special instruction. Nevertheless, Chinese doctrines were introduced and corrupted men's hearts. Even though these teachings resembled those of China itself, they were of the kind which heard in the morning are forgotten by evening. Our country in ancient times was not like that. It obeyed the laws of Heaven and earth. The emperor was the sun and moon and the subjects the stars. If the subjects as stars protect the sun and moon, they will not hide it as is now the case. Just as the sun, moon, and stars have always been in Heaven, so our imperial sun and moon, and the stars his vassals, have existed without change from ancient days, and have ruled the world fairly. However, some knaves appeared,[6] and as a result the emperor is diminished in power, and his subjects too have fallen off. The *Age of the Gods* is where we may gain a knowledge of this. To discover it, we should carefully examine the words and thoughts in the ancient poetry, and thereby see clearly into the oldest writings.

MOTOORI NORINAGA
The True Tradition of the Sun Goddess

This excerpt is from Motoori's *Precious Comb-box* (*Tama kushige*), the contents of which are meant to "comb" out the snarls of intellectual confusion. In it he upholds the traditional account of the divine creation in all its unembellished simplicity while rejecting the rationalistic cosmogony of the Chinese. The Sun Goddess is a universal deity as well as a national one, but she has shown special favor to the Japanese and guides them to a special destiny.
[From *Motoori Norinaga Zenshū*, VI, 3–6]

The True Way is one and the same, in every country and throughout heaven and earth. This Way, however, has been correctly transmitted only in our Imperial Land. Its transmission in all foreign countries was lost long ago in early antiquity, and many and varied ways have been expounded, each country representing its own way as the Right Way. But the ways of foreign countries are no more the original Right Way

[6] Not identified; refers perhaps to the Fujiwara family and all others who have usurped power from the emperor.

than end-branches of a tree are the same as its root. They may have resemblances here and there to the Right Way, but because the original truth has been corrupted with the passage of time, they can scarcely be likened to the original Right Way. Let me state briefly what that one original Way is. One must understand, first of all, the universal principle of the world. The principle is that Heaven and earth, all the gods and all phenomena, were brought into existence by the creative spirits of two deities—Takami-musubi and Kami-musubi. The birth of all humankind in all ages and the existence of all things and all matter have been the result of that creative spirit. It was the original creativity of these two august deities which caused the deities Izanagi and Izanami to create the land, all kinds of phenomena, and numerous gods and goddesses at the beginning of the Divine Age. This spirit of creativity [*musubi*, lit., "union"] is a miraculously divine act the reason for which is beyond the comprehension of the human intellect.

But in the foreign countries where the Right Way has not been transmitted this act of divine creativity is not known. Men there have tried to explain the principle of Heaven and earth and all phenomena by such theories as the yin and yang, the hexagrams of the Book of Changes, and the Five Elements. But all of these are fallacious theories stemming from the assumptions of the human intellect and they in no wise represent the true principle.

Izanagi, in deep sorrow at the passing of his goddess, journeyed after her to the land of death. Upon his return to the upper world he bathed himself at Ahagiwara in Tachibana Bay in Tsukushi in order to purify himself of the pollution of the land of death, and while thus cleansing himself, he gave birth to the Heaven-Shining Goddess who by the explicit command of her father-God, came to rule the Heavenly Plain for all time to come. This Heaven-Shining Goddess is none other than the sun in heaven which today casts its gracious light over the world. Then, an Imperial Prince of the Heaven-Shining Goddess was sent down from heaven to the middle kingdom of Ashihara. In the Goddess' mandate to the Prince at that time it was stated that his dynasty should be coeval with Heaven and earth. It is this mandate which is the very origin and basis of the Way. Thus, all the principles of the world and the way of humankind are represented in the different stages of the Divine Age. Those who seek to know the Right Way must therefore pay careful attention to the stages of the Divine Age and learn the truths of existence. These aspects of the various stages are embodied in the ancient traditions of the Divine Age. No one knows with whom these ancient traditions began, but they were handed down orally from the very earliest times and they refer to the accounts which have since been recorded in the *Kojiki* and the *Nihongi*. The accounts recorded in these two scriptures are clear and explicit and present no cause for doubt. Those who have interpreted these scriptures in a later age have contrived oracular formulae and have expounded theories which have no real basis. Some have become addicts of foreign doctrines and have no faith in the wonders of the Divine Age. Unable to understand that the truths of the world are contained in the evolution of the Divine Age, they fail to ascertain the true meaning of our ancient tradition. As they base their judgment on the strength of foreign beliefs, they always interpret at their own discretion and twist to their own liking anything they encounter which may not be in accord with their alien teachings. Thus, they say that the High Heavenly Plain refers to the Imperial Capital and not to Heaven, and that the Sun Goddess herself was not a goddess nor the sun shining in the heavens but an earthly person and the forebear of the nation. These are arbitrary interpretations purposely contrived to flatter foreign ideologies. In this way the ancient tradition is made to appear narrow and petty, by depriving it of its comprehensive and primal character. This is counter to the meaning of the scriptures.

Heaven and earth are one; there is no barrier between them. The High Heavenly Plain is the high heavenly plain which covers all the countries of the world, and the Sun Goddess is the goddess who reigns in that heaven. Thus, she is without a peer in the whole universe, casting her light to the very ends of heaven and earth and for all time. There is not a single country in the world which does not receive her beneficent illuminations, and no country can exist even for a day or an hour bereft of her grace. This goddess is the splendor of all splendors. However, foreign countries, having lost the ancient tradition of the Divine Age, do not know the meaning of revering this goddess. Only through the speculations of the human intelligence have they come to call the sun and the moon the spirit of yang and yin. In China and other countries the "Heavenly Emperor" is worshiped as the supreme divinity. In other countries there are other objects of reverence, each according to its own way, but their teachings are based, some on the logic of inference, and some on arbitrary personal opinions. At any rate, they are merely man-made designations and the "Heavenly Ruler" or the "Heavenly Way" have no real existence at all. That foreign countries revere such non-existent beings and remain unaware of the grace of the Sun Goddess is a matter of profound regret. However, because of the special dispensation of our Imperial Land, the ancient tradition of the Divine Age has been correctly and clearly transmitted in our country, telling us of the genesis of the great goddess and the reason for her adoration. The "special dispensation of our Imperial Land" means that ours is the native land of the Heaven-Shining Goddess who casts her light over all countries in the four seas. Thus our country is the source and fountainhead of all other countries, and in all matters it excels all the others. It would be impossible to list all the products in which our country excels, but fore-most among them is rice, which sustains the life of man, for whom there is no product more important. Our country's rice has no peer in foreign countries, from which fact it may be seen why our other products are also superior. Those who were born in this country have long been accus-tomed to our rice and take it for granted, unaware of its excellence. They can enjoy such excellent rice morning and night to their heart's content because they have been fortunate enough to be born in this country. This is a matter for which they should give thanks to our shining deities, but to my great dismay they seem to be unmindful of it.

Our country's Imperial Line, which casts its light over this world, rep-resents the descendants of the Sky-Shining Goddess. And in accordance with that Goddess' mandate of reigning "forever and ever, coeval with Heaven and earth," the Imperial Line is destined to rule the nation for eons until the end of time and as long as the universe exists. That is the very basis of our Way. That our history has not deviated from the in-structions of the divine mandate bears testimony to the infallibility of our ancient tradition. It can also be seen why foreign countries cannot match ours and what is meant by the special dispensation of our country. For-eign countries expound their own ways, each as if its way alone were true. But their dynastic lines, basic to their existence, do not continue; they change frequently and are quite corrupt. Thus one can surmise that in everything they say there are falsehoods and that there is no basis in fact for them.

Wonder

This passage explains the inadequacy of human reason to comprehend the wondrous manifestations of the power of the gods, and mocks at the Confucian pretention to have found a rational answer to every problem. It is taken from the *Arrowroot* (*Kuzubana*), so entitled because this plant creeps humbly along the ground but yields a pretty blossom and a nutritious starch, which, when fermented, produces a stimulating liquor. Motoori suggests that his ideas, simple and unpretentious though they may be, are nevertheless food and stimulus for thought. This dialogue was written in answer to an attack on the Shinto revival by the Confucianist, Ichikawa Tatsumaro (d. 1795).

[From *Motoori Norinaga Zenshū*, V, 459–62]

Objection: You are obstinate in insisting that the Sun Goddess is the sun in heaven. If this is so, perpetual darkness must have reigned everywhere before her birth. The sun must have been in heaven since the beginning of the universe [before the birth of the Goddess].

Motoori: First of all, I cannot understand why you say that I am obstinate. That the Sun Goddess is the sun in heaven is clear from the records of the *Kojiki* and the *Nihongi*. If it is so beyond any doubt, is not the person who raises an objection the one who is obstinate? This Sun Goddess casts her light to the very extremities of the universe, but in the beginning it was in our Imperial Land that she made her appearance, and as the sovereign of the Imperial Line, that is, of the Imperial Land, she has reigned supreme over the Four Seas until now. When this Goddess hid herself in a cave in heaven, closing its doors, darkness fell over the countries of the world. You ask why darkness did not reign everywhere before her birth, a question a child might well ask. It seems childish indeed when a question which might spring from the doubts of a child is asked with such insistence by you. But this very point proves that the ancient happenings of the Divine Age are facts and not fabrications. Some say that the records are the fabrication of later sovereigns, but who would fabricate such shallow sounding, incredible things? This is a point you should reflect upon seriously.

The acts of the gods cannot be measured by ordinary human reasoning. Man's intellect, however wise, has its limits. It is small, and what is beyond its confines it cannot know. The acts of the gods are straightforward. That they appear to be shallow and untrue is due to the limitation

of what man can know. To the human mind these acts appear to be remote, inaccessible, and difficult of comprehension and belief. Chinese
teachings, on the other hand, were established within the reach of human
intelligence; thus, to the mind of the listener, they are familiar and intimate and easy of comprehension and belief. The Chinese, because they
believe that the wisdom of the Sage [Confucius] was capable of com-
prehending all the truths of the universe and of its phenomena, pretend
to the wisdom of the Sage and insist, despite their small and limited
minds, that they know what their minds are really incapable of knowing.
But at the same time they refuse to believe in the inscrutability of the
truth, for this, they conclude, is irrational. This sounds clever, but on the
contrary, it betrays the pettiness of their intelligence. If my objector would
rid himself of such a habit and reflect seriously, such a doubt as he has
just expressed would disappear of itself.

It will be recalled that when Izanagi made his way to the nether region, he carried a light because of the darkness there, but while he lived
in the actual world, he did not. The nether world is dark because it has
to be dark; the actual world is clear because it has to be clear. Thus, there
was light in the actual world before the birth of the Sun Goddess, although the reason why it is so cannot be fathomed. In the commentaries
on the *Nihongi* there are references to luminous human beings of the
days of creation who cast light about them, but these references were
derived from the Buddhist scriptures. There is also mention of a deity
of firefly light, but this was an evil deity, and his case cannot be taken as
a typical one. There are otherwise no traditions about deities of light, and
thus we have no way of knowing what light there was for illumination.
But presumably there was light for reasons beyond the reach of human
intelligence. Why then did darkness prevail when the Sun Goddess hid
herself behind the door of the rocky cave? It was because it had been
determined that with the birth of the Sun Goddess the whole space of the
universe should come within her illumination, and that henceforth there
would be no light without her illumination. This is the same sort of
inscrutable truth as the case of the descent of the Imperial Grandchild
from Heaven after which communication between Heaven and earth
was completely severed. There are many other strange and inscrutable
happenings in the Divine Age, which should be accepted in the same way.
The people of antiquity never attempted to reason out the acts of the

gods with their own intelligence, but the people of a later age, influenced by the Chinese, have become addicts of rationalism. Such people appear wise, but in reality are quite foolish in their suspicion and skepticism about the strange happenings of the Divine Age which are quite different from the happenings of the human age. The fact is that even the things of the human age are, in reality, strange and wondrous, but because we are accustomed to their present form and have always lived in their midst, we cease to be aware of their wondrous quality. Consider, for example, how this universe goes on. Is the earth suspended in the sky or attached to something else? In either instance it is a wondrous thing. Suppose it is attached to something else, what is there under it to support it? This is something which cannot be understood. Thus in China, although there are many theories, they all end in wonder. Among them is a theory called the global theory which says that the earth is round and that it is enveloped in space and hangs in the sky. It sounds most plausible but ordinary reasoning tells us that despite the fullness of the ether in the sky this land and the great oceans cannot remain suspended and motionless in the sky. Thus, this theory too is nothing more than an expression of wonderment. Another theory says that space consists of ether only and that it has no form of its own. This too sounds plausible, but if ether fills the outer space, is there a limit to its extension or not? If it has no limit there is no way of determining its circumference or its center or where in it the earth is situated. The earth cannot stop except at the dead center of space. If, on the other hand, the extension of ether is limited, then it must assume the shape of a ball, raising the question about the definite point around which it condenses itself. Then again, what is there to cause it to condense? Thus we see that this theory too is an expression of the strange and the wondrous.

Man, living in such a strange and wondrous universe, wonders not about its mysteries but only about the wonders of the Divine Age, saying there is no reason for them. If this is not senseless, what is?

Consider also the human body: it has eyes to see, ears to hear, a mouth to speak, feet to walk, and hands to do a thousand things. Are they not truly wonderful? Birds and insects fly in the sky, plants and trees bloom and bear fruit—they are all wonderful. When insentient beings change into sentient beings such as birds and insects, or when foxes and badgers take on human form—are these not the strangest of all strange things? Thus, the universe and all things therein are without a single exception strange and wondrous when examined carefully. Even the Sage would be incapable of explaining these phenomena. Thus, one must acknowledge that human intelligence is limited and puny while the acts of the gods are illimitable and wondrous. But it is indeed amusing that there are people who respect and believe in this Sage as one who had illuminated every truth of the universe and its phenomena, when in fact he explained only those things within the boundaries of his own intelligence.

The beginnings of such a vastly wondrous universe and all its phenomena must be even more wonderful. The Chinese explain it in terms of yin and yang, but they have failed to explain why yin and yang operate in such a manner—which only adds to the wonder of the beginnings of the universe. Or one might say that the universe had no beginning, just as it will have no end; but if things existed which had no beginning, it would be even more strange and wondrous. If my objector would reflect upon the above things, his doubts would disappear of themselves. If his doubts are still insoluble, I shall cite examples nearer to him. Mice and martens can see in darkness as well as in broad daylight. By what manner of light do they see? There are also birds which see things well at night but cannot see them in daylight. Such things cannot be explained by the usual reasoning. The objector has said that there was no reason for light to exist in the Divine Age, but can he say that there was a reason for such light not to exist? What is your answer? Even in the case of lowly birds and animals there is a reason beyond reason. Is there any need to say more about our imperial forebears at the beginning of the universe?

The Error of Rationalism
[From *Kuzubana* in *Motoori Norinaga Zenshū,* V, 463–66]

Objection: The scholar [Motoori] treats this country as if it were different from other countries.

Motoori: The objector also says at the end of the book that I want "to put our country outside the universe." I cannot understand what he means, but I surmise from what he says before and after that he is criticizing me for my statement that the Sun Goddess, who is the sun in heaven, was born in our country. . . .

I shall not reiterate here the details of the theory that the Sun Goddess is the sun in heaven and that she was born in our land. But because of the absence of the correct transmission of this fact in foreign lands, men there do not know about the genesis of the sun and the moon. They had a theory [in China] that the sun and the moon were the eyes of P'an Ku, which is a remnant of the true ancient tradition, but in China, where everyone is addicted to sophistry, such an interpretation was regarded as fantastic, and it was discarded. Instead, the sun and the moon were declared to be, on pure personal conjecture, the spirits of yin and yang. The theory of P'an Ku's eyes is an instance of the transmission to and modification in a foreign country of the tradition that the Sun Goddess was born of the ablution of Izanagi's eyes. It is only a fragmentary survival, but it is superior to any conjectural theory.

Leaving aside for the moment the question as to which is superior, let us first make a distinction between the Chinese and the Japanese views. From the Chinese point of view, the Japanese view is wrong, and from the Japanese point of view, the Chinese view is wrong. But the objector advances only the Chinese view and attempts to universalize it, even denying the antiquity of our Imperial Land. Is this not prejudiced and arbitrary? To this he might reply that the universe is one, that there is no distinction between a Chinese and Japanese point of view, and that narrow partiality lies in attempting to make such distinctions. However, the objector, in advancing only the Chinese view and casting doubt on the antiquity of our Imperial Land, himself makes such a distinction and shows partiality to China. . . . Even if there were no distinctions among the countries, it would still be proper for the various countries of the world, each with its own traditions and its point of view, to maintain their views according to their own traditions. Our Imperial Land in particular is superior to the rest of the world in its possession of the correct transmission of the ancient Way, which is that of the great Goddess who casts her light all over the world. It is treasonable malice to urge that we discard that transmission in favor of a senseless foreign view which, moreover, insists that our ancient transmission is a fantasy and a fabrication. . . .

Then again, his assertion that I represent the sun as something different from the sun of other countries is a ridiculous statement. How can the sun be different in other countries if I say that the Sun Goddess was born in our country and shines over all other countries? . . . Again, he says that the gods in Heaven regard all things equally and bestow their blessings impartially on them all. That is quite so, and yet our Imperial Land is the land where the Sky-Shining Goddess was born and where her descendants reign supreme; thus, it is superior to all other countries and cannot be regarded as the same.

Objection: The Sage, Confucius, has been looked up to as Heaven itself by tens of millions of people.

Motoori: This fact demonstrates that the Chinese, dynasty after dynasty, have been deceived by the Sage, who really does not deserve such credit. If adoration by the many is the mark of superiority, then it must be said that Shinran, the founder of the Ikkō Sect, is superior to the Sage, for the present-day followers of the Ikkō Sect revere their founder far more deeply than Confucians adore Confucius. . . .

Sages are superior to other people only in their cleverness. The fact is that they were all impostors. Among them the least blameworthy was Confucius. He was respectful of the Chou dynasty, for he was born in the Chou. That he deplored the impositions and irregularities of the feudal lords is a thing deserving of praise. But Mencius, whom the Confucianists revere as a sage in the same class with Confucius, was quite different. While professing the kingly way, he encouraged revolt wherever he went. He was no less evil a person than T'ang and Wu.[1]

The Fact of Evil

A fundamental error of Confucianism and Buddhism, according to Motoori, is their attempt to transcend evil, death, and human sorrow by subtle rationalization. These are basic facts of human existence, he says, which must be faced in all their stark reality.

[From *Tama Kushige* in *Motoori Norinaga Zenshū,* VI, 9–11]

All things in life—great and small, their very existence in the universe, even man himself and his actions—are due to the spirits of the gods and their disposition of things. In general, there are various kinds of gods—

[1] According to the Confucian *Book of Documents* T'ang and Wu were founders of the Shang and Chou dynasties, who asserted that the rulers they deposed had lost the Mandate of Heaven by their misconduct.

noble, mean, good, bad, right, and wrong. So it is that things in life are not always lucky and good: they are mixed with the bad and the unfortunate. Internecine wars break out occasionally and events not in the interest of the world or of mankind take place. Not infrequently, good or bad fortune befalls a man contrary to the principles of justice. Such things are the acts of the evil deities. The evil deities are those who do all manner of evil, moved by the spirit of the deity Magatsubi who was born of the pollution of the land of death, of which the God Izanagi had cleansed himself. When such evil deities flourish and are unchecked, there are times when even the protective powers of the shining deities prove inadequate. This has been true since the Divine Age.

Why is it that life does not consist solely of the good and the right, and that the evil and the wrong are necessarily a part of it? Here again there is a basic reason, fixed in the Divine Age and recorded in the *Kojiki* and the *Nihongi*. It is, however, a long story, difficult to relate here in detail. But a word or two should be said about the pollution of the land of death. The land of death is situated beneath the ground at the bottom of the earth. Thus, it is also called the "baseland" or the "netherland." It is an extremely dirty and evil land, where the dead go. In the beginning, Izanami, after her death, made her way there and partook of a cooked substance of the land called *yomotsuhegui,* which caused her to be defiled. Because of the pollution, she could never afterwards return to the upper world and she soon became the deity of evil and wickedness. Since it was this pollution which brought forth Magatsubi, it is well to bear in mind that pollution should be scrupulously avoided in life.

Now in life, everyone, noble or base, good or bad, must go to this land of death at the expiration of his life. This is indeed a sorrowful thing. It may seem to be too flat a statement and devoid of any logical basis, but it stems from traditions held since the Divine Age, traditions containing wondrous truths which defy comprehension by the ordinary mind. In foreign countries many doctrines have been contrived to explain the reason for man's life and death, but these are either mere human speculations or else contrivances cleverly made to appeal to human credulity. They sound plausible but are in fact fabrications. Man-made explanations in general seem plausible enough, unlike truths transmitted from ancient times which sound shallow and illogical. But human intelligence has its limits and there are many things it cannot fathom. Thus it is that man, not knowing that these shallow and ludicrous sounding traditions actually contain wondrous and profound truths, continues to doubt them and at the same time believes in plausible-seeming fabrications. This is tantamount to believing in one's own mind rather than in facts, which is indeed ludicrous.

Upon his death man must leave everything behind—his wife and children, relatives and friends, house and property—and depart forever from the world he has known. He must of necessity go to that foul land of death, a fact which makes death the most sorrowful of all events. Some foreign doctrines, however, teach that death should not be regarded as profoundly sorrowful, while others assert that one's actions and attitude of mind in this life can modify the situation after death. So comprehensive and detailed are these explanations that people have been deluded into thinking they are true. Once faith is established in these beliefs, grief over death is regarded as a superstition. Those who hold them profess to be ashamed of being concerned about death, and they try not to be superstitious or emotional about it. Some write deathbed poems to express their sense of supreme enlightenment. These are all gross deceptions contrary to human sentiment and fundamental truths. Not to be happy over happy events, not to be saddened by sorrowful events, not to show surprise at astonishing events—in a word, to consider it proper not to be moved by whatever happens—are all foreign types of deception and falsehood. They are contrary to human nature and extremely repugnant to me. Death in particular is and should be a sorrowful event. Even the deity Izanagi who had created the land and all things thereon, and who had first shown the way of life in this world, wept sorrowfully like a little child when death overtook his wife and, longing for her, followed her even to the land of death. That is an expression of true human nature and sentiment. The truth requires that man too must act likewise.

In antiquity, before the confusion caused by the introduction of alien doctrines, man was honest. He did not indulge in the sophistication of inventing various and pointless theories about where he would go after death. He simply believed in the truth that at death he would go to the land of death, and death was cause for him to weep in sorrow. Now this may have no bearing on government, but it helps in understanding the relative truth of our Imperial Way and that of foreign lands.

In foreign lands where it is not known that the occurrence of evil and wicked things in life is the result of the acts of evil deities, attempts have been made to explain man's fortunes—good, bad, or undeserved—in terms of the doctrine of causality and retribution [Buddhism]. Then again they have dismissed the question of man's destiny, by saying that it is Heaven's mandate or Heaven's way [Confucianism]. The doctrine of causality and retribution, as stated above, was invented for expediency's sake and does not merit serious consideration. The doctrine of Heaven's mandate, or Heaven's way, was nothing more than an excuse made in ancient China by men like T'ang and Wu to justify, where no cause for justification existed, the treacherous overthrow of their sovereigns and the seizure of their domains. If that was Heaven's mandate or Heaven's way, then there should have been no irregularities at all in connection with it. But actually there were many irregularities.[2] Why?

Good and Evil in the Tale of Genji

Before Motoori became involved in the Neo-Shinto movement, he had devoted himself to the study of Japanese literature, the interpretation of which provided the basis for much of his later thought. The next selections are from his *Tama no Ogushi*, a study of Lady Murasaki's *Tale of Genji*. The novel he viewed in a surprisingly "modern" light: it is a record of human experience as we find it, not necessarily as we should wish it to be. It is just such a realistic appreciation of the emotional life of man that makes the *Genji* one of the greatest expressions of the Japanese spirit and provides the key to all that is truest and best in the Japanese national life.

[From *Motoori Norinaga Zenshū*, VII, 472–88]

There have been many interpretations over the years of the purpose of this tale. But all of these interpretations have been based not on a consideration of the nature of the novel itself but rather on the novel as seen from the point of view of Confucian and Buddhist works, and thus they do not represent the true purpose of the author. To seize upon an occasional similarity in sentiment or a chance correspondence in ideas with Confucian and Buddhist works, and proceed to generalize about

[2] That is, men of virtue such as Po I and Shu Ch'i protested against this usurpation.

the nature of the tale as a whole, is unwarranted. The general appeal of this tale is very different from that of such didactic works. [p. 472]

. . . .

Good and evil as found in this tale do not correspond to good and evil as found in Confucian and Buddhist writings. . . . Good and evil extend to all realms. Even with the human being good and evil are not necessarily limited to his thinking and his conduct. Rank and position imply good and evil; thus, the noble person is regarded as good, the lowly as bad. In the *Tale* persons of high rank are spoken of as good, while in common parlance there are such expressions as "of good family" and "of good or bad standing." Thus it is too that we speak of good or bad features of one's face. Again, longevity, wealth, and prosperity are all good things, while short life, poverty, failure, loss of material things, illness, and disaster are all bad things. In addition to these strictly human aspects of good and evil, there is good and evil in such things as dress, furniture, housing, and in fact in all things. Thus, it is not only in the psychological and ethical realms of life that we find good and evil. Again, good and evil are not constant—they change according to time and circumstance. For example, an arrow is good if it penetrates its object, while armor is good if it is impenetrable. In the heat of a summer day coolness is good, while in the cold of winter heat is good. For the man who treads the road at night darkness is bad, but for the one who seeks to conceal himself moonlight is bad. In such a way all things may be good or bad. Thus too the good and bad in man's mind and in his acts may not be as opposed to each other as they seem: they differ according to the doctrines one follows. What Confucianism deems good Buddhism may not; and what Buddhism considers good Confucianism might regard as evil. Likewise, references to good and evil in the *Tale* may not correspond to Confucian or Buddhist concepts of good and evil. Then what is good or evil in the realm of human psychology and ethics according to the *Tale of Genji?* Generally speaking, those who know the meaning of the sorrow of human existence, i.e., those who are in sympathy and in harmony with human sentiments, are regarded as good; and those who are not aware of the poignancy of human existence, i.e., those who are not in sympathy and not in harmony with human sentiments, are regarded as bad. Regarded in this light, good and evil in the *Tale* may not appear to be especially different from that in Confucianism or

Buddhism. However, if examined closely it will be noted that there are many points of difference, as, for example, in the statement about being or not being in harmony with human sentiment. The *Tale* presents even good and evil in gentle and calm terms unlike the intense, compelling, dialectical manner of Confucian writings.

Since novels have as their object the teaching of the meaning of the nature of human existence, there are in their plots many points contrary to Confucian and Buddhist teaching. This is because among the varied feelings of man's reaction to things—whether good, bad, right, or wrong —there are feelings contrary to reason, however improper they may be. Man's feelings do not always follow the dictates of his mind. They arise in man in spite of himself and are difficult to control. In the instance of Prince Genji, his interest in and rendezvous with Utsusemi, Oborozukiyo, and the Consort Fujitsubo are acts of extraordinary iniquity and immorality according to the Confucian and Buddhist points of view. It would be difficult to call Prince Genji a good man, however numerous his other good qualities. But the *Tale* does not dwell on his iniquitous and immoral acts, but rather recites over and over again his profound awareness of the sorrow of existence, and represents him as a good man who combines in himself all good things in man. . . .

For all that, the *Tale* does not regard Genji's misdeeds as good. The evil nature of his acts is obvious and need not be restated here. Besides, there is a type of writing which has as its purpose the consideration of such evils—in fact, there are quite a few such writings—and an objective story therefore need not be used for such a purpose. The novel is neither like the Buddhist Way which teaches man to attain enlightenment without deviating from the rightful way, nor like the Confucian Way which teaches man how to govern the country or to regulate one's home or one's conduct. It is simply a tale of human life which leaves aside and does not profess to take up at all the question of good and bad, and which dwells only upon the goodness of those who are aware of the sorrow of human existence. The purpose of the *Tale of Genji* may be likened to the man who, loving the lotus flower, must collect and store muddy and foul water in order to plant and cultivate the flower. The impure mud of illicit love affairs described in the *Tale* is there not for the purpose of being admired but for the purpose of nurturing the flower of the awareness of the sorrow of human existence. Prince Genji's conduct is like the lotus flower which is happy and fragrant but which has its roots in filthy muddy water. But the *Tale* does not dwell on the impurity of the water; it dwells only on those who are sympathetically kind and who are aware of the sorrow of human existence, and it holds these feelings to be the basis of the good man. [pp. 486–88]

Love and Poetry

In this piece from an early work, *Sekijō shishuku-gen* (freely: *Observations from Long Years of Apprenticeship to Poetry*), Motoori acclaims Japanese poetry for its spontaneous expression of the deepest human emotions and justifies its defiance of Confucian canons of emotional restraint. Characteristically, Motoori recognized the worth of any poetry, early or late, which satisfied this criterion, whereas his mentor Kamo Mabuchi had held that in all poetry after the *Manyōshū* the Japanese spirit had been corrupted by Chinese influence.

[From *Motoori Norinaga Zenshū*, VI, 524–29]

Question: Why are there so many love poems in the world?

Answer: The oldest love poems are found in the *Kojiki* and the *Nihongi*, but the dynastic anthologies are particularly conspicuous for the great number of love poems which they contain. In the *Manyōshū* there are sections . . . devoted entirely to love poems. . . . Even in the Chinese *Book of Odes* love songs are prominent. Why is this so? It is because love, more than any other emotion, stirs the human heart deeply and demands an outlet in poetry. It is to love poems that we must look for lines which are profoundly expressive of human emotion.

Question: Generally speaking, man seems to be constantly concerned, not so much with love but rather with personal success and the acquisition of wealth, in which he appears to be completely and unreasonably absorbed. Why is it that there are no poems expressive of these sentiments?

Answer: There is a distinction between emotion and passion. All the varied feelings of the human heart are emotions, but those among them which seek for something in one way or another are passions. These two are inseparable, passions being in general a kind of emotion. Only such feelings as sympathy for others, sadness, sorrow, and regret are specifically called emotions. But as far as poetry is concerned, it comes only from emotion. This is because emotion is more sensitive to things and more deeply compassionate. Passion is absorbed only in the acquisition of things; it does not move one deeply or intimately. Thus, it has no capacity for tears at the sight of flowers or the song of birds. The desire to acquire wealth is an example of passion. It is so alien to the awareness of the sorrow of existence that there can be no outpouring of poetry from it. Although love has its origin in passion, it is a deep emotion which no living thing can avoid. And as man is most highly capable of understanding the meaning of the sorrow of existence, it is he who is most deeply moved—sometimes unbearably—by the sentiment of love. Outside of love where there is awareness of the sorrow of existence, there is poetry. And whereas it became the practice in later times to suppress emotion—for emotion was regarded as less profound than passion, a sign of a faint heart, and therefore a shameful thing—poetry alone retained the spirit of antiquity and continued to express truthfully and without adornment the real sentiments of the human heart. Nor has poetry felt constrained to apologize for femininity or faintheartedness. In later times poets, in order to enhance the charm of poetry, have emphasized awareness of the sorrow of existence and have turned against themes of passion. Passion is not a fit subject for poetry. Thus, poems such as those in praise of wine found in the third volume of the *Manyōshū* and so common in Chinese poetry are unappealing, if not odious. They evoke no affection and hold no attraction, because passion is regarded as tainted and not conducive to fine sentiment. Why is it that in other countries [meaning China] the feeling of emotion is regarded as something shameful while base passion is regarded as something admirable?

Question: In the Chinese work, the *Book of Rites,* it is stated that love is a cardinal passion of man. Conjugal sentiment is deep, for it is the feeling of husband for wife and wife for husband, and this is as it should be. But love in poetry is not always confined to love between man and wife. A man in the privacy of his own room yearns for the woman who is not acceptable to his parents; another, in the intimacy of the bedchamber, gives his love to a woman betrothed to another. Such conduct is licentious and wicked; yet it is regarded as an exquisite example of love. Why?

Answer: It has been stated above that the human heart is susceptible to love—no one can avoid it. Once involved in and disturbed by it, the wise and foolish alike frequently behave illogically in spite of themselves, and they end by losing control of the country,[3] and ruining their bodies and their reputations. That has been the case in numberless instances

---

[3] It is characteristic of Confucian teaching, which is addressed primarily to the ruling class, that it is most concerned with the political consequences of moral failings.

in the past and it is so in the present. And this occurs despite the fact that everyone fully realizes that such behavior is evil and that one must guard against becoming wildly infatuated. But not all men are sages. Not only in love but also in their daily thought and conduct the good does not always prevail; in fact, the bad often does. Love, of all the things in life, is most difficult to suppress in spite of every effort to control it. And man, even with the realization that conduct contrary to the dictates of his own mind is evil, is helpless to control it; of this there are numerous instances. Within the heart, unnoticed by others, there may be a fancy for someone else even though outwardly one appears quite sober and admonishes others to beware of love. If one searches the bottom of one's heart it is impossible not to find love there, especially the type of love forbidden by man. And try as one might to suppress it, there will be only melancholy and bewilderment in one's heart. As love is thus unreasonable, the love poems which come forth on such occasions are especially touching. It is also natural that there should be many love poems which suggest impropriety and licentiousness. Be that as it may, poetry follows the principle of the sorrow of existence and attempts to express without adornment the bad as well as the good. Its aim is not to select and arrange for the heart that which is good or bad. To advise against and check evil is the duty of those who govern the country and teach the people. While unruly love should be strongly cautioned against, it is not the responsibility of poetry to teach such discipline. The aim of poetry is different: it aims to give expression to an awareness of the poignancy of human life and should not be judged on any other basis. This is not to say that poetry applauds evil conduct or implies that it is good. It only avers that poems, as a medium for the expression of emotion, are admirable. All forms of literature including the novel should be looked upon and appreciated in this light and an attempt made to grasp the spirit of their purpose. For further reference I have dwelt upon this point separately and at greater length in my study of the *Tale of Genji,* which includes quotations from every chapter and explanatory notes. From this tale one can understand the spirit of poetry.

Question: Chinese poetry and other forms of Chinese literature are rarely devoted to accounts of love, but our literature abounds in them, including many instances of licentious behavior involving the high and the low alike. Yet, no one condemns this as evil. Is it because there is a taste for the frivolous and the voluptuous in our national character?

Answer: Man's predilection for love is the same now as it has been in the past, and it is the same here as it is elsewhere. An examination of Chinese historical accounts indicates that that country has had more than its share of licentious affairs. The Chinese, however, customarily subject all things to long, tedious moralistic judgments. In particular, love affairs have been judged by would-be scholars as something contemptible and despicable. Chinese poetry, likewise, has been subjected to this same national tendency; it has a taste only for the heroic, manly spirit and speaks not of the effeminate sentiments and sinful aspects of love, which it regards as shameful. This aspect of Chinese poetry is only its edited, ornamented, and outward appearance and not the true revelation of the human heart. But in a later age readers of such poetry have accepted it without serious study as expressive of the true situation. It is ridiculous to believe on this basis that the people of that country are less susceptible to the temptations of love than the people of other countries.

In general our countrymen are generous and not particularly discerning or critical. They have not engaged in painstaking and persistent disputations on the good or the bad in men. Instead they have transmitted in speech and in writing things as they were without adornment. This is particularly true of our poetry and novels, which have as their aim the expression of a sensitivity to human existence; they are calm, straightforward revelations of the varied feelings of men in love.

Again, our national histories written on Chinese models show no special distinction from their Chinese prototypes. It is erroneous to ignore these national histories and to fail to discern what is so clearly written in them, just as in their Chinese prototypes; or to adjudge the Japanese solely on the basis of the poetry and novels, as being especially susceptible to the temptations of love. Even the *Wei chih,* a Chinese history which may not be wholly reliable on all matters, says that the Japanese are not sexually licentious. Not only in love but in all other things as well there have been many scoundrels in China. The Chinese persistently warn against evil; yet, there are many evil men there because the country is bad. In our country, on the other hand, man's conduct has neither been excessively praised nor excessively decried; it has been dealt with calmly and straightforwardly. Thus, we do not make much of evil men in our country. And this is due to the fact that our country is the land of the gods.

[33]

Question: Monks should never indulge in love affairs; yet poetry does not censure them for it. In fact, there are many love poems by monks in the dynastic anthologies, and they continue to write them freely even today. Why?

Answer: Everyone knows very well that the Buddha warned sternly against licentious passions and that it is a matter which monks must scrupulously observe. Even today involvement in love is considered highly deplorable. However, the determination of the morality of such acts should be left to those who belong to the various orders. Poetry is a different thing. It attempts neither to trespass on the teachings of Confucius and Buddha nor to pass moral judgments. Its aim is merely to express a sensitivity to human existence, and its method is to give expression to the overflowing sentiments of the heart. As for monks who have forsaken the world and have entered an order, it is proper that they abide strictly by the teachings of the order, and that they do not conduct themselves licentiously even to the slightest degree. This is particularly true of their outward behavior, which they must maintain with utmost firmness. But the human sentiment of monks does not differ from that of laymen simply because they have become monks; for monks are neither all incarnations of the Buddha and Boddhisattvas, nor can they, short of achieving enlightenment, rid themselves completely of the defilement of worldly life. The sentiment of love is apt to linger in their hearts—but this is as it should be. It is nothing shameful or worthy of reproach. They may even lose their minds over love and commit errors they should not commit, but such are common occurrences in everyday life. Buddha emphasized the commandment in this respect because it is a general weakness and one which is apt to lead people astray. For the people to believe that monks look like Buddha, and for the monks themselves to pretend that they look like Buddha, is a grave sin. I shall use a parable about a holy man in order to explain that psychology. The holy man, seeing the autumnal leaves at the peak of their glory, thought them beautiful, but meeting an attractive woman on the road, he passed by without casting a glance in her direction. Think of his behavior on these two occasions. The tinted autumnal leaves are no less a thing of charm of this world than the beautiful woman, and thus the holy man should not have given his attention to them. But such an attraction is momentary, unlike a woman's charm which has the special capacity of captivating the human heart and of obstructing the attainment of salvation in the life hereafter. Thus the monk may admire the leaves but should not so much as cast a glance in the direction of the woman. His behavior, therefore, was correct, but to say that it was sincere and came from the bottom of his heart would be a gross deceit. If tinted leaves have charm which is limited and does not stir the human heart as deeply as a woman's personal charm, which is unlimited and beguiling to the human heart, it stands to reason that the human heart which admires the limited charm of the tinted leaves cannot help but admire the unlimited charms of a woman. It is as if a hundred ounces of gold were desirable but not a thousand. That is simply illogical. If a beautiful woman does not stir his heart even slightly, he is indeed a Buddha; otherwise, he is inferior in emotional capacity to the bird and the insect and may even be likened to the rock and the tree, which are devoid of feelings. Since a monk does not have a wife and must constantly discipline the passions which strain and distract his mind, it follows that his love poems are more expressive of feelings than those of the laity. There is an ancient anecdote which says that an abbot of Shiga temple was once permitted to hold the hand of a certain royal concubine while composing a poem called "Tamahabaki" [broom corn]. This is a most touching incident and one in keeping with a monk's feelings. To give vent in poetry to the unruly thoughts, long pent up in one's heart, is in accord with the spirit of "laying open one's heart" and of "confession," is it not? At any rate, as long as poetry is poetry, it needs no regulation.

HIRATA ATSUTANE

If Motoori Norinaga is to be credited with having made of the National Learning a subject worthy of a great scholar's attention, and thereby lent the largely inarticulate Shinto religion the authority of a canon of sacred writing, it remained for Hirata Atsutane (1776–1843) to assert the supremacy of Shinto over all other religions and branches of learning. A curious blend of real learning and an often irrational bigotry produced in Hirata an ultranationalistic type of scholarship which was to exert a powerful emotional effect on the Japanese.

Little is known of Hirata's early years. He ran away from his home in the north of Japan at the age of nineteen, and made his way to Edo, where for several years he eked out a hand-to-mouth existence with menial jobs. In 1801, at the age of twenty-five, he became interested in National Learning, a few months too late to meet Motoori, who died earlier in the same year. To Motoori's respect for the Japanese classics Hirata brought a contempt and hatred for Buddhism and Confucianism which extended at times to all things foreign. Motoori had sought to prove that there was a place for Shinto; Hirata now insisted that there was room for nothing else, but he extended the boundaries of Shinto to embrace almost all other forms of knowledge.

One of the most unusual aspects of Hirata's doctrines was the place held in it by Western learning and ideas. Although Hirata was at pains to revile the nations of the West whenever the necessity arose of proving that Japan was uniquely blessed, he also occasionally expressed a grudging admiration for Western science and even for Western theology. He himself was a practicing physician, and studied Dutch medical books in Japanese translation. He was fascinated by what he knew of Western astronomy, partially at least because of its relation to the Shinto cosmogony. Thus he welcomed the Copernican theory, saying that it confirmed ancient Japanese traditions which exalt the importance of the sun.

Most curiously, Hirata borrowed at times from Christian theological works. Such books had been banned in Japan for almost two hundred years, but Hirata managed to secure copies of at least three written in Chinese by Catholic missionaries in Peking. In one early (but never published) essay he very slightly adapted the arguments advanced by the Jesuit priest Matteo Ricci in support of Christianity against Confucianism in such a way that they became arguments for the supremacy of Shinto. It was an amazing instance of his determination to strengthen Shinto by all possible means.

It is debatable how much of Christianity remained in Hirata's theology as it finally evolved. The importance of a Creator God (in this case Takami-musubi) seems to partake of Christian influence, as does Hirata's insistence on the certainty of an agreeable afterworld for those who merit it, unlike the gloomy realm of pollution which Motoori saw as the final destination of all men. Hirata also borrowed from Confucianism, Taoism, and even Buddhism (which he so detested), when additional ammunition was needed in his battle for Shinto.

Hirata's zeal at times was so great as to transgress the bounds of rationality and even of honesty. He seriously interrogated frauds who claimed to have visited the moon or to have lived among the mountain elves, noting with satisfaction whenever their statements confirmed Shinto doctrine. He declared that the Japanese had writing before its introduction from China and produced as evidence a script which proved to be the fifteenth-century Korean alphabet. The fact that the ancient Japanese chronicles make no mention of the Flood, so prominently described in the Bible, led Hirata to assert that this was proof that Japan is situated higher than all the inundated countries. These and many other instances leave us wondering whether he was intellectually dishonest or merely overcredulous.

Hirata's writings became powerful weapons in the struggle to arouse a national consciousness among the Japanese. By their very simplicity, by their appeal to what seemed obvious and immediate to the ordinary man, and through the supreme value placed on sheer emotionalism, the Neo-Shinto teachings won many adherents among those unmoved by more subtle or complex doctrines. The idea that Japan is first among the nations because the sun rises and shines on it first seems bizarre to us, but undoubtedly made better sense to unsophisticated peasant minds in nineteenth-century Japan, which had a more intimate association with the sun than with the other peoples of the world. That this and other naïve notions of Hirata were listened to by a large and sympathetic audience is shown by the leading part these ideas were to play in the Restoration and subsequent chauvinist movements of modern Japan.

HIRATA ATSUTANE

On Japanese Learning

This and the following three selections are from Hirata's *Summary of the Ancient Way* (*Kodō Taii*, 1811).
[From *Hirata Atsutane zenshū*, I, 5–7]

People commonly speak of "learning" as if all learning were one and the same; in point of fact, however, there are many different kinds of learning, each of which is centered around one particular discipline. Japanese learning itself may be divided into some seven or eight categories, the most important of which is Shinto, the Way of the Gods. We may also mention the study of poetry; the study of the legal code;

the study of *The Tales of Ise* or *The Tale of Genji,* to which some scholars devote their chief attention; and the study of history, which deals with the events of the successive reigns of emperors. These various disciplines may in turn be divided into smaller groupings. Chinese studies, to which the Confucian scholars dedicate themselves, have their schools, and Buddhism is divided into sects. In the study of astronomy and geography known as *rangaku,* which is the learning of Holland, and in medicine there are also schools, both traditional and Dutch. One may see how many types of learning are to be found.

If it is asked which of them is the greatest, we must answer, though it may seem slightly presumptuous, that no learning can equal that of Japan. It is easy to see why this is true. The Confucianists learn the Four Books and the Five Classics or the Thirteen Classics and similar books. Having once perfunctorily run their eyes over the pages of these works and learned how to compose a bit of poetry and prose in Chinese, they qualify as Confucian scholars. It is really not very difficult to read so limited a number of books and to acquire the rudimentary knowledge of Chinese composition which they possess. And yet this is the general level of those who pass for Confucian scholars.

Compared to these Confucian scholars, the Buddhist priests are of a much broader learning, for they are required to read the more than 5,000 volumes of the canon—enough books to make at least seven packloads for a strong horse. Even assuming that they do not read the entire collection but only a tenth of it, this still amounts to at least twice what the Confucian scholars are supposed to read. Moreover, since it is not considered a defect in a Confucian scholar if he neglects to read Buddhist books, he naturally never does, with some very rare exceptions. The Buddhists on the other hand must study Confucian books from their childhood days in order to learn Chinese characters, and they write Chinese prose and poetry just as Confucian scholars do.

Buddhist learning is thus broader in scope than Confucian, but Japanese learning is even more embracing. All the various types of learning, including Confucianism and Buddhism, are joined in Japanese learning, just as the many rivers flow into the sea, where their waters are joined. Because of the diversity and number of the different parts of Japanese learning, people are often bewildered and at a loss to evaluate it. Unless, therefore, we can distinguish accurately the elements which make up this vast amalgam of learning, the excellence of the true Way will remain obscure. . . . We must be aware of such matters in order to appreciate the pure and righteous Way of Japan. Japanese should study all the different kinds of learning—even though they be foreign—so that they can choose the good features of each and place them at the service of the nation. We may properly speak not only of Chinese but even of Indian and Dutch learning as Japanese learning: this fact should be understood by all Japanese who delve into foreign studies.

The Land of the Gods
[From *Kodō Taii* in *Hirata Atsutane zenshū*, I, 22–23]

People all over the world refer to Japan as the Land of the Gods, and call us the descendants of the gods. Indeed, it is exactly as they say: our country, as a special mark of favor from the heavenly gods, was begotten by them, and there is thus so immense a difference between Japan and all the other countries of the world as to defy comparison. Ours is a splendid and blessed country, the Land of the Gods beyond any doubt, and we, down to the most humble man and woman, are the descendants of the gods. Nevertheless, there are unhappily many people who do not understand why Japan is the land of the gods and we their descendants. . . . Is this not a lamentable state of affairs? Japanese differ completely from and are superior to the peoples of China, India, Russia, Holland, Siam, Cambodia, and all other countries of the world, and for us to have called our country the Land of the Gods was not mere vainglory. It was the gods who formed all the lands of the world at the Creation, and these gods were without exception born in Japan. Japan is thus the homeland of the gods, and that is why we call it the Land of the Gods. This is a matter of universal belief, and is quite beyond dispute. Even in countries where our ancient traditions have not been transmitted, the peoples recognize Japan as a divine land because of the majestic effulgence that of itself emanates from our country. In olden days when Korea was divided into three kingdoms, reports were heard there of how splendid, miraculous and blessed a land Japan is, and because Japan lies to the east of Korea, they said in awe and reverence, "To the East is a divine land, called the Land of the Rising Sun." Word of this eventually spread all over the world, and now people everywhere refer to Japan as the Land of the Gods, irrespective of whether or not they know why this is true.

[39]

The Creator God

[From *Kodō Taii* in *Hirata Atsutane zenshū,* I, 27–28]

If we examine the origins of the name Mi-musubi given to two of the gods, it is clear from facts recorded in the annals of the divine age that the name stems from their miraculous creative power. We are also informed by the positive declaration of the gods of the sun and the moon that Takami-musubi [1] must be credited with the creation of Heaven and earth, that he is a god of incomparable power, and that he without doubt resides in Heaven and reigns over the world. Despite the pellucidly clear nature of these truths, scholars whose minds have become damaged by Chinese and Indian learning (as well as people who in their ignorance display impious disbelief) do not understand that the very fact of their own birth is immediately attributable to the creative power of this god. They persist in their skepticism and declare that the ancient truths are merely legends peculiar to Japan which they refuse to believe. These truths, however, are by no means confined to Japan. In many other countries it is believed that the seed of man and all other things owe their existence to the powers of this god.

As proof of this we may cite different foreign traditions. In the ancient Chinese legends, where this god is referred to as Shang Ti or T'ien Ti, it is recorded that he resides in Heaven and reigns over the world, and that man was created by him. Moreover, the legend states that it was Shang Ti who implanted in men's hearts such true principles as humanity, righteousness, decorum, and wisdom. This legend is preserved in general form in ancient works like the *Book of Odes,* the *Book of Documents,* and the *Analects,* as all can plainly see who take the trouble to look. However, since the Chinese are of an irreverent disposition, some perverted scholars assert that the ancient legends are merely parables, and voice other such theories. I have elsewhere dealt with this matter in detail. [2]

In the ancient Indian legends the god Musubi is called Brahma the Creator. Here again we find him described as residing in the extremely lofty heaven of the thirty-three devas, [3] and it is stated that he reigns over

[1] Hirata usually does not distinguish between the two "Musubi" gods, Takami-musubi and Kami-musubi, but tends to regard them as two aspects of one god.

[2] In *New Discussion of the Gods* (*Kishin Shinron,* 1805), Hirata's earliest major work.

[3] Trayastrimshās.

the world and that the heavens and earth, man and all things were created by him. The most ancient traditions have it that no god is as holy as he. However, in later times a man named Shākyamuni appeared who invented what he called Buddhism, a religion to suit his own tastes. He deceived men with his so-called divine powers, which were actually a kind of black magic. The false opinion was spread that Buddha was more sacred than Brahma, and even learned priests were deceived by the lie. No one now is left in India who knows the truth.

Far to the west of India there are numerous other countries, and in each of them there are traditions of a god of Heaven who created the heavens and earth, man and all things. This may be known from reading Dutch books.

Thus, in all countries, as if by common consent, there are traditions of a divine being who dwells in Heaven and who created all things. These traditions have sometimes become distorted, but when we examine them they afford proof of the authenticity of the ancient traditions of the Imperial Land. There are many gods, but this god stands at the center of them and is holiest of all.

Dutch Learning
   [From *Kodō Taii* in *Hirata Atsutane zenshū*, I, 53]

The men of the countries of Europe sail at will around the globe in ships which recognize no frontiers. In Holland, one of the countries of Europe (though a small one), they consider astronomy and geography to be the most important subjects of study because unless a ship's captain is well versed in these sciences it is impossible for him to sail as he chooses to all parts of the world. Moreover, the Dutch have the excellent national characteristic of investigating matters with great patience until they can get to the very bottom. For the sake of such research they have devised surveying instruments as well as telescopes and helioscopes with which to examine the sun, moon, and stars. They have devised other instruments to ascertain the size and proximity of the heavenly bodies. It may take five or ten years or even a whole lifetime for such research to be completed; when problems cannot be solved in one lifetime, scholars write down their own findings and leave the solution for their children, grandchildren, and disciples to discover, though it may require generations.

With their scientific instruments the Dutch attempt to determine the properties of things. Unlike China, Holland is a splendid country where they do not rely on superficial conjectures. When the Dutch come across matters which they cannot understand no matter how much they may ponder over them, they say that these are things beyond the knowing of human beings, and belong to *Gotto* [God], and that only with divine powers could such matters be comprehended. The Dutch thus never resort to wild conjectures. Their findings, which are the result of the efforts of hundreds of people studying scientific problems for a thousand, even two thousand years, have been incorporated in books which have been presented to Japan. I have seen them and that is how I happen to be able to write of them.

Ancient Japanese Ethics

In his *Indignant Discussion of Chinese Books* (*Seiseki Gairon,* c. 1810) Hirata is occupied mainly in denouncing such Confucian scholars as Dazai Jun, who had proclaimed the superiority of China.

[From *Hirata Atsutane zenshū,* I, 96–97]

Let me present a few of the arguments advanced by scholars of Chinese learning. First of all, we may cite Dazai Jun, who wrote in *Bendōsho,* "In Japan there was originally no such thing as a Way. As proof of this there is the fact that no native Japanese words exist for the concepts of humanity, righteousness, decorum, music, filial piety, and fraternal affection. There certainly must have been a Japanese word for everything which originally existed in Japan, and the absence of such terms proves that the concepts were also lacking."

This opinion, shocking though it is, is not confined to this particular Confucian scholar. Far from it—the majority of the Confucian pedants and other scholars partial to things Chinese are overjoyed and infatuated with the idea that China possesses the teachings of a Way, and proclaim that in ancient Japan there were no teachings like those of China. But however much they may heap indignation on Japan, all that they assert is utterly in error. Humanity, righteousness, filial piety, and the rest are all principles governing the proper conduct of man. If they are always automatically observed and never violated, it is unnecessary to teach them. If they are the invariable standard of behavior, what need is there for a "Way?" . . .

[42]

The ancient Japanese all constantly and correctly practiced what the Chinese called humanity, righteousness, the five cardinal virtues and the rest, without having any need to name them or to teach them. There was thus no necessity for anything to be especially constituted as a Way. This is the essentially Japanese quality of Japan, and one where we may see a magnificent example of Japan's superiority to all other countries of the world. In China, as I have already had frequent occasions to mention, there were evil customs from the very outset, and human behavior, far from being proper, was extremely licentious. That is the reason why so many sages appeared in ancient times to guide and instruct the Chinese. . . . From this we may see that the very fact that in ancient Japan there was no Way is the most praiseworthy feature of the nation, and that it is the shame of a country if it has had to invent a Way for the guidance of the people.

The Art of Medicine

In *Shizu no Iwaya* (1811) Hirata gives a good summary of Western medicine as known in Japan at the time, together with more general remarks on the relations between medicine and Shinto. In the following extract he discusses why the arts of medicine did not develop independently in Japan.
[From *Hirata Atsutane zenshū*, I, 22]

The art of medicine, though introduced to Japan from abroad, appears originally to have been taught to foreign countries by our own great gods. Later, because of the special needs it meets, this art came to be widely practiced in Japan, and though it may be said to have once been of foreign origins, we are not obliged to dislike it for that reason. Nevertheless it is true that the art of medicine developed to such a high degree in China by way of a quite natural reaction to the rampant and pernicious maladies which resulted from the evil character of the country itself. The spread in Japan since middle antiquity of Confucianism and Buddhism, both of them exceedingly troublesome doctrines, has worsened and confused men's minds, and as a result of the attendant increase in the number of things to worry about, various maladies which were unknown in ancient times have become prevalent. The Chinese methods of treatment were perfectly suited to deal with such maladies and are therefore now in general employ. Just as in countries where there are numerous bandits the government establishes severe laws to punish them, when pernicious maladies are first detected people versed in medicine make their appearance to combat them. In countries where there are many doctors there are also many deadly sicknesses, and as the doctors gradually grow more proficient, the sicknesses become proportionately more difficult to cure.

Life After Death

Most of Hirata's works are filled with lavish praise for Motoori Norinaga, but in the *Pillar of the Soul* (*Tama no Mihashira*, 1812) he disputed Motoori's view that the souls of the dead all go to Yomi, a dark region of pollution. It has been suggested that unlike Motoori, Hirata had no residual faith in the abiding grace of Amida Buddha, and that he therefore envisaged a pleasanter Shinto afterworld than Motoori had described.

[From *Hirata Atsutane zenshū*, II, 73–75, 77–78, 81–85, 88, 90–91]

Accounts of the afterworld are so confused that it is only natural that they arouse bewilderment. Even my teacher did not escape this confusion. His view that the gods and men, good and evil alike, all go to the land of Yomi when they die, was a mistaken one, owing mainly to his insufficient examination of the evidence. . . . The view that after men die their souls go to Yomi is part of a tradition which was introduced to Japan from abroad for which there is no attestation whatsoever in our ancient past. . . .

Someone asked me in this connection, "In the Izumo Chronicles there is an account of a cave known as the Hole of Yomi. Anyone who dreams that he is going to this cave is certain to die. Is this not proof that dead spirits go to Yomi?"

I answered, "When a man dies his corpse becomes foul beyond all recognition and it then belongs to Yomi. The dream thus is a sign that after death the body is to be buried in the earth. It is not a sign that the soul is to go to Yomi. . . . Proof that men's souls do not all go to Yomi may be discovered not only in the facts transmitted to use from the Divine Age, but from an examination of how it happens that people are born and what actually occurs after death. Men owe their lives to their parents, but that they can be created at all is due to the wonderful, miraculous creative power of the gods, who form man of air, fire, water, and earth, and having infused a soul in him, give him life. After a man's death the water and earth in him become his corpse, which is left behind, but the soul flies off with the air and fire. This is because fire and air belong to the sky just as surely as earth and water belong to the ground. [Hirata's note: This is one reason why we know that all human souls do not go to Yomi. Since the soul is bestowed on man by the god Musubi, by nature it should return to Heaven. However, I have not yet found positive evidence or old traditions to prove that this is true of all men.] . . .

There are people who claim that they have come back to life many days after their deaths, and who describe Heaven and hell, but I have never heard of any who claimed to have been to Yomi and seen it. Once there was a woman who said she had visited Heaven and hell. I administered some medicine to her and personally examined her. I discovered that she had in fact been duped by some Buddhist cant. . . .

The old legends that dead souls go to Yomi cannot be proven. Then, it may be asked, where do the souls of Japanese go when they die? It may be clearly seen from the purport of ancient legends and from modern examples that they remain eternally in Japan and serve in the realm of the dead governed by Ōkuninushi-no-kami. This realm of the dead is not in any one particular place in the visible world, but being a realm of darkness and separated from the present world, it cannot be seen. . . . The actions of men can be perceived from the realm of the dead, but from the visible world it is not possible to see this realm of darkness. . . . The darkness, however, is only comparative. It should not mistakenly be imagined that this realm is devoid of light. It has food, clothing, and houses of various kinds, similar to those of the visible world. Proof of this may be found in accounts, preserved in both Japanese and Chinese books, in which a living person has occasionally returned to tell of the realm of the dead. Some self-important scholars may conclude that the realm of the dead does not exist, simply because they cannot see it, but this is exceedingly foolish.

People of this world, wherever they may live and however be employed, go to the realm of darkness when they are dead, and their souls become gods, differing in the degree of excellence, virtue, and strength according to the individual. Those of superior powers are capable of feats in no way inferior to those of the gods of the Divine Age, and do not differ from those gods in their power to inform men of future events. . . .

[45]

After death the soul leaves the body and resides in the area of the grave, a fact attested by countless accounts in Chinese and Japanese sources of both ancient and modern times of miraculous occurrences by spirits in the vicinity of graves. The resting place of the soul after death appears to have been a matter of concern in all times to all people, but in Japan this question has been discussed only under foreign influence. The ancient Japanese never pondered such matters. . . . Some say that the soul goes to the filthy realm of Yomi, but there is not a shred of evidence that this is the case. My teacher was inadvertently in error when he said that the soul went there. His own soul has not gone to Yomi. I, Atsutane, have definitely determined where his soul resides. It dwells in peace and calm amid the spirits of scholars of former times, who wait in attendance on him. Together they write poems and essays and study afresh errors in their teachings. . . .

The place where my teacher's spirit dwells is Mt. Yamamuro. . . . He lived there during his life and fixed upon this mountain as his eternal resting place. How then can it be doubted that his spirit dwells there? How can we imagine that it has gone to the filthy land of Yomi?

CHAPTER XXIII

REFORMERS OF THE LATE TOKUGAWA PERIOD

In view of the shogunate's efforts to channel all thought and discussion within certain prescribed limits, we could understand it if the Japanese had shown little awareness of their true situation during the early nineteenth century and little inclination to speak about it. But despite the prohibition on heterodox teaching in 1790, the restrictions on intellectual contact with the West, and the penalties which attached to any direct criticism of government policies, there was a surprising degree of intellectual ferment and diversity of opinion in regard to the very problems which the Tokugawa had chosen to ignore or proved incapable of meeting. With the more and more frequent appearances of the "black ships" of the West in Japanese waters, as well as with worsening economic conditions manifested in the impoverishment of both peasants and samurai, expressions of dissatisfaction increased as the new century began. Especially was this true in the northern regions of Japan where fears of Russian expansion and economic troubles were most acutely felt.

What is perhaps most significant about the three reformers we shall consider here is that their responses to the challenge of a new age reflected very much their own past. Thus in two of these cases we find a notable willingness to learn from the West, to the extent that this was possible through contact with the Dutch in Nagasaki, combined with the sort of fierce nationalism that had risen steadily throughout the Tokugawa Period. In another case we find a very practical and resourceful attempt to deal with agricultural problems associated with wholly traditional attitudes in the domain of religion and ethics. In this respect we have a foreshadowing of the compromises and adjustments which were to be made in the subsequent period of rapid, wide-scale modernization.

A typical example of this man of the future, who would have one foot in the old world and another in the new, was Honda Toshiaki from the west coast province of Kaga. As a mathematician, ship captain, and scholar, he concerned himself with the economic strengthening of Japan and with her survival in a world of expanding imperialism. Another example is Satō Nobuhiro from Dewa in the north, who had an unusual heritage in that he represented the fifth generation of a family of experts in horticulture and mining in northern Japan. A keen student of Western science and a passionate nationalist, he worked out in later years a complete program of national reorganization along totalitarian lines. The third was Ninomiya Sontoku, a poor farm boy from the hinterland of Edo, who by dint of strenuous personal effort and experimentation tried to raise agriculture to the point where it would no longer be at the mercy of nature, and in so doing elevated human labor to the dignity of a new religious cult.

HONDA TOSHIAKI AND THE DISCOVERY OF EUROPE

The long reign of peace under the Tokugawa Shogunate was kind to many peaceful intellectual pursuits, among them mathematics. Very early in the eighteenth century Seki Kōwa (1642–1708) is said to have arrived simultaneously with Newton and Leibnitz at the mathematical problems of integral and differential calculus and their solution. As the shogunate was concerned at that time with calendar reform and also with the preparation of new maps of the country, there was a real need for men with training in mathematics. The rising tide of mercantilism, with its emphasis on navigation, likewise helped to make this field of study popular. Schools were opened here and there by Seki's followers in important towns and feudal domains. At the age of eighteen, Honda's biographer says that he made his way to Edo in order to study mathematics under a famous master of the time. His progress was such that at the age of twenty-four he was able to open his own school and became known as a first-rate mathematician in his own right.

Not content with the native Japanese system of mathematics, Honda decided to study Dutch, in the hope that a knowledge of the language would open to him the secrets of Western mathematics. Other Japanese of his day were studying Dutch in order to read books of medicine, astronomy, and military science. Indeed, many of the best minds of the late eighteenth century in Japan were turning to the West for new information and guidance as the isolation of the country grew increasingly oppressive. That they chose to study Dutch rather than any other Western language was dictated by the fact that since 1639 the Dutch had been the only Europeans permitted to remain in Japan, and it was towards their trading station at Nagasaki that many young Japanese looked for knowledge. At the time there were no decent dictionaries, and the difficulties besetting the would-be scholar of Dutch were enormous, but with great determination and expense of energy some of them were able to gain enough proficiency in the language to be able to make significant contributions in many fields. It was the example of such men which helped to make possible the amazing Japanese assimilation of Western techniques in later years.

Honda's interest in Dutch mathematics moved to a study of astronomy and navigation, sciences closely connected with mathematics, and from them to more general considerations of the importance of shipping and trade (which depend on a knowledge of navigation). He was convinced that Japan's economy was at a standstill, and only by breaking out of her self-imposed isolation could she achieve greatness. His books are filled with ambitious programs and suggestions in which he sought to incorporate the new knowledge from the West.

No matter how diverse were the subjects he chose to write upon, Honda never failed to use or display his knowledge of mathematics wherever possible. In some cases his penchant for mathematical formulations of economic and social problems, together with his impatient disregard of the niceties of conventional prose, make it difficult for the reader to follow him. And it is sometimes painfully apparent that he has a fondness for multiplying statistics, often quite unnecessarily, merely in order to magnify his conclusions and stagger the reader. But it is also true that at times his laborious computations produce significant results, such as his conclusions concerning the relation of population growth and food supply, which correspond to those of his English contemporary Malthus.

Honda's chief program of action, as enunciated in his work *A Secret*

Plan for Governing the Country, was centered around the so-called "four imperative needs" of Japan—gunpowder, metals, shipping, and development of overseas possessions. Honda was interested in gunpowder primarily for its use in blasting new channels for rivers, part of his program for improving transportation within the country, rather than for its use in warfare. By metals he referred to both the precious ones which, in mercantile fashion, he sought to attract to Japan, and to the base metals, the use of which he advocated in place of wood, so as to reduce loss to rot and fire. His views on shipping and on the development of overseas possessions are given in the readings.

Honda devoted almost equal attention to such matters as sweeping plans for the aggrandizement of Japan and to the problems of daily living faced by settlers of the proposed colonies. In all things he attempted to regulate himself by what he conceived to be the dictates of practical use. For example, he favored abolishing the use of cumbersome Chinese characters in writing Japanese, and the adoption instead of the more practical Western alphabet. He decried the impressionistic renderings of nameless mountains often found in Japanese paintings, and praised instead Dutch realistic painting which, he thought, lent itself better to pedagogic purposes. He hoped that by taking advantage of the benefits of Western science Japan could shake off its long somnolence and emerge as the "England of the East." He wrote,

How may Japan become the greatest nation in the world? She should profit by the arts of civilization which she has learned during the 1,500 years that have elapsed since the time of the Emperor Jimmu. She should move her capital to the country of Kamchatka. (It is located at 51° N. Lat., the same as London, so the climates must be similar.) She should build a great stronghold on Saghalien. . . . Once cities spring up in Saghalien and Kamchatka, the momentum will carry on to the natural development of the islands to the south, and the growing prosperity of these regions will raise the prestige of the Japanese government to new heights. This, in turn, will lead to the acquisition of the American islands, which are Japan's possessions manifestly.

This outspoken imperialism was voiced in 1798, at a time when Japanese were forbidden by law to leave their country, and only a few castaways had ever visited foreign shores. Honda's program may at points seem excessively crude, and when he assumes that the climate of Kamchatka must be the same as that of London, he may excite our smiles. Nevertheless, even in such instances he also compels our admiration by his bold use of Western knowledge—though sometimes it was misinformation—in his attempt to help Japan out of the economic stagnation which he so deplored.

HONDA TOSHIAKI

SECRET PLAN FOR MANAGING THE COUNTRY

Shipping

[From Keene, *The Japanese Discovery of Europe,* 166–70]

By shipping I mean the transport of and trade in the products of the whole country by means of government-owned ships, and the relief of the hunger and cold of all people afforded by these instruments of supplying each region with what it needs. Shipping and foreign trade are the responsibility of the ruler and should not be left to the merchants. If shipping is left entirely in the hands of merchants, they will act as their greed and evil purposes dictate, thereby disturbing commodity prices throughout the country. Prices then fluctuate enormously, and the farmers find it difficult to survive. If this situation is remedied by using government-owned ships for transport and trade, the prices of commodities will be stabilized naturally and the farmers relieved.

As long as there are no government-owned ships and the merchants have complete control over transport and trade, the economic conditions of the samurai and farmers grow steadily worse. In years when the harvest is bad and people die of starvation, the farmers perish in greater numbers than any other class. Fields are abandoned and food production is still further reduced. There is then insufficient food for the nation and much suffering. Then the people will grow restive and numerous criminals will have to be punished. In this way citizens will be lost to the state. Since its citizens are a country's most important possession, it cannot afford to lose even one, and it is therefore most unfortunate that any should be sentenced to death. It is entirely the fault of the ruler if the life of even a single subject is thereby lost.

All the many varieties of troubles, disasters, and crimes found among the common people are a product of their unhappiness and anger over fluctuations in commodity prices. Such fluctuations are caused by the inadequacy of sea transport, which in turn is caused by the fact that the ruler controls no ships, and there is no government service. It cannot be estimated how greatly the prerogatives of the ruler are thereby impaired. Shipping and trade are now the business of merchants. Under this system no distinction is made between the interests of the merchants and the duties of the ruler. By developing the techniques of shipping it would become possible to equalize prices throughout the country, thus helping both the samurai and the farmers. Food production would increase steadily which, in turn, would make the nation prosperous.

It is obviously impossible to feed the thousands of people living in a great city with only the food that can be brought in by coolie labor or on the backs of beasts; unless food is transported in ships the population will go hungry. But when shipping is controlled, as is at present the case, by merchants, it will lead in the end to disaster; this must be changed. [pp. 166–67]

. . . .

Some daimyo have now ceased to pay their retainers their basic stipends. These men have had half their property confiscated by the daimyo as well, and hate them so much that they find it impossible to contain their ever accumulating resentment. They finally leave their clan and become bandits. They wander lawlessly over the entire country, plotting with the natives who live on the shore, and thus entering a career of piracy. As they become ever more entrenched in their banditry one sees growing a tendency to revert to olden times.[1]

It is because of the danger of such occurrences that in Europe a king governs his subjects with solicitude. It is considered to be the appointed duty of a king to save his people from hunger and cold by shipping and trading. This is the reason why there are no bandits in Europe. Such measures are especially applicable to Japan, which is a maritime nation, and it is obvious that transport and trade are essential functions of the government.

Ships which are at present engaged in transport do not leave coastal waters and put out to sea. They always have to skirt along the shore, and can navigate only by using as landmarks mountains or islands within visible range. Sometimes, as it inevitably happens, they are blown out to sea by a storm and lose their way. Then, when they are so far away

---

[1] A reference to the *bahan*, Japanese pirates who were at their strongest in the fifteenth and sixteenth centuries.

from their familiar landmarks that they can no longer discern them, they drift about with no knowledge of their location. This is because they are ignorant of astronomy and mathematics, and because they do not possess the rules of navigation. Countless ships are thereby lost every year. Not only does this represent an enormous annual waste of produce, but valuable subjects also perish. If the methods of navigation were developed, the loss at sea of rice and other food products would be reduced, thus effecting a great saving. This would not only increase the wealth of the nation, but would help stabilize the prices of rice and other produce throughout Japan. The people, finding that they are treated equally irrespective of occupation and that the methods of government are fair, would no longer harbor any resentment, but would raise their voices in unison to pray for the prosperity of the rulers. By saving the lives of those subjects who would otherwise be lost at sea every year, we shall also be able to make up for our past shame, and will keep foreign nations from learning about weak spots in the institutions of Japan from Japanese sailors shipwrecked on their shores. Because of these and numerous other benefits to be derived from shipping, I have termed it the third imperative need. [pp. 168–70]

Colonization

[From Keene, *The Japanese Discovery of Europe*, pp. 170–78]

If the islands near Japan were colonized they would make highly desirable places. By such colonization numerous possessions—some sixty or more—would be created, which would serve not only as military outposts for Japan, but would also produce in abundance metals, grain, and fruit, as well as various other products, thus greatly adding to Japan's strength. I presume that run-of-the-mill officials must be thinking that colonization could be effected only at the expense of the ruler, and the authorities are not in the least inclined to spend any government money on developing farmland. This is the way mediocre minds always react.

The order to be followed in colonizing territories is as follows: First, ships are dispatched to ascertain the location of the islands to be taken, and to measure their extent. The natural products of the islands are investigated, and the native population estimated. Then, when it is known about how many provinces the islands would make if colonized, the actual work is begun. If the natives are still living in caves, they are taught about houses. A house should be built for the tribal chief. Those natives without implements or utensils should be supplied with them. By helping the natives and giving them everything they desire, one will inspire a feeling of affection and obedience in them, like the love of children for their parents. This is true because they are moved by the same feelings that pervade the rest of the world, barbarians though they may be considered.

The way to compensate for the expenses involved in colonization lies in taking the natural products of the islands and shipping them to Japan. Trading marks a beginning of compensation for those expenses. Even barbarians do not expect to ask favors and give nothing in return. The products they offer represent a commencement of taxation. Since every island has wooded areas, there will always be some value in the lumber which can be taken from the islands, even after a great many years. The value of other products besides lumber would be too great to calculate. It is the task of the ruler-father to direct and educate the natives in such a manner that there will not be a single one of them who will spend even one unprofitable day. This matter should not be put off for another moment; it is a vital state duty.

At this point we must discuss the foundation of colonization—the sciences of astronomy and mathematics. In Japan these sciences are not as yet fully known, and there are few men who understand their significance. Even in China the principles of astronomy and mathematics have roughly been understood since the arrival of a number of Europeans late in the seventeenth century.[2] If, in connection with colonization projects, ships cross the seas without reference to the principles of astronomy and mathematics, there is no way to tell how much easier sea travel is than land travel. The name of the book in which the natural laws behind these principles are contained is *Schatkamer*,[3] a European work. One may learn from the latitude of a particular island what its climate is like throughout the year. Or, without actually visiting an island, one can predict in this way whether it will prove fertile. This may be done with certainty; false tales need not be believed.

[2] Honda is a century out—late sixteenth century would be more accurate.

[3] Possibly the *Schatkamer of te Konst der Stuur-Lieden* by Klaas de Vries, a navigator's handbook frequently reissued in Holland. The book was known in Japan before the country was opened. Cf. Hayashi, "A List of Some Dutch Astronomical Works," p. 44.

The key to colonization is to establish a system [4] with long-range objectives as to future profit and loss. By encouraging the good customs of the natives and eliminating their bad ones, it is possible to have them maintain human dignity. They should never be permitted to forget the generosity of the Japanese ruler. This is how colonization should be set about, but Japan persists in her bad habit of imitating old Chinese usages. Very few of the government authorities possess any real knowledge of astronomy or mathematics, and it is because of their ignorance that whenever there is talk of colonizing the northern territories, as occasionally happens, the project is never carried through. It is Japan's misfortune that her officials are misled by foolish tales about these great countries, which are actually far superior to Japan, and consequently do not take advantage of great opportunities for profitable ventures. This is a matter of especial regret because there have been Russian officials in the islands inhabited by the Ainu since about 1765. They have displayed such diligence in their colonization efforts that eighteen or nineteen Kurile islands and the great land of Kamchatka have already been occupied. Forts are said to have been built at various places and a central administration established, the staff of which is regularly changed, and which rules the natives with benevolence. I have heard that the natives trust them as they would their own parents.

In Japan, on the other hand, this system is as yet not followed. It is forbidden to carry from the country seeds for the five cereals or edged tools for use in building houses. It is forbidden to teach Japanese to any natives. These are supplemented by a host of other prohibitions. It is a most lamentable system which has as its object keeping barbarians forever in their present condition. Since the Russians operate under a system which provides that their own subjects are sent out to live among the natives, it is only to be expected that the Ainu look up to the Russian officials as gods and worship them. [pp. 170–72]

. . . .

When the Ezo islands are colonized they will make worthwhile places which will yield several times as much produce as Japan does today. Although there are other islands both to the east and west which should

[4] *Seido*, here translated "system," is a difficult word; it means more or less that which can be established by means of laws.

also be Japanese possessions, I shall not discuss them for the moment. At this crucial time when the Ezo islands are being seized by Russia, we are faced with an emergency within an emergency. When, as now, Japan does not have any system for colonizing her island possessions, there is no way of telling whether they will be seized by foreign countries or remain safe. This is not the moment for neglect; such actions by foreign powers may lead to the destruction of our national defense. With the establishment of a system of colonization, a knowledge of navigation will naturally develop among Japanese, but if navigation, shipping, and trade continue to be considered the occupation of merchants, the natives of our island possessions are doomed to an eternal want of civilization. The fact that the Ainu are living in a state of barbarity has been regarded by Russia as affording a fine opportunity for her to devote her energies to the colonization of the islands, a timely undertaking. The lack of a colonization system has kept Japanese rule from the island, and has meant that the natives are unaware of the goodness of the ruler of Japan. Because of this ignorance they have been quick to become subject to Russia.

So important is colonization that I have termed it the fourth imperative need. [p. 178]

SATŌ NOBUHIRO AND TOTALITARIAN NATIONALISM

Like Honda Toshiaki, Satō Nobuhiro (1769–1850) was a northerner from that side of the country facing the Sea of Japan. Dewa was his native province, the same province from which came the militant Neo-Shintoist, Hirata Atsutane. Two things appear to have been uppermost in his mind: the economic rehabilitation of the country in order to rescue it from poverty and starvation, and the building-up of Japan's military power in the face of frequent visits by "Black Ships" of the West in Japanese waters. For Satō, as for Honda and a few others, a drastic renovation of the national life seemed urgently necessary. And in truth, no thinker even of late nineteenth-century Japan came forward with a more complete and detailed program of reform than Satō did. His *Confidential Memoir on Social Control* (*Suitō hiroku*) contains a complete program of political, economic, and cultural reconstruction, which was the fruit of a long life of freedom and independent study, of broad learning and special training, such as few men enjoyed in his time.

Besides a solid grounding in Chinese culture, common to the leading thinkers of the later Tokugawa Period, he could draw on a large store of experience and experimentation in the fields of agriculture, horticulture, forestry, and mining, which had been accumulated by five generations in his own family. Of the five, his father and grandfather in particular had become real specialists, and to them he owed much of his expert knowledge in the development of natural resources, which formed the basis of his economic rehabilitation program. This family heritage Nobuhiro added to by intensive study of the Dutch language, for him the gateway to a knowledge of Western mathematics, astronomy, geography, history, navigation, and artillery. That his knowledge of Western astronomy was quite impressive is shown in his *Essays on Creation and Cultivation* (*Yōzō kaiku-ron*); and using Dutch sources he was able to write a *Brief History of the Western Powers* (*Seiyō rekkoku-shiryaku*). In addition, he wrote a general survey of the oceans, and several handbooks on the use of artillery. Satō also claimed to have conducted experiments on a motor boat propelled by fire, and on a new type of explosive. It was studies such as these that impelled him to write about military and naval reorganization of the country and to develop his imperialistic program of world union. ·

Satō was not satisfied with a knowledge gained from books, and he took every opportunity to travel around the country, from the land of the Ainu in the northeast to Kyushu island in the southwest. His personal observations of the feudal domains are contained in his *Lands and Climates* (*Shokoku fudoki*), an important source of first-hand geographical information.

Thus Satō may be considered a worthy representative of the rationalistic and empirical strain in Tokugawa thought. The other important trend in this period, nationalism, he represents to an equal or perhaps greater degree. Free of any feudal allegiance, he tended to think in terms of the nation as a whole and not of the interests of a single domain. Therefore it is not surprising that in his later years he should have come under the influence of the extreme nationalist and Neo-Shinto leader, Hirata Atsutane. With his knowledge of Western astronomy, Satō assumed that the sun is the center of our universe, and so Japan, with the Sun-Goddess as its progenitrix, must be the sovereign land of the entire world. Further he claimed that the oldest annals of Japan, the *Kojiki,* is the true book of revelation. In it he found the truth concerning the triple godhead: the Sovereign God and Center of Heaven (*Amenominaka-nushi*), the August Spirit of Vitality (*Takami-musubi*), and the August Spirit of Fertility (*Kami-musubi*). According to Satō, the highest truth in the three realms of nature (Heaven, earth, and mankind) is the law of vitality and fertility. And this law of vitality and fertility, personified in two of the three godheads, assumed an enduring form in the Sun-Goddess, as sovereign of the solar system and forbear of the Divine rulers of the Divine Land. It is this law of vitality and fertility, according to Satō, which must be the basis of all political, economic, and cultural reconstruction of the nation.

Satō's program of reconstruction dwells on what he calls "three essentials and six indispensables." The state which aims at upholding the aforementioned principle must have a Department of Education (*Kyōkadai*), a Department of Religion (*Shinji-dai*), and a Department of Justice. In regard to the Department of Religion it is worth noting that for Satō the gods and goddesses in the national pantheon are those who have made signal contributions to the divine way of vitality and fertility, and who are installed in the pantheon so that their example may inspire loyalty and devotion to this principle.

Satō, however, insists most emphatically on the importance of education as the basic function of the state. The Educational Department includes a ministry of education and a state university, exercising an exclusive right to choose the curriculum, select teachers, and perform other necessary duties without any outside intervention. The university would have ten standing divisions: Philosophy, Religion, Social Institutions, Music, Law, Military Defense, Medicine, Astronomy, Geography, and Foreign Languages. All government officials should be graduates of the university. The Education Department would also have under its jurisdiction provincial schools, one in each district that yields 20,000 *koku* of rice; these will admit all children at the age of eight, regardless of their social status. The provincial school in turn will have under its jurisdiction an institute of general relief, four free dispensaries, six asylums for poor children, forty playgrounds, and twenty kindergartens. The benefits of education at the expense of the state must go to every member of society.

Under the three departments come six administrative bureaus. They are: 1) a Bureau of Basic Affairs (*Honji-fu*), and by basic affairs Satō meant agriculture; 2) a Bureau for the Development of Natural Resources (*Kaimotsu-fu*), which includes forestry and mining among other things; 3) a Bureau of Construction and Manufacture; 4) a Bureau of Commerce and Treasury, which will control the exchange of all commodities through local offices of price control (*Heijunkan*), and will also act as financial agent of the state, providing funds for all state expenses and relief activities (Satō insists that these functions be in the hands of trained civil servants and not of merchants); 5) an Army Bureau having complete control of unskilled labor, with offices in important defense districts of the country; and 6) a Navy Bureau controlling sea ports, waterways, and adjacent islands essential to the defense of the country. Satō thinks that all fishermen and seafarers should come under the jurisdiction of the Navy Bureau, along with sixteen coast defense forces of 3,200 men and seventy-two outer defense forces with 35,000 men. The entire population would come under the jurisdiction of one or another of these government bureaus, and would be divided into eight classes along functional lines.

For Satō the real salvation of the country from the menace of poverty can never be obtained while the Japanese are limited to their own home islands. The law of vitality and fertility demands that the nation move on and spread all over the world. The world is one and is ruled by the simple principle of production and procreation; it is the destiny of Japan and the duty of all Japanese to produce and procreate so as to become the first nation of the world.

SATŌ NOBUHIRO

Preface to *The Essence of Economics* (*Keizai Yōroku*)

The empirical strain in Satō's thought is brought out in this preface, which is largely autobiographical. Though some recent historians have doubted whether Satō's immediate forbears contributed as much to the technological development of agriculture, mining, and manufacturing as he claims here, it is clear at least that he regards advances in these fields as dependent on the steady and systematic accumulation of empirical knowledge. Since Satō places a premium on first-hand observation, much of this account is a travelogue of his and his

[59]

father's "field-trips" throughout Japan, studying the topography and economic geography of different regions. Finally he tells of his increasing interest and employment in matters of military defense.

[From *Keizai taiten*, XVIII, 174–78]

My family had lived for generations in Okachi County, Dewa Province, where it had held an hereditary estate. Having lost its estate in the debacle of 1600,[1] it turned to medicine as its profession. In later days my grandfather, Fumai-ken, himself saw tens of thousands made homeless by recurring famines, and scores die of starvation. He was grief-stricken and thought: "The profession of medicine is of minor importance if it cannot save the masses. I should like to find a way to save the people from the dire afflictions of cold and hunger in times of national poverty and distress." Thus began his interest in the study of economics. Taking precedence in his studies was the management of agriculture, followed by mining, the manufacture of various commodities and improvement of methods of manufacturing. In his desire to improve the methods of manufacturing, he traveled widely through the provinces, calling upon experts in the various fields, and seeking advice from stone cutters, jewelers, mine managers, coal workers, kiln owners, brick makers, fishermen, trap setters, paper makers, weavers, dyers, masons, smiths, coppermen, woodcutters, sawyers, arrowhead makers, lacquer artisans, sheath makers, tea masters, brewers, candy experts, and beverage makers. He inquired of each the principles of his trade.

He also traveled to remote mountains and distant valleys, forded rivers and crossed lakes, and explored gold mines and oil wells. After more than forty years of laborious, indefatigable research, and leaving his tracks nearly everywhere in the country, he passed away at Ani copper mine in Akita County, Dewa, in 1732. Among his works there are *New Book on Natural Resources* (*Kaikoku shinsho*) in twelve chapters, and *Secret of Tracing Ores* (*Sanso hiroku*) in two chapters. The *New Book on Natural Resources* explains the principles of economics and the secret of developing natural resources, and it constitutes the basis of our family program of study. Its aim, in a few words, is to discuss how to develop our land, which is in a primeval state, so as to yield products contributing to the enrichment of our country. It is similar to plans proposed for the development of Ainuland [Hokkaidō]. It examines minutely the particulars of

[1] The defeat of Ieyasu's enemies at Sekigahara.

topography, the taking of measurements, and the marking of boundaries, and it explains their techniques. As for the *The Secret of Tracing Ores,* it describes the physiognomy of mountains which should yield gold, silver, copper, iron, tin, lead, cinnabar, mercury, jade, precious stones, verdigris, sulphur, and alum. It also explains how to determine the presence of gold, silver, or other metals in mountains by their shape and the color and quality of their soils and rocks. It further discusses how to find veins of metal and how to determine the logical sequence of veins of various metals. Moreover, as it deals with the kinds and amount of metal deposits, estimating the height or depth at which they may be found, and the degree of difficulty to be expected in their excavation, it enables one to calculate beforehand the suitability of a particular mountain for mining and prospects of success. It also suggests through a consideration of the natural topography the existence and course of water veins on and under mountains and points out the secret of cutting tunnels to keep the pits dry. Thus, the work has been of incalculable value to mining engineers who have closely guarded its secrets. As this study of mountain physiognomy existed in the past only in name and not in fact, there have been many instances of miners making all kinds of wild claims, deceiving and luring the people into bankruptcy. Indignant over this situation, my grandfather spent over forty years of careful study to write this book which he then presented to his followers. As a result of his study mountain physiognomy has become a science, providing a standard for students to rely upon. Today, those who espouse the science of mountain physiognomy in Dewa, Mutsu, Iyo, Tajima, and Iwami are, for the most part, followers of my grandfather.

When Fumai-ken was still alive he ordered my father, Gemei-ka, to develop and improve the science of economics and natural resources, which he did. Upon my grandfather's death my father also traveled about the country for more than forty years in his study at this subject, and he wrote the *Theory of Developing Resources* and *Lectures on Economics* in thirteen chapters, *Mountain Physiognomy, Illustrated,* in one chapter, and *Management of Miners* in two chapters. In the spring of Temmei 1 [1781], when my father journeyed to Matsumae, I accompanied him to the land of the Ainu. I spent the year at Matsumae, seeing the land with my own eyes, studying its climate, and inspecting its various products. In the spring of Temmei 2 [1782] we crossed over from Matsumae to Tsugaru, from where we toured Nambu, Sendai, Sōma and the entire seacoast of Mutsu. That fall we re-entered the Sendai region via Nihonmatsu and Fukushima, and traversing a by-road called Koyasugoe, at year's end we returned home to Akita where we observed the New Year. In the spring of Temmei 3 [1783] we left home to go to the silver mines of Shinjō, and in the summer of that year we toured the province of Dewa, climbing the Chōkai, Gassan, Haguro, and Hayama mountains. We inspected the natural features and products of Shōnai and Mogami fiefs, Yamagata, Kamiyama, and Yonezawa fiefs. That fall we reached Aizu where we scaled Iide and Bandai, and encircled Lake Inashiro. Wherever we went in Aizu we inspected the soil and the products. In October of that year we passed through Hidama Pass to reach Nasu County in Shimotsuke Province. We scaled Mt. Takahara and stopped for several days at the gold mine located at its foothills where my father taught the natives how to grow mushrooms. At year's end we arrived at Nikkō and greeted the New Year at the village of Kujira where a disciple of my father, Sarubashi Kai-no-Kami, had his residence.

During the early spring of Temmei 4 [1784] we traversed on foot and examined the natural products of the mountains and valleys of Nikkō, beginning with Kurokami. Then we took leave of Sarubashi and made our way to the copper mine of Ashio where there were disciples of my father and grandfather. My father had made a visit to this place to consider a method of extracting silver from copper, and in answer to the invitation of the villagers of Nitamoto who wished to develop a tin mine. The output of the Ashio copper mine in recent years had been extremely small and the mines had deteriorated considerably. My father remained there for more than a hundred days. In the heat of the waning summer, he contracted dysentery, and medicines proving ineffective, he passed away at an inn on the third day of August.

On his deathbed he advised me that, were I to return to my native place after his death, I would live out my life exactly like a plant and the scholarship gained by the labors and hardships of my father and grandfather through two generations would all come to naught. "Although you are but a youth," he said, "you seem to be intelligent. It is my wish that you go to Edo, study the science of economics and of natural resources under a competent teacher, carry out the cherished wishes of your father and grandfather by succeeding to the family profession, and carry this science to its completion."

I was at the time a mere youth of sixteen, and I knew not what to do. I gave heed, however, to my father's injunction and went to Edo to become a pupil of the Master Udagawa Genzui, or Kaien. I heard lectures on natural history, both descriptive and functional. I received training in the reading and translation of Dutch. And from the Master Inoue Chū, or Bubi-en, and from my friend Kimura Taizō, I learned astronomy, geography, mathematics, and surveying.

Then I shouldered my basket and set out on an extensive trip around the country. I visited towns and cities as well as remote mountains and ravines, searching for plants and products, and covering by foot more than sixty provinces. Besides economics and natural resources, I was able to acquire training in such military arts as the making of armor, the making of bows and arrows, and the use of artillery and fireworks. In Bunka 3 [1806] I returned to the Eastern Capital and took up residence on Yanagi Street in Kyōbashi.

In 1808 I went to Awa Province where I devoted my attention largely to fireworks and to devising numerous inventions. It was here also that I wrote *An Historical Survey of Eastern Nations* in two chapters, and *My Idea of Real Military Science* in seven chapters (which was enlarged to thirteen chapters in Bunsei 4 [1821] and the title changed to *My Idea of Military Science*). I also studied the mathematical principles of firing by gunpowder and wrote the *Theory of Firearms* in two chapters. It was in Awa too that I experimented with new weapons of my own invention for use in military expeditions, coastal defense and naval warfare, and wrote the book, *How to Use Three Types of Firearms* in three chapters. Moreover, after painstaking study of military matters, I perfected a method of applying firepower to offensive action, and I built a ship propelled by firepower as well as two types of miraculous bullets which I called the New Thunder and the Golden-purple Bell. In this way I was able to complete my plans for the maritime defense of our nation.

In 1809 I left Awa to return to Edo, but in the following year I again left Edo to retire to Mamezuka village in Shimōsa. I made this move because during my stay in Awa I had gained a sudden notoriety as an inventor of devices relating to maritime defense, and officials in the service of the various fiefs and other curious persons flocked to my residence every day, forming large groups of carriages before my gate. My wife, fearing the unforeseen consequences of so great a notoriety for a *rōnin* such as I, constantly urged me to live in retirement.

Since my retirement I have become interested in a school of thought called Japan's Ancient Way, which is espoused by a fellow native of Dewa, Hirata Atsutane. As I studied carefully the traditions of our heavenly gods and earthly deities, the purity of our origins, our manifest national purpose, and the principles for the evolutionary improvement of all things on earth has become clear to me, so that I have been able to perfect and complete my family's program of studies.

Thereupon, using my grandfather's *New Book on Natural Resources* and my father's *Development of Natural Resources* as a basis, and adding to them what I myself had gained through constant study and research, I have collected the various principles and theories of my family's studies in the following works: *Essays on Creation and Cultivation* in three chapters, *The Pillar of Heaven* in three chapters, and *Compendium of Economics* in eighty chapters. The drafts of these works are ready now, and when proofread they will become a family legacy entrusted to the safekeeping of my children.

The following passage from *Questions and Answers Concerning Restoration of the Ancient Order (Fukko-hō montō-sho)* amplifies the preceding account of Satō's activities as an economic, military, and technical adviser to various feudal lords.
[From *Keizai taiten,* XIX, 98–99]

In the beginning of the Kansei Era [1789–1801] I had an audience with the Lord of Tsuyama. I discussed with him methods of making his domain prosperous, and I wrote for him a book in two volumes on the subject of reforms. Later, during my visit to Kazusa Province, I discussed fishing methods with the natives of the coast of Tsukumo and showed them ways of maintaining a fishing economy. Early in the Bunka Era [1804–1818] I became adviser to Chief Officer Shūdō of Awa fief, and visiting in the city of Tokushima I participated in discussions on coastal defense and wrote *Theory of Firearms* in two chapters, *How to Use Three Types of Firearms* in three chapters, and a *Brief History of Western Countries* in three chapters. In addition I discussed the subject of unifying the world, wrote a fifty-chapter book on *How to Control the Ocean,* helped to cast many cannons, and thus spent three years in Awa. I then went to Owari where I remained for a year and where I wrote the *Development of Natural Resources* in seven chapters. The following year I returned to my native village and assisted the Satake family in opening a sea route on the Pacific for the transporting of Akita products to Edo. The following year I went to Edo and took up residence at Nakabashi. When I wrote *How to Administer Satsuma* in behalf of Igai, the Chief Officer of Satsuma fief, who had enrolled as my student, the Lord of Satsuma who read the tract was so pleased he sent me an honorarium in the personal care of Yamamoto Rihei and Tanaka Shichibei. I then went to the Lord's residence at Takanawa to pay my respects and stayed for more than ten days at the home of the Chief Officer Igai. As he asked me many questions in great earnestness about agriculture, I later wrote and presented him with a copy of *Agricultural Problems* in ten chapters. The venerable Lord was again highly pleased and made me a present of three male and three female pigs. I assigned their care to one of my pupils, Aida Gihei. Their numbers increased many times. Later, I took up residence at Daizudani in southern Shimōsa where I lectured on economics and agriculture and began the revision of the works on agriculture written by my forebears.

The Population Problem

The great increase in Japan's population during the peaceful years of Tokugawa rule created a problem the magnitude of which few even of thinking Japanese appreciated. Satō, feeling that population growth was in accordance with natural law and the divine spirit of creativity, called for fuller employment of Japan's resources and increased food production, while opposing limitation of the birth rate or infanticide. The passage is from his *Essence of Economics* (*Keizai yōroku*).

[From *Keizai taiten,* XVIII, 433–34]

Since the Middle Ages agricultural guidance in the various provinces has been on the decline, there having been no appointment of farm experts to study and to assist the people in the development of natural resources. Thus, despite the beauty of our country and the abundance of fertile land, the exhaustion of the soil and the lack of new attempts at cultivation have led to a scarcity of products, which are hardly sufficient to feed and

[65]

clothe the populace of the country. This, in turn, has led to difficulty in rearing children and to the secret practice of infanticide. The practice is particularly widespread in the northeast and in the eastern regions. It is also widespread in the Inland Sea region, Shikoku and Kyushu, but there the children are killed before their birth, thus making it appear that there is no infanticide. The one place where infanticide seems to be extremely rare is Echigo, but in its stead the practice prevails on a large scale of selling girls over seven or eight years of age to other provinces for prostitution. In fact, girls for prostitution is a kind of "special product" of Northern Echigo. Some consider this practice inhuman, but to think so is a great mistake. It is far more humane than either abortion or infanticide. I was told that long ago in Central Asia there was a large country whose king killed 3,300 children annually to obtain their livers, with which he made a medicine for the kidney to be used for sexual purposes. No one who is told of this practice can help but feel a sense of shock and revulsion. When first I heard of it, I too was greatly shocked, but later, as I reflected on it deeply, it occurred to me that while the king's act of slaying 3,300 children annually was indeed inhumane, it was not as barbarous as the practice of infanticide which is prevalent today. In Mutsu and Dewa alone, the number of children killed annually exceeds sixty or seventy thousand. And I have not yet heard of anyone who deplores this situation. I find it nonetheless an unspeakable state of things. . . . That infanticide is so widespread in the various provinces cannot be attributed to the inhumanity of the parents. In the final analysis, it must be attributed to the ruler who lacks compassion, who is unaware of his duty as deputy of Heaven to help the people, who does not study the science of developing natural resources, who does not appoint agricultural experts, and who fails to carry out a program of agriculture which would encourage farmers to exert their utmost. Under such rule agricultural yields are meager and the condition of the land poor. Human beings are the beloved children of heaven. If rulers fail to carry out the teaching of service to Heaven, and permit the slaying of several tens of thousands of children year after year, who knows what Heaven will not do? If this state of affairs continues, divine punishment is inevitable. Therefore the ruler of the land must not fail to adopt methods for the achievement of national prosperity.

Total Government

This plan for the total utilization and control of natural and human resources, contained in Satō's *Confidential Memoir on Social Control* (*Suitō
hiroku*), seems frighteningly modern and yet owes much to Confucian social
ideals and the already well-developed Chinese pattern of centralized government. Here he extends and adapts it to the complex requirements of his own
society in order to exploit fully the potentialities of technological developments.
Though he anticipates considerable innovation from the West, Satō characteristically regards this political reform as the fulfillment of the ancient (Chinese)
ideal of a rationally ordered society in a universe governed by natural law
(already set forth in his *Restoration of the Ancient Order* [*Fukko-hō*], 1846).
That this would also be in accord with Divine Law and Providence, as understood through Shinto traditions, is made clear in other writings to follow.

This passage concerns the chief agencies of government which Satō would
put in control of the economic life of the nation. Since it would involve a
complete reorganization of the four-class system and military government of
his day, Satō treated this plan as private and confidential rather than appear
to be taking issue publicly with established Tokugawa policy.

[From *Keizai taiten*, XVIII, 635–36]

The Six Ministries should be the Ministry of Fundamental Affairs,[2]
Ministry of Development, Ministry of Manufacture, Ministry of Finance,
Ministry of the Army, and Ministry of the Navy. This system is similar to
the Six Offices of the Chou government and the Six Departments of the
T'ang dynasty in China. However, the systems of the Chou and T'ang
dynasties governed the people by dividing them into four classes: the
ruling class, the farmer, the artisan, and the merchant. After much
thought, I have come to the conclusion that in a four-class system there
are some matters which do not come under effective control of the government and possibilities for the development of industry cannot be
exploited to their fullest extent. In this way, we neglect some of the great
resources which nature has bestowed upon us.

In order to promote government "in the service of Heaven," [3] it should
be done on the basis of the occupations of all the people, who should be
classified into groups with similar functions. The country's industries
should be divided into eight groups, namely: plant-cultivation, forestry,

[2] Signifies "agriculture," traditionally regarded as the mainstay of the state.
[3] This means something much like "in accordance with natural law."

[67]

mining, manufacturing, trading, unskilled occupations, shipping, and fishing. The people, once classified into these eight groups, would then be assigned to the Six Ministries. Each person would be assigned to one occupation and attend diligently to his own occupation. The law should strictly prohibit anyone from trying his hand at another occupation. Those who cultivate plants should be assigned to the Ministry of Fundamental Affairs, foresters and miners to the Ministry of Development, craftsmen to the Ministry of Manufacture, traders to the Ministry of Finance, unskilled labor to the Ministry of the Army, and the boatmen and fishermen to the Ministry of the Navy. Thus, the six Ministries will care for the groups of people assigned to them, inducing them to study their occupations and making them devote their attention constantly and exclusively to the performance of their occupations without faltering or becoming negligent, and to the fullest extent of their energies. In this way, as the months and the years pass, each industry will acquire proficiency and perfect itself, providing steadily increased benefits for the greater wealth and prosperity of the state.

If, as in the systems of the Chou and the T'ang, the people are divided into four classes for purposes of administration, the division, although clear and distinct in appearance, in practice leads inevitably to confusion. This is because the ruling class concerns itself exclusively with the administration of government and national defense, giving no attention to the production of goods from land or sea, and placing the burden of production for the entire country on the other three groups: the farmers, craftsmen, and the merchants. As a small number of groups must assume a large number of industries, the merchant has to take on some of the functions of the farmer, forester, artisan, and the fisherman. Each trade is left largely uncontrolled, and thus is unable to develop any skill and ingenuity. Profits dwindle from year to year, and some people have to turn over their businesses to others losing house and home as well. The number of homeless destitutes gradually increases, and leads in the end to the decline of the nation itself. This is a matter of the greatest magnitude, requiring serious thought and investigation.

Moreover, when the people are divided into eight groups, each group should be segregated and mixed residence not permitted, as in the ancient rule of [the early Chinese statesman] Kuan Chung of Ch'i. If this system is followed the people will learn their trades from the period of their adolescence, and even without being formally instructed they will become familiar with their trades. Thus, the number of specialists will naturally increase.

Creation and Cultivation (*Yōzō Kaiku Ron*)

Satō's economic and technological studies, pursued in a rationalistic and empirical spirit, had been devoted to increasing the production and utilization of goods. In his later years, under the influence of Hirata Atsutane, Satō's rationalism was joined to Shinto vitalism. He now saw productivity and the technological transformation of nature as themselves implicit in the natural order. Indeed, to Satō they have a metaphysical basis in the primordial gods, the Spirit of Vitality and Spirit of Fertility.

[From *Keizai taiten*, XVIII, 106–8]

For rulers to employ every means in their power for the sake of agriculture—including the study of natural law,[4] astronomy, surveying of land and sea, determining latitude and longitude, examining climate, distinguishing the nature of soils, reclaiming paddy fields and farms, rectifying boundaries, repairing irrigation ditches, building and repairing embankments, preparing for drought and rain, tilling and harrowing with infinite care, and cultivating with earnestness—is the way to carry out the divine will of creation and to assist in the cultivation of nature. These are what we call the thirteen laws of agricultural management.

If the thirteen laws of agricultural management were conscientiously carried out, then all things would produce an abundant harvest. These products would then be brought under the control of a system of allocation and distribution. In this manner the goods and wealth of the land would be accumulated, and the way would be opened for civilizing the countries of the world. If we strive to teach service to Heaven, all living people will enjoy the benefits of benevolent rule. To be well-versed in agricultural management, to bring all products under a single control, and to endeavor to spread education are what we call the Three Essentials of Economics.

When the head of a nation carries out satisfactorily these Three Essentials, production will increase greatly, there will be a flow of money and

[4] Lit. "the principles (or laws) of Heaven."

wealth, the whole country will prosper, all the people will be rich and happy, and suffering due to poverty will be unknown. Then what harm would there be in having a large family? Then and only then can the teaching of gratitude for divine favors be promoted and the foul custom of infanticide be eradicated. Only in this way can talents be developed, military defense be perfected, and laws enforced. Therefore if the government is conscientious in this respect, the innate goodness of all men will assert itself. Acts of violence will decrease gradually, moral discipline will gradually improve, and the population will increase greatly. . . .

Let us respectfully examine the annals of the Divine Age. Prior to the creation of heaven and earth there were three godheads: the Lord of the Center of Heaven, the Spirit of Vitality, and the Spirit of Fertility. These three together were the fountainhead of all creation.

Then in the beginning of creation one original energy manifested itself in the midst of the great void of fusion and confusion. Because of the divine act of creation what was heavy was separated from what was light, and what was clear was separated from what was foul; and the ethereal essence was condensed in the center and the upper heaven was completed.

Confidential Plan of World Unification (Kondō Hisaku)

As a prelude to his plan of world empire Satō pursues further the theme above: reconciliation of Shinto creation legends and the naturalistic cosmology of the Chinese which had already been incorporated into the *Nihongi*. Here the pivotal concept is Heaven (*ten*), which embraces both nature and the divine, so that the will of the Shinto gods is readily identified with the natural law (Heaven's law) of the Chinese and the West.

World rule by Japan is to result from: 1) divine favor, in the form of natural geographical advantages; 2) a capacity for rational organization of the world's resources; and 3) a divine spirit among the Japanese, such that their superior moral fiber is sufficient to overcome all obstacles. Echoes of these arguments were to be heard in the twentieth century from Japanese militarists, who counted heavily on Japanese "spirit" to offset the material preponderance of the West.

[From *Keizai taiten*, XVIII, 567–69]

Our Imperial Land came into existence at the very beginning of the earth and it is the root and basis of all other countries of the world. Thus, if the root is attended to with proper care, the entire world will become its prefectures and counties,[5] and the heads and rulers of the various countries will all become its ministers and servants. According to the scriptures of the Divine Age, the imperial progenitors, Izanagi and Izanami, instructed Susanoo [The Impetuous Male Deity] that "our rule extends over the eight hundred folds of the blue immense." And thus we learn that to make clear the divine teaching of production and procreation and thereby to set the peoples of the entire world at peace was, from the very beginning, the principal and urgent mission of our heavenly country. My earlier works, the *Compendium of Economics* (*Keizai taiten*) and the *Outline of Heaven's Law* (*Tenkei yōroku*), examined the divine teaching of creation with the purpose of uniting the entire world in peace.

The salvation of the people of the world is an immense task which requires, first of all, a clear knowledge of geography and the state of affairs in the countries of the world. If measures are not taken to bring the actual state of affairs into harmony with Heaven's will, the principle and teaching of production and procreation cannot be put into effect. And therefore the study of geography is imperative.

Let us now examine the situation of our country in terms of the geography of the countries of the world. It extends from 30° N latitude to 45° N latitude. Its climate is temperate, its soil fertile, and it is not without a variety of crops which produce abundant harvests. Facing the ocean on four sides, for convenience of ocean transportation it has no equal among the nations of the world. Its people, living on sacred land, are superior, excelling those of other countries for bravery and resoluteness. In truth they are fully capable of holding the reins of the world. From this position of strength they could majestically command the world in every direction, and by virtue of the awesome prestige of this Imperial Land they could readily subjugate the puny barbarians and unify the world under their control. Ah, how boundless have been the blessings of the creator on our Imperial Land!

However, even in our Imperial Land, since the descent from heaven of the Imperial Grandson, rulers have disobeyed the laws and teachings of the Divine Age. They have squandered many years in pleasure, idleness,

[5] The process of empire building is described as it had taken place in China, where the feudal states of antiquity were absorbed into the Ch'in empire as centrally administered prefectures and counties.

and unbridled dissipation, setting their hearts on beautiful women instead of heroic women, and thus shortening their own lives. They have also neglected their duties toward the industry and economy of the nation, while they indulged instead in useless undertakings. There has been no harmony between husband and wife, and household management has suffered. Brothers have quarreled with each other and relatives have killed one another, resulting in the decline of state and society. The ruler did not act like a ruler, nor the subject like a subject. The providential plan initiated by Onamochi and Sukuna-hikone was abandoned and the national polity remained in a state of decline for a long time. Thus magic and Buddha's teachings came into vogue, and no one was left who knew the true teaching of old. The ignorant masses of this corrupt age, having been informed of the vastness of China and India on the one hand, while seeing on the other the smallness of their heavenly land and the weakness of its power, have been convulsed with laughter when they heard my arguments for the unification of the world, telling me that I lack a sense of proportion. They have no awareness that heaven has ordained our country to command all the nations. . . .

In terms of world geography our Imperial Land would appear to be the axis of the other countries of the world, as indeed it is. Natural circumstances favor the launching of an expedition from our country to conquer others, whereas they are adverse to the conquest of our country by an expedition from abroad. The reason why an expedition from our country could be executed more easily than one from abroad is as follows. Among the nations of the world today, no country compares with China in immensity of territorial domain, in richness of products, and in military prestige. Yet, even though China is our neighbor and very close to us, there is no way for her to inflict harm on us, try as she might to conquer us with all the resources of her country. Should a reckless despot dare to send a great force against us—like Kublai of the barbarous Mongols who mobilized the entire manpower of his country to send against us—we in our heavenly land need have no fear. On the contrary, we will inflict great damage on China. She may make a second attempt but will be incapable of making any more. If our nation should attempt to conquer China, however, with proper spirit and discipline on our part China would crumble and fall like a house of sand within five to seven years. This is because the cost to our country of dispatching a military expedition will be small while for China it would be so great as to be prohibitive. Moreover, her people would be exhausted with ceaseless running from one end of the country to another. Thus, for Japan to attempt to open other countries, her first step must be the absorption of China.

As already noted above, China, despite her great strength, cannot oppose our country. Needless to say, the other countries likewise cannot oppose us, for by the grace of nature Japan is so situated as to be able to unify the countries of the world. I am, therefore, going to explain in this work how China can be subjugated. After China is brought within our domain, the Central Asian countries, as well as Burma, India, and other lands where different languages are spoken and curious costumes are worn, who yearn for our virtues and fear our power, will come to us with bowed heads and on hands and knees to serve us.

NINOMIYA SONTOKU: AGRARIAN REFORM AND COOPERATIVE PLANNING

Fuji no shirayuki wa	The white snow on Fuji
Asahi ni tokeru	Melts in the morning sun,
Tokete nagarete	Melts and runs down
Mishima ni ochiru	To Mishima,
Mishima jorōshū no	Where Mishima's prostitutes
Keshō no mizu.	Mix it in their make-up.

Ninomiya Sontoku (1787–1856), who grew up within sight of Mt. Fuji, must have hummed this popular ballad on occasion, and might have mused upon what it meant. The white snow is beautiful to look at, but it can only become of use to man by melting and running down to the foot of the mountain where men habitate. The Japanese often speak of the "underground activity of water" (chikasuigyō) as a simile for self-effacing service on the lowest level of human life. And Sontoku's lifelong service was something akin to that of water. He never wanted to be a government official, nor did he offer to serve as a political adviser. Starting life as a tiller of the soil, he always remained one. But at the same time he did much to improve the farmer's life by teaching and practicing a creed which may be summed up in these few articles: first, manual labor is the worthiest of human activities since it brings to fruition the creative labors of the gods; second, the law of averages in nature requires a sort of planned agrarian economy, whereby something is set aside from good harvests to tide over bad years; third, agrarian life is essentially communal and its success depends upon unselfish, cooperative activity in an organization through which the savings of some members may be made available for the use of others; and last, human life must be conceived as a continuing act of thanksgiving for the providence of Heaven, earth, and man.

This creed, and the indefatiguable labors of Ninomiya Sontoku to rescue his fellow farmers from the vagaries of nature, won for him the affectionate title, "Peasant Sage of Japan." A popular ivory image of Sontoku represents him as a hard-working and affable youth with a happy, smiling face. But a wooden portrait kept in his home and a drawing now placed in the Ninomiya shrine at Odawara, represent him as a man of rugged physique and rough features, with a look of unshakeable determination. This is the man to whom shrines have been built as to a guardian angel in the rural districts around modern Tokyo.

At first glance it might seem hard to reconcile Ninomiya's deep sense of gratitude to nature with his constant emphasis on the need for planning against the vagaries of nature. But to his mind the seeming irregularities of nature are in no way arbitrary or capricious. Natural calamities indeed occur without regard to immediate human desires; but they are aspects of an inexorable natural order that works ultimately for the good of man, providing that man does his share. Man cannot rescue himself from the miseries of a hazardous livelihood by crying out against Nature. He must instead be ready to understand the conditions set by Nature, and take them into account in the planning of his life. This requires, above all and before all, the virtue of honesty (*shisei*),[1] which to Ninomiya meant not only a recognition of law and order in human relationships, but also a wholehearted acceptance of the order of Nature. And one of the things which must be accepted as a law of the universe is the necessity for human labor. Hard work is just as much a part of the natural order as the rising and setting of the sun or the alternation of the seasons. Every year, every month, every day and every hour has an incalculable value to the forwarding of human life. Therefore idleness cannot

[1] The "Absolute Sincerity" of the Confucian classic, the Mean.

be tolerated. "The root of virtue is found in labor," he once said, "and the loss of virtue comes from idleness."

Labor also makes man what he is, for civilization and human advancement are nothing but the cumulative achievements of human labor. The Japanese nation itself is only what generation after generation of forbears have made of it through their loving labors. Ninomiya expresses this idea in a poem that bespeaks the rising tide of Neo-Shintoist concepts in early nineteenth-century Japan:

Furu michi ni	The beaten path
Tsumoru ko no ha wo kakiwakete	Is covered with fallen leaves; Brush them aside
Amaterasu kami no	And see the footprints
Ashiato wo miru	Of the Sun-goddess

The practical side of Ninomiya's teaching is embodied in his own system of economic planning. Farmers are apt to feel the seeming indifference, or even cruelty, of nature during a year of poor harvest. This will be felt most keenly by those whose existence is most precarious, who are living from day to day or from harvest to harvest at the limit of their resources. The only solution for them is to think and plan in long-range terms. In other words, man must try to see things in somewhat the same way Nature does, and statistics, based on the law of averages, is what enable him to do this. Ninomiya thus urges his fellow farmers to compile their own statistics of crop yields over a ten-year period or longer. With this they can arrive at a fairly reliable estimate of their average annual income, and budget their expenses accordingly. The major portion of Ninomiya's collected works, which run to thirty-six volumes, is devoted to the budgets or formulas (*shioki*) which he worked out for various individuals, village communities, feudal domains, and even for the shogunate. They represent probably the most detailed case studies of agrarian problems and the most immediately practical solutions for them attempted in the Tokugawa Period.

Ninomiya's system of planning or budgeting, however, was not conceived in terms of immediate personal needs alone. Definite provision had to be made for contributing to the welfare of others, especially of posterity. Just as the individual shares in the life of a community and benefits from the contributions of his predecessors, so must he contribute to the general welfare. Since the welfare of each individual is bound up with that of the community, the sufferings of some, if unaided in times of distress, will eventually affect the lives of others and hold back the progress of all. The mark of a civilized community is the provision which it makes for mutual aid. In agrarian communities this should take the form of a voluntary credit union. Ninomiya gave these societies which he organized the name "Society for the Repayment of Virtue." Thus was acknowledged the debt which each man owes to his fellows and to his forbears for their contributions to the general welfare.

If there is anything original in the teachings of Ninomiya it is these simple formulations for long-range planning and mutual aid in the agrarian community. These are by no means insignificant contributions, as the Westerner may realize if he considers that the depressed condition of agriculture in many Oriental countries still calls urgently for more of the planning, cooperative enterprise and short-term farm credit he tried to promote. But Ninomiya's espousal of such techniques would not alone explain the success of his movement or the lasting impression he made upon the Japanese peasantry. We must recognize that he was as much as anything else a religious leader, though he did not consider himself to have been favored by any special insight or inspiration, or by the sort of education which might command respect among the people. He had no formal instruction, and in reading his life story one is impressed by the fact that he took from his reading only what he had already learned from life. His thought does not bear the mark of any established tradition, and yet it seems to have absorbed much from existing cults which would contribute to his purpose. Thus he once said that his teaching was one-half Shinto, one-quarter Buddhist, and one-quarter Confucianist. That his creed does combine the most practical aspects of these doctrines is not hard to see: the emphasis upon honesty or sincerity, a cardinal virtue in Confucianism and one which the Neo-Shintoists valued to the exclusion of almost all others in their bare, impoverished system of thought; the emphasis upon thanksgiving, which is important in both Pure Land Buddhism and Shinto; the same insistence upon disciplined and devoted service which Nichiren had called for in the name of the Lotus and the nation; and finally the self-reliance which Zen had inculcated in its followers. Above all Ninomiya must have showed the poor peasant the effectiveness of these ideas in action. While others talked and wrote about them, he worked at them. His accomplishments in rescuing numerous communities from poverty and ruin, starting with nothing more than his native wit and willingness to work hard, became the inspiration for many others after him who joined together to solve their problems in a self-reliant but selfless spirit.

NINOMIYA SONTOKU
The Repayment of Virtue

Ninomiya devoted himself more to the practical realization of his teachings than to writing about them. Though his collected works run to thirty-six volumes, they contain for the most part his detailed analyses and solutions of the economic problems of various domains. For his more general beliefs we must refer to the accounts kept by disciples of his conversations with them, or else to the simple slogans and formulas which he found so effective in spreading his ideas among people who, like himself, had had little formal education. The use of Chinese characters in the original formulation achieves a special effect—a combination of pithiness and neat parallelism—largely lost in translation.

Through the following refrain runs the theme of man's dependence upon nature and society and his obligation to repay that debt.

[From Hōtoku-kun 4 in Ninomiya Sontoku ō zenshū, Seikatsu Genri Hen, p. 309]

The origin of father and mother depends upon the will of heaven and earth.

The origin of the human body depends upon its being given birth to and cared for by father and mother.

The succession to children and grandchildren depends upon the sincere solicitude of husband and wife.

The wealth and rank of father and mother depend upon the labor and achievements of their forbears.

The wealth and rank of ourselves depends upon the accumulated goodness of father and mother.

The wealth and rank of children and grandchildren depends upon our own labor and effort.

The growth and preservation of our selves depend upon three things: food, clothing, and shelter.

The three necessities of food, clothing, and shelter depend upon [the products of] field and farm, woods and forests.

[The products of] field and farm, woods and forest, depend upon the labor and cultivation of the people.

This year's food and clothing depend on the production of last year.

Next year's food and clothing depend on the exertions and hardships of this year.

Year in and year out we must be ever mindful of the repayment of virtue.

The Practice of Repayment

[From Fukuzumi Masae, *Hōtokugaku naiki* 7 in *Ninomiya Sontoku ō zenshū*, XXXVI, 864–65]

The teaching of the Repayment of Virtue is a practical teaching. In practicing it the three most important things are to labor, to be thrifty, and to pass something on to others. To labor means to work hard at one's own occupation; to be thrifty means to keep the family income clearly in mind and to live within that income; to pass something on to others means to practice the five forms of sharing according to one's own means. These are what I call the Three Duties of my school. These duties are like a tripod, which needs each one of its legs and fails to fulfill its function if one is lacking. A man may labor hard at his occupation, but if he is not thrifty it will be labor wasted. A man may be thrifty, but if he is not also hardworking, he will be unable to produce anything and he will have a sense of guilt toward Heaven and earth. Lastly, even though a man be both hardworking and thrifty, if he does not pass something on to others, he will be lacking in humanity and may fall into miserliness. Industry and thrift are practiced only for the sake of passing something on to others.

The Way of Nature

One of the most interesting aspects of Ninomiya's teaching is that he stresses the maximum utilization of the gifts of nature without suggesting in any way that man should seek to dominate or exploit nature. Thus, in contrast to Satō Nobuhiro, he does not think in terms of technological progress but rather of fulfilling nature's own plan through rational management and human industry. Less of a scientist and engineer than Satō, and more of an ethical or religious reformer, Ninomiya puts his faith in voluntary effort on the part of the individual instead of in state controls.

[From *Sangyō jizen dan* in *Ninomiya Sontoku ō zenshū*, I, 951–52]

Here is a man who wants to eat rice in order to feed his body and sustain life. The best thing for him to do is to cultivate rice. Now rice culture follows the seasons. Seeding starts at the end of spring, and transplant-ing, hoeing, fertilizing, and other kinds of care are given in the summer. When the rice is ripe in autumn, it is cut and taken in before winter arrives. After threshing, apportionment of the grain is made so that there will be enough for needs throughout the year, avoiding excess now and deficiency later. This is the quickest way to get rice to eat. Though some might consider it too long a process, I can assure you that there is no other proper way to obtain rice for the people. If you work hard and faithfully at this great task, you will be free from hunger and starvation from generation to generation. Do not ask for any short cut. In the final analysis Heaven has its own natural way of doing things, and in order to obtain rice the only proper procedure is to cultivate rice plants. In the cultivation of rice plants, too, there is a proper procedure, which involves the sowing of seeds. Remember that rice plants never produce rice plants, and rice seeds never produce rice seeds. First the seeds must grow into plants and then the plants produce seeds. From the beginning of crea-tion there has always been this endless process of transformation and transmigration.[1]

> So let our labor bring benefits
> Equally to all,
> That all as one may attain the Buddha-mind
> And go on to live in the land of Bliss.

The "Pill" of the Three Religions
[From Fukuzumi Masae, *Ninomiya ō yawa* in *Ninomiya Sontoku ō zenshū*, XXXVI, 820-23]

Old Ninomiya once said, "I have long pondered about Shinto—what it calls the Way, what are its virtues and what its deficiencies; and about Confucianism—what its teaching consists in, what are its virtues and

[1] The idea of transmigration is associated in the author's mind with the Kegon doctrine of the interdependence of all things and with the adaptation of this theme to the Amidist doctrine of the "circulating Nembutsu," whereby the merits of each individual are applied to the salvation of all. Thus Ninomiya is prompted to add the poem which follows, adapting the same theme to his teaching of the supreme value of human labor. It is just in this way that he claimed to be a synthesizer of existing religions.

deficiencies; and also about Buddhism—what do its various sects stand for, and what are their virtues and deficiencies. And so I wrote a poem:

Yo no naka wa	The things of this world
Sute ajirogi no	Are like lengths
Take-kurabe	Of bamboo rod
Sore kore tomo ni	For use in fish nets—
Nagashi mijikashi	This one's too long,
	That one too short.

"Such was my dissatisfaction with them. Now let me state the strong and weak points of each. Shinto is the Way which provides the foundation of the country; Confucianism is the Way which provides for governing the country; and Buddhism is the Way which provides for governing one's mind. Caring no more for lofty speculation than for humble truth, I have tried simply to extract the essence of each of these teachings. By essence I mean their importance to mankind. Selecting what is important and discarding what is unimportant, I have arrived at the best teaching for mankind, which I call the teaching of Repaying Virtue. I also call it the 'pill containing the essence of Shinto, Confucianism and Buddhism.' " . . .

Kimigasa Hyōdayū asked the proportions of the prescription in this "pill," and the old man replied, "One spoon of Shinto, and a half-spoon each of Confucianism and Buddhism."

Then someone drew a circle, one half of which was marked Shinto and two quarter-segments labeled Confucianism and Buddhism respectively. "Is it like this?" he asked. The old man smiled. "You won't find medicine like that anywhere. In a real pill all the ingredients are thoroughly blended so as to be indistinguishable. Otherwise it would taste bad in the mouth and feel bad in the stomach." [pp. 822–23]

. . . .

The old man said: "The Buddhists say that this life is temporary and only the life hereafter is important. Nevertheless, we have obligations to our masters, our parents, our wives, and our children. Even if we could renounce this world, leaving behind our masters and parents and wives and children, still our bodily life goes on. And as long as our bodily life goes on, we cannot do without food and clothing. In this world you cannot get across the river or sea without paying the boat fare. So Saigyō says in his poem:

Sute hatete	Having renounced all,
Mi wa naki mono to	I feel myself utterly nonexistent,
Omoedomo	And yet when it snows,
Yuki no furu hi wa	I know
Samuku koso are	How cold I am!" [p. 820]

The Society for the Repayment of Virtue

This society was organized by one of Ninomiya's leading disciples, Fukuzumi
Masae, to further the work of his master, and eventually spread all over Japan.
The following account of its organization and activities was written in 1912.
[From Yoshimoto, *A Peasant Sage of Japan*, pp. 227–31]

"Men who wish to render thanks to Heaven by benefiting mankind as
much as they can; men who wish to reform villages in order to help the
poor; man who wish to sow the seeds of goodness that they may enjoy
its lovely flowers and noble fruit; of such men does the 'Hōtokusha'
consist." So wrote Fukuzumi Masae, a great disciple of Sontoku.

This Hōtokusha ("Society for Returning Virtue") was organized by
Fukuzumi according to Sontoku's instructions, and consisted of a Central
Society and many branches which have since spread all over Japan. [The
central organization was on the principle of Sontoku's Hōtoku office,
or "Hōtoku Yakusho," as it was called, of which Sontoku said, "The
spirit of the Hōtoku office, if pictured, would be like an august deity
shedding a holy light and filled with love and compassion for the common people. No other picture would do justice to its subject."]

The purpose of the Hōtokusha is to help the poor and to aid them to
unite in helping one another, first by opening their hearts and developing goodness of character among them, and secondly by assisting them
to open up wild lands, improve irrigation and roads, repair bridges and
river banks, and, in general, by doing all that is of benefit to the poor.
It begins by helping the poorest and encouraging and rewarding the good.
The function of the Central Society is to give financial help as well as
advice to the branches, so its members are well-to-do persons who freely
give their money and services in order to show their gratitude to Heaven
by helping their fellow men, and they expect no material reward for
themselves.

The Branch Societies consist of poorer men who pay a small subscrip-

[81]

tion known as the "Nikka-sen" or "Daily Subscription Money," laying aside from day to day a certain amount of their regular earnings, or the product of extra labor, though it be but a farthing a day, to be paid into the Society monthly. The money thus subscribed by the poor, together with money received from the Central Society, forms a fund from which loans are made to members requiring capital for sound productive enterprises, such as improving their trade or industry. No interest is charged, because the purpose of the Society is to help the needy. Sontoku once compared the virtue of lending money, without interest, to the sun "When the sun rises industry awakes. Officials take up their duties, farmers till their fields, merchants buy and sell, and all men work at their various employments. So when money is lent without interest farmers who were sitting idle for lack of implements set to work on their farms, merchants who were lying asleep because they had no money to buy goods get up and open their shops again, the weak become strong, and the poor become rich. The sun rises and sets daily and corn grows, trees blossom, fruit ripens, and in 365 rounds of the sun all the needs of man are satisfied. Even so is the virtue of money lent without interest —farmers and merchants prosper, and the idle become industrious."

Zenshukin, "Seed-of-goodness Money," is a fund formed from occasional contributions of members, and is employed in charity and various public benefits. The following extracts from an old cashbook of a branch indicates the source of such contributions:

CONTRIBUTIONS TO ZENSHUKIN

Yen	Sen	
3	0	Amount saved by economizing expenses on marriage ceremony of donor's sons.
9	50	Proceeds of sale of unnecessary clothing in donor's family.
5	0	Share of profit from keeping pigs.
2	0	Proceeds of sale of three trees planted for the purpose five year ago.
1	25	Amount saved by economizing in traveling expenses.
0	75	Amount saved by giving up drinking *sake*.
0	37	Amount realized by selling pipes and tobacco, donor having given up smoking.
0	25	Proceeds of nightwork making rope.
0	65	Proceeds of sale of a silver hairpin.

The Hōtokusha is virtually a Cooperative Credit Society founded with a high moral purpose, and it has proved a great boon to the poorer classes of people. Its organization at the present time is not precisely the same as at its inception, having been more or less modified to meet the changing circumstances of the times and the various needs of different localities, but in spirit and in general principles it remains as it was at its origin.

CHAPTER XXIV

THE DEBATE OVER SECLUSION AND RESTORATION

After 1739 Russian ships were seen in Japanese waters with increasing frequency. A report was brought home by waifs that the Russians had established a school of navigation at Irkutsk in 1764, and that a Japanese language department had been added in 1768. The Russian government was not alone in its persistent efforts to open Japan's closed door; in 1808 the English ship *Phaeton* humiliated the shogunate by forcing its way into the port of Nagasaki; and the commissioner of the port had to commit suicide as a result of the disgrace. The country was already in turmoil when Commodore Perry of the United States arrived in 1853 at Uraga Bay near the shogunal capital to demand that Japan be opened to navigation and trade. This was only five years after the United States had annexed California. Literally defenseless, the shogunate had no choice but to accept a treaty stipulating that two ports be opened. This was a complete reversal of the long-established shogunate policy of excluding foreigners, and provoked an uproar from one end of the country to the other. The mounting discontent and agitation pointed unmistakably to the downfall of the tottering shogunate. From the raging debate on the open-door three main points of view emerged. The Mito schoolmen, headed by Lord Nariaki and eloquently spoken for by Fujita Tōko and Aizawa Seishisai, came to be known as the group which advocated "reverence to [meaning eventually "restoration of"] the emperor and repulsion of foreigners" (*sonnō-jōi*). A more conciliatory group advocated "union of the civil authority [Kyoto Court] and military authority [Edo Shogunate]" (*kōbu gattai*) in order to strengthen the nation politically; in the cultural sphere it called for the adoption of Western science and art while preserving Oriental ethics. The most important spokesman for this view was Sakuma Shōzan (1811–1864), later victim of assassination at the hands of a political opponent, who set forth the shogunal policy of opening the country in order to learn Western techniques indispensable for the defense of the country. There was a third group which believed that the salvation of the country would come not from the mere adoption of certain techniques or tactics, but only from a complete renovation of national life through a system of education based on Western civilization and science. This group had as its predecessors such leaders as Sugita Gempaku and Takano Chōei. In the latter half of the nineteenth century Fukuzawa Yukichi was its foremost leader and spokesman, with "independence and self-respect" (*dokuritsu jison*) as his slogan.

THE LATER MITO SCHOOL

"Revere the Emperor, Repel the Barbarian"

The Mito school, as we have already seen, was inaugurated in the seventeenth century by Tokugawa Mitsukuni for the purpose of compiling an official history of Japan. This work, however, remained in preliminary draft during Mitsukuni's lifetime, and was not in fact put into final form until the early years of the present century. Meanwhile, in the eighteenth and early nineteenth centuries, the Mito branch of the Tokugawa family rose steadily in influence, partly owing to the great prestige acquired through its sponsorship of a project in which many illustrious scholars participated. Its political fortunes rose especially after Nariaki succeeded to leadership of the family, and his son became a candidate for the office of shogun in the absence of an heir in the main Tokugawa line. But the rising political power of Mito was also due in no small measure to the simple and forceful doctrines disseminated by its leading schoolmen. These were dramatized in the slogans: "Shinto and Confucianism are one!" (*Shinju-funi*), "Literary and military [training] are not incompatible" (*Bumbu-fugi*), and "Loyalty to sovereign and loyalty to parents are one in essence" (*Chūkō-ippon*).

Here was a program designed to conciliate and unite the principal religious, intellectual, and political elements in the country against the threat from outside. But what answer had these men to the great question of the moment: "How are the foreigners to be dealt with?" To under-

[85]

stand their answer we must review Japanese history as the Mito men themselves were doing in their compilation of the *Dai-Nihon-shi*. The office of shogun, which the Tokugawa held, had its inception in the subjugation of the Ainu, then called the "Northern Barbarians." Generals commissioned by the imperial court to undertake campaigns of suppression were designated "Barbarian-subjugating Generalissimo" (*Sei-i tai shōgun*), subsequently abbreviated to simply Generalissimo (*Shōgun*). The original function of the shogunate was, then, to cope with the barbarians. But the Tokugawa were obviously unable to discharge this responsibility. By yielding to the demands of the barbarians from America, the shogunate had abandoned its trust and forfeited its authority to rule. In this predicament the Mito branch of the Tokugawa, one of three specially appointed to guard the interests of the ruling house, was in a logical position to take the lead in salvaging the situation. Its solution, as set forth by Aizawa Seishisai (1782–1863) and Fujita Tōko (1806–1855), was to deal with the new barbarians as vigorously and contemptuously as earlier barbarians had been dealt with.

In his *New Proposals* (*Shinron*) Aizawa puts the issue in this form. "In the defense of the state through armed preparedness, a policy for peace or for war must be decided upon before all else. If there is indecision on this point, the people will be apathetic, not knowing which way to turn. Morale will deteriorate while everyone hopes for peace that cannot materialize. The intelligent will be unable to plan; the brave will be unable to stir up their indignation. Thus day after day will be spent allowing the enemy to mature his plans. Waiting until defeat stares one in the face is due to an inner sense of fear that prevents resolute action. In the days of old when the Mongols were insolent, Hōjō Tokimune stood resolute. Having beheaded the Mongol envoy, he ordered his generals to summon the army for war. Emperor Kameyama, majestic as he was, prayed at the Ise Shrine and offered his life for the salvation of the country. Thereupon the men who were called upon to sacrifice themselves responded by defying death in a body, as if the entire nation were of one mind. Their loyalty and patriotism were such as to bring forth a storm and hurricane that smashed the foe at sea. 'Put a man in a position of inevitable death, and he will emerge unscathed,' goes the saying. The ancients also said that the nation would be blessed if all in the land lived as if the enemy were right on the border. So I say, let a policy for peace or for war be decided upon first of all, thus putting the entire nation into the position of inevitable death. Then and only then can the defense problem be easily worked out."[1]

This is what came to be known as the policy of "repelling the barbarians" (*jōi*). But Aizawa felt, even though he could not openly declare it, that the shogun lacked the authority to make a final decision in favor of such a policy. The historical studies of the Mito school had already established that the descendants of the Sun Goddess were the ordained rulers of the Land of the Rising Sun. So with Aizawa, as with Nariaki and Tōko, reverence for and loyalty to the sovereign (*sonnō*) must be the rallying cry for the entire nation in putting up a unified front against the growing threat of the Western barbarians. On this point the Mito spokesmen joined hands with the Neo-Shintoists. Aizawa mentions the special features of Japanese geography and history; that the country was created by Heavenly forebears and is located at the center of the world; that ever since the descent of the Sun Goddess the country has been ruled by a single line of her descendants; that in Japan loyalty to the sovereign and filial piety to parents form the basis of all morality, so that the people will live happily and die happily for the sake of the emperor and their parents. This is the nucleus of the Japanese nationalistic ideology that later came to be known as the "national polity" (*kokutai*).

Because of the introduction of Buddhism in earlier times, the people had lost sight of the basic truths of history and had become lax in the observance of the fundamental duties of loyalty and filial piety. Throughout the medieval period confusion and disorder became almost the rule, until Hideyoshi and Ieyasu pacified the country. "Thus the whole land and the entire population came under a single control and all as one paid respect to the benevolence of the Heavenly court while at the same time obeying the commands of the shogunate. Peace reigned supreme over the nation. Because of the prolonged peace, however, signs of weakness and sluggishness have appeared: the rulers of fiefs are easygoing; they make no provision for times of need and destitution; reckless people are left to themselves and go unpunished; foreign barbarians stand by off our coasts awaiting their chance. . . . But all the people, high and low, are intent only upon their own selfish gain, with no concern for the security of the nation. This is not the way to preserve our national

[1] Takasu, *Shinron kōwa*, p. 253.

[87]

polity. When a great man assumes leadership, he is only concerned lest the people be inactive. Mediocre leaders, thinking only of easy peace, are always afraid of the people's restlessness. They see to it that everything appears quiescent. But they let barbarians go unchecked under their very eyes, calling them just 'fishing traders.' They conspire together to hide realities, only to aggravate the situation through half-hearted inaction. Standing on high and surveying the scene in order to practice delaying tactics with an intelligent air seems to me a sure way of carrying us all to an inevitable catastrophe. . . . If instead the shogunate issues orders to the entire nation in unmistakable terms to smash the barbarians whenever they come into sight and to treat them openly as our nation's foes, then within one day after the order is issued, everyone high and low will push forward to enforce the order. . . . This is a great opportunity such as comes once in a thousand years. It must not be lost." [2]

Such is the clarion call of Aizawa's *New Proposals* (*Shinron*), which before the Second World War was acclaimed as one of the two immortal essays on militant loyalty and patriotism, the other being Yamaga Sōko's *Historical Evidence of the Central Kingdom* (*Chūchō jijitsu*).

AIZAWA SEISHISAI
Preface to the *New Proposals* (*Shinron*)

The *New Proposals* of Aizawa Seishisai, written in 1825, represents the first declaration of the creed of the Mito school, which until that time had confined itself to the writing of history and avoided political controversy. The crisis brought on by the appearance of Western ships in Japanese waters, and in particular the detention of crewmen from a British whaler in the Mito domain (1824), called forth this explicit statement of doctrines which had a powerful impact on their times.

[From Takasu, *Shinron kōwa*, 1–10]

Our Divine Land is where the sun rises and where the primordial energy originates. The heirs of the Great Sun have occupied the Imperial Throne from generation to generation without change from time immemorial. Japan's position at the vertex of the earth makes it the standard for the nations of the world. Indeed, it casts its light over the world, and the distance which the resplendent imperial influence reaches knows no limit.

[2] Takasu, *Shinron kōwa*, pp. 71–72.

Today, the alien barbarians of the West, the lowly organs of the legs and feet of the world, are dashing about across the seas, trampling other countries underfoot, and daring, with their squinting eyes and limping feet, to override the noble nations. What manner of arrogance is this!

The earth in the firmament appears to be perfectly round, without edges or corners. However, everything exists in its natural bodily form, and our Divine Land is situated at the top of the earth. Thus, although it is not an extensive country spatially, it reigns over all quarters of the world, for it has never once changed its dynasty or its form of sovereignty. The various countries of the West correspond to the feet and legs of the body. That is why their ships come from afar to visit Japan. As for the land amidst the seas which the Western barbarians call America, it occupies the hindmost region of the earth; thus, its people are stupid and simple, and are incapable of doing things. These are all according to the dispensation of nature. Thus, it stands to reason that the Westerners, by committing errors and overstepping their bounds, are inviting their own eventual downfall. But the vital process of nature waxes and wanes and Heaven may be overcome by the collective strength of men in great numbers.[1] Unless great men appear who rally to the assistance of Heaven, the whole natural order will fall victim to the predatory barbarians, and that will be all.

If, today, we should discuss a far-sighted program in the public interest, the public will stare at one another in astonishment and suspicion, for the public has been weakened by time-worn tales and become accustomed to outdated ideas. In [Sun Tzu's] *Art of War* it says: "Do not rely on their not coming upon you; rely on your own preparedness for their coming. Do not depend on their not invading your land; rely on your own defense to forestall their invasion."

Let, therefore, our rule extend to the length and breadth of the land, and let our people excel in manners and customs. Let the high as well as the low uphold righteousness [duty]; let the people prosper, and let military defense be adequate. If we proceed accordingly and without committing blunders, we shall fare well however forceful may be the invasion of a powerful enemy. But should the situation be otherwise, and

---

[1] According to Confucian theory Heaven, Earth, and Man form a harmonious Triad, the balance of which may be temporarily upset by the evil actions of men.

should we indulge in leisure and pleasure, then we are placing our reliance where there is no reliance at all.

Some say that the Westerners are merely foreign barbarians, that their ships are trading vessels or fishing vessels, and that they are not people who would cause serious trouble or great harm. Such people are relying on the enemy not coming and invading their land. They rely on others, not upon themselves. If I ask such people about the state of their preparedness, about their ability to forestall an invasion, they stare blankly at me and know not what to say. How can we ever expect them to help save the natural order from subversion at the hands of the Western barbarians?

I have not been able to restrain my indignation and my grief for this state of affairs. Thus, I have dared to set forth what the country should rely on. The first section deals with our national polity, in which connection I have called attention to the establishment of our nation through the loyalty and filial piety of our divine forbears. I have then emphasized the importance of military strength and the welfare of the people. The second section deals with the general situation, in which I have discussed the trend in international affairs. The third is on the intentions of the barbarians, in which I have discussed the circumstances of their designs upon us. The fourth is on defense, wherein I have discussed the essentials of a prosperous and militarily strong nation. The fifth presents a long-range plan wherein a method for the education of the people and the uplifting of their customs are mapped out. These five essays are written with the fervent prayer that in the end Heaven will triumph over man. They represent the general principles to which I have pledged my life in the service of Heaven and earth.

The National Polity

The opening portion of Aizawa's work presents his central conception of the national polity (*kokutai*), probably the most potent concept in modern Japanese nationalism because it so effectively brings together Shinto mythology and Confucian ethics of the *bushidō* variety. Note how, from beginning to end, Aizawa identifies the Sun Goddess with Heaven, which presides over the moral order of the Confucian universe, attributes to her the promulgation of the moral law and political order among men, and equates the Confucian virtues of loyalty and filial piety with Shinto worship and thanksgiving. For

[90]

this reason *kokutai* has simultaneous religious, moral, and political overtones. It embraces the "national structure," especially the imperial institution; the "national basis" as found in the divine origins of the country and the dynasty; and the "national character" as embodied in those moral virtues which were considered indispensable to social unity and order.

[From Takasu, *Shinron kōwa*, pp. 13–20]

The means by which a sovereign protects his empire, preserves peace and order, and keeps the land from unrest is not the holding of the world in a tight grip or the keeping of people in fearful subjection. His only sure reliance is that the people should be of one mind, that they should cherish their sovereign, and that they should be unable to bear being separated from him. Since Heaven and earth were divided and mankind first appeared, the imperial line has surveyed the four seas generation after generation in the same dynasty. Never has any man dared to have designs on the imperial position. That this has been so right down to our own time could scarcely have been by mere chance.

The duty of subject to sovereign is the supreme duty[2] in Heaven and earth. The affection between parent and child is the quintessence of kindness (*on*)[3] in the land. The foremost of duties and the quintessence of kindness pervade everything between Heaven and earth, steadily permeating the hearts of men and enduring forever without change. These are what the sovereign relies upon above all in regulating Heaven-and-earth and maintaining order among the people.

Of old, when the Heavenly progenetrix [Amaterasu] established the state on a foundation as broad as Heaven, her position was a Heavenly position, and her virtues were Heavenly virtues, and with these she accomplished the Heavenly task of bringing order into the world. All things great and small were made to conform with Heaven. Her virtue was like that of the jewel, her brightness was like that of the mirror, and her awesome power was like that of the sword.[4] Embodying the benevolence of Heaven, reflecting the radiance of Heaven, and showing forth the awesome power of Heaven, she beamed majestically over the whole realm. When she bequeathed the land to her imperial grandson and personally bestowed the Three Regalia on him, these were taken

[2] Or principle of righteousness.
[3] Implying especially a strong sense of indebtedness for favors received.
[4] The Three Imperial Regalia.

to be symbols of the Heavenly office, giving form to the Heavenly virtue, and taking the place of Heaven's own hand in the performance of the Heavenly functions. Subsequently they were handed down to unbroken generations; the sanctity of the imperial line being such that no one dared violate it. The status of sovereign and subject was clearly defined, and the supreme duty [of loyalty to the Throne] was thereby made manifest.

When the Heavenly progenetrix handed down the Divine Regalia, she took the treasured mirror and giving her benediction, said: "Looking at this is like looking at me." Countless generations, bearing this in mind, have revered the mirror as the divine embodiment of the Heavenly progenetrix. Her holy son and divine grandson looked into the treasured mirror and saw in it a reflection. What they saw was the body bequeathed to them by the Heavenly progenetrix, and looking at it was like looking at her. Thus, while reverently worshiping her, they could not help feeling an intimate communion between gods and men. Consequently how could they not but reverence their ancestors, express their filial devotion, respect their own persons [as something held in trust], and cultivate their own virtue? Even so, as the love between parent and child deepens, the quintessence of kindness becomes fully manifest.

The Heavenly progenetrix, having thus established human morality on these two principles, imparted her teachings to endless generations. The obligations of sovereign and subject, parent and child—these are the greatest of Heaven's moral obligations. If the quintessence of kindness is achieved within and the highest duty is manifest without, loyalty and filial piety will be established and the great Way of Heaven and man will be brilliantly shown forth. By loyalty honor is done to those worthy of honor; by filial piety affection is shown to parents. It is truly by these means that the hearts of the people are made as one, and high and low are made to cherish one another.

But how is it that these superlative teachings are preserved without being propagated in words and how is it that the people practice them daily without being conscious of them? [5] As the Heavenly progenetrix resides in Heaven and beams majestically upon the earth below, so

[5] The question implies that these truths have a mysterious power so that they may be perpetuated in the life and experience of the people even though they have not been committed to writing. The subsequent passage explains how this mysterious power operates.

Heaven's descendant below manifests to the utmost his sincerity and reverence in order to repay his debt to the Heavenly ancestor. Religion and government being one,[6] all the Heavenly functions which the sovereign undertakes and all the works that he performs as the representative of Heaven are means of serving the Heavenly forebear. Revering the ancestor and reigning over the people, the sovereign becomes one with Heaven. Therefore, that his line should endure as long as Heaven endures is a natural consequence of the order of things. And thus, in expressing their supreme filial piety, successive sovereigns have maintained the imperial tombs and performed ceremonies of worship to their ancestors. They have manifested to the full their sincerity and reverence by observing the whole system of rites, and have fulfilled their duty of repaying the debt to their progenetrix and of reverencing their ancestors by performing the Great Thanksgiving Ceremony. This ceremony consists in the first tasting of the new grain and the offering of it to the Heavenly god[s].

The Danger from the West

The following excerpt from the *New Proposals* is preceded by a discussion of the principle known as "retracing the descent and repaying the original debt" (*hanshi hōhon*) which affirms the divine descent of the imperial house and the gratitude of the Japanese people for the blessings of the gods. According to Aizawa this principle was inculcated by the original Shinto teaching and reinforced by Confucianism from China. Later, however, it declined owing to the spread of superstitious beliefs identified as Shamanism, and of Buddhism, unorthodox Confucian teachings and Christianity.

[From Takasu, *Shinron kōwa*, pp. 90–95]

Thus, our ancestral teaching has been muddled by the shamans, altered by the Buddhists, and obscured by pseudo-Confucians and second-rate scholars who have, through their sophistries, confused the minds of men. Moreover the duties of sovereign and minister and of parent and child have been neglected and left undefined in their teachings. The great Way of Heaven and man are nowhere to be found in them.

In the past those who have attracted popular attention and confused the thinking of the populace with their improper teaching have only been

---

[6] The early Japanese word for government (*matsuri-goto*) is a compound based on the word for religious rite (*matsuri*), indicating a close association of political and religious functions.

people of our own realm. But now we must cope with the foreigners of the West, where every country upholds the law of Jesus and attempts therewith to subdue other countries. Everywhere they go they set fire to shrines and temples, deceive and delude the people, and then invade and seize the country. Their purpose is not realized until the ruler of the land is made a subject and the people of the land subservient. As they have gained momentum they have attempted to foist themselves on our Divine Land, as they have already done in Luzon and Java. The damaging effects of their heresies go far beyond anything done by those who attack from within our own land. Fortunately, our rulers were wise and our ministers alert, and thus were able to perceive their evil designs. The barbarians were killed and exterminated, and there has been no recurrence of this threat. Thus, for two hundred years, the designing and obstinate fellows have been prevented from sowing their seeds in our soil. That the people have been free from the inflammatory teaching of the barbarians has been due to the great virtue of our government. . . .

Recently, there has appeared what is known as Dutch Studies, which had its inception among our official interpreters [at Nagasaki]. It has been concerned primarily with the reading and writing of Dutch, and there is nothing harmful about it. However, these students, who make a living by passing on whatever they hear, have been taken in by the vaunted theories of the Western foreigners. They enthusiastically extol these theories, some going so far as to publish books about them in the hope of transforming our civilized way of life into that of the barbarians. And the weakness of some for novel gadgets and rare medicines, which delight the eye and enthrall the heart, have led many to admire foreign ways. If someday the treacherous foreigner should take advantage of this situation and lure ignorant people to his ways, our people will adopt such practices as eating dogs and sheep and wearing woolen clothing. And no one will be able to stop it. We must not permit the frost to turn to hard ice. We must become fully aware of its harmful and weakening effects and make an effort to check it. Now the Western foreigners, spurred by the desire to wreak havoc upon us, are daily prying into our territorial waters. And within our own domain evil teachings flourish in a hundred subtle ways. It is like nurturing barbarians within our own country.[7] If confusion reigns in the country, and depravity and ob-

---

[7] Lit. the "Central Kingdom," the usual Chinese name for China.

sequiousness among the people, could this land of ours still be called the Central Kingdom? Would it not be more like China, India, or the Occident? After all, what is the "basis" [8] of our nation?

The Source of Western Unity and Strength
[From Takasu, *Shinron kōwa,* pp. 198, 215]

The Western barbarians have independent and mutually contending states, but they all follow the same God. When there is something to be gained by it, they get together in order to achieve their aims and share the benefits. But when trouble is brewing, each stays within his own boundaries for self-protection. So when there is trouble in the West, the East generally enjoys peace. But when the trouble has quieted down, they go out to ravage other lands in all directions and then the East becomes a sufferer. Russia for instance, having subjugated the Western plains, turned eastward to take over Siberia and penetrate the Amur River region. But as the Manchus were still strong in China, the Russians could not attain their objectives and had to turn their aggressive designs toward the land of the Ainu. [p. 215]

. . . .

As to the Western barbarians who have dominated the seas for nearly three centuries—do they surpass others in intelligence and bravery? Does their benevolence and mercy overflow their own borders? Are their social institutions and administration of justice perfect in every detail? Or do they have supernatural powers enabling them to accomplish what other men cannot? Not so at all. All they have is Christianity to fall back upon in the prosecution of their schemes. . . . When those barbarians plan to subdue a country not their own, they start by opening commerce and watch for a sign of weakness. If an opportunity is presented, they will preach their alien religion to captivate the people's hearts. Once the people's allegiance has been shifted, they can be manipulated and nothing can be done to stop it. The people will be only too glad to die for the sake of the alien God. They have the courage to give battle; they offer all they own in adoration of the God and devote their

---

[8] Refers to the "national polity" (*kokutai*), especially as found in the divine origins of the country and the dynasty, and as embodied in those moral virtues which are considered indispensable to social unity and order.

resources to the cause of insurrection.[9] The subversion of the people and overthrowing of the state are taught as being in accord with the God's will. So in the name of all-embracing love the subjugation of the land is accomplished. Though greed is the real motive, it masquerades as a righteous uprising. The absorption of the country and conquest of its territories are all done in this fashion. [p. 198]

THE OPENING OF JAPAN FROM WITHIN

In the atmosphere of impending crisis which pervaded Japan in the mid-nineteenth century, the Mito slogan, "Revere the Emperor, Repel the Barbarian" was to prove remarkably effective in rallying nationalistic sentiment around a single center, the imperial house. Yet the very simplicity and generality of this appeal rendered it susceptible of conflicting interpretations and left many questions unanswered, which, as events brought nearer the final crisis in foreign relations, were to be resolved in an unexpected manner. Thus for some of the Mito leaders, themselves prominent members of the Tokugawa family and desirous of strengthening its position rather than abandoning it, the expression "Revere the emperor" had represented a call to national unity, and not what it later became to proponents of the imperial Restoration: a call for surrender to the emperor of functions long performed by the shogunate. Similarly, the cry "Repel the barbarian," which at first gave vent to a xenophobic rejection of all intercourse with the West, was in a few years' time sufficiently moderated to allow for "opening of the country" as the only practicable way of building up Japan's strength against the West. In the rapid evolution of Japanese thinking about these questions, Sakuma Shōzan (1811–1864) and his disciple Yoshida Shōin (1830–1859) stand as important links between the old order and the new.

SAKUMA SHŌZAN: EASTERN ETHICS AND WESTERN SCIENCE

A samurai from mountainous Shinano province, Sakuma Shōzan (or Zōzan) completed his Confucian classical studies at Edo under Satō

[9] Referring to the uprising of Christians at Shimabara, near Nagasaki, in 1637–38.

Issai, a noted scholar and literary stylist who taught under the aegis of the orthodox Hayashi school but was deeply influenced by the intuitionist philosophy of Wang Yang-ming. Sakuma's own writings, and those of his disciple Yoshida, betray this same influence in their stress upon the inseparability of knowledge and action. Sakuma nonetheless felt that his master had gone too far in the direction of subjectivism, to the neglect of Chu Hsi's objective "investigation of things." That he subsequently became interested in Western science and technology, however, was not a purely logical development from this early concern for Chu Hsi's "investigation of things." He devoted himself mainly to the teaching of classical studies until suddenly thrust into a situation requiring much more practical knowledge than he possessed. In 1841, his lord, Sanada Yukitsura, who had considerable influence in shogunate circles by reason of both his family connections and his personal talents, was appointed to its highest council of advisers and put in charge of Japan's coastal defenses. As a trusted counsellor of his lord, Sakuma found himself confronting squarely the most difficult and fateful question of the day; how to deal with the threat of Western naval power in Japanese waters.

Though a believer in "Revering the Emperor and Repelling the Barbarian," Sakuma was not blinded by this antiforeignism to the realities of the situation, but immediately launched into the study of Western gunnery as it was taught by two Japanese pioneers in this field, Takashima Shūhan and Egawa Tan'an. The eight-point program which he subsequently submitted to Lord Sanada as the basis for shogunate policy reveals both his firm adherence to the seclusion policy and his espousal of technical developments from the West.

1. Fortifications must be erected at all strategic points on the coast and equipped with adequate artillery.
2. The export of copper through the Dutch must be suspended and the metal used for casting thousands of guns for distribution to all points.
3. Large merchant ships must be built, so as to prevent the loss of rice through the wreck of small coastal vessels which are all that the exclusion edicts allow.
4. Maritime trade must be supervised by capable officials.
5. Warships of foreign style must be constructed and a force of trained naval officers built up.
6. Schools must be established throughout the country and a modern education provided, so that "even the most stupid men and women may understand loyalty, piety, and chastity."

7. Rewards and punishments must be made clear, and government must be conducted benevolently but firmly, so as to strengthen the popular mind.

8. There must be established a system of selecting and employing men of ability in official posts.[1]

While noting Sakuma's bold advocacy of Western military methods, we must not regard his references to Confucian virtues and precepts as mere lip service to tradition. To him they represented the indispensable basis for any program of reform, since support for this stupendous national undertaking could only be guaranteed by intensifying the moral indoctrination of the people and improving the quality of government so as to insure popular backing.

Sakuma's proposals met with strong opposition, however, and when his lord was finally forced to relinquish his high place in shogunate councils, Sakuma found himself free to devote his full energies to Western studies. This involved learning Dutch, so as to have direct access to sources of knowledge made available only through the Dutch trading mission at Deshima. Following an encyclopedia in Dutch translation, for instance, he experimented in the making of glass and the refining of certain chemicals. By 1848 he had become proficient enough to cast cannon and small arms. These activities, and the steps he also took to improve animal husbandry in his native region, were supported by Lord Sanada to develop and strengthen his own fief of Matsushiro. They also served to make Sakuma more widely known as a leader in the adoption of Western methods.

Meanwhile, through his lord and others high in the Edo government, Sakuma continued to press for the building up of land fortifications and a Western-type navy. Unsuccessful in this, he still had the satisfaction of seeing his hopes for a modern navy carried forward by one of his disciples, Katsu Awa (or Kaishū, "Sea-vessel"), who later studied naval science and construction in the United States, and as first Navy Minister in the Meiji regime became known as "the father of the Japanese Navy."

Another disciple of Sakuma during these years was the aforementioned Yoshida Shōin, who met a far different fate in his attempt earlier to go abroad for study. With the encouragement of his teacher, Yoshida had tried to stow away on one of Perry's ships in 1854, only to be turned over to the shogunal authorities and be imprisoned for violating the Seclusion

---

[1] As summarized by Sansom in *The Western World and Japan*, p. 254.

Laws. Sakuma himself would probably have been punished far more severely for his part in this "crime" had not influential persons interceded to avert the death penalty for both him and his disciple. After less than a year in jail, each was released in the custody of his clan for domiciliary confinement.

Undeterred and irrepressible, Sakuma continued to take an active part in the debate on political and military questions. His prison diary had ended with this statement, echoing a famous utterance of Confucius:

At twenty I realized I had a part to play in the life of my state.
At thirty I realized I had a part to play in the life of the entire nation.
At forty I realized I had a part to play in the life of the entire world.[2]

Up to this time Sakuma's advocacy of Western methods had still not implied that Japan itself should be opened to the West. In 1858, however, the signing of a commercial treaty with the United States brought to an end the seclusion policy of the shogunate. Accepting this state of affairs, Sakuma eventually became known as an active proponent of the new policy of "opening the country" (*kaikoku-ron*), to which the Tokugawa were now unavoidably committed. Meanwhile, opposition to the shogunate and to intercourse with the West centered increasingly around the emperor at Kyoto, and Sakuma, fearing the effects of this cleavage on Japan's capacity to resist Western encroachment, devoted his efforts to bridging the gulf between the two courts. In the early 1860s a compromise party appeared in both Edo and Kyoto calling for collaboration between the shogunate and the imperial court under the slogan "Union of Civil and Military [Government]" (*Kōbu gattai*). The aim of this movement was on the one hand to uphold the policy of "opening the country," and on the other to grant a greater voice in government to the imperial court and its supporters among the so-called "outer daimyō." In the interests of such a compromise, Sakuma offered his services as an emissary from the shogunate to the Kyoto court, convinced that he could persuade the emperor of the necessity of "opening the country." It was on this mission to Kyoto that Sakuma suddenly met death at the hands of assassins from the southwestern fief of Chōshū, who were bitterly opposed to the Tokugawa and any move toward reconciliation.

Beside being identified with the policy of "opening the country" to the

[2] *Analects*, II, 4.

West and the movement for "Union of Civil and Military Government," Sakuma's name is remembered especially in connection with a slogan he made famous, "Eastern ethics and Western science" (*Tōyō no dōtoku, Seiyō no gakugei*). In these few words Sakuma summed up his faith in the compatibility of the Oriental (mainly Confucian) ethical heritage with the new technical knowledge of the West. No doubt, in so acclaiming the respective virtues of East and West, Sakuma failed to sense the latent contradictions between them, the frictions which might develop, and the difficulty of keeping each to the sphere of influence he had assigned it. Nevertheless his simple formula was more than just the hasty contrivance of a desperate man, hoping, in the face of overwhelming Western superiority, to salvage something from the wreckage of his own civilization. It satisfied at least two of the basic conditions for Japan's survival in the modern world: the need for developing military power sufficient to hold off the West, while at the same time preserving that unity of national purpose and action which, under the circumstances, could only spring from common and well-established traditions. Thus the formula proved workable enough to serve a whole generation of leaders during the Meiji Restoration, and to provide the basis for a modernization program of unparalleled magnitude in the late nineteenth century. What is noteworthy in this is not that the pursuit of these two aims brought them into continual conflict, but that Japan's leaders and her people, adhering as much to traditional values as they were guided by the vision of a modernized nation, should have managed to hold these contradictions and conflicts sufficiently within limits so as not to disrupt the whole enterprise.

It should be mentioned in passing that Sakuma was not the only man of this era in world history to hit upon such an answer to the predicament of Orientals suddenly confronted with the power and expanding energy of the West. In China, during the last half of the nineteenth century, essentially the same solution was advanced under the slogan "Chinese learning to provide the [moral] basis, Western learning to provide the [technical] means" (*Chung-hsüeh wei t'i, Hsi-hsüeh wei yung*).[3] This is not the place to enter into a general comparison of these

---

[3] See Teng and Fairbank, *China's Response to the West*, Ch. V and XVII. Wei Yüan (1794–1856) is probably the first exponent of this point of view in China, though it was not formulated in these terms until much later. Sakuma Shōzan, in his work *Seiken-roku*,

two movements which sought to encourage the adoption of Western technology (especially the production of modern arms) while reaffirming traditional moral teachings. Still we cannot fail to observe that the attempt made in China was to be far less successful in promoting rapid modernization than in Japan. Whatever the reasons for this, it is significant that in neither case do we find the claims of tradition so incompatible with the requirements of modernization that the one could be advanced only at the direct expense of the other. In China, while it is true that the weight of certain customs and traditions impeded reform, there is no evidence that the marked lag in modernization was linked to a strong reassertion of native traditions in thought and conduct; on the contrary, Confucianism itself seems to have ebbed in vitality and influence in the midst of a general trend toward the disintegration of Chinese society. In Japan, on the other hand, as the nation took giant strides toward Westernization, far from abandoning her most cherished ideals, she seemed for a time to gain new strength from them. At least this is so of the men who were to guide Japan's destinies in the latter half of the nineteenth century. Retaining a vital faith in their national heritage, they were able not only to perpetuate it but even to extend in some ways its hold on the people, employing for this purpose the very techniques of modern mass education and improved means of communication adopted from the West. For leaders such as these, who made a place in the modern world for the Land of the Rising Sun, there was probably no single figure in recent history who provided a more inspiring example of traditional virtues than did Sakuma's pupil Yoshida Shōin.

SAKUMA SHOZAN
Reflections on My Errors (Seiken-roku)

This book was written as if to record Sakuma's reflections while in prison, though it was actually committed to writing after his release. Ostensibly a piece of self-examination, it is in fact a vigorous self-defense, dealing in turn with his fundamental Confucian beliefs, the need for pursuing Western studies, and the justification for his political activities. Because of his outspoken criticism

mentions having read a work of Wei's on China's defense policies in 1850–51, and asserts that each of them had arrived at the same general conclusion independently. Sakuma's memorial on Japanese maritime defense was drawn up in the winter of 1842–43, while Wei completed his *Sheng-wu chi* in the summer of 1842.

of the existing regime, it was not published until after the author's death and the fall of the shogunate.

[From Terry, *Sakuma Shōzan and His Seiken-roku,* pp. 58–86]

In the summer of Kaei 7, the fourth month (May, 1854), I, Taisei, because of an incident, went down into prison. During my seven months of imprisonment I pondered over my errors, and, as a result, there were things that I should have liked to say concerning them. However, brush and ink-stone were forbidden in the prison, and I was therefore unable to keep a manuscript. Over that long period, then, I forgot much. Now that I have come out, I shall record what I remember, deposit the record in a cloth box, and bequeath it to my descendants. As for publicizing what I have to say, I dare do no such thing.

. . . .

2. Take, for example, a man who is grieved by the illness of his lord or his father, and who is seeking medicine to cure it. If he is fortunate enough to secure the medicine, and is certain that it will be efficacious, then, certainly, without questioning either its cost or the quality of its name, he will beg his lord or father to take it. Should the latter refuse on the grounds that he dislikes the name, does the younger man make various schemes to give the medicine secretly, or does he simply sit by and wait for his master to die? There is no question about it: the feeling of genuine sincerity and heartfelt grief on the part of the subject or son makes it absolutely impossible for him to sit idly and watch his master's anguish; consequently, even if he knows that he will later have to face his master's anger, he cannot but give the medicine secretly.

. . . .

16. Although my family branch was poor, I grew up with plenty to eat and with warm clothing to wear. I never underwent the tempering of cold and hardship. I was therefore always afraid that in the event of a national emergency I would have difficulty bearing the attendant difficulties in everyday living, such as privations in food and drink. However, last summer, when the American ships suddenly arrived, and Edo was put on strict guard, I managed military affairs in the mansion belonging to my *han,* and, although I got no sleep for seven days and nights, my spirits grew higher and higher. This year, I was condemned and sent to prison. For several weeks I have eaten meager food, licked salt, and received the same treatment as men under heavy punishment.

However, I have kept calm and have managed to become content with my lot. Moreover, my spirit is active, and my body is healthy. To have tried myself somewhat on these two points is of no small profit. My ordeal can thus be called a heavenly blessing.

. . . .

20. The gentleman has five pleasures, but wealth and rank are not among them. That his house understands decorum and righteousness and remains free from family rifts—this is one pleasure. That exercising care in giving to and taking from others, he provides for himself honestly, free, internally, from shame before his wife and children, and externally, from disgrace before the public—this is the second pleasure. That he expounds and glorifies the learning of the sages, knows in his heart the great Way, and in all situations contents himself with his duty, in adversity as well as in prosperity—this is the third pleasure. That he is born after the opening of the vistas of science by the Westerners, and can therefore understand principles not known to the sages and wise men of old—this is the fourth pleasure. That he employs the ethics of the East and the scientific technique of the West, neglecting neither the spiritual nor material aspects of life, combining subjective and objective, and thus bringing benefit to the people and serving the nation—this is the fifth pleasure.

. . . .

27. All learning is cumulative. It is not something that one comes to realize in a morning or an evening. Effective maritime defense is in itself a great field of study. Since no one has yet thoroughly studied its fundamentals, it is not easy to learn rapidly its essential points. Probably this fact explains why even if you take hold of a man's ear and explain these essential points to him, he does not understand.

28. The principal requisite of national defense is that it prevents the foreign barbarians from holding us in contempt. The existing coastal defense installations all lack method; the pieces of artillery that have been set up in array are improperly made; and the officials who negotiate with the foreigners are mediocrities who have no understanding of warfare. The situation being such, even though we wish to avoid incurring the scorn of the barbarians, how, in fact, can we do so?

. . . .

30. Of the men who now hold posts as commanders of the army, those who are not dukes or princes or men of noble rank, are members of

wealthy families. As such, they find their daily pleasure in drinking wine, singing, and dancing; and they are ignorant of military strategy and discipline. Should a national emergency arise, there is no one who could command the respect of the warriors and halt the enemy's attack. This is the great sorrow of our times. For this reason, I have wished to follow in substance the Western principles of armament, and, by banding together loyal, valorous, strong men of old, established families not in the military class—men of whom one would be equal to ten ordinary men—to form a voluntary group which would be made to have as its sole aim that of guarding the nation and protecting the people. Anyone wishing to join the society would be tested and his merits examined; and, if he did not shirk hardship, he would then be permitted to join. Men of talent in military strategy, planning, and administration would be advanced to positions of leadership, and then, if the day should come when the country must be defended, this group could be gathered together and organized into an army to await official commands. It is to be hoped that they would drive the enemy away and perform greater service than those who now form the military class.

. . . .

35. Mathematics is the basis for all learning. In the Western world after this science was discovered military tactics advanced greatly, far outstripping that of former times. This development accords with the statement that "one advanced from basic studies to higher learning." In the *Art of War* of Sun Tzu, the statement about "estimation, determination of quantity, calculation, judgment, and victory" has reference to mathematics. However, since Sun Tzu's time neither we nor the Chinese have ceased to read, study, and memorize his teachings, and our art of war remains exactly as it was then. It consequently cannot be compared with that of the West. There is no reason for this other than that we have not devoted ourselves to basic studies. At the present time, if we wish really to complete our military preparations, we must develop this branch of study.

. . . .

40. What do the so-called scholars of today actually do? Do they clearly and tacitly understand the way in which the gods and sages established this nation, or the way in which Yao, Shun, and the divine emperors of the three dynasties governed? Do they, after having learned the rites and music, punishment and administration, the classics and

governmental system, go on to discuss and learn the elements of the art of war, of military discipline, of the principles of machinery? Do they make exhaustive studies of conditions in foreign countries? Of effective defense methods? Of strategy in setting up strongholds, defense barriers, and reinforcements? Of the knowledge of computation, gravitation, geometry, and mathematics? If they do, I have not heard of it! Therefore I ask what the so-called scholars of today actually do.

· · · ·

42. Learning, the possession of which is of no assistance and the lack of which is of no harm, is useless learning. Useful learning, on the other hand, is as indispensable to the meeting of human needs as is the production of the light hemp-woven garment of summer and the heavy outer clothing of winter.

· · · ·

44. We say that this nation has an abundance of gold, and of rice and millet. However, our territory is not large, and after the internal needs of the country have been met there is hardly any surplus of the materials produced here. Such things as the need for coastal defense arise from without. To install several hundred defense barriers, to construct several hundred large warships, and to cast several thousand large artillery pieces, will call for vast expenditures. Again, all these things are not permanently durable: every ten or twenty years they will have to be repaired, reconstructed, or improved. Externally, there will be the need for funds with which to carry on relations with foreign countries, and, internally, the expense of necessary food supplies for our own country. Where can money for these sorts of things be obtained? If a family in financial distress receives many guests, and frequently prepares feasts for them, its resources will be dissipated to the point where it can no longer continue to carry on these activities. How does the present position of the nation differ from the plight of this poor family? With what tactics can such a situation be overcome? Those who sincerely wish to conduct the affairs of state well must make careful plans in advance.

· · · ·

46. At the time when my former lord assumed office in the government, and later, when he took charge of coastal defense, the English barbarians were invading the Ch'ing empire, and news of the war was sensational. I, greatly lamenting the events of the time, submitted a plan

in a memorial. That was, actually, in Tempō 13, the eleventh month [December, 1842–January, 1843]. Later I saw the *Sheng-Wu Chi* of the Chinese writer Wei Yüan.[1] Wei had also written out of sorrow over recent events. The preface to the book was composed in the seventh month of the same year [August–September, 1842]; and while Wei thus wrote only four months before I submitted my memorial, the two of us, without having had any previous consultation, were often in complete agreement. Ah! Wei and I were born in different places and did not even know each other's name. Is it not singular that we both wrote lamenting the times during the same year, and that our views were in accord without our having met? We really must be called comrades from separate lands. However, Wei says that China from ancient times until the present has had naval defense, but has had no naval warfare; therefore, as the method of defense against attacks from the sea, she should strengthen fortified towns and clear fields, in order to be able to push back the landing invaders. I, on the other hand, wish to promote to the full the teaching of techniques for using armored warships and to form a plan of attack whereby an enemy could be intercepted and destroyed, in order that the death sentence may be given to the plunderers before they have reached the country's shores. That is the only point of difference between Wei and me.

47. In order to master the barbarians there is nothing so effective as to ascertain in the beginning conditions among them. To do this, there is no better first step than to be familiar with barbarian tongues. Thus, learning a barbarian language is not only a step toward knowing the barbarians, but also the groundwork for mastering them. When the various nations on one pretext or another began sending ships frequently to the territory around Sagami and Awa, I thought it genuinely difficult to find out facts about them. As a result, I felt the desire to compile a lexicon in several volumes, translating other languages into Japanese, in order to teach the tongues of the various European countries. Also, since we have long had trade relations with Holland, and since many of us already know how to read the books used in that country, I wished to publish the Dutch section first. Before this, there had been an order from

[1] Scholar and associate of Commissioner Lin Tse-hsü, whose attempt to suppress the opium trade at Canton led to the war with the British. Wei's book, *Sheng-wu Chi* (*Record of Imperial Military Exploits of the Manchu Dynasty*) was finished just after the signing of the Treaty of Nanking ending the Opium War. [Ed.]

the government to the effect that all books to be published must undergo official inspection. Therefore, in the winter of Kaei 2 [1849–1850], I came to Edo, submitted my manuscript, and requested permission to publish it. The affair dragged on for a year, and I was ultimately unable to obtain permission. During the time I was in the capital I first secured Wei's book and read it. He also wished to set up schools in his country primarily for the translation of foreign documents and the promotion of a clear understanding of conditions among the enemy nations, in order to further the cause of mastering the enemies. In this too his opinion concurred with mine. I do not know, however, whether or not his country has put his words into effect.

48. The main requirement for maritime defense are guns and warships, but the more important item is guns. Wei included an article on guns in his *Hai-kuo T'u-shih* [*sic*].[2] It is for the most part inaccurate and unfounded; it is like the doings of a child at play. No one can learn the essentials of a subject without engaging personally in the study of it. That a man of Wei's talent should fail to understand this is unfortunate. I deeply pity Wei that in the world of today, he, ignorant of artillery, should have unwittingly perpetrated these errors and mistakes on later generations.

49. Last summer the American barbarians arrived in the Bay of Uraga with four warships, bearing their president's message. Their deportment and manner of expression were exceedingly arrogant, and the resulting insult to our national dignity was not small. Those who heard could but gnash their teeth. A certain person on guard in Uraga suffered this insult in silence, and, having been ultimately unable to do anything about it, after the barbarians had retired, he drew his knife and slashed to bits a portrait of their leader, which they had left as a gift. Thus he gave vent to his rage. In former times Ts'ao Wei of Sung, having been demoted, was serving as an official in Shensi, and when he heard of the character of Chao Yüan-hao, he had a person skillful in drawing paint Chao's image. Ts'ao looked at this portrait and knew from its manly appearance that Chao would doubtless make trouble on the border in the future. Therefore Wei wished to take steps toward preparing the border in advance, and toward collecting together and examining men of

[2] Correct name *Hai-kuo t'u-chih* (*Illustrated Gazetteer of the Maritime Countries*), compiled by Lin Tse-hsü and Wei Yüan, 1841.

ability. Afterwards, everything turned out as he had predicted. Thus, by looking at the portrait of his enemy, he could see his enemy's abilities and thereby aid himself with his own preparations. It can only be regretted that the Japanese guard did not think of this. Instead of using the portrait, he tore it up. In both cases there was a barbarian; in both cases there was a portrait. But one man, lacking the portrait, sought to obtain it, while the other, having it, destroyed it. Their depth of knowledge and farsightedness in planning were vastly different.

. . . .

52. Formerly, with one or two friends, I took a trip to Kamakura; at length, we sailed over the sea past Arasaki to Jōgashima; we lodged at Misaki, continued on past Matsuwa, and stopped over at Miyata. Then, having stayed a time at Uraga, we went up to Sarugashima, viewed Kanazawa, went out to Hommoku, and returned to Edo. In the course of this trip I stopped at about ten places where barricades had been set up in preparation against an invasion from the sea. However, the arrangement of them made no sense, and none of them could be depended on as a defense fortification. Upon discovering this, I unconsciously looked up to Heaven and sighed deeply; I struck my chest and wept for a long time. Edo is the throat of the nation, and, while Futtso-no-su, as its lip, may be called a natural barrier, the mouth opening into the sea is still broad. From the outset, it would be difficult without warships and naval troops to halt an enemy transgression or attack. Now, without any real effort, these foolish walls and mock parapets have been thrown up high above the surface of the sea, only to display to the foreign nations our lack of planning. If during these times the nations to east and west sent ships to pay us a visit, how could they take us seriously? There is no point in criticizing the mediocrity of the lower officials. But what is to be done if even those who ride on golden saddles with ornate saddle-cloths, who wear brocade and feast on meat, and who call themselves high class, fail to recognize the great plan for the nation, but instead use up the country's wealth on this useless construction work. If barbarian ships arrived in force, how could we either defend against them or defeat them? After my trip, I felt the urge to write a petition discussing the things that should and should not be done in maritime defense, with the hope that I might be of assistance in this time of emergency. I completed my manuscript and requested my former lord for permission to submit

it. He refused, and I gave up my plan. This was in the early summer of Kaei 3 [1850]. Four years later, as I had predicted, the affair of the American barbarians arose. At the time when my former lord stopped my memorial, he was probably acting out of the fear that I might be punished for impertinence. His benevolence in protecting me was truly great. If he were in the world today and were informed that I have been imprisoned, his grief would be profound!

YOSHIDA SHŌIN AND THE VALUE OF DEATH

Torajirō   Torajirō—
Nijū-ikkai mōshi   Twenty-one times a death-defier!

Yoshida Torajirō (better known by his pen-name, Shōin), whose heroism drew such acclaim as this from young Japanese of the Meiji Restoration and even won admiration abroad through the writings of Robert Louis Stevenson, was born in the southwestern fief of Chōshū and adopted into the family of a samurai in rather humble circumstances. His father, a military instructor, found it necessary to divide his time between teaching and cultivating the soil in order to earn a frugal living, and Yoshida, who succeeded to the direction of his father's school at a very young age, always remained a peasant at heart—earnest, unsophisticated, and alive with the raw energy of the earth. From his father, also, he inherited a deep devotion to the precepts of Yamaga Sokō, whose teachings on the code of the warrior (later known as *bushidō*) had been handed down in the family school. He also acquired a close acquaintance with the principles of military science as set forth in the ancient Chinese classic, Sun Tzu's *Art of War*. Perhaps an even more decisive influence on Yoshida was the book of Mencius, whose high idealism, strong assertion of the inherent worth of the individual, and staunch opposition to arbitrary authority instilled in Yoshida a lively sense of his own mission in the world and an impatience with all external restraints.

An avid learner, and impressed by Sun Tzu's *Art of War* with the importance of military intelligence, Yoshida traveled about picking up what information he could about the West in Nagasaki and from such progressive teachers as Yokoi Shōnan and Sakuma Shōzan. On a trip to northern Japan he also visited the school at Mito which was proclaiming Japan's divine mission to turn back the West and found a world empire under the legitimate imperial dynasty. After the failure of Yoshida's ill-planned attempt to stow away on one of Perry's ships, which ended in his being confined to his native fief, Yoshida was permitted by his indulgent feudal lord to resume teaching. With Mencius as his main text, he stressed the latter's implicit justification of revolt against an unworthy and incompetent ruler, and pointed to the shogun's failure to fulfill the function indicated by his title of "Barbarian-subduing Generalissimo" (*Sei-i tai shōgun*). Throughout the ranks of the aristocracy, however, he found a similar incapacity to assume the responsibilities of leadership in the crisis facing Japan. Yoshida became convinced that only among those close to the soil and untainted by the corruption of wealth and high office could be found men selfless and fearless enough to overthrow the regime. To arouse these stalwarts of the countryside only dedicated leadership and an inspiring example of the true warrior spirit were needed.

Yoshida's call to action had in it the essential ingredients of a modern revolution: the overthrow of the hereditary feudal aristocracy and the raising up of the Japanese common man to a role of vital importance. Here were the seeds of epochal changes to be brought about by the Restoration—the abolition of feudalism, emancipation of the serfs, the arming of the peasantry in modernized forces—changes initiated by such youthful leaders and former disciples of Yoshida as Kido Kōin, a key figure in the dismantling of feudalism; Itō Hirobumi, framer of the Meiji Constitution; and Yamagata Aritomo, father of the modern Japanese army. But theirs was a revolution aiming more at the revitalization of national leadership than at the correction of social injustice or overturning of the social order. If Yoshida's dissatisfaction with the status quo was inspired by class consciousness at all, it did not concern the rights of any economic group but the heavy responsibilities and high destiny of the true samurai.

Typically, therefore, Yoshida's mind ran not to planning and organizing for political action, but to some spectacular act of bravery which would dramatize the need for selfless leadership. Thus he conceived the idea of assassinating the shogun's emissary to the imperial court, whose mission was to secure the emperor's approval for a treaty with the United States. Considering his impetuosity and the previous failure of his ill-considered plans, it is not surprising that this daring plot should have been detected and smashed. Sent a prisoner to the shogunate capital at Edo, Yoshida was beheaded in 1859 at the age of thirty. But in death his dreams were fulfilled: he became a hero to a whole generation and his self-sacrifice the spark which fired the minds and hearts of Japan's new revolutionary leaders. Reverently his patriotic disciples, including Itō and Kido, bore home his last remains, and with deep emotion young Japanese of the new era repeated the two poems which were his last testament in prison:

Oya wo omō	The son's solicitude for his mother
Kokoro ni masaru	Is surpassed by
Oyagokoro	Her solicitude for him.
Kyō no otozure	When she hears what befell me to-day,
Ika ni kikuran	How will she take it?

Kaku sureba	That such an act
Kaku naru mono to	Would have such a result
Shiri nagara	I knew well enough.
Yamu ni yamarenu	What made me do it anyhow
Yamato damashii	Was the spirit of Yamato.

YOSHIDA SHŌIN

On Leadership

[From *Zenshū*, II, 25–26; III, 145; V, 239, 334; VIII, 146]

What is important in a leader is a resolute will and determination. A man may be versatile and learned, but if he lacks resoluteness and determination, of what use will he be? [VIII, 146]

. . . .

Once the will is resolved, one's spirit is strengthened. Even a peasant's will is hard to deny, but a samurai of resolute will can sway ten thousand men. [V, 239]

. . . .

One who aspires to greatness should read and study, pursuing the True Way with such a firm resolve that he is perfectly straightforward and open, rises above the superficialities of conventional behavior, and refuses to be satisfied with the petty or commonplace. [II, 26]

· · · ·

Once a man's will is set, he need no longer rely on others or expect anything from the world. His vision encompasses Heaven and earth, past and present, and the tranquility of his heart is undisturbed. [III, 145]

· · · ·

Life and death, union and separation, follow hard upon one another. Nothing is steadfast but the will, nothing endures but one's achievements. These alone count in life. [V, 334]

· · · ·

To consider oneself different from ordinary men is wrong, but it is right to hope that one will not remain like ordinary men. [II, 25]

On Being Direct
[From *Zenshū*, III, 239]

In relations with others, one should express resentment and anger openly and straightforwardly. If one cannot express them openly and straightforwardly, the only thing to do is forget about them. To harbor grievances in one's heart, awaiting some later opportunity to give vent to them, is to act like a weak and petty man—in truth, it can only be called cowardice. The mind of the superior man is like Heaven. When it is resentful or angry, it thunders forth its indignation. But once having loosed its feelings, it is like a sunny day with a clear sky: within the heart there remains not the trace of a cloud. Such is the beauty of true manliness.

Arms and Learning

These excerpts mark two important stages in Yoshida's intellectual development: first, when he was led by his studies in military science to seek a deeper knowledge of classical philosophy; and second, when he realized the vital importance of first-hand knowledge of the West. It is characteristic of him that this latter realization should be expressed in typically Confucian terms.
[From *Zenshū*, II, 145; IV, 115]

Those who take up the science of war must not fail to master the [Confucian] Classics. The reason is that arms are dangerous instruments and not necessarily forces for good. How can we safely entrust them to any but those who have schooled themselves in the precepts of the Classics and can use these weapons for the realization of Humanity and Righteousness? To quell violence and disorder, to repulse barbarians and brigands, to rescue living souls from agony and torture, to save the nation from imminent downfall—these are the true ends of Humanity and Righteousness. If, on the contrary, arms are taken up in a selfish struggle to win land, goods, people, and the implements of war, is it not the worst of all evils, the most heinous of all offenses? If, further, the study of offensive and defensive warfare, of the way to certain victory in all encounters, is not based on those principles which should govern their employment, who can say that such a venture will not result in just such a misfortune? Therefore I say that those who take up the science of war must not fail to master the Classics. [II, 145]

. . . .

What I mean by the "pursuit of learning" is not the ability to read classical texts and study ancient history, but to be fully acquainted with conditions all over the world and to have a keen awareness of what is going on abroad and around us. Now from what I can see world trends and conditions are still unsettled, and as long as they remain unsettled there is still a chance that something can be done. First, therefore, we must rectify conditions in our own domain, after which conditions in other domains can be rectified. This having been done, conditions at court can be rectified and finally conditions throughout the whole world can be rectified. First one must set an example oneself and then it can be extended progressively to others.[1] This is what I mean by the "pursuit of learning." [IV, 115]

Facing Death
[From *Zenshū,* I, 101; IV, 238; VIII, 299]

From the beginning of the year to the end, day and night, morning and evening, in action and repose, in speech and in silence, the warrior must

[1] This type of reasoning follows the opening text attributed to Confucius in the *Great Learning.*

keep death constantly before him and have ever in mind that the one death [which he has to give] should not be suffered in vain. In other words [he must have perfect control over his own death] just as if he were holding an intemperate steed in rein. Only he who truly keeps death in mind this way can understand what is meant by [Yamaga Sokō's maxim of] "preparedness." [IV, 238]

. . . .

If the body dies, it does no harm to the mind, but if the mind dies, one can no longer act as a man even though the body survives. [VIII, 299]

. . . .

If a general and his men fear death and are apprehensive over possible defeat, then they will unavoidably suffer defeat and death. But if they make up their minds, from the general down to the last footsoldier, not to think of living but only of standing in one place and facing death together, then, though they may have no other thought than meeting death, they will instead hold on to life and gain victory. [I, 101]

Selfishness and Heroism

Through the following passages runs a strong undercurrent of antagonism toward the idle rich, which is inspired by the traditional disapproval of self-indulgence found in Confucianism and Buddhism. Here Yoshida stands as a link between the old samurai ideal of frugality and self-sacrificing service, and these same virtues as exemplified by peasant soldiers in the service of the twentieth-century Japanese nationalism.

The first passage is a commentary on a poem by the Chinese poet Li Po, who points out that the most beautiful things in the world, the beauties of nature, are no one's private possession and may be enjoyed by all free of charge.

[From *Zenshū*, IV, 175; V, 315; VI, 164; IX, 239, 286, 297]

Nowadays everyone lives selfishly and seeks only the leisure in which to indulge his own desires. They look on all the beauties of nature— the rivers and mountains, the breeze and the moon—as their own to enjoy, forgetting what the shrine of the Sun Goddess stands for [i.e., that everything is held in trust from Heaven]. The common man thinks of his life as his own and refuses to perform his duty to his lord. The samurai regards his household as his own private possession and refuses to sacrifice his life for his state. The feudal lords regard their domains as their own and refuse to serve King and Country. Unwilling to serve King and Country, at home they cherish only the objects of desire and abroad they willingly yield to the foreign barbarian, inviting defeat and destruction. Thus the scenic beauties they enjoy will not long remain in their possession. [IV, 175]

. . . .

As things stand now the feudal lords are content to look on while the shogunate carries on in a highhanded manner. Neither the lords nor the shogun can be depended upon [to save the country], and so our only hope lies in grass-roots heroes.[2] [V, 315]

. . . .

When I consider the state of things in our fief, I find that those who hold official positions and receive official stipends are incapable of the utmost in loyalty and patriotic service. Loyalty of the usual sort—perhaps, but if it is true loyalty and service you seek, then you must abandon this fief and plan a grass-roots uprising. [IX, 239]

. . . .

It seems hopeless, hopeless. Those who eat meat [at public expense] are a mean, selfish lot, and so the country is doomed. Our only hope lies in the grass-roots folk who eat our traditional food [i.e., rice]. [VI, 164]

. . . .

If Heaven does not completely abandon this land of the Gods, there must be an uprising of grass-roots heroes. [IX, 297]

. . . .

If the plan [to intercept the shogunate emissary to the Kyoto court] is to be carried out, it can only be done with men from the grass roots. To wear silk brocades, eat dainty food, hug beautiful women, and fondle darling children are the only things hereditary officials care about. To revere the emperor and expel the barbarian is no concern of theirs. If this time it should be my misfortune to die, may my death inspire at least one or two men of steadfast will to rise up and uphold this principle after my death. [IX, 286]

[2] *Sōmō eiyū,* lit. "grass-clump heroes."

FUKUZAWA YUKICHI, PIONEER OF WESTERNIZATION

"Here lies," the epitaph on a monument to Fukuzawa reads, "a man of self-reliance and self-respect with a world-wide vision." And it is probably safe to say that no other Japanese in those turbulent pre-Restoration days had such wide vision as Fukuzawa Yukichi (1834–1901) did, nor in the reconstruction period which followed did any Japanese of his renown and ability live the life of an independent commoner with such native dignity.

Born in the Kyushu province of Bungo which had produced such progressive thinkers as Miura Baien and Hoashi Banri, Fukuzawa came from the lower levels of the feudal aristocracy. Always alert and energetic, he set about the study of Dutch very early in life, and then became a pioneer student of English. As early as 1860 he took advantage of an opportunity to visit America with a shogunate mission, made a return visit in 1867, and in between traveled through European countries, especially England. When at last he took up writing and lecturing about Western civilization and its achievements, it was on the basis of a wider firsthand knowledge of the West than any other Japanese of his time could boast. Hale, handsome, and of a sanguine nature, his personality radiated a lively enthusiasm that lent itself to the conveying of his ideas to others. Around him in his little school of Keio he drew ambitious young Japanese in growing numbers, men who were to become leaders of the new Japan in its work of political, economic, and social reconstruction. As a writer he probably excelled any of his contemporaries in versatility and persuasiveness. Among Confucians, Sorai had been the most proficient and forceful writer; among Buddhists, Rennyo had been the most eloquent. But Fukuzawa combined Sorai and Rennyo in one style with which he proclaimed the gospel of a new civilization. His books sold in millions of copies, bringing him a fortune and giving him the financial independence which enabled him to live the life of a commoner without having to accept a position in the government. It also provided him with the means to establish a newspaper through which he could voice his opinions on current questions with complete freedom.

Fukuzawa's influence was the greater because of the practical and popular character of his writings. He aimed less at converting the scholarly elite to a new philosophy than at conveying to great numbers of Japanese his enthusiasm for the tangible advantages of life in the West. Nonetheless these advantages were not wholly of a material sort. Fukuzawa's appreciation of Western civilization was surprisingly broad, and while he lacked any deep knowledge of its background or traditions, he sensed that the meaning of the West was to be found as much in the moral tales told to its children or in the procedure for running meetings as in treatises on natural or political science. If there is any single influence from the West which Fukuzawa most clearly exemplified and fostered it is British utilitarianism and liberalism, a trend especially strong in the early decades of the Restoration. Linked closely to this was the prevailing belief in human progress through the wider application of the methods of the natural sciences. Increasingly toward the end of his life, however, Fukuzawa expressed the conviction that moral and religious regeneration of the Japanese was indispensable to their future progress.

Fukuzawa was never a Confucian, because the fastidious formalism and rigidity of Neo-Confucianism repelled him, though he did admire its orderliness and balance. Nor in spite of his appreciation for the simplicity, straightforwardness, and patriotism inculcated by Shinto, could he accept it as a genuine religion or personal faith. As for Buddhism, he came close to Zen in his insistence upon the dignity of man and upon facing the hard realities of life, but preferred a life of abundance to the poverty and frugality of Zen. The Shinran sect's emphasis upon universal salvation rather than enlightenment for the few had great appeal to him; for the otherworldliness of Jodoism, however, he had no taste at all. In Christianity what drew his wholehearted approval was its high regard for womanhood and also the high standard of personal morality it maintained. On the other hand he also had occasion to condemn the arrogance and impatience of many missionaries who were almost totally ignorant of the historic culture of the nations they sought to convert.

Among the scientific studies he took special pains to promote in his Keio school, physics stood foremost, since he thought it the basis of all scientific inquiry. His interest in it was so deep and genuine that he sent his first son to America as a step toward further promotion of this line of inquiry. Next to physics came economics; indeed, Keio University became a symbol for economic research in Japan even during Fukuzawa's lifetime. Later Fukuzawa supported the medical researches of Kitazato Shibasaburō, the leading Japanese authority in bacteriology at that time. Today the medical department of the University, with its Rockefeller-sponsored hospital, stands near Meiji shrine in Tokyo as one of the foremost medical schools in the country. In this way the self-made leader of modern Japan, without official position or organized political support, helped reconstruct his country and build institutions through which others could achieve "independence and self-respect."

FUKUZAWA YUKICHI
Excerpts from His *Autobiography*

This book was dictated in 1898 shortly before Fukuzawa's death and was later translated into English by a grandson, Kiyooka Eikichi, under the title *The Autobiography of Fukuzawa Yukichi* (Tokyo, 1934). These selections pertain to his first visits to America and Europe, and to his founding of a private school for Western studies and also of a private newspaper.

[From the *Autobiography of Fukuzawa Yukichi,* pp. 118–44, 222–31, 326–60]

I am willing to admit my pride in this accomplishment for Japan. The facts are these: It was not until the sixth year of Kaei (1853) that a steamship was seen for the first time; it was only in the second year of Ansei (1855) that we began to study navigation from the Dutch in Nagasaki; by 1860, the science was sufficiently understood to enable us to sail a ship across the Pacific. This means that about seven years after the first sight of a steamship, after only about five years of practice, the Japanese people made a trans-Pacific crossing without help from foreign experts. I think we can without undue pride boast before the world of this courage and skill. As I have shown, the Japanese officers were to receive no aid from Captain Brooke throughout the voyage. Even in taking observations, our officers and the Americans made them independently of each other. Sometimes they compared their results, but we were never in the least dependent on the Americans.

As I consider all the other peoples of the Orient as they exist today, I feel convinced that there is no other nation which has the ability or the courage to navigate a steamship across the Pacific after a period of five years of experience in navigation and engineering. Not only in the Orient would this feat stand as an act of unprecedented skill and daring. Even Peter the Great of Russia, who went to Holland to study navigation, with all his attainments in the science could not have equalled this feat of the Japanese. Without doubt, the famous Emperor of Russia was a man of exceptional genius, but his people did not respond to his leadership in the practice of science as did our Japanese in this great adventure. [pp. 118–19]

. . . .

On our part there were many confusing and embarrassing moments, for we were quite ignorant of the customs and habits of American life. . . . Things social, political, and economic proved most inexplicable. One day, on a sudden thought, I asked a gentleman where the descendants of George Washington might be. He replied, "I think there is a woman who is directly descended from Washington. I don't know where she is now, but I think I have heard she is married." His answer was so very casual that it shocked me.

Of course, I knew that America was a republic with a new president every four years, but I could not help feeling that the family of Washington should be regarded as apart from all other families. My reasoning was based on the reverence in Japan for the founders of the great lines of rulers—like that for Ieyasu of the Tokugawa family of shoguns, really deified in the popular mind. So I remember the intense astonishment I felt at receiving this indifferent answer about the Washington family. As for scientific inventions and industrial machinery, there was no great novelty in them for me. It was more in matters of life and conventions of social custom and ways of thinking that I found myself at a loss in America. [pp. 121–25]

. . . .

While we were in London, a certain member of the Parliament sent us a copy of a bill which he said he had proposed in the House under the name of the party to which he belonged. The bill was a protest against the arrogant attitude of the British minister to Japan, Alcock, who had at times acted as if Japan were a country conquered by military force.

One of the instances mentioned in the bill was that of Alcock's riding his horse into the sacred temple grounds of Shiba, an unpardonable insult to the Japanese.

On reading the copy of this bill, I felt as if "a load had been lifted from my chest." After all, the foreigners were not all "devils." I had felt that Japan was enduring some pointed affronts on the part of the foreign ministers who presumed on the ignorance of our government. But now that I had actually come to the minister's native land, I found that there were among them some truly impartial and warm-hearted human beings. So after this I grew even more determined in my doctrine of free intercourse with the rest of the world. [pp. 138–39]

. . . .

During this mission in Europe I tried to learn some of the most commonplace details of foreign culture. I did not care to study scientific or technical subjects while on the journey, because I could study them as well from books after I had returned home. But I felt that I had to learn the more common matters of daily life directly from the people, because the Europeans would not describe them in books as being too obvious. Yet to us those common matters were the most difficult to comprehend.

For instance, when I saw a hospital, I wanted to know how it was run— who paid the running expenses; when I visited a bank, I wished to learn how the money was deposited and paid out. By similar firsthand queries, I learned something of the postal system and the military conscription then in force in France but not in England. A perplexing institution was representative government.

When I asked a gentleman what the "election law" was and what kind of an institution the Parliament really was, he simply replied with a smile, meaning I suppose that no intelligent person was expected to ask such a question. But these were the things most difficult of all for me to understand. In this connection, I learned that there were different political parties—the Liberal and the Conservative—who were always "fighting" against each other in the government.

For some time it was beyond my comprehension to understand what they were "fighting" for, and what was meant, anyway, by "fighting" in peace time. "This man and that man are 'enemies' in the House," they would tell me. But these "enemies" were to be seen at the same table, eating and drinking with each other. I felt as if I could not make much out of this. It took me a long time, with some tedious thinking, before I could gather a general notion of these separate mysterious facts. In some of the more complicated matters, I might achieve an understanding five or ten days after they were explained to me. But all in all, I learned much from this initial tour of Europe. [pp. 142–44]

THE GROWTH OF A PRIVATE SCHOOL

It was during the fourth year of Keio (1868) that I moved my school from Teppozu to Shinsenza in the Shiba ward. Now that it had taken on somewhat the status of a regular school, I gave it the name of Keio-gijuku, after the name of the era. Students who had scattered during the unsettled times were now returning and the school again prospered. . . . At that time all of the schools formerly supported by the government of the shogun had been broken up and all their teachers had scattered. The new regime had no time yet to concern itself with education. And so the only school in the whole country where any real teaching was being done was Keio-gijuku. . . . Indeed, I think it was until after the abolition of the clan system and organization of prefectural government that Keio remained the only school specializing in European studies. . . .

The final purpose of all my work was to create in Japan a civilized nation, as well equipped in both the arts of war and peace as those of the Western world. I acted as if I had become the sole functioning agent for the introduction of Western culture. It was natural then that I would be disliked by the older type of Japanese, and suspected of working for the benefit of foreigners.

In my interpretation of education, I try to be guided by the laws of nature in man and the universe, and I try to coordinate all the physical actions of human beings by the very simple laws of "number and reason." [1] In spiritual or moral training, I regard the human being as the most sacred and responsible of all orders, unable therefore, in reason, to do anything base. So in self-respect, a man cannot change his sense of humanity, his justice, his loyalty, or anything belonging to his manhood even when driven by circumstances to do so. In short, my creed is that a man should find his faith in independence and self-respect.

[1] By this he seems to have meant mathematics and rational inquiry as applied to such fields as accounting, economics, physical sciences, etc. [Ed.]

From my own observations in both the Occidental and Oriental civilizations, I find that each has certain strong points and weak points bound up in its moral teaching and scientific theory. But when I examine which excels the other as to wealth, armament, and general well-being, I have to put the Orient below the Occident. Granting that a nation's destiny depends upon the education of its people, there must be some fundamental difference in the education of the Western and Eastern peoples.

In the education of the East, so often saturated with Confucian teaching, I find two points lacking; that is to say, the lack of studies in "number and reason" in material culture, and the lack of the idea of independence in the spiritual culture. But in the West I think I see why their statesmen are successful in managing their national affairs, and the businessmen in theirs, and the people generally ardent in their patriotism and keen in their family circles.

I regret that in our country I have to acknowledge that people are not formed in these two principles, though I believe no one can escape the laws of "number and reason," nor can anyone depend on anything but the doctrine of independence as long as nations are to exist and mankind is to thrive. Japan could not assert herself among the great nations of the world without full recognition and practice of these two principles. And so I reason that Chinese philosophy as the root of education was responsible for our obvious shortcomings. . . .

It is not only that I hold little regard for the Chinese teachings, but I have even been endeavoring to drive its degenerate influences from my country. It is not unusual for scholars in Western learning and for interpreters of languages to make this denouncement. But too often they lack the knowledge of Chinese which would make their attacks truly effective. But I know a good deal of Chinese, and I have given real effort to the study of it under a strict teacher. And I am familiar with most of the references made from histories, ethics, and poetry. Even the peculiarly subtle philosophy of Lao Tzu and Chuang Tzu, I have studied after hearing my teacher lecture on them. All of this experience I owe to the great scholar of Nakatsu, Shiraishi. So, while I frequently pretend that I do not know much, I often take advantage of the more delicate points for attack both in my writings and speeches. I realize that I am a pretty disagreeable opponent of the Chinese scholars—"a worm in the lion's body."

The true reason of my opposing the Chinese culture with such a vigor is my belief that as long as the old retrogressive doctrine of the Chinese school remains at all in our young men's minds, our country can never enter the rank of civilized nations of the world. In my determination to save our coming generations from the detrimental influence, I was prepared even to face, single-handed, the Chinese scholars of the country as a whole. [pp. 222–31]

MY PRIVATE LIFE

I do not think it is particularly to be commended that I have a harmonious home and that I am faithful to my wife, for ours is not the only happy family there is. I am not fool enough to take pride in living a clean life as if that were the only and final purpose of a man's career. But strange is the reaction of society, for what I take to be simply ordinary behavior proves to be exemplary influence at times, and in unexpected quarters.

In the beginning my reputation in my lord's household was very bad, for I was simply an upstart samurai who had studied some foreign sciences, traveled in strange lands, and was now writing books to advocate very unconventional ideas; moreover I was finding fault with the venerable Chinese culture—a very dangerous heretic. I can imagine the kind of reports made about me to the inner household.

But when years passed and times had changed, the whole country turning inevitably toward the new culture, my clan came to find that this Fukuzawa was not so spiteful a person as was thought, and that he might really prove useful in some way. A certain chancellor named Shimazu Yutaro was the first to see the situation and speak well of me in the feudal household.

At that time there was a certain lady dowager in the household whom people called Horen-in Sama. She was of very noble lineage, having come from the great house of Hitotsu-bashi, and now at her advanced age she was held in particular respect by the whole household.

In conversing with this lady, Shimazu described much of the medicine and navigation and other sciences of the Western lands; also the customs which were very different from our own. The most remarkable of all the Western customs, he told her, was the relation between men and women; there men and women had equal rights, and monogamy was the strict rule in any class of people—this, at least, might be a merit of the Western customs.

The lady dowager could not help being moved by this conversation, for she had had some unhappy trials in earlier days. As if her eyes were suddenly opened to something new, she expressed a desire to make the acquaintance of Fukuzawa. When I was admitted to her presence, she found that I was quite an ordinary man—though often called a heretic, I had no horns on my head nor tail beneath my formal skirt. So she gradually began to place confidence in me. Many years later Shimazu told me all about this, and then I learned how I was first admitted to the inner household of the lord.

By this incident I am inclined to think that the doctrine of monogamy does have a great deal of power in society though it usually passes unnoticed. There are people who hold that it is ridiculous to advocate the abolishing of polygamy in this age. But that is a poor excuse of those who are in the midst of difficulties. The doctrine of monogamy is not pedantic. I am sure that the majority of people in present-day Japan agree with it. Especially the ladies of the higher society are all on my side. So I intend to work as long as I live for the abolition of the unhealthy custom. It does not matter whom I may have to encounter. I will attempt to make our society more presentable if only on the surface. [pp. 326–28]

I DEVELOP A NEWSPAPER

To speak very honestly, the first reason for my avoiding a government post is my dislike of the arrogance of all officials. It might be argued that they need to put on dignity in their office. But in reality they enjoy bullying.

The titles of nobility ought to have been given up with feudalism, but those men in office would keep them, thus contriving to place distinction between officials and ordinary men as if the former belonged to a nobler race of people than the latter. Anyone joining this nobler group would have to lord it over the commoner as a natural consequence whether he considered it right or not. While he may bully those below him, he must at the same time receive the bullying of those above him. This would be a foolish game.

As long as I remain in private life, I can watch and laugh. But joining the government would draw me into the practice of those ridiculous pretensions which I cannot allow myself to do.

The second reason, which cannot be but distasteful for me to go into, is the low moral standard of the average officials. They live in large houses, dress well, and are often very generous. They may show a splendid spirit in their political activities, clean and courageous. But in private life they have the sad habit of affecting the Chinese "heroes,"[2] disregarding the restraint that is a part of a man's moral duty. They would keep concubines in their own houses, committing the crime of polygamy, but they seem to feel no shame about it; they would not even endeavor to hide it. I must say that these men are promoting the new civilization on one hand and practicing the debased customs of the old on the other. So I cannot help feeling that they are in this regard below my standards and practice.

As long as I am keeping these men at a distance, they are not particularly objectionable. I do not mind meeting them for occasional business and social intercourse. But working together under the same roof and becoming really a member among them—that is another thing. I may be fastidious and narrow, but again, it is my nature, and I am as I am.

Still a third reason that kept me from taking office was the sad memory I had of these men at the time of the Restoration. When the crisis came and the shogun returned to Yedo defeated, great was the uproar from all his retainers and adherents. Hundreds volunteered suggestions and plans for the shogunate cause: "This great régime of three hundred years begun by the sacred ancestor of the Tokugawa must not be abandoned in a day"; "As loyal followers of the house of Tokugawa, we must not forget the three hundred years of benevolence bequeathed to us"; "Who are these men from Satsuma and Choshu, now attempting to attack us? Descendants of the men whom our ancestors overcame in the battle of Sekiga-hara. How can we bend our knees before them and bring shame to our proud forebears?"

Spirit ran high. Some tried to throw up a defense line on the Tokaido highway. Others entered ships of war and withdrew to plan some counterattack. Many sought audience with the shogun to plead for a last stand against the oncoming forces. In the intensity of their ardor many raised their voices and wept. It was indeed like an exposition of patriots and would-be martyrs.

[2] A type of swashbuckler is meant here.

But after all, their zealous efforts bore no fruit; the shogun decided to surrender and retire. When his government was finally dissolved, some of the still ardent and undaunted escaped north to Hakodate; others led bands of soldiers and carried on chance fighting in the northern provinces, while still others concealed their humiliation in their bosoms and went with the shogun in his retirement to Shizuoka.

The most ardent of these loyal partisans began to call Tokyo the "land of the traitors." They would not even eat a piece of cake if it came from Tokyo. In going to bed at night they would not lie down with their heads pointing towards the capital. They would not even mention the word "Tokyo," nor listen to it spoken, lest it pollute their mouth and ears. Their actions were much like those of the faithful brothers in Chinese history—Po I and Shu Chi.[3] And Shizuoka seemed to have become the Shou Yang mountain of the new era.

But one year passed, then two years—the "Po Is" and "Shu Chis" were probably beginning to feel the scarcity of "bracken" on "Shou Yang mountain." First they came down to the foot of the "mountain"; then they entered the "land of the traitors." And furthermore, it was not long before they appeared at the seat of the new government and were seeking office!

With no apparent embarrassment the once resolute "Po Is" and "Shu Chis" and the former vengeful counterrevolutionists, along with nearly everybody else in the empire, calmly presented themselves at the government headquarters and asked for employment. I wonder how they greeted the officials—the one time "traitors." They could hardly have spoken the usual salutation, "For the first time I behold your honored countenance," for the two sides had had frequent quarrels a few years before. Probably they composed themselves and said, "We are humble citizens of Japan whom, we think, you already know."

At any rate, they were received cordially enough, it seems, for in accordance with the old precept, "a highminded man never speaks of past misfortunes," these regenerated men from the old shogunate were all taken into the new government—all past bitterness forgotten. Now, this would seem a state of things for congratulation; hardly would anyone expect me to find fault with it. Nevertheless, I have something to say about it.

[3] They remained loyal to their defeated king and starved to death in the mountains rather than accept any favors from the new ruler.

First of all, consider the essential basis of the division between them. Suppose the truth were that the shogunate had held the policy of free foreign intercourse; and suppose the imperialist party had been opposed to this. Then if, after the triumph of the imperialists in the dispute, they had come to see their own error and turned to adopt the policy of open intercourse, once held by their adversaries; and the shogunate, seeing their own policy adopted by the new government, had decided to join forces with it—if this supposition were the truth, I should certainly have nothing to find fault with.

But the truth is that at the time of the Restoration there was no one who argued on this point. The conduct of the shogunate party was entirely derived from the ancient doctrine of the retainer's duty to his master and the three hundred years of the Tokugawa regime which they had inherited. Yet when the old regime was lost, the retainers apparently felt that the basis of their stand was also gone. They turned around and offered their services to the new government, their one-time enemy, without the least show of embarrassment.

There should be no shame in being defeated in a dispute. I have no mind to accuse a man for having once made an error of judgment. But it seems to me that when a man fails in a dispute, it is his part to take his defeat and retire from active society. But there was nothing like that with these men. They have sought high positions in the rival government, and having obtained them, are proud. After all, the loyalists are not to be trusted; the doctrine of loyalty is a fickle idea. I should be much happier to remain an independent citizen than to associate with this kind of unreliable men.

Not that I believe in criticizing the career of others, but knowing the circumstances too well, I cannot help feeling sorry for the shifty, fainthearted group who once called themselves the loyal retainers of the shogun. This, again, may be my fastidiousness, but it is one of the reasons why I am free from political ambition.

Now for the fourth reason—putting aside the matter of political allegiance and doctrine, I disliked that rush and disorderly struggle for office which passed through the whole country at the beginning of the new government. Not only the samurai, who of course have been accustomed to holding offices, but even the sons of merchants and farmers—men with any kind of education at all were swarming together like insects around some fragrant food. Some who could not be appointed officials sought other connections for profit as if there could be no chance in the world for anyone outside the government. Nobody seemed to realize there was any virtue in human independence.

Many a time a young man returning from study abroad has come to me and has imparted his belief in an independent career, saying he would not think of relying on a government post. I usually listen to his proud declaration with half credulity. And sure enough, after a while I learn that the same young man has been appointed clerk in a certain department—sometimes he has been lucky enough to be placed in the higher office of a province.

Of course I have no business to be criticizing the choice of a man's career, but I have the feeling that this fallacy of the Japanese people is an evidence of the surviving influence of the Chinese teaching. To point out this fallacy to our people and lead them in the right way of modern civilization, someone must be an example. The independence of a nation springs from the independent spirit of its citizens. Our nation cannot hold its own if the old slavish spirit is so manifest among the people. I felt determined to make an example of myself whatever the consequence of my endeavor might be. If I should be the poorer for it, I should live poorer; if I chanced to make money, I should spend it as I wished. At least I would not depend upon the government or its officials. [pp. 331-37]

. . . .

In the fifteenth year of Meiji (1882) I began to publish a newspaper which I called the *Jiji-shimpō*. It was the year following the political outbreak which had so stirred the country; and many of my alumni [4] had urged me to start a paper.

I could see that our society was rapidly changing. The ever increasing competition was bringing about more and more of bitter rivalry and disputes. Recently the government had experienced a very provoking quarrel inside itself.[5] It was logical to expect similar reaction in subsequent economic and industrial rivalry. The greatest need in such a time is for an instrument of nonpartisan, unbiased opinion. But it is easy to make satisfying theories about nonpartisan opinion and not so easy to realize it in practice, for the usual man, conscious of his own personal

---

[4] Of Keio University, which he had founded. [Ed.]
[5] The struggle between Itō and Ōkuma, ending in the latter's resignation in 1881. [Ed.]

interests, cannot lightly throw off his partisanship. As I looked about the country I decided to myself that there were not many besides myself who were independent in living, and who possessed worthwhile ideas in their heads, and who could yet be free from political and business ambitions.

With this reasoning I set myself to the task of establishing a newspaper which became the *Jiji-shimpō*. After I had determined on this project, I paid no attention to certain friends who appeared to warn me of the difficulty in such an undertaking. I decided that it should be entirely my own work, no help coming from outside whether the circulation be large or small. As I originated the paper, so I could destroy it. Even if I were to fail, I should not feel any regret or false shame; nor would my family suffer in the least. Thus forewarned and forearmed, I started publication with no regard for outside criticism. The journal has continued to be successful up to this day.

In editing the paper I encouraged the reporters to write bravely and freely. I have no objection to any severe criticism or extreme statements, but I warned them that they must limit their statements to what they would be willing to say to the victim face to face. Otherwise, they are what I would call *kage-benkei* [shadow-fighters] attacking from the security of their columns. It is very easy for *kage-benkei* to fall into mean abuses and irresponsible invectives which are the eternal shame of the writer's profession. [pp. 344–46]

A FINAL WORD ON THE GOOD LIFE

After all, the present is the result of the past. This glorious condition of our country cannot but be the fruit of the good inheritance from our ancestors. We are the fortunate ones who live today to enjoy this wonderful bequest. Yet I feel as though my second and greater ambition has been attained, for everything that I had hoped for and prayed for has been realized through the benevolence of Heaven and the virtues of those forebears. I have nothing to complain of on looking backward, nothing but full satisfaction and delight.

However, it seems that there is no end to man's capacity for desire. I can still point out some things I am yet hoping for. Not ideas in foreign diplomacy nor developments in our constitutional government—all these I leave to the statesmen. But I should like to put my further efforts towards elevating the moral standards of men and women of my land to make them truly worthy of a civilized nation. Then I should like to encourage a religion—either Buddhism or Christianity—to pacify the minds of a large number of our people. And thirdly, I wish to have a large foundation created for the study of both the physical and meta-physical sciences.

It is these three things that I wish to see accomplished during the remaining years of my life. Though a man may grow old, he should keep active as long as he has his health both of mind and body. And so I intend to do all that lies within my power as long as it is granted to me. [pp. 359–60]

CHAPTER XXV

THE MEIJI ERA
(1868-1912)

With the restoration of imperial rule under the young Emperor Meiji in 1868, Japan stepped up greatly the program of modernization already begun by the shogunate. Within a few decades, as the first Asian nation to bring herself abreast of the West, she came to hold a position of leadership and influence that was quite new to her. For centuries the Japanese had lived in the shadow of China; for over two hundred years they had been almost wholly cut off from the world. Now they found themselves a center of world attention, feared, admired, and imitated by backward nations seeking to benefit from Japan's example.

Yet in so vigorously responding to the challenge of the West, the Japanese had put their own way of life to a severe test. No one could predict, at the outset, the ultimate effects upon it of Japan's sudden and full exposure to the dynamic influences of Western ideas and institutions. Both by the opening of her own doors and by the sending of her ablest sons abroad for study, Japan was soon thrust into new worlds of thought and action—into the political world of Rousseau and the French Revolution, of British liberalism and the statism of Prussia; into the economic world of Malthus, Smith, Mill, and List; into the intellectual world of Kant, Hegel, Darwin, Huxley, and Spencer. It would not be long before each new current in Western thought would have its native spokesmen in Japan, its great works made available in translation. In the meantime there would be foreign advisers in the government, Western scholars teaching in the new universities, and young Japanese in great numbers studying abroad. Henceforth, in the minds of many in the rising generation the word of a Western philosopher or sociologist would carry far more weight than all the classics of the East.

Whatever the manifold effects of Western influence, however, they were not so deep or direct as to displace soon those traditional concepts

[131]

which had played a vital role in the Restoration itself. Not only is this true of the great mass of uneducated and inarticulate opinion, but it is especially true of the handful of men whose attitudes and ideals largely guided the course of Meiji Japan. If any group may be considered representative of the nation as a whole in this period, it is not the scholars or writers who sought to grasp the whole new world in one embrace, but this very uncommon band of leaders who proved themselves in action to have achieved a workable synthesis of new and old, East and West. Not since the seventh century, when a band of Sinophiles around the Throne tried to remake Japan on the Chinese model, had all aspects of Japanese life been so much altered by political action or Japanese thinking so much directed along lines laid down by a few master planners. As to just where those lines should run the ruling oligarchy itself was by no means always clear, but that their bold program of state action would inevitably make them leaders in the fields of economics, education, journalism, and even social reform, as well as in politics, was evident from the very outset. And even apart from the preponderant role of the state in initiating changes on such a wide scale, outside the government too an important part was played by men with the same samurai traditions of leadership as those in power. Their circumstances or convictions might keep them from taking office but not from pioneering in new fields of private endeavor.

LEADERS OF THE RESTORATION AND RENOVATION

The over-all aim of the Meiji leaders, and of the country as a whole, is found in the slogan "Enrich the nation and strengthen its arms." To build up Japan's military power and gain equality with the Western powers was undoubtedly the most urgent desire of her samurai leaders. Still it is significant that they should have understood, as a necessary counterpart and even a prerequisite to this, the importance of "enriching the nation"; of strengthening its economy, developing its industry and commerce, more fully utilizing its human resources, and improving its social and political institutions. Progress in certain of these phases of reform may have lagged behind others in the forced march toward modernization, but at least recognition was given to Japan's problem in all its magnitude. In principle no phase of life, no segment of society, was to be sacrificed to the juggernaut of military power. Thus the Meiji Restoration promised to remedy not only the weakness of Tokugawa arms, but also the economic weaknesses of the shogunate to which Japanese writers of the eighteenth and nineteenth centuries had increasingly drawn attention.

In the accomplishment of this ambitious goal the Meiji leadership displayed two striking characteristics: a readiness to try new methods and push ahead with them boldly, coupled with a tenacious adherence to traditional ideals and virtues. Only if both of these attitudes are kept in mind, can we appreciate how much actual progress was made, and how nevertheless the new nation could still have been more a product of its own past than of its recent contact with the West. The Restoration movement appealed at the start to the idea of reviving the golden age of imperial rule before the onset of feudalism and military government. This ideal was as much the product of recent invention as of earlier tradition, but the slogan used by the ideologists of the Restoration, "Restore the old order" (*fukko,* a phrase in the Neo-Confucian vocabulary which came down to them from Sung dynasty China), harked back to ancient times when the imperial power had been raised to new heights of glory by the wholesale adoption of Chinese institutions and ideals. Some of these same institutions, and much of their spirit, was to be preserved in the new regime.

Another important characteristic of the Meiji leadership, suggested by its capacity to bring together such divergent conservative and reformist tendencies, is its moderation. This did not exhibit itself, certainly, in any disinclination to take strong action, or in a mere desire to compromise between opposing extremes. It was marked rather by a constructive and determined pursuit of certain positive goals, from which these leaders refused to be turned away by doctrinaire slogans or partisan clamor. Thus this quality of moderation reflected a common acceptance of certain ultimate values, such as loyalty to the emperor and the nation, on the part of men who might differ widely on the best means of serving them, and it owed much to a sense of solidarity or esprit de corps among the samurai elite, who had long been conditioned to disciplined and concerted action. Meiji Japan was certainly not without its rugged individualists and rebellious spirits, even in the ranks of the samurai. It lacked neither extremists of the left and right, nor those who stood where the very extremities of left and right conjoined. Even the samurai tradition of violent political action was vigorously perpetuated, as the long record of political assassinations and uprisings right down to the Second World War amply demonstrates. Yet in the midst of this Japan maintained a remarkably steady course toward her goal of "Enriching the nation and strengthening its arms." For this, and for simultaneous progress along so many fronts, credit must go to that group of men whose strong convictions and ambitions were combined with an equally strong sense of moderation, cohesion, and national loyalty.

As we turn to the actual work of building a new Japan, therefore, our attention must shift from those laying the intellectual foundations of the future, as the priests and scholars we have examined in the past had done for the Meiji Era, and instead be focused on the outstanding personalities and momentous decisions which were to shape the immediate present. First of all we take up the great symbol of Japan's modernization, the Emperor Meiji, and three leaders who became known as the "Triumvirate of the Restoration." Thereafter we shall be concerned with three broad movements which contributed to Japan's emergence as a modern state: the development of constitutional government, of party politics, and of the army as a powerful force in Japan's national life.

THE ENLIGHTENED RULE OF EMPEROR MEIJI

Little is known about the Emperor Meiji, owing to the aura of sanctity which always surrounded his person and activities. He was raised in the comparative seclusion of the Kyoto court, which for centuries had maintained a ceremonial existence withdrawn from the realities of Japanese life. But even after his removal to the former shogunate capital, thenceforth known as Tokyo, the "Eastern Capital," the young Emperor remained apart from the world; his assumption of actual rule, though making him much more a center of national attention, hardly brought him into closer touch with his subjects. The traditional view of the Throne as representing a divine and mystical power, exalted far beyond the reach of ordinary men, not only persisted but was greatly heightened by the role this monarch played in the government of the country. It

[134]

was a role much in keeping with his personality and temperament, insofar as we can discern them. Modest and reserved, but exceedingly conscientious in attending to matters of state, the Emperor worked quietly and without any impulse to dominate. He relied heavily upon his advisers, as the Confucian conception of the wise sovereign called for him to do, and was always ready to hear different points of view. Yet when momentous decisions had to be made, his own judgement commanded the respect of counsellors who might be deeply divided among themselves. Indeed there is no reason to question the sincere admiration for the Emperor expressed by the statesmen who served him most closely. In a situation which conferred great power and influence upon a single person, a man less understanding and self-disciplined might well have drawn the resentment of government leaders and encouraged attempts to limit imperial authority by constitutional means. As it was these leaders no doubt felt more secure in the service of a sympathetic and patient ruler than of a fickle public. They therefore joined all the more willingly in raising the Throne to a position of overwhelming prestige and inviolability.

In such a position the Emperor Meiji effectively symbolized and inspired two of the most powerful forces for social unity in the new Japan. One of these was nationalism, a sentiment already well-nourished in Tokugawa times and requiring little stimulus from the West, but which quickly grew into an all-pervasive creed and cult. Often enough in the modern world such nationalism has taken on a religious character. In Japan, with the help of Neo-Shintoism and a tradition of imperial absolutism inherited from the Chinese, a nationalistic cult centered upon the God-Emperor became in fact the most widely accepted and compelling belief among the people. Increasingly, as a result of the profound changes affected by the Meiji leadership, the lives and activities of the Japanese were organized around the imperial house and directed to the fulfillment of its divine mission. But national consciousness and emperor worship would have been powerless to move Japan's millions without the strong support of Confucian ethics, which provided the order and discipline Shinto theology lacked. Of this vital moral force, too, the Emperor was more than a passive symbol. His personal tutor and mentor was a Confucian scholar of the old school. In the imperial rescripts by which his thoughts and wishes were made known to his subjects, Meiji spoke less

[135]

like a modern chief of state than like the ancient sage-king, imparting moral guidance to his children and exhorting them diligently to practice the traditional virtues. Today this may appear to have been no more than a convenient and accepted means of keeping people in line. It remains a fact, however, that the leaders of the regime, no less than the Emperor's humblest subjects, submitted to the requirements of this exacting code and in their basic outlook were more profoundly influenced by Confucian philosophy than by any Western school of thought.

In recognizing the vital role of tradition, however, we must not neglect the central fact of Meiji's rule—that it brought Japan out of the feudal past and into the modern world. Indeed, this long reign from 1868 to 1912 was best known for its enlightened and progressive character. The name Meiji, which means "enlightened or illustrious rule," was originally a reign title, only posthumously applied to the sovereign himself. Yet no one questioned the appropriateness of this name for the ruler who became known, even to reformers in nineteenth century China, as a symbol of the modern East. If subsequently the imperial institution has been able to withstand the shocks of the twentieth century, and survive in the esteem of the people, it is due largely to the prestige won for it by Meiji, in demonstrating that the Throne could be a constructive and steadying force in the new era.

The Charter Oath

Of all the declarations made in the name of the Emperor Meiji the Charter Oath of April 1868 best symbolized the progressive side of his reign. It was drawn up by a few young advisers, representative of the low-ranking samurai who provided the real leadership of the Western clans opposed to the Tokugawa. Generally hostile to the old aristocracy and eager to make room for new leadership, they nevertheless confined themselves to a statement of general principles which might attract the most support to the Restoration by assuring everyone of a part in the new regime, while threatening no one with a diminution of his power. Its vagueness, reminiscent of the constitution of Prince Shōtoku, was by no means wholly a defect, but left room for adjustment in a rapidly changing situation. Thus the deliberative assembly referred to in the first article was in early drafts of the Oath specifically to be a council of the feudal clans, but in its final form was general enough to be applicable even after the abolition of feudalism, when advocates of parliamentary government often invoked its authority.

[From *Meiji boshin,* pp. 81–82]

By this oath we set up as our aim the establishment of the national weal on a broad basis and the framing of a constitution and laws.

1. Deliberative assemblies shall be widely established and all matters decided by public discussion.

2. All classes, high and low, shall unite in vigorously carrying out the administration of affairs of state.

3. The common people, no less than the civil and military officials, shall each be allowed to pursue his own calling so that there may be no discontent.

4. Evil customs of the past shall be broken off and everything based upon the just laws of Nature.

5. Knowledge shall be sought throughout the world so as to strengthen the foundations of imperial rule.

The Constitution of 1868

The Constitution of June 1868, hastily drawn up to implement the Charter Oath, throws light on the original intentions of the Restoration leadership. Articles II, III, V, and IX make it clear that the framers were influenced by Western concepts of representative government and the separation of powers, though the provisions to this effect soon proved unworkable and inoperative. The significance of the other articles lies in their attempt to assert the supremacy of the imperial government throughout the land and reserve certain powers to it without directly attacking feudal authority. In the same way, while reaffirming the principle of noble rank, the intent is to enhance the position of those at court and limit the social prerogatives of the feudal aristocracy. The appendices to this document, not reproduced here, set forth a governmental organization based largely on the model of a centralized state imported from China in the seventh century. This was, in fact, better suited to the kind of strong government administered by the ruling oligarchy than were the democratic institutions of the West, with which Japanese had no real familiarity or experience.

[From *Meiji boshin,* pp. 87–89; McLaren, *Japanese Government Documents,* pp. 8–10]

The first article, deleted here, restates the Charter Oath as a preamble to the main text.

II. All power and authority in the empire shall be vested in a Council of State, and thus the grievances of divided government shall be done away with. The power and authority of the Council of State shall be threefold, legislative, executive, and judicial. Thus the imbalance of authority among the different branches of the government shall be avoided.

III. The legislative organ shall not be permitted to perform executive functions, nor shall the executive organ be permitted to perform legislative functions. However, on extraordinary occasions the legislative organ may still perform such functions as tours of inspection of cities and the conduct of foreign affairs.

IV. Attainment to offices of the first rank shall be limited to princes of the blood, court nobles, and territorial lords, and shall be by virtue of [the sovereign's] intimate trust in the great ministers of state. A law governing ministers summoned from the provinces (*chōshi*) shall be adopted, clan officials of whatever status may attain offices of the second rank on the basis of worth and talent.

V. Each great city, clan, and imperial prefecture shall furnish qualified men to be members of the Assembly. A deliberative body shall be instituted so that the views of the people may be discussed openly.

VI. A system of official ranks shall be instituted so that each [official] may know the importance of his office and not dare to hold it in contempt.

VII. Princes of the blood, court nobles, and territorial lords shall be accompanied by [no more than] six two-sworded men and three commoners, and persons of lower rank by [no more than] two two-sworded men and one commoner, so that the appearance of pomp and grandeur may be done away with and the evils of class barriers may be avoided.

VIII. Officers shall not discuss the affairs of the government in their own houses with unofficial persons. If any persons desire interviews with them for the purpose of giving expression to their own opinions, they shall be sent to the office of the appropriate department and the matter shall be discussed openly.

IX. All officials shall be changed after four years' service. They shall be selected by means of public balloting. However, at the first expiration of terms hereafter, half of the officials shall retain office for two additional years, after which their terms shall expire, so that [the government] may be caused to continue without interruption. Those whose relief is undesirable because they enjoy the approval of the people may be retained for an additional period of years.

X. A system shall be established for levying taxes on territorial lords, farmers, artisans, and merchants, so that government revenue may be supplemented, military installations strengthened, and public security maintained. For this purpose, even persons with rank or office shall have taxes levied upon them equivalent to one thirtieth of their income or salaries.

XI. Each large city, clan, and imperial prefecture shall promulgate regulations, and these shall comply with the Charter Oath. The laws peculiar to one locality shall not be generalized to apply to other localities. There shall be no private conferral of titles or rank, no private coinage, no private employment of foreigners, and no conclusion of alliances with neighboring clans or with foreign countries, lest inferior authorities be confounded with superior and the government be thrown into confusion.

The Imperial Rescript on Education

If the preceding documents bespeak the more progressive side of Meiji's rule, the following represents the strong traditionalist element which he also symbolized. Copies of this rescript were distributed to every school in Japan and hung alongside the Emperor's portrait, where all made obeisance to them. In such awe were they held that on occasion teachers and principals risked their lives to rescue them from burning buildings. All moral and civic instruction after 1890 was based on the principles—largely Confucian—set forth here. Issuance of the rescript at that time reflected a powerful reaction to the Westernizing tendencies of the early Meiji Period, yet there can be no doubt that this type of thinking was already strongly prevalent and only reinforced by the systematic indoctrination of the new public schools.

This rescript was the work of many hands, as were most of Emperor Meiji's pronouncements, but principally those of Inoue Kowashi, a Kumamoto samurai known for his Chinese learning and later minister of education.

[From Kikuchi, *Japanese Education,* pp. 2–3]

Know ye, Our subjects:

Our Imperial Ancestors have founded Our Empire on a basis broad and everlasting, and have deeply and firmly implanted virtue; Our subjects ever united in loyalty and filial piety have from generation to generation illustrated the beauty thereof. This is the glory of the fundamental character of Our Empire, and herein also lies the source of Our education. Ye, Our subjects, be filial to your parents, affectionate to your brothers and sisters; as husbands and wives be harmonious, as friends true; bear yourselves in modesty and moderation; extend your benevolence to all; pursue learning and cultivate arts, and thereby develop intellectual faculties and perfect moral powers; furthermore, advance public good and promote common interests; always respect the Constitution and observe the laws; should emergency arise, offer yourselves courageously to the State; and thus guard and maintain the prosperity of Our Imperial Throne coeval with heaven and earth. So shall ye not only be Our good and faithful subjects, but render illustrious the best traditions of your forefathers.

The Way here set forth is indeed the teaching bequeathed by Our Imperial Ancestors, to be observed alike by Their Descendants and the subjects, infallible for all ages and true in all places. It is Our wish to lay it to heart in all reverence, in common with you, Our subjects, that we may all attain to the same virtue.

October 30, 1890

KIDO KŌIN AND THE NEW REGIME

The real leadership of the new regime came not from among the feudal lords of the rebellious states, but from very young, low-ranking samurai who had furnished the zeal and drive which made the Restoration a success. Answering very closely to Yoshida Shōin's description of the "grass-roots hero" who would rise up and overthrow the effete aristocracy, they possessed the samurai sense of leadership and hierarchical order, but no great love for the feudal system which favored hereditary right over individual merit. Nevertheless, they brought into the new government a strong spirit of clannishness, which kept power in the hands of a ruling oligarchy dominated by Satsuma and Chōshū.

A Chōshū samurai and disciple of Yoshida Shōin, Kido Kōin (1833-1877) realized early the futility of his fellow-clansmen's violent anti-foreign demonstrations while they remained militarily so weak. Though physically frail and of an introspective temperament, he showed remarkable energy and genius in modernizing the Chōshū forces and leading them against the Shogunate. Moreover he was an able negotiator, who engineered the coalition of forces which eventually overthrew the Tokugawa. And when the Emperor had reassumed the powers formerly held by the shogun as military overlord of a feudal Japan, it was Kido who saw the necessity for abolishing feudalism itself, if the new imperial government were to possess the power proper to a modern state.

KIDO KŌIN
The Voluntary Surrender of the Feudal Domains

Rather than precipitate a civil war over this issue, Kido used his talents of persuasion to convince the daimyo of the victorious coalition that they should surrender their fiefs as a patriotic gesture. The other feudal lords could then hardly refuse to follow suit. The text of the surrender offer bespeaks the overriding importance in Kido's mind of a single centralized authority.

[From *Meiji bunka zenshū,* vol. 2; McLaren, *Japanese Government Documents,* pp. 29–32]

Your servants venture to address Your Majesty with profound reverence. We respectfully suggest that two things are essential to Your Majesty's administration. There must be one national polity and one sovereign authority. Since the Imperial Ancestor founded the country and established a basis of government, there has been one imperial line for countless generations without change, making the farthest limits of heaven and earth its realm and all mankind its subjects. This is what is meant by the national polity. And the sole power of giving and taking away ranks and fiefs, by which the foundation is maintained, makes it impossible for a foot of ground to be held for private ends, or for one subject to be wantonly robbed. This is what is meant by sovereign authority. . . .

Here the memorial describes the usurpation of imperial authority by the shogunate and the establishment of independent domains under the great feudal houses.

It was commonly said [by members of these families]: "These possessions of ours were gained by the military power of our ancestors." But wherein did this differ from defying the death penalty to plunder the imperial storehouses and steal their treasures? If a man were to break into a storehouse, others would know him to be a robber, yet no one thought it strange when these families plundered lands and robbed people. Is this not a great confounding of principle?

Now that we are about to establish an entirely new form of government, the national polity and the sovereign authority must not in the slightest degree be yielded to subordinates. The place where your servants live is the emperor's land, and those whom they rule are the emperor's people. How can these be made the property of subjects? Your servants accordingly beg respectfully to surrender their fiefs to Your Majesty. They ask that the court act on the basis of what is right, giving what should be given and taking away what should be taken away; and that Your Majesty issue edicts redisposing of the enfeoffed land of our clans. Furthermore, they ask that the court lay down regulations regarding all things, from the administration of troops to uniform and military equipment, so that everyone in the empire both great and small shall be caused to submit to one [authority]. Thus, in the future, in name and in fact our country can begin to take its place among the nations of the world.

As this is the most urgent affair of the day, Your Majesty's servants also share the responsibility for dealing with it. Therefore, Your Majesty's servants, though they are without judgment, dare to present their foolish opinions for Your Majesty's consideration.

Observations on Returning from the West, 1873

As one of the drafters of the Charter Oath, Kido is said to have insisted on the fourth article: "Evil customs of the past shall be broken off and everything based on the just laws of Nature." On his visit to Europe, which he made as a member of the official Iwakura mission in 1871, Kido was still more greatly impressed by the backwardness of his own people in comparison to the West. To achieve thoroughgoing reform would require years of patient effort and freedom from military involvements. While not necessarily abandoning any of his ultimate aspirations for the expansion of Japanese power, Kido opposed war in Korea or Formosa in order to concentrate on internal reform. Nevertheless, the speed and ruthlessness with which the government pushed some of these changes, and especially the commutation of samurai pensions, offended his sense of justice and he withdrew from the government. Thereafter until his premature death at the age of forty-three he remained in peaceful opposition to, but spurned open rebellion against, the regime now dominated by Ōkubo.

The statement of Kido which follows shows the evolution of his thinking from an initial concern for centralized authority to one for the exercise of that authority according to law. In this sense he remained true to the progressive impulses of the Restoration and was a herald of the constitutional movement in later decades. What struck Kido most in the West were the constitutional processes which limited those in power and provided a sound basis for orderly change. Indeed in a long preamble to the passage quoted here he asserts as a universal law of history that the rise and fall of nations is determined by their fidelity to constitutional order.

[From *Shōgiku Kido-kō den,* II, 1563–68; McLaren, *Japanese Government Documents,* pp. 571–75]

It was thought advisable, as early as the spring of 1868 when the northern provinces were still unsubdued, to summon together at the palace all the officials and nobles of the empire. The Emperor then prayed to the gods of Heaven and earth and pronounced an Oath containing five clauses, which was thereupon published throughout the empire, indicating to what end the Constitution should tend, and guiding the ideas of the people in one fixed direction. The heading of this Oath states: "By this Oath We set up as Our aim the establishment of the national weal on a broad basis and the framing of a constitution and laws." This led at last to granting the petitions for leave to restore the fiefs to the Emperor, which occasioned the abolition of feudal titles and the unification of the divided national authority. Is not all this consonant with the prevailing view in the powerful countries of the five great continents? And if this be so, then surely we must consider those five clauses as the foundation of our Constitution. Now the Constitution is a thing which sets on a firm basis the weal of the entire nation, which prevents officials from taking unauthorized steps on their own judgment, and which by placing under one control all the business of administration, renders it necessary that all measures conform to it. Is there at the present time any subject of the empire who does not gratefully acknowledge its profound and farsighted policy and admire the loftiness of the Emperor's views?

However, in enlightened countries, though there may be a sovereign, still he does not hold sway in an arbitrary fashion. The people of the whole country give expression to their united and harmonious wishes, and the business of the State is arranged accordingly, a department (styled the government) being charged with the execution of their judgments, and officials appointed to transact business. For this reason all who hold office respect the wishes of the whole nation and serve their country under a deep sense of responsibility, so that even in extraordinary crises, they take no arbitrary step contrary to the people's will. The strictness [of the constitution] of these governments is such as I have just described, but as an additional check upon illegal acts, the people have parliamentary representatives whose duty it is to inspect everything that is done and to check arbitrary proceedings on the part of officials. Herein lies the best quality of these governments. But if the people are not yet sufficiently enlightened, it becomes necessary, at least for a time, that the Sovereign should by his superior discernment anticipate their unanimous wishes and act for them in arranging the affairs of State and in entrusting to officials the execution of their wishes. By this means he will gradually lead them forward in the path of enlightenment. Such a course is consonant with natural principles, and I am inclined to believe that the thought of the Emperor when he inaugurated by an oath his energetic policy was based on this idea. My belief is that although Japan is not yet ready for parliamentary inspection of the affairs of state, in the importance of its laws and the magnitude of its affairs it is no different from those countries of Europe and America the conduct of whose governments embodies the will of the people. It is important that our officials should not be forgetful of their responsibility and should take as their model our five-clause Constitution. . . .

Every citizen's object in life is to preserve his natural liberty by exercising his rights, and to assist in carrying on the government by sharing its obligations. Therefore, [these rights and obligations] are specified exactly in writing and men bind themselves by a solemn promise to permit no infringement of them, but to act as mutual checks on each other in maintaining them. These writings are what we call laws. The laws grow out of the Constitution, for the Constitution is the root of every part of the government, and there is nothing which does not branch out from it. For this reason, every country, when the time comes for changing its constitution, bestows on it the greatest care and the ripest consideration and ascertains to the full the general wishes. No new measures are put in force unless they are imperatively called for by the circumstances, [nor are any adopted] lightly or hastily. In a country whose sovereign generously decides to meet the wishes of the people, the greatest care must be taken to ascertain them with accuracy, the internal conditions of the country must be profoundly studied, what the people produce must be taken into account, and, most important of all, policies must be suited to the degree of civilization of the people.

Again, in ordering the affairs of a nation, its strength must be taken into account. If not, one good will be converted into a hundred evils. The poor man's son who tries to rival the son of the rich man ruins his property and his house, and in the end does not make a show equal to his rival. Those who order the affairs of a nation should remember, before taking action, to consider the due sequence of measures, and should proceed by gradual steps in nourishing its strength, for no nation ever attained to a perfect state of civilization in a single morning. . . .

When I consider the results of the measures of the past few years with reference to the present condition of our country it appears to me that the trend of the times still lacks direction. The people's minds are perversely turned in one direction, and instead of exercising their rights, many of them mimic idly the arts of civilization; instead of discharging their responsibilities to the state, they are much given to ill-judged pretensions to enlightenment. The consequence is that although they are gradually acquiring the outward appearance of refinement, and the old rustic coarseness is gradually changing, they have not suddenly become enlightened in their hearts.

The Need for News of the West

To raise the general cultural level of his people Kido believed that they must be better informed of conditions and developments in the West. In December of 1871 he wrote to Shinagawa Yajirō, who had been sent by the government to observe the Franco-Prussian War, asking his cooperation in a project for the dissemination of news about the West in Japan. It is significant that Kido, though a member of the ruling oligarchy, recognized that more could be accomplished through an independent, private organization than through an official propaganda agency.

[From *Shōgiku Kido-kō den*, II, 1394–1402]

It is my plan to open a news office which will publish all the news—both domestic and foreign—for the edification of our people in every province and fief. I feel that it will contribute to their enlightenment. I therefore request you to write me at every opportunity on anything that will help educate our people, starting with accounts of the great war between the countries. As our country's cultural standard is considerably lower than that of the countries of Europe, I hope that you will make the articles as easy as possible for our people to read. As you know, our people —eight- or nine-tenths of them—are obdurate and stubborn. Thus, if this

[145]

newspaper office is opened by the government, they will suspect that it is at the government's disposal, and they will pay little attention to it. Therefore, I should like to have it opened as if the government had nothing to do with it. I feel that it should be permitted to discuss the government's affairs to a certain degree—and even critically, if there is anything unreasonable about them. I mention this, of course, in the event of such an exigency.

The other day one of your letters from New York reached me. Some of the information in it has already appeared in foreign language newspapers, but as it also contained news yet unknown to us, I submitted it to His Majesty's attention. That letter contained much that was highly instructive; and therefore I wish you to bear in mind my plans for a news office and to discuss it with Samejima. If it is feasible I should like to have Samejima write me steadily on the affairs of European countries which would be of interest to our people. I shall forthwith forward them to the news office to be published. Kindly inform Mori Kinnojō, who has been dispatched to America, and Nawa Kan, who has accompanied him, about our plans for this newspaper office. If they will write about America and on other matters of interest to our people, and send them to my address I shall forward them for publication in the same newspaper. I shall be especially obliged if you will be good enough to make the arrangements with Nawa.

[Excerpts from Shinagawa's reply to Kido:]

Because of Your Excellency's advice on the occasion of my appointment to go abroad, I did not entertain the thought of going home after a mere glance at Europe. I was anxious to do something for my country, when the thought occurred to me to start a newspaper. Immediately upon my arrival in America, Yamamoto Jinsuke and I went directly to a newspaper office to pay a visit. We were shown the printing presses and were told of the importance of the newspaper in the daily life of the people. A subsequent visit I made to England, Germany, and France increased my convictions about the indispensability of the newspaper to contemporary life. Such was my enthusiasm in this regard that Ōyama and others have been calling me "Newspaper." As I have been looking forward to the day when I could return to my country and start a newspaper of my own, the coincidence in our plans of which I learned from Your Excellency's letter made me jump with joy. I shall be praying from this side of the world for the success of Your Excellency's publication venture. When European newspapers are translated for publication under Your Excellency's personal direction, the benefits to the country, if I may be permitted to say, would far exceed any that might come from the addition of two or three Ministers to the State Council.

SAIGŌ TAKAMORI AND THE SAMURAI SPIRIT

The oldest among the "Triumvirate" of the Restoration and its most popular figure, Saigō Takamori (1827–1877), was the military leader of the Satsuma forces which joined with Kido and the Chōshū armies to overthrow the Tokugawa. A giant for a Japanese—almost six feet tall and weighing two hundred pounds—he had enormous shoulders, a bull-neck with a collar size of nineteen and a half, and large piercing eyes under big bushy eyebrows. So commanding was he in appearance that it is said almost everyone introduced to him "bowed his head in spite of himself." But he was known less for his fearsome appearance than for his heartiness, which attracted young men to him in great numbers; and for his magnanimity and forbearance, which, when he was chief of staff of the imperial armies at Edo, caused him to spare the shogunate capital from the final carnage of war.

After the Restoration, Saigō enjoyed great popularity and the unique rank of field marshal, but he proved to have less influence in government councils than those who urged rapid changes in Japanese society to which he was opposed. Disturbed especially by the treatment of the old warrior class and by a process of Westernization which he felt would undermine traditional values, he wished to strengthen the position and spirit of the samurai by employing them to improve Japan's military situation. Japan could not resist the West, he was convinced, unless she had Korea and China at her side. Fearing Russia especially, he felt that Korea must be won over quickly, by force if necessary. In the face of obvious hostility from the Korean government, however, Saigō favored first sending an ambassador whose certain execution by the contemptuous Koreans would provide ample pretext for war. As the emissary who would thus meet death he offered himself.

When his plan was rejected in favor of Ōkubo's policy of peace and internal reform, Saigō withdrew from the government along with other prominent Restoration leaders in 1873. Having often in earlier years suffered patiently in exile for his royalist convictions and activities, he was prepared to retire quietly to Satsuma and bide his time. Nevertheless when his more hot-blooded followers became involved in open resistance to government forces, his sense of loyalty and comradeship impelled him to join them. With the crushing of that rebellion in 1877, the life that Saigō had hoped to give to his country he gave up for his friends. But his death, much like that of Yoshida Shōin, made him a hero to future generations of Japanese patriots. The soldiers who later gave their lives on the battlegrounds of Asia, and the *kamikaze* suicide pilots of the Second World War, were spiritual descendants of Saigō Takamori, the death-defying ambassador.

SAIGŌ TAKAMORI
Letters to Itagaki on the Korean Question

In the summer of 1873 Saigō wrote his friend Itagaki a total of eight letters on the Korean question. The three which follow reflect not only his contempt of danger but also his simplicity of speech and taste and his repugnance for display. Though Saigō eventually broke with the government on this issue and died an enemy of the state, it was for these qualities that he was subsequently honored with a pardon from the emperor and regarded by later generations as a martyred hero whose life exemplified the samurai spirit.
[Ōkawa, *Dai Saigō zenshū*, II, 736–56]

July 29 [1873]
Thank you so much for coming all the way to visit me the other day. Has any decision been made on Korea, now that Soejima is back? If the meeting has yet to take place, I should like to be present despite my illness if I am informed on what day I may attend. Please let me know.

When a decision is at last reached, what will it involve if we send troops first? The Koreans will unquestionably demand their withdrawal and a refusal on our part will lead to war. We shall then have fomented a war in a manner very different from the one you originally had in mind. Would it not be far better therefore to send an envoy first? It is clear that if we did so the Koreans would resort to violence, and would certainly afford us the excuse for attacking them.

[1] Soejima Taneomi, foreign minister, returned from China on July 26.

In the event that it is decided to send troops first, difficulties may arise in the future [elsewhere]. Russia has fortified Saghalien and other islands, and there have already been frequent incidents of violence. I am convinced that we should send troops to defend these places before we send them to Korea.

If it is decided to send an envoy officially, I feel sure that he will be murdered. I therefore beseech you to send me. I cannot claim to make as splendid as envoy as Soejima, but if it is a question of dying, that, I assure you, I am prepared to do. [pp. 736–38]

August 14 [1873]
Should there be any hesitation at your place with reference to my being sent, it will mean further and further delays. I ask you therefore please to cut short deliberations, and to speak out in favor of my being sent. If we fail to seize this chance to bring us into war, it will be very difficult to find another. By enticing the Koreans with such a gentle approach we will certainly cause them to furnish us with an opportunity for war. But this plan is doomed to fail if you feel it would be unfortunate for me to die before the war, or if you have any thoughts of temporizing. The only difference is whether [my death comes] before or after the event. I shall be deeply grateful to you, even after death, if you exert yourself now on my behalf with the warm friendship you have always shown me. [pp. 751–52]

August 17 [1873]
Last evening I visited the Prime Minister's residence and discussed my plan with him in great detail. . . . However, I could not help feeling uneasy when he said that he would wait until the return of the [Iwakura] mission. I have never meant to suggest an immediate outbreak of hostilities. War is the second step. Even under the present circumstances grounds for starting a conflict might be found from an examination of international law, but they would be entirely a pretext, and the people of the nation would not accept them. If, on the other hand, we send an envoy to tell the Koreans that we have never to this day harbored hostile intentions, and to reproach them for weakening the relations between our countries; at the same time asking them to correct their arrogance of the past and strive for improved relations in the future, I am sure that

the contemptuous attitude of the Koreans will reveal itself. They are absolutely certain, moreover, to kill the envoy. This will bring home to the entire nation the necessity of punishing their crimes. This is the situation which we must bring to pass if our plan is to succeed. I need hardly say that it is at the same time a far-reaching scheme which will divert abroad the attention of those who desire civil strife, and thereby benefit the country. The [adherents of the] former government will lose the opportunity to act, and having to refrain from creating any internal disturbance, will lose the country once and for all. [pp. 754–56]

The following poem, not a part of the above letter, is believed to have been composed by Saigō during one of his periods of exile on an island off the coast of Kagoshima.
   [*Dai Saigō zenshū*, III, 1201]

Shikishima no	I am a boat
Michi ni	Given to my country;
Waga mi o sute obune	If the winds blow, let them!
Kaze fukaba fuke	If the waves rise, let them!
Nami tataba tate.	

ŌKUBO TOSHIMICHI AND THE KOREAN QUESTION

A less colorful figure than Saigō, his boyhood friend, Ōkubo (1830–1878) was as selflessly dedicated to politics as Saigō was to war. It was this basic difference in outlook and political aptitude which eventually brought a cleavage over the Korean issue between these two fellow-clansmen who had been such close colleagues in the Restoration movement. Ōkubo's consuming passion was internal order and systematic progress, which were incompatible with Saigō's plans to direct Japanese energies abroad. As the personification of those virtues which were to distinguish the Meiji bureaucrat, Ōkubo had long-range vision, unshakable tenacity, and a remarkable gift for spotting young men of talent who could help realize his plans. Particularly noteworthy was his ability to transcend clan loyalties and bring to his side capable lieutenants from other fiefs, such as Itō of Chōshu and Ōkuma of Hizen. Ōkubo had already become the driving force and chief engineer of Japan's modernization, when the final defeat of the Satsuma rebellion created the conditions for fulfilling his master plan of internal development. But unexpectedly this task was left to his protégés when Ōkubo died at the hands of an assassin in 1878. The three heroes of the Restoration, Kido, Saigō, and Ōkubo, had all died in the prime of life within a year of each other, but thanks to the foresight of Ōkubo the men who were to carry on their leadership in the long reign of Meiji were well prepared for their job.

ŌKUBO TOSHIMICHI
Reasons for Opposing the Korean Expedition

It was the sort of cold reasoning presented in the following paper by Ōkubo, which won out in the councils of state over Saigō's impetuous and dramatic call for war in Korea. The date of this document is not known, but it is believed to have been prepared for Prince Sanjō, then presiding over the council of state, in the early fall of 1873.

[From Kiyozawa, *Ōkubo Toshimichi,* pp. 28–31]

The most mature consideration and forethought is essential in order to govern the nation and to protect the land and the people. Every action, whether progressive or conservative, should be taken in response to the occasion, and if it develops unfavorably should be abandoned. This may entail shame, but it is to be endured; justice may be with us, but we are not to choose that course. We must act as our greatest needs dictate, taking into account the importance of any problem and examining the exigencies. We have here the problem of dispatching an envoy to Korea. The reasons why I am in no great haste to subscribe to the proposal come from much careful and earnest reflection on the problem. The gist of my arguments is as follows:

I. Because of His Majesty's supreme virtue, sovereignty has been restored and extraordinary achievements have been made to bring about today's prosperity. However, His Majesty's reign is still young and the foundations of his reign are not yet firmly laid. The sudden abolition of feudal fiefs and the establishment of prefectures are indeed a drastic change unusual in history. A look at the situation in the capital seems to indicate that the change has been accomplished. But in the remote sections of the country there are not a few who have lost their homes and property and who are extremely bitter and restless because of this measure. . . . Within the last two years, how many scenes of bloodshed have taken place unavoidably? Due to their misunderstanding of the purport of public proclamations, or their misgivings about rising taxes, the ignorant, uninformed people of the remote areas have become easy victims of agitation and have started riots. A careful consideration of these facts constitutes the first argument against any hasty action regarding Korea.

II. Government expenditure today is already tremendous, and there is the difficulty of matching the annual revenues with the annual expenditures. To start a war and to send tens of thousands of troops abroad would raise expenditures by the day to colossal figures; and should war be prolonged, expenditures will continue to soar so as to necessitate heavy taxes, or a foreign loan, with no prospect of repayment, or the issuance of paper notes with no hope of redemption. . . . Our loans from foreign countries now exceed five million, but we have no definite plan for their repayment. Even if a definite plan is evolved, the undertaking of the Korean venture would, in all likelihood, lead to a considerable deviation from our plans. It would be so disastrous as to preclude any chance of salvation. This constitutes my second reason against any hasty action regarding Korea.

III. The government's present undertakings intended to enrich and strengthen the country must await many years for their fulfillment. These projects, in the areas of the army, navy, education, justice, industry, and colonization, are matters which cannot be expected to produce results overnight. To launch a meaningless war now and waste the government's efforts and attention needlessly, increase annual expenditures to enormous figures, suffer the loss of countless lives, and add to the sufferings of the people so as to allow no time for other matters, will lead to the abandonment of the government's undertakings before their completion. In order to resume these undertakings, they would have to be started anew. . . . This is the third reason against the hasty commencement of a Korean war.

IV. In looking at the sum total of our country's exports and imports there is an annual shortage of exports of approximately one million. This deficit must be made up in gold. If gold in such quantity leaves the country, there will be a corresponding decrease in the gold reserves of the country. At the present time the currency in use in the country consists of gold and paper. If gold is reduced it will, of itself, impair the credit of the government, reduce the value of the paper notes, and cause considerable hardship to the people. It will produce a situation for which there may be no remedy later. . . . If now, without examining the wealth or poverty of our country, or without clarifying the strength or weakness of our army, we should hastily launch a war, our able-bodied youths would be subjected to hardships both at home and abroad, and their parents, out of worry and trouble, would lose their will to be thrifty or to work hard. . . . It would lead inevitably to the impoverishment of our country. Such a state of affairs would be a matter of serious concern, which constitutes the fourth reason against any hasty venture in Korea.

V. Turning to foreign relations, we note that for our country Russia and England occupy the position of foremost and greatest importance. Russia, situated in the north, could send her troops southward to Saghalien and could, with one blow, strike south. . . . Thus, should we cross arms with Korea and become like the two water-birds fighting over a fish, Russia will be the fisherman standing by to snare the fish. This is a matter for constant vigilance and constitutes the fifth reason against a hasty venture in Korea.

VI. England's influence is particularly strong in Asia. She has occupied land everywhere and has settled her people and stationed her troops thereon. Her warships are poised for any emergency, keeping a silent, vigilant watch, and ready to jump at a moment's notice. However, our country has been largely dependent on England for its foreign loans. If our country becomes involved in an unexpected misfortune, causing our stores to be depleted and our people reduced to poverty, our inability to repay our debts to England will become England's pretext for interfering in our internal affairs which would lead to baneful consequences beyond description. . . . This is the sixth reason against hasty action in Korea.

VII. The treaties our country has concluded with the countries of Europe and America are not equal, there being many terms in them which impair the dignity of an independent nation. The restraints they impose may bring some benefit, but there are, on the other hand, harmful aspects to these treaties. England and France, for example, on the pretext that our country's internal administration is not yet in order and that it cannot protect their subjects, have built barracks and stationed troops in our land as if our country were a territory of theirs. Externally, from the standpoint of foreign relations, is this not as much a disgrace as it is internally, from the standpoint of our nation's sovereignty? The time for treaty-revision is well-nigh at hand. The ministers in the present government, by giving their zealous and thorough attention, must evolve a way to rid the country of its bondage and to secure for our country the dignity of an independent nation. This is an urgent matter of the moment which provides the seventh reason why a hasty venture in Korea should not be undertaken.

.I have argued in the foregoing paragraphs that a hasty Korean war should not be precipitated. . . . Prior to the dispatch of an envoy, the question of whether or not to embark on a war should be settled. Should the decision be to wage war, then more than a hundred thousand men for the campaign abroad and for the defense of the country should be raised. Moreover, additional tens of thousands of men should be called to escort the envoy. Although it is difficult to estimate in advance the enormous cost of ammunition, weapons, warships, transports, and other expenses, it may well reach into tens of thousands daily. Even if the campaign makes a favorable start, it is unlikely that the gains made will ever pay for the losses incurred. What will happen should the campaign drag on for months and years? Suppose total victory is gained, the entire country occupied, and the Koreans permitted to sue for peace and to indemnify us. Still, for many years, we shall have to man garrisons to defend vital areas and to prevent their breach of the treaty terms. When the entire country is occupied it is certain that there will be many discontented people who will cause disturbances everywhere, making it well-nigh impossible for us to hold the country. In considering the cost of the campaign, and of occupation and defense of Korea, it is unlikely that it could be met by the products of the entire country of Korea. Then there is Russia, and there is China. Although it is argued, on the basis of one or two conversations between officials or on the tacit understanding of officials, that Russia and China will not interfere in the Korean affair, there is no actual document to confirm it. Even if such a document existed, who can say that the governments of these two countries will not plot and take advantage of the opportunity to bring about a sudden and unexpected calamity. It is certainly no difficult matter to find an excuse to break a prior promise. If we permit the initiation of such a great venture, blithely and with no consideration for such an eventuality, we shall in all probability have cause for much regret in the future. . . .

Some argue that the arrogance of Korea toward our country is intolerable. But as far as I can see, the reasons for the sending of an Envoy Extraordinary seem to be to look for a positive excuse for war by having him treated arrogantly and discourteously. We would then dispatch troops to punish them. If this be the case, it is clear that this venture is to be undertaken, not because the situation makes it unavoidable or because there is no other way, but rather because the honor of the country will have been sullied and our sovereignty humiliated. I consider such a venture entirely beyond comprehension, as it completely disregards the safety of our nation and ignores the interests of the people. It will be an incident occasioned by the whims of individuals without serious evaluation of eventualities or implications. These are the reasons why I cannot accept the arguments for the undertaking of this venture.

ITŌ AND THE CONSTITUTION

A fundamental aim of the reforms undertaken in Meiji Japan was to win the respect of the Western nations, and to redeem the Japanese from the humiliation suffered by the forcible opening of the country. It was under Itō Hirobumi (1841–1909) that Japan accomplished this aim, first, by establishing a constitutional regime embodying the rule of law; second, by demonstrating her new military strength in the Sino-Japanese War of 1894; and shortly thereafter, by winning revision of the unequal treaties imposed upon Japan only a few decades before. Of these achievements the adoption of a constitution had the most far-reaching significance; it also illustrated the manner in which Meiji Japan, typified by Itō, kept one eye on the West and the other on its own national individuality. This individuality Itō and his colleagues referred to as Japan's "national polity" (*kokutai*), a term which, as we have seen, embraced both its political structure and the distinctive moral values considered to underlie it. Itō's own life was intimately bound up with both of these.

The fact that Itō was once a "barefoot boy," who rose through an aristocratic society to the heights of power, has a peculiar significance in his case. It is not that he came from a lowly stratum of society where the humblest samurai was almost indistinguishable from the peasant, but that as part of his rigorous induction into the code of the warrior his teacher insisted that he go barefoot, prepared as any footsoldier must be to endure whatever hardships may come. (This practice, incidentally, is said to account for Itō's unusually big feet.) From this teacher also, and from his next mentor, Yoshida Shōin, both of whom died for their convictions, he learned to be ready for death at any time. Like so many other Restoration leaders who met violent ends, Itō eventually died at the hands of an assassin.

Thus strongly imbued with the Confucian ideals of loyalty and self-discipline to be put to the service of the Throne, Itō was at the same time convinced by Shōin of the need for acquiring a firsthand knowledge of the West. This he accomplished by working his way to Europe as a deckhand on an English ship in 1862, in defiance of the Tokugawa seclusion laws. On his return he became a leading advocate in Chōshū of learning to live with the West, and after the Restoration an effective member of the inner group of government leaders seeking to reform Japan along Western lines. A second visit to the West as virtual chief-of-staff to the Iwakura mission gave him a further opportunity to study the economic and political organization of the most advanced Western nations, and also to cement his relationship with Ōkubo, who increasingly dominated government councils in those years.

After Ōkubo's assassination, however, when Itō's colleague, Ōkuma, pressed for a change from oligarchical rule to representative government, Itō became the leader of the bureaucratic group which opposed any immediate step in this direction, and instead proposed an extended study of constitutional systems which might be suited to Japan's needs. Entrusted by the emperor with conducting such a study in 1881, after Ōkuma's ouster from the government, Itō took his constitutional commission on another tour of the West, during which his admiration for the new Germany of Bismarck and his sympathy with Prussian statism became apparent. Even so the Prussian state served less as a model for the Japanese constitution finally enacted in 1889 than as a means of dignifying an arrangement which had already taken shape in Itō's mind. He had been convinced from the outset that the emperor should be the axis of the new constitutional order, since the whole Restoration movement had centered on the Throne and it alone of native political institutions remained in the modern age as a bulwark and symbol of Japan's traditional political structure (*kokutai*). Itō was also determined that the new parliament should not be so powerful that it could disrupt the strong leadership provided in the past by the clan oligarchy—the group of former samurai around him whose traditions of leadership, Spartan discipline, and *esprit de corps* had equipped them so well to face the challenges of the modern world. Thus when the new Constitution was promulgated by the emperor, it affirmed the rule of the imperial house as "eternal," the emperor as "sacred" and "inviolable," and the constitution as an "immutable fundamental law" granted to the people by virtue of "the supreme prerogative inherited from our imperial ancestors." Moreover, the ministers of state were left responsible to the emperor alone and not to parliament. The army and navy too remained under direct imperial command, instead of being answerable to the civil administration.

But if the new constitution followed a pattern already well established in Japan more than it did any Western system, Itō's frequent references to the Prussian example and German constitutional theories are nonetheless significant. It was important to him that the new regime, besides conforming to the Japanese traditions Itō valued most, also be "modern." For years he had listened to the exponents of Western liberalism identify themselves with progress and represent popular sovereignty as the basis of the most advanced societies. Now, having just returned from the West for which these progressives claimed to speak, he could meet them on their own ground. It was his opponents who were behind the times, Itō implied, and his own point of view which had the sanction of political scientists and constitutional authorities in Germany, the rising star on the Western horizon.

Was this, then, the only value which the West had for Itō? Had the young reformer of the Meiji Restoration become merely an adroit defender of the status quo, a confirmed bureaucrat who used his knowledge of the West only to outmaneuver the opposition and block any changes which might seriously threaten his own power? Not by any means. Itō thought of himself always as a middle-of-the-roader, and, though he had resisted the pressure of impatient progressives on the constitutional question, he also showed himself capable of taking a firm stand against the more reactionary elements in the government. After all, it was under his auspices that the first parliament east of Suez had come into being, and he believed firmly in its potential usefulness to the nation. It is true that he saw the Diet's function as service to the emperor, contributing its share to the harmonious workings of the Confucian family-state. But he also recognized that the new political party system could exert a decisive influence on the balance of power, and when in 1900 reactionary, military-minded bureaucrats sought to curtail that influence, Itō did not hesitate to give up his powers as prime minister and take the lead in organizing a new political party. Thereafter he emphasized increasingly the importance of the people's exercise of their political rights—as a duty more than as an inherent power, yet still as an indispensable element in Japan's national life. For a Confucian traditionalist to stress the importance of the people was not wholly unprecedented, but to attach such a high value to their active participation in politics was. Itō obviously had been impressed by the West's fuller development of its human potential, and he looked upon the more active role of his own people as an asset, not a danger, to the country.

Perhaps to some extent this attitude reflected his own sense of personal accomplishment in rising from the humble role of footsoldier to the highest offices of the land. In any case, when this four-time premier became Viceroy of Korea in the last years of his life—achieving even the unfulfilled ambition of that other former footsoldier, Hideyoshi—he could not suppress a certain boyish delight in being permitted, for the first time, to wear the resplendent uniform of a field-marshal.

ITŌ HIROBUMI

Memorandum of Ōkubo's Views on Constitutional Government

The guiding principles of Japan's constitutional regime had already been suggested by Ōkubo in a series of discussions within the government during the early years of the Restoration. Ōkubo believed that constitutional government for Japan was desirable and inevitable, but he wished to steer a middle course between despotism and democracy toward a limited monarchy based on traditional Confucian ideals—the course Itō himself tried to steer. Dated 1873, this brief memorandum found in Itō's private collection and in his own handwriting, records Ōkubo's views on the subject.

[From Tokutomi, Ōkubo Kōtō Sensei, p. 253]

Since the Restoration it has been the aim of our government to excel the nations of the whole world. Still, the administration, following conventional and long-established customs, preserves the form of a despotic monarchy. This form may well be applicable for the present . . . but it must not be insisted upon for the future. If this be so, must our government assume the form of a democracy? I say no. . . . Democracy must not be adopted, nor should despotic monarchy be retained. In the framing of a constitution our aims should be determined by the ideal of a government which conforms with our country's geography, customs and sentiments of the people, and the spirit of the times.

When our forebears founded our country, their government had only the people in mind. It was a government dedicated to the people. Likewise, the people maintained the government for their sovereign. Therefore, a constitutional government which is eminently fair and just, and which is neither the private domain of the sovereign nor of the people, should be one of joint effort by both the sovereign and the people, with the rights of the sovereign above defined and the rights of the people below limited.

From an Address on the Constitution to the Conference of Presidents of Prefectural Assemblies, February 15, 1889
[From *Itō Hirobumi den,* II, 651–57]

The Constitution recently promulgated is, needless to say, a constitution by imperial grant. As you well know, the term "imperial grant" means that it was initiated by the sovereign himself and that it was sanctioned and granted to his subjects by the sovereign. It is my hope that you will always remember this fact—and inscribe it in your hearts—that this Constitution is the gift of a benevolent and charitable emperor to the people of his country.

Our Constitution consists of seven chapters and seventy-six articles, and as you have probably read and re-read it carefully, there is no need now to discuss it article by article. Let me, therefore, take this occasion to compare our Constitution with those of other countries. The differences between our Constitution and their constitutions are considerable. For example, Chapter I which clarifies sovereignty in connection with the prerogative of the sovereign has no parallel in the constitutions of other countries. The reason for this difference can be understood at a moment's reflection. Our country was founded and ruled by the emperor himself since the very beginning of our history. Thus, to state this fact in the opening article of the Constitution is truly compatible with our national polity. And this fact distinguishes our Constitution in structure and form from those of other countries.

Chapter II states the rights enjoyed by subjects and the duties owed by them. The rights properly due to subjects within the limits of the law are generally enumerated there without exception. Chapter III prescribes the system of deliberative assembly to be established so that the emperor in the exercise of his constitutional rights, might consult in advance with the representatives of his subjects and obtain their cooperation and consent. As for the other chapters and articles, there is no need for any special comment. . . .

It may be asked why is it necessary to establish a diet to deliberate on the pros and cons of government? In the first place, the enactment of law requires consultation with representatives of the subjects. Secondly the fixing of the state budget, i.e., the annual income and expenditures requires the discussion of the many. The annual revenues of the state treasury consist of taxes levied on the people, and as the annual revenues are used to meet the expenditures necessary for the existence of the state the consultation and decision of the diet should, in all fairness, be asked This, in short, is the most valid reason for the establishment of a diet to deliberate on the pros and cons of government. One may see that in our Constitution these two elements are provided for systematically.

In explaining the nature of our government, it must be said that . . its control and operation rests on sovereignty, which, in our country, is united in the august person of the emperor. . . . In Europe at a time when controversy raged on the subject of sovereignty in the medieval period Montesquieu advanced the theory of the separation of powers. Separation of powers, as you know, is the division of the three powers of legislation, justice, and administration into three independent organs However, according to a theory based on careful study and on actual experience and advanced by recent scholars,[1] sovereignty is one and indivisible. It is like the human body which has limbs and bones but

---

[1] No doubt Itō had in mind such authorities as the German von Gneist and the Austrian von Stein.

whose source of spiritual life is the mind. Thus, present-day scholars who discuss sovereignty agree in general that it is one and indivisible. That this theory coincides with our interpretation of sovereignty based on our national polity (*kokutai*) is significant.

On the Constitution of 1889

These excerpts from a speech by Itō just after adoption of the Constitution stress the peculiar circumstances surrounding this development in Japan as compared with Western experience. It is significant that he should try to establish a greater antiquity for representative government in Germany than in England, in order to assert the superiority of that system which in spirit was closest to his own.

[From McLaren, *Japanese Government Documents*, pp. 617–22]

If we reflect upon the history of civilization in this country it will be perceived, I think, that while several influences have been at work, still the introduction of such alien religious systems as Confucianism and Buddhism, which were largely instrumental in elevating our people, and the development of such works as have conduced to their welfare, have been due to the benevolent guidance and encouragement of the sovereign. We may therefore say with truth that the civilization which we now possess is a gift from the Throne. . . .

I shall now proceed to discuss the subject of the participation of the people in the government of the state. It is only by the protection of the law that the happiness of the nation can be promoted and the safety of person and property secured, and to attain these ends the people may elect their representatives and empower the latter to deliberate on laws with a view to the promotion of their own happiness and the safeguarding of their rights. This, gentlemen, is enacted by the Constitution, and I think you will agree that it constitutes a concession to the people of a most valuable right. Under an absolute system of government the sovereign's will is his command, and the sovereign's command at once becomes law. In a constitutional country, however, the consent of that assembly which represents the people must be obtained. It will be evident, however, that as the supreme right is one and indivisible, the legislative power remains in the hands of the sovereign and is not bestowed on the people. While the supreme right extends to everything, and its exercise is wide and comprehensive, its legislative and executive functions are undoubtedly the most important. These are in the hands of the sovereign; the rights pertaining thereto cannot be held in common by the sovereign and his subjects; but the latter are permitted to take part in legislation according to the provisions of the Constitution. In a country which is under absolute rule the view of the sovereign is at once law; in a constitutional country, on the other hand, nothing being law without a concurrence of views between the sovereign and the people, the latter elect representatives to meet at an appointed place and carry out the view of the sovereign. In other words, law in a constitutional state is the result of a concord of ideas between the sovereign and subject; but there can be no law when these two are in opposition to each other. . . .

If we trace back to its origin the principle of a representative body, we find that it first manifested itself among an ancient German people. It has been, and still is indeed, affirmed that it is a growth of the English people, but it is not so in fact, for in an old German law, that in the levying of a tax the taxpayer should be consulted, we find the germ of the popular representative principle. The system prevailing in England must be an offshoot from the seedling that appeared in Germany, and from which the principle developed largely in later times in the west of Europe, though it never gained a hold in the central and eastern parts. Till about a century ago it was held that representative bodies should have a monopoly of the legislative right, and the theory of thus dividing the supreme right found much favor. But this conclusion has been held to be illogical by modern scholars. They say the state is like a human body. Just as one brain controls the diverse actions of the limbs and other parts, so should one supreme power superintend and control all the other members of a nation, though such members may play various parts in the whole. This view is perhaps in its turn a little antiquated, but it is sufficient to show the absurdity of the tripartite theory which maintains that the representative body should monopolize the right of legislation. If we remember that the legislative right is a part of the supreme prerogative and that the latter is the sole possession of the emperor, it will be apparent that no such monopoly is possible. But the sovereign may permit the representative body to take part in the process of practically applying the legislative right. Since the tripartite theory lost favor it has come to be recognized that the supreme right must be vested in one person and be indivisible. . . .

If we look back into the history of the world to the origin of the representative body, we shall find that the principle has undergone an extraordinary degree of development. At the Restoration the institution, then well grown in Europe, was by an enlargement and extension of the scope of our national policy adopted in Japan. Now, by carefully adapting the principle to our national characteristics, manners, and customs, and by retaining what is excellent and discarding what is faulty, we are about to put into practice a system of constitutional politics that is without rival in the East. And this leads us not unnaturally to discuss briefly the English constitution, which in many quarters has been thought worthy of imitation. I shall, however, speak solely of the difference in the history and evolution of the two constitutions, and shall not attempt to define their relative merits. In England there is no codified constitution, and you must bear in mind how the English people obtained the so-called Great Charter. The nobles of England, as you no doubt are aware, not only form a large section of the population, but they were, and are still, powerful. The sovereign of that day, having engaged in unnecessary warfare with a foreign country, levied heavy burdens on the people, which policy led to much discontent. But the complaints were not confined to the mass of the people; the nobles were also angered by the monarch's actions and refused to obey his commands. Eventually they combined and required him to sign the Magna Carta; he at first refused but was at length compelled by force to comply. You will see then that while it is quite true that the king had oppressed the people, as a matter of fact this Magna Carta pledge was extorted from him by the nobles at the point of the sword. The case of Japan is totally different. The most cordial relations prevail between the Throne and the people while our Constitution is granted. The position of our court cannot be at all compared with that of England when the Magna Carta was granted, for we know that our Imperial House has a single aim—the welfare and happiness of the nation. Not only were there no such discontented barons in this country, but our feudal lords, great and small, joined in requesting the Crown to take back the military and political rights which for centuries they had enjoyed. Could any two things be more radically different than the origins of the English and Japanese Constitutions? If the English people felicitate themselves on the influence exercised in promoting and developing the national welfare and interest, by a Charter given under such ominous circumstances as was theirs, how much more should we congratulate ourselves on having received from our benevolent sovereign, under the most happy and peaceful auspices, the Constitution of the Japanese empire! . . .

The course which lies now before the Japanese empire is plain. Both ruler and ruled should apply their efforts smoothly and harmoniously to preserve tranquility; to elevate the status of the people; to secure the rights and promote the welfare of each individual; and finally, by manifesting abroad the dignity and power of Japan, to secure and maintain her integrity and independence.

Reminiscences on the Drafting of the New Constitution

These observations first appeared in Japanese in 1908 and the following year in this English translation. Written just before Itō's death, they present the framing of the Constitution in a new perspective, reflecting the development of Itō's own position with respect to the changing political scene. His earlier role he sees as that of a moderator between impatient radicals and die-hard reactionaries, one who upholds what is of value in the Japanese tradition and seeks patiently to remedy its evils. He credits the Emperor Meiji, too, with acting on the whole in favor of liberalism and progress.

For the sake of brevity his opening remarks are paraphrased in the first paragraph below.

[From Ōkuma, *Fifty Years of New Japan*, I, 122–31]

The advent of Commodore Perry, followed by a rapid succession of great events too well known to be repeated here, roughly awakened us to the consciousness of mighty forces at work to change the face of the outside world. We were ill-prepared to bear the brunt of these forces, but once awakened to the need, were not slow to grapple with them. So, first of all, the whole fabric of the feudal system, which with its obsolete shackles and formalities hindered us in every branch of free development, had to be uprooted and destroyed. The annihilation of centrifugal forces taking the form of autocratic feudal provinces was a necessary step to the unification of the country under a strong central government, without which we would not have been able to offer a united front to the outside forces or stand up as a united whole to maintain the country's very existence.

SOURCES OF JAPANESE CIVILIZATION AND CULTURE

I must, however, disabuse my readers of the very common illusion that there was no education and an entire absence of public spirit during feudal times. It is this false impression which has led superficial observers to believe that our civilization has been so recent that its continuance is doubtful—in short, that our civilization is nothing but a hastily donned, superficial veneer. On the contrary, I am not exaggerating when I say that, for generations and centuries, we have been enjoying a moral education of the highest type. The great ideals offered by philosophy and by historical examples of the golden ages of China and India, Japanicized in the form of a "crust of customs," developed and sanctified by the continual usage of centuries under the comprehensive name of *bushidō,* offered us splendid standards of morality, rigorously enforced in the everyday life of the educated classes. The result, as everyone who is acquainted with Old Japan knows, was an education which aspired to the attainment of Stoic heroism, a rustic simplicity and a self-sacrificing spirit unsurpassed in Sparta, and the aesthetic culture and intellectual refinement of Athens. Art, delicacy of sentiment, higher ideals of morality and of philosophy, as well as the highest types of valor and chivalry— all these we have tried to combine in the man as he ought to be. We laid great stress on the harmonious combination of all the known accomplishments of a developed human being, and it is only since the introduction of modern technical sciences that we have been obliged to pay more attention to specialized technical attainments than to the harmonious development of the whole. Let me remark, *en passant,* that the humanitarian efforts which in the course of the recent war were so much in evidence and which so much surprised Western nations were not, as might have been thought, the products of the new civilization, but survivals of our ancient feudal chivalry. If further instance were needed, we may direct attention to the numbers of our renowned warriors and statesmen who have left behind them works of religious and moral devotions, of philosophical contemplations, as well as splendid specimens of calligraphy, painting, and poetry, to an extent probably unparalleled in the feudalism of other nations.

Thus it will be seen that what was lacking in our countrymen of the feudal era was not mental or moral fiber, but the scientific, technical, and materialistic side of modern civilization. Our present condition is not the result of the ingrafting of a civilization entirely different from our own, as foreign observers are apt to believe, but simply a different training and nursing of a strongly vital character already existent.

It was in the month of March, 1882, that His Majesty ordered me to work out a draft of a constitution to be submitted to his approval. No time was to be lost, so I started on the 15th of the same month for an extended journey to different constitutional countries to make as thorough a study as possible of the actual workings of different systems of constitutional government, of their various provisions, as well as of theories and opinions actually entertained by influential persons on the actual stage itself of constitutional life. I took young men with me, who all belonged to the élite of the rising generation, to assist and to cooperate with me in my studies. I sojourned about a year and a half in Europe, and having gathered the necessary materials, in so far as it was possible in so short a space of time, I returned home in September, 1883. Immediately after my return I set to work to draw up the Constitution. I was assisted in my work by my secretaries, prominent among whom were the late Viscount K. Inouyé, and the Barons M. Itō and K. Kanéko, and by foreign advisers, such as Professor Roesler, Mr. Piggott, and others.

PECULIAR FEATURES OF THE NATIONAL LIFE

It was evident from the outset that mere imitation of foreign models would not suffice, for there were historical peculiarities of our country which had to be taken into consideration. For example, the Crown was, with us, an institution far more deeply rooted in the national sentiment and in our history than in other countries. It was indeed the very essence of a once theocratic State, so that in formulating the restrictions on its prerogatives in the new Constitution, we had to take care to safeguard the future realness or vitality of these prerogatives, and not to let the institution degenerate into an ornamental crowning piece of the edifice. At the same time, it was also evident that any form of constitutional régime was impossible without full and extended protection of honor, liberty, property, and personal security of citizens, entailing necessarily many important restrictions on the powers of the Crown.

EMOTIONAL ELEMENTS IN SOCIAL LIFE OF PEOPLE

On the other hand, there was one peculiarity of our social conditions that is without parallel in any other civilized country. Homogeneous in race, language, religion, and sentiments, so long secluded from the outside world, with the centuries-long traditions and inertia of the feudal system, in which the family and quasi-family ties permeated and formed the essence of every social organization, and moreover with such moral and religious tenets as laid undue stress on duties of fraternal aid and mutual succor, we had during the course of our seclusion unconsciously become a vast village community where cold intellect and calculation of public events were always restrained and even often hindered by warm emotions between man and man. Those who have closely observed the effects of the commercial crises of our country—that is, of the events wherein cold-blooded calculation ought to have the precedence of every other factor—and compared them with those of other countries, must have observed a remarkable distinction between them. In other countries they serve in a certain measure as the scavengers of the commercial world, the solid undertakings surviving the shock, while enterprises founded solely on speculative bases are sure to vanish thereafter. But, generally speaking, this is not the case in our country. Moral and emotional factors come into play. Solid undertakings are dragged into the whirlpool, and the speculative ones are saved from the abyss—the general standard of prosperity is lowered for the moment, but the commercial fabric escapes violent shocks. In industry, also, in spite of the recent enormous developments of manufactures in our country, our laborers have not yet degenerated into spiritless machines and toiling beasts. There still survives the bond of patron and protégé between them and the capitalist employers. It is this moral and emotional factor which will, in the future, form a healthy barrier against the threatening advance of socialistic ideas. It must, of course, be admitted that this social peculiarity is not without beneficial influences. It mitigates the conflict, serves as the lubricator of social organisms, and tends generally to act as a powerful lever for the practical application of the moral principle of mutual assistance between fellow citizens. But unless curbed and held in restraint, it too may exercise baneful influences on society, for in a village community, where feelings and emotions hold a higher place than intellect, free discussion is apt to be smothered, attainment and transference of power liable to become a family question of a powerful oligarchy, and the realization of such a régime as constitutional monarchy to become an impossibility, simply because in any representative régime free discussion is a matter of prime necessity, because emotions and passions have to be stopped for the sake of the cool calculation of national welfare, and even the best of friends have often to be sacrificed if the best abilities and highest intellects are to guide the helm. Besides, the dissensions between brothers and relatives, deprived as they usually are of safety-valves for giving free and hearty vent to their own opinions or discontents, are apt to degenerate into passionate quarrels and overstep the bounds of simple differences of opinion. The good side of this social peculiarity had to be retained as much as possible, while its baneful influences had to be safeguarded. These and many other peculiarities had to be taken into account in order to have a constitution adapted to the actual condition of the country.

CONFLICT BETWEEN THE OLD AND NEW THOUGHTS

Another difficulty equally grave had to be taken into consideration. We were just then in an age of transition. The opinions prevailing in the country were extremely heterogeneous, and often diametrically opposed to each other. We had survivors of former generations who were still full of theocratic ideas, and who believed that any attempt to restrict an imperial prerogative amounted to something like high treason. On the other hand there was a large and powerful body of the younger generation educated at the time when the Manchester theory was in vogue, and who in consequence were ultra-radical in their ideas of freedom. Members of the bureaucracy were prone to lend willing ears to the German doctrinaires of the reactionary period, while, on the other hand, the educated politicians among the people having not yet tasted the bitter significance of administrative responsibility, were liable to be more influenced by the dazzling words and lucid theories of Montesquieu, Rousseau, and other similar French writers. A work entitled *History of Civilization*, by Buckle, which denounced every form of government as an unnecessary evil, became the great favorite of students of all the higher schools, including the Imperial University. On the other hand, these same students would not have dared to expound the theories of Buckle before their own conservative fathers. At that time we had not yet arrived at the stage of distinguishing clearly between political opposition on the one hand, and treason to the established order of things on the other. The virtues necessary for the smooth working of any constitution, such as love of freedom of speech, love of publicity of proceedings, the spirit of tolerance for opinions opposed to one's own, etc., had yet to be learned by long experience.

DRAFT OF THE CONSTITUTION COMPLETED

It was under these circumstances that the first draft of the Constitution was made and submitted to His Majesty, after which it was handed over to the mature deliberation of the Privy Council. The Sovereign himself presided over these deliberations, and he had full opportunities of hearing and giving due consideration to all the conflicting opinions above hinted at. I believe nothing evidences more vividly the intelligence of our august Master than the fact that in spite of the existence of strong undercurrents of an ultra-conservative nature in the council, and also in the country at large, His Majesty's decisions inclined almost invariably towards liberal and progressive ideas, so that we have been ultimately able to obtain the Constitution as it exists at present.

Speech on the Restoration and Constitutional Government

Delivered in the intimate atmosphere of a homecoming celebration, this speech by Itō in his native town of Hagi on June 2, 1899, was an attempt to explain in the language of the layman the guiding principles of the Restoration and the Constitution. He stresses that in order to win for Japan a place of equality in the world community it was necessary to raise the general level of the Japanese people to that of other civilized peoples, which has been attempted through the adoption of certain Western institutions and freedoms. Since these rights have been granted to the people by the emperor, in a manner compatible with the traditional "national polity" (*kokutai*), the duties or obligations attached to these rights are emphasized more strongly than the enjoyment of personal liberties. Nevertheless, Itō insists that the future of constitutional government in Japan depends upon the responsible exercise of these rights by the people. Thus, just prior to his entry into party politics, he shows an increased realization of the importance of popular support for the government.

[From *Itō-kō zenshū,* Vol. II, Pt. 2, pp. 142–49]

When our enlightened emperor decided to accept the open-door principle as an imperial policy . . . it became a matter of urgent necessity to develop the intellectual faculties of our people and to increase their business activities. This led to the abolition of the feudal system and made it possible for the Japanese people to live in a new political environment and to have diverse freedoms. . . . The first of these freedoms was the freedom of movement, followed by the freedom to pursue an occupation of one's own choosing. Moreover, the freedom to study at any place of one's choosing was given to all. There was also granted freedom of speech in political affairs. Thus, the Japanese today enjoy freedom, each according to his own desires, within the limits of the law. These rights belong to people who live in a civilized government. If these rights are withheld and their enjoyment refused, a people cannot develop. And if the people cannot develop, the nation's wealth and the nation's strength cannot develop. . . . But the fact is that because of the imperial policy of the open-door, we have established a government which is civilized. And as we have advanced to such a position, it has become necessary to establish a fixed definition of the fundamental laws. This, in short, is the reason for the establishment of constitutional government.

A constitutional government makes a clear distinction between the realms of the ruler and the ruled, and thereby defines what the people and the sovereign should do; that is, the rights which the sovereign should exercise and the rights which the people should enjoy, followed by the procedure for the management of the government. According to the Constitution the people have the right to participate in government, but this right is at once an important obligation as well as a right. Government is a prerogative of the emperor. As you will be participating in government—which is the emperor's prerogative—you must regard this right as the responsibility of the people, the honor of the people, and the glory of the people. It is therefore a matter of the greatest importance.

In this connection what all Japanese must bear in mind is Japan's national polity [*kokutai*]. It is history which defines the national polity; thus the Japanese people have a duty to know their history. . . . The national polity of the various countries differs one from another, but it is the testimony of the history of Japan to this day that the unification of the country was achieved around the Imperial House. So I say that the understanding of the national polity of Japan is the first important duty of our people.

In the next place we must know the aims and the policies of our country. Political parties may have their arguments, and others may have their views about the government, but they must be kept within the bounds of the aims and policies of the government. What then is the aim of the nation? It is the imperial aim decided upon at the time of the Restoration of imperial rule. . . . The aim of our country has been from the very beginning, to attain among the nations of the world the status of a civilized nation and to become a member of the comity of European and American nations which occupy the position of civilized countries. To join this comity of nations means to become one of them, but in this connection, we must consider the rights and duties attendant upon membership. Among fellow men of civilized nations there is a thing called common justice. To become a member of this comity of nations it is necessary to respect this common justice. Generally speaking, all Oriental countries—China and Japan included—have the habit of holding foreign countries in contempt and of holding their own country in esteem. But in carrying on relations according to civilized standards of common justice, it is done according to a procedure of mutual equality without contempt for the other and esteem for oneself, or vice versa. . . .

From the standpoint of the sovereign power, that is, the emperor's prerogative to rule the country, the people are one and equal under the constitutional government. They are all direct subjects of the emperor. The so-called "indirect subjects" no longer exist. This means that the Japanese people have been able to raise their status and to achieve for themselves a great honor. They now have the right to share in legislative rights, which come from the emperor's sovereign powers, and to elect and send representatives. Having the right to send representatives they can, indirectly, voice their opinions on the advisability and the faults of their country's administration. Thus, every member of the nation—be he a farmer, craftsman, or merchant—must become familiar beforehand with the merits and demerits of questions of government. Not only on questions of government, but also on matters concerning his own occupation, the citizen must give due thought and become prosperous. When every man becomes wealthy, the village, the county, and the prefecture in turn become wealthy, and the accumulated total of that wealth becomes the wealth of Japan. The expansion of military strength and the promotion of national prestige depend upon the power of the individual members of the country. Therefore, in order to promote the development of military strength and national prestige, it is only proper

[171]

and necessary to diffuse education so that the people can understand the changes and improvements with respect to their government and their society. In a constitutional government the occasions for secrecy are few —except for laws not yet proclaimed—in contradistinction to a despotic government. The principle of keeping the people uninformed in order to make them obedient has no place here. To inform them well so that they will serve well is the way of constitutional government. . . .

Since government is concerned with the administration of the country as a whole it does not follow that its acts are always favorable to all individuals. The nation's affairs, of their own nature, are not personal and concerned with the individual. They must be carried out according to the nation's aims, the nation's prestige, and the nation's honor. It is for this reason that the people have an obligation to understand the nation's aims. They must regard the nation as their own, meet the military obligation to defend it and to pay for the cost of defending it. And what happens when this cost is paid? In the past the people remitted their payments to the authorities above, beyond which they were no longer concerned. It is not so today. Government is conducted today so that one may know clearly how the money is spent and what relation the payments have to the state of the nation. If one believes that an expenditure is unwise, he may readily avail himself of the freedom of speech which he possesses as a citizen and raise his voice in objection. To resolve a situation in which the opinions of the people are so diverse as to seem impossible of reaching a decision we have established a parliament to make the decision on the basis of majority rule of its members. If you do not send representatives who are well informed on matters of government, the rights which you have earned by great effort will prove ineffective in practice.

ŌKUMA AND POLITICAL DEMOCRACY

One of the chief contributions to the Meiji Constitution, a close aide of Itō once acknowledged, was made by a man who had no hand in its preparation—Ōkuma Shigenobu. His memorial in 1881, calling for establishment of representative government under a constitution, resulted in Ōkuma's abrupt dismissal from the government after years of distinguished service, but it also won from the emperor a promise that parliamentary government would be inaugurated within ten years. Thereafter, though Ōkuma found himself a perennial leader of the opposition, the fact that even in this role he should have contributed greatly to the building of political democracy in Japan tells us much about the man and his age. If Itō may be taken as the great symbol of cohesive unity, stability, and continuity in Meiji Japan, Ōkuma represents constructive opposition, vigorous but gradual reform, and optimistic acceptance of the West. More than all of these, however, he represents that characteristic of Meiji Japan which perhaps best accounts for its rapid progress along Western lines: its capacity to hold contending forces in a dynamic balance and foster the growth of new and varied activities contributing to the national welfare—in short, its diversity in a vital unity.

The Restoration, we should remember, was the work of a coalition rather than of a single dominant power. From the beginning it brought together diverse interests in a common cause. One of the least of the states so joined in the coalition of southwestern fiefs was that of the Nabeshima family in Hizen, whose sole contribution to the top leadership of the movement was Ōkuma (1838–1922). Born in a samurai family near Nagasaki, the only port which had remained open to the West in Tokugawa times, Ōkuma absorbed much of its cosmopolitan and mercantile spirit. His knowledge of Dutch and English, acquired early, together with his powers of speech, forceful personality and impressive size, all recommended him for his first assignment under the new regime handling foreign relations in Nagasaki. Subsequently he became the government's leading expert in both financial matters and foreign affairs. Had his own fief been stronger and Ōkuma less dependent on the support of other clan leaders, such as Kido, from Chōshū, and then Ōkubo, from Satsuma, he might well have emerged as the dominant figure within the ruling oligarchy after Ōkubo's assassination. Fortunately for the future of Japanese democracy, however, when the alliance of Satsuma and Chōshū bureaucrats forced him from the government over the constitutional issue, Ōkuma's great talents and personal prestige were unexpectedly put to the service of the political party movement.

Ōkuma was not, however, the first champion of this movement in Meiji Japan. The real pioneer had been Itagaki Taisuke (1837–1919), a Tosa samurai who had left the government along with Saigō over the

Korean issue seven years earlier. First he organized several patriotic societies, which combined ultranationalism and a concern for the welfare of ex-samurai with the egalitarian slogans and radical reformism of the French Revolution. Then Itagaki founded Japan's first political association on a national basis, the Liberal Party. Attempting to carry on open political activity in a part of the world which had known as its nearest equivalent only factionalism at court or covert conspiracy, the Liberal Party nevertheless proved an unsuccessful blend of divergent political traditions. Itagaki's followers were radical enough to be distrusted by the majority of Japanese, but still so steeped in the feudal past that democracy to them meant primarily a wider sharing of political power among the heirs of the feudal aristocracy. The rather factious opposition of the Liberals themselves lent substance to the view that their party was a pressure group advancing the personal ambitions of political "outs," a vestige of the old feudal struggle for position and power.

In any case Ōkuma, who regarded the Liberals as an irresponsible opposition, and was more sympathetic to the gradualism and orderly progress of the British than to the revolutionary extremism of the French Revolution, chose to establish his own organization, the Progressive Party, to work for orderly change in the direction of British constitutional democracy. In the 1880s his party fared little better than the Liberals, owing to the government's repressive acts and some of the same internal weaknesses which had afflicted their rivals. But there can be no doubt that Ōkuma spoke for a much wider segment of Japanese opinion than Itagaki, and one which grew with the years. After the inauguration of parliament in 1889, it was Ōkuma who led the struggle to make the government representative of and responsible to the parties in the Diet. Throughout the late years of Meiji his prestige and influence as the champion of representative government rose, until it reached a peak with his appointment as premier in the First World War. During the heyday of the political parties, in the late 'teens and 'twenties, the liberal statesmen who largely dominated the national scene were often his protégés, and the succession to party leadership even after the Second World War could still be traced back to this towering figure.

The measure of Ōkuma's liberalism, however, is not to be found in the record of his political acts or policies alone. Indeed, his continued respect for imperial institutions, his ready acceptance of Itō's Constitution as a sound basis for further progress, and his strong nationalism, kept Ōkuma from pursuing a course of invariable opposition to the ruling bureaucracy and involved him in compromises hardly consonant with a doctrinaire liberalism. It was, nevertheless, wholly in conformity with his larger view of the new Japan and the needs of a democratic society that Ōkuma diverted some of his tremendous energies from party politics to other spheres of national life. Almost simultaneously with his founding of the Progressive Party Ōkuma had established a new university, Waseda, aiming to develop a new type of citizen whose conception of service to the state would not be narrowly political or bureaucratic. This represented a fundamental departure from the traditional Confucian ideal of the educated man whose success was chiefly to be found in government service. Whereas Tokyo Imperial University reflected the philosophy of Itō and served as a training ground for government officials, Waseda was premised on a belief in educational pluralism, on the value of private institutions neither subject to government control nor conforming to a single pattern. It is particularly to the credit of Ōkuma, moreover, that he lent his support to other private institutions besides his own, including Japan Women's College and Doshisha University, the latter founded by an outstanding Christian convert, Joseph Neesima.

Three significant features of Waseda reflect Ōkuma's range of interests and associations. One is that, while the graduates of Tokyo Imperial University virtually monopolized government office, Waseda graduates became leaders in journalism. In this respect Ōkuma contributed substantially to a field of endeavor in which his close friend and ally, Fukuzawa Yukichi, had already pioneered. In turn, Japanese journalism gave strong support to political democracy by informing and mobilizing public opinion. The second significant feature is that as a private institution Waseda relied heavily on financial support from the business world, one of its principal benefactors being Baron Iwasaki, the head of the Mitsubishi interests. But it was also Japanese business, stimulated to no small degree by the policies which Ōkuma had pursued in the early years of Meiji, which became closely identified with the political parties of the twentieth century. Thirdly, Waseda was known for its international outlook, as was Ōkuma throughout his career. Especially in his later years, he who had borne the chief responsibility for revision of the unequal treaties found foreign affairs and international relations his consuming interest. His ardent nationalism neither inhibited his frank acceptance of the West, nor required him to denigrate other cultures than his own. The new Japan, he believed, had drawn strength both from its own best traditions and from the enormous contributions of Western civilization. For the last six years of his life, therefore, he met regularly with a group of Waseda professors to work on a vast study, *The Reconciliation of Eastern and Western Civilization*. Through such varied and forward-looking activities as these, Ōkuma, in association with some of the newest and most vital movements of his time, helped to give democracy strong roots in Japanese society.

ITAGAKI TAISUKE

Memorial on the Establishment of a Representative Assembly

This petition, submitted on January 17, 1874, by Itagaki and eight associates, followed shortly upon the former's resignation from the government because of his defeat along with Saigō on the Korean issue. It touched off a long debate and public agitation for representative government throughout the '70s
[From Itagaki, *Jiyū-tō-shi*, I, 86–89; McLaren, *Japanese Government Documents*, pp. 426–32]

When we humbly reflect upon the quarter in which the governing power lies, we find that it is not the Imperial House above, nor the people below, but the officials alone. We do not deny that the officials revere the Imperial House, nor that they protect the people. Yet, the manifold decrees of the government appear in the morning and are changed in the evening, the administration is influenced by private considerations, rewards and punishments depend on personal favor or disfavor, the channel by which the people should communicate with the government is blocked, and they cannot state their grievances. We hope in this manner to rule the country, yet even an infant knows that this cannot be done. We fear, therefore, that if a reform is not effected the state will be ruined. Unable to resist the promptings of our patriotic feelings, we have sought to devise a means of rescuing it from this danger. We find this means to consist in developing public discussion in the empire. The means of developing public discussion is the establishment of a council-chamber chosen by the people. Then a limit will be placed on the power of the officials, and high and low will obtain peace and prosperity. We ask leave then to make some remarks on this subject.

The people whose duty it is to pay taxes to the government have the right of sharing in their government's affairs and of approving or condemning. Since this is a universally acknowledged principle, it is not necessary to waste words in discussing it. . . .

How is the government to be made strong? By the people's being of one mind. We shall not cite events of the distant past to prove this, but shall illustrate it with the governmental change of last October. How great was the peril! Why does our government stand alone? How many of the people of the empire rejoiced at or grieved over the change in the government of last October? Not only was there neither grief nor joy on account of it, but eight or nine out of every ten people in the empire were utterly ignorant that it had taken place, and they were only surprised at the disbanding of the troops. The establishment of a council chamber chosen by the people will create community of feeling between the government and the people, and they will unite into one body. Then and only then will the country become strong. . . .

We are informed that the present officials . . . are generally averse to progress and call those who advocate reforms "rash progressives." . . . If "rash progress" means measures which are heedlessly initiated, then a council chamber chosen by the people will remedy this heedlessness. Does it mean the want of harmony between the different branches of the administration, and in times of change, the postponement of urgent matters in favor of those less urgent, so that the measures carried out are wanting in unity of plan? Then the cause of this is the want of a fixed law in the country and the fact that the officials act in accordance with their own inclinations. These two facts suffice to show why it is necessary to establish a council chamber chosen by the people. Progress is the most beautiful thing in the world, and is the law of all things moral and physical. Men actuated by principle cannot condemn this word "progress," so their condemnation must be intended for the word "rash"; but the word "rash" has no application to a council chamber chosen by the people. . . .

Another argument of the officials is that the council chambers now existing in European and American states were not formed in a day, but were only brought into their present state by gradual progress, and there-fore we cannot today copy them suddenly. But is this true only of council chambers? It is the same with all branches of knowledge, science, and mechanical arts. The reason why [foreigners] developed them only after the lapse of centuries is that no examples existed previously and they had to be discovered by actual experience. If we can select from among their examples, why can we not apply them successfully? If we were to postpone using steam engines until we had discovered for ourselves the principles of steam, or postpone laying telegraph lines until we had discovered the principles of electricity, the government should by the same token never set to work.

Address on Liberty

Itagaki is known as the foremost apostle of liberty in the Meiji Period, a sort of Japanese Patrick Henry who is remembered especially for his dramatic declaration, just after being stabbed by an assassin, "Itagaki may die, but liberty will never die." It is noteworthy, therefore, that in this address to members of his Liberal Party in 1882, Itagaki should stress liberty as a means to achieving greater national unity, requiring a strong sense of personal re-sponsibility and discipline in the promotion of the public interest. This emphasis upon social responsibility rather than individual freedom probably reflects not only his own samurai origins but also the difficulties he experienced in achieving some sort of party discipline.

[From Itagaki, *Jiyū-tō-shi*, II, 442–48; McLaren, *Japanese Government Documents*, pp. 605–13]

When the country was under the feudal system the people were kept in submission by the military power of their lords and had no voice in their own government. The rulers did not govern with the consent of the common people, and the people did not participate in national affairs. Moreover, the people were like slaves, so they felt remote from the nation and lacked the slightest sense of community among themselves. Even the samurai, though they enjoyed the status of citizens, conceived their sole duty as obedience to the commands of their lords, and ignored all other obligations. Each one harbored a spirit of individuality, and all were lacking in a feeling of community. They were aware of their own personal freedom, but they knew nothing of public freedom. Society within the country was maintained solely by means of the ties between lord and subject, so that if the ties were broken, the total absence of harmony among people could not be repaired. Freedom was likely to degenerate into extravagant license and [no one] knew how to bend his personal freedom in order to extend it into public freedom. . . .

Capable men acted despotically; they wished to control others, so they did not allow the others to govern themselves. On the other hand, those who were without power and were ruled by others accepted submission to tyranny as their lot; they cherished the spirit of dependence, and had no will to freedom. Deprived of self-government and self-protection, they wished to depend on others. They joined forces with other men, but knew nothing of enlisting in a cause. The old abuses of our country's tyranny were almost ineradicable. . . .

In the Middle Ages the system of governing divided everyone into two classes, the samurai and the people. The samurai occupied the position of rulers, while the people were the ones whom they ruled. Hereditary tradition creates common custom. Power was vested solely in the rulers, and the samurai made it their business to participate in the affairs of state, so they were well versed in political theory; the people on the other hand accepted being ruled as their lot, and had nothing to do with affairs of state, so they were deficient in political theory. Since this system of government was fostered for so many years, the ignorant masses declined in the knowledge of political theory, and in the end had none at all. Though it has been said that the people of our country never developed political thought, this is true only of the ignorant masses. The political thought of the informed classes developed to a very high level. Truly the difference in the appreciation of politics between our informed and ignorant classes is as wide as the distance between heaven and earth. To maintain balance and harmony between them is most difficult, for as the wise add to their wisdom the foolish progress in their ignorance. . . .

Our national education is of three kinds, Shinto, Confucian, and Buddhist. The first is a relic of the old theocratic rule, and was long of valuable assistance to the ancient sovereign administration. Buddhism is an imported creed, and almost became the state religion, but was always subservient to politics, holding that government and religion have the same end. Confucianism, too, mixed politics and ethics. It laid down a single path both for disciplining oneself and for governing the country, and set forth the doctrine that the government was like a teacher or father and should instruct the people. Thus government and religion have usurped each other's domain and have interfered on the one side

with the private life of the people and on the other with the administra
tion of public affairs, doing injury to both. . . .

In order for our party to organize a constitutional government and
perfect the freedom of all, each individual must cast away selfishness and
assume a spirit of community. The people must become accustomed to
banding together by depending on one another. A nation and its government exist so that all the people may pool their strength and guard
their rights. Hence, if a man wishes to enjoy liberty through the protection of his government he must strive to acquire a national liberty. If an
individual can live satisfactorily in a state of isolation without caring for
the common weal, he may be as selfish and extravagant as he pleases
without sacrificing any of his personal freedom. Nevertheless, people can
only enjoy life by mixing with their fellows and depending on the community, and therefore their aim should be to secure civil liberty by making mutual concessions. The extension of national liberty is the means
by which individual liberty is perfected and is the basis of social organization. The people of our country are deficient in community spirit; each
holds to his own individuality. Their ignorance of the fact that individual
liberty has been compromised for the sake of public freedom has caused
the perpetuation of despotism. Therefore, the only way to correct this
abuse is to give the people the right of participating in government, to
move forward in national unity, and to foster the understanding that
there is no disparity between public and private benefit. . . .

The aim of our party is to work for self-discipline, not the control of
others. Ruling others is easy, but self-control is hard. Everyone prefers
ease to hardship, but those who undertake to lead society should leave
the easy way to others and take the difficult way for themselves. . . .

If our party wishes to cement its union and vanquish its opponents,
each member should suppress his spirit of independence and strengthen
mutual confidence. In this way the cause will be furthered without creating factions around individuals. The freedom to which we so earnestly
aspire is the principle which pervades Heaven and earth, and not merely
a selfish attribute. A party centered around one individual alone is nothing but a private faction, but one that bands together in mutual trust and
cooperation around a cause can be called a public party. . . . If each of
its members holds firmly to his own principles and the party is unified
behind a cause rather than an individual, then even if the individual
should die, the cause will live on.

One urgent need of our party is to enlist the strength of the masses. In general, men of intelligence are highly liberal, men of wealth tend toward conservatism, and men of experience value their own opinions. Thus in the people we find many grades of opinion, but as long as their object is identical with our own, we should do our best to draw them to ourselves, caring nothing for minor differences of opinion. For example, even among those who agree that there should be a change in the form of government and that people should be permitted to participate in politics, [there are differences of opinion] as to whether the legislature should have one chamber or two, or whether suffrage should be universal or restricted by property qualifications. The decision of such questions can well be postponed until the form of government has been reconstituted. . . . In Western nations political parties contend with one another, and each one tests its principles thoroughly. Often the intensity of party strife is conducive to party welfare, but this is because these parties are well established and mature. Since our party is newly organized and imma-ture, we must not follow their example. It would be a great mistake for our new, immature party to thrash out its principles thoroughly and thus fall into disputes over trifles. . . .

The object of our union is to institute a form of government wherein the people shall have a voice in public affairs. Public opinion is the axis around which government policy should revolve. On its prosperity or decay depends the prosperity or decay of the government. For its promo-tion and a simultaneous inauguration of a beneficial policy we must edu-cate the people in politics. The means by which good government and the happiness of the people can be assured is for the governed to control their rulers through the force of public opinion and prevent them from using their power arbitrarily. If those who are governed lack political knowledge and are ignorant of the technique by which public opinion can be made to control their rulers, even a good government and just laws can suddenly degenerate into despotism and oppression, and the people will be deprived of their just benefits.

Good governments depend on good people. Therefore, to reform the government and ensure lasting benefits from it, we should reform the national character and foster good people. We cannot hope for reform of the national character so long as the educated and the ignorant classes are so far apart in their understanding of politics as to lack a feeling of con-cord with each other. Therefore, our party should help the educated lead the ignorant and the ignorant to follow the educated onward, and thus spread political understanding and establish the welfare of the people on a sound foundation. . . .

The West has achieved its present enlightened systems of government and constitutions by gradual maturation in accordance with the law of nature. If our country, already of advanced age, wants to overtake the West, it must take a short cut. The hidebound Confucianists are likely to say: "How can one govern a country without first disciplining oneself and putting one's own house in order?" Or: "The enlightenment of the West has come about in accordance with the law of nature. How can our country attain civilization by a short cut?" This is an obstinate way of looking at things. Human affairs are living things and should not be treated as though they were dead. Our party must not adopt such obsolete and uninformed opinions, but must work to increase the speed of national progress and thus overtake the West. . . .

Our party desires a liberal, not an interfering, government. The interference of a government with the private affairs of the people is due to its ignorance of the distinction between politics and religion or between public and personal matters. Government interference means the loss of independence. Our party should discriminate between politics and religion, and oppose government interference with private affairs. Propagation of liberal principles by our party is a public, not a private, venture. Those who agree with us in public matters are good friends of liberty, and, although they may not be in harmony with us in private affairs, we can still be in perfect accord with them otherwise. On the other hand, those who, no matter how intimate they may be with us privately, oppose the cause of liberty, cannot tread the same road with us.

OZAKI YUKIO

Factions and Parties

The significance of the foregoing address by Itagaki to the Liberal Party may be more readily appreciated in the light of these observations on Japanese party politics made later, in 1918, by the veteran progressive leader Ozaki Yukio.
[From Ozaki, *The Voice of Japanese Democracy*, pp. 93–94]

Here in the Orient we have had the conception of a faction; but none of a public party. A political party is an association of people having for its exclusive object the discussion of public affairs of state and the enforcement of their views thereon. But when political parties are transplanted into the East, they at once partake of the nature of factions, pursuing private and personal interests instead of the interests of the state—as witnessed by the fact of their joining hands by turns with the clan cliques or using the construction of railways, ports and harbors, schools, etc., as means for extending party influence. Besides, the customs and usages of feudal times are so deeply impressed upon the minds of men here that even the idea of political parties, as soon as it enters the brains of our countrymen, germinates and grows according to feudal notions. Such being the case, even political parties, which should be based and dissolved solely on principle and political views, are really affairs of personal connections and sentiments, the relations between the leader and the members of a party being similar to those which subsisted between a feudal lord and his liegemen, or to those between a "boss" of gamblers and his followers in this country. A politician scrupulous enough to join or desert a party for the sake of principle is denounced as a political traitor or renegade. That political faith should be kept not *vis-à-vis* its leader or its officers but *vis-à-vis* its principles and views is not understood. They foolishly think that the proverb "A faithful servant never serves two masters: a chaste wife never sees two husbands" is equally applicable to the members of a political party. In their erroneous opinion, it is a loyal act on the part of a member of a party to change his principles and views in accordance with orders from headquarters, while in the event of headquarters changing their views it is unfaithful to desert them.

ŌKUMA SHIGENOBU

Suggestions to the Emperor, 1881

The proposals below, moderate and inoffensive though they may seem today, marked an important turning point in the history of the Meiji government, since they forced the issue of constitutionalism within the ruling regime. Though Ōkuma was compelled to resign from the government for having pressed his case, he won from the emperor a positive assurance that steps would be taken toward the establishment of representative government.

[From Watanabe, *Ōkuma Shigenobu*, p. 61]

1. That the date of the opening of a national deliberative body be proclaimed.

[183]

2. That due regard be given to the wishes of the people in the appointment of prominent ministers of the government.

3. That there be a distinction between offices for party men and offices for career men.

4. That a constitution be instituted at the emperor's direction.

5. That representatives be elected at the end of the 15th year of Meiji [1882], and that a national deliberative body be convened at the beginning of the 16th year [1883].

6. That policies for its administration be determined.

On the Launching of the Progressive Party

This interview was conducted by Fujita Ichirō, a reporter for the *Tokyo Nichi Nichi,* and published March 18, 1882. Ōkuma had been a member of the government until October of the previous year.

[From Watanabe, *Ōkuma Shigenobu,* pp. 87–88]

Question. On October 18 of last year, Your Excellency informed me that you intended to become a model of those who resigned by imperial command from the Meiji government. You expressed the opinion that no one as yet had left office properly, and you promised to set an example. I recorded your statement and have never forgotten it. Since then I have seen from time to time in the newspapers accounts of your activities, saying variously that you intended to go to Shimōsa and begin a land reclamation project, or that you would travel abroad. Each time I have read such an article I have been pleased, for it showed you still held to the views you expressed to me. However, I have been rather perturbed to read now that you plan to organize a political party. Is this in fact true? If it is true, there is likely to be criticism of Your Excellency. I have also felt obliged to mention it.

Answer. It is quite true that I intend to organize a political party. I did indeed inform you last year that I planned to set an example for those resigning by imperial command from the Meiji government. How could I forget it? I referred by "setting an example" to the proper way of leaving office. When I appeared at the Council of State last year to announce to its members that I was leaving the government, I asked them to remember that whether I was in or out of office my principles would not change. This fact is well known to everyone at court. I should never dream of behaving like Itagaki Taisuke who, barely a few months after he left the Cabinet over the Korean Expedition, submitted a memorial to the Throne for the establishment of a popularly elected parliament.[1] I left the government over principles, and I shall appeal to the people on those principles. There is nothing improper about such a course. My close observation of recent conditions in Japan convinces me that the formation of political parties and the discussion of political issues must not come to a halt, but must continue to expand from day to day.

Again, the behavior of members of existent political parties cannot but be of grave concern to both of us. They attack anyone belonging to the government—down to the last provincial official or policeman—without examining individual merits. They believe that popular rights are won by opposing the government. The worst such offenders are in the Liberal Party. If left to themselves they will in the end destroy society. Unworthy though I am, I wish to take it upon myself as a private citizen to correct this situation, and by preserving the security of the nation offer my thanks to the emperor. How could it be supposed that I acted as a mere mischief-maker?

To the Members of the Progressive Party

Ōkuma delivered the following address at the founding of the Progressive Party, on March 14, 1882, to explain its purposes. His real forte was public speaking, not writing, and this eloquent statement of his gospel of progress is characteristic of the rhetorical style for which he was famous.
[From Watanabe, *Ōkuma Shigenobu*, pp. 92–95]

The magnificent achievement of the Restoration had as its object the destruction of the monopoly of political power by a few families. Is it not the true function of our government to pursue this original concept to its ultimate realization by exerting itself on behalf of the dignity and prosperity of the Imperial Household and the happiness of the entire people? Nay, is it not incumbent on the Meiji government to encourage the whole nation to work as one man for these ends? But have the various cabinet ministers in fact the moral qualities to achieve this? Have they

[1] Ōkuma implies here that Itagaki is opportunistic; that he did nothing to help the establishment of a deliberative assembly while in the government and in a position to do so. Ōkuma also suggests the impropriety, for one who had had intimate knowledge of the studies and deliberations conducted within the government on this question, of making political capital out of it through a widely publicized memorial.

been performing their duties as they should? The discerning people of the nation surely know the true state of affairs.

I was one of those who labored in support of the glorious work of the Restoration in order that the monopoly of the political power of the empire by the few families might be destroyed, and I do not imagine that my adherence to these principles will change in the future. Nay, I hope always to work with an ever firmer resolve for the achievement of the glorious work of the Restoration; for the laying of a foundation for our empire which will last through all eternity; and for the everlasting preservation of the dignity and prosperity of the Imperial Household and the happiness of the people.

There are some who, though they style themselves the party of "respect for the Emperor" and wear the trappings of that virtue, actually seek mainly to establish a few families as the bulwark of the Imperial Household or else to protect the Imperial Household with troops. The extremists of this group would push the sovereign to the very forefront, and make him bear directly the brunt of the administration. They would by their support of the Imperial Household place it in a position of danger.

Is it actually possible to promote the dignity and prosperity of the Imperial Household by such means? No, it is not possible to promote the dignity and prosperity of the Imperial Household by such means. Even if it were possible, the prosperity would be transitory, and such fleeting glory could not satisfy me. I need hardly say that a way does exist for preserving the dignity and prosperity of the Imperial Household, and that rules exist which would ensure that the entire nation enjoy happiness. If this way and these rules are not discovered, we may wish for the one and hope for the other result, but we will never obtain either. Gentlemen, if any among you do not desire that our party reform the government and lead it forward, that it preserve the everlasting dignity and prosperity of the Imperial Household and seek the realization of the eternal happiness of the people, I do not wish to travel farther with you. The chains which bound us within our country have been sundered and will not be fastened again. The tides of progress from abroad reach us unhindered, and their strength is enormous. Today, when public opinion is universally inclined to progress, any attempt to run counter to this trend should be dismissed with scorn. Indeed, an examination of natural principles shows that reform and progress are the invariable law of all crea-tion. Consider any objects, whatever their species, and you will see that not one but advances from crude to refined, and from coarse to pure; each improves without cease from day to day, and progresses from month to month. To resist these forces stubbornly or to attempt to oppose the grand scheme of Nature is surely a mistake. . . .

Ever since the early days of the Meiji Era I have considered political reform to be my personal responsibility. I participated in the adminis-tration of the Restoration government and, as far as my feeble powers permitted, I worked for reform and progress. My greatest regret is that I have not been able fully to satisfy my own hopes, and that I have ac-cordingly disappointed you gentlemen frequently in yours. However, the course of our empire is at last pointed in the direction of progress. . . . Political reform and progress is the unanimous wish of our party and has ever been my abiding purpose. It must, however, be achieved by sound and proper means. . . . Some, the spiritual descendants of Rousseau,[2] would seek to arrive by direct action at their ultimate objectives, but such en-deavors would upset the social order and end by actually impeding po-litical reform. Our party entertains no such desire. We seek political reform and progress by sound and proper means, and hope to reach our objectives step by step. Because we desire reform and progress by such means, if any among you follow Rousseau and would re-enact the violent drama of the Jacobins in the hope of achieving precipitous changes, I re-ject your support and have no wish to travel farther with you. And while I am emphatic in my rejection of precipitous changes, I feel it is impor-tant to distinguish our party from those which mask their real conserva-tism by pretending to stand for gradual progress.

Our party is the party which stands for political progress. We wish to effect by sound and proper means political reform and progress as com-plete as possible. We differ categorically from those parties which fail to act when the occasion demands it, and which under the guise of work-ing for gradual progress seek private advantage through deliberate pro-crastination.

Party Politics and Public Opinion

The following has a historical as well as a political interest: it was the first recording made of a speech by a modern Japanese leader for the purpose of

[2] Itagaki and his followers.

wider public consumption. When the suggestion was made to him by his supporters, he at first questioned the rectitude of using such a method to reach a larger audience, remarking, "It is like acting!" Later, however, he acceded and the recording was made on March 2, 1915, while Ōkuma was Premier.

Ōkuma's warning of the dangers that lie ahead if public opinion is not exerted to clean up party politics, almost prophesies the fate of party government in the 1920s and '30s.

[From *Ōkuma kō hachijūgonen-shi*, III, 234–36]

The rights and duties given to the people by the Constitution are of great importance. The Constitution itself is the basis whereon our nation is built. And the rights of the people as subjects, that is, the duties of the people given by the Constitution, are a matter of vital importance. Among them, the most important is that of participating in elections. The complaints we hear today throughout the country about high taxes and the maladministration of government are like those of the servile people of the autocratic period. Under the Constitution nothing is performed—including the collection and spending of taxes, the prescription of the rights and duties of the people, and the making of all laws—without the approval of the Diet. . . . Remember that His Majesty, the Emperor Meiji, handed over to the people an extremely important key. What foolishness it is to allow this priceless key, which controls the state and which influences legislation, to be stolen by mean, vulgar, and designing men, who bring misfortune upon the people and cause endless complaints. Yet these misfortunes are retribution for the people's own errors, for their own lack of self-respect. Why do they not value their rights more? . . .

Now the allied powers of England, France, and Russia are engaged in war against the great power of Germany. Our empire is in the process of effecting a great change in the present world situation. Without a doubt our empire is advancing toward the attainment of a status of parity with the most civilized nations of the world. What foolishness it is, at such a time, to engage in petty quarrels based on political partisanship in our internal relations and in financial matters, as well as on the question of national defense and in other matters of government. There is a need to mobilize the great power of public opinion against such practices and to crush them. The unquestionable fact of the evils of all of our political parties to date—despite their disavowals—is present everywhere. This should be the reason, on the eve of the election, to move the people to a firm resolve. It is my hope that the power of public opinion will make its influence felt. It is my faith that if the people arouse themselves and re-solve to carry out their sacred obligation to the state the elections will prove very effective. Japan is now at a turning point. If Japan errs in her steps, such important matters as her national destiny, her honor and her reputation, would be affected. This I believe is a matter to which our people must give serious thought. In this connection I recognize the great power of public opinion. It is my faith that the power of public opinion controls the destiny of our country.

Education—A Pluralistic View

In contrast to Itō, who was closely identified with the state-supported Imperial University of Tokyo and provided its graduates with a virtual monopoly of bureaucratic posts, Ōkuma was a vigorous exponent of independent educational institutions. In 1882, after his withdrawal from the government, he helped to found Waseda University and later gave this speech during a fund-raising campaign in January 1901.

[From *Ōkuma kō hachijūgonen-shi*, II, 547]

Although the State expends a great deal of effort for common education, it is extremely doubtful whether it is beneficial to carry out higher education in state-maintained institutions. The State has the power to do so, but there are times when the aims of the State are actually those of the government in power and they are not truly representative of the aims of the people. There may also be times when the aims of the State are in error.

If a state is the creation of an aggregation of people, it is difficult to maintain that it will not on occasion fall into error. Thus, I feel that all kinds of schools are necessary—governmental, public, and private. And as they vie with each other in their search for truth, they will illuminate the truth and will in the end bring forth new doctrines. It is my belief that Waseda University will develop to a greater or lesser degree its own characteristics in comparison with the Imperial University and other institutions and will, in the competition for study and research, exert a wholesome influence over education in general.

Citizenship in the New World

On October 17, 1913, the thirtieth anniversary of the founding of Waseda University, Ōkuma set forth his conception of the educated man, combining the intellectual independence and practical knowledge of the West with the social virtues of Confucianism.

[From *Ōkuma kō hachijūgonen-shi*, III, 426–29]

The true aims of education of Waseda University are the realization of the independence of study, the practical application of study, and the cultivation of model citizens. As Waseda University considers independence of study its true aim, it has emphasized freedom of investigation and originality of research with the hope that it might contribute to the world's scholarship. As the practical application of study is also one of Waseda University's aims, it has taught, along with the study of theory for its own sake, ways to apply theory in practice. It hopes thereby to contribute to progress. As the making of model citizens is also an aim of Waseda University, it expects to cultivate good, loyal subjects of our constitutional empire who will be self-respecting, promote the welfare of their own families, prove useful to state and society, and who will participate widely in world affairs.

This requires an explanation. The civilization of the world never remains stationary. It progresses from day to day. All the ideas and sentiments and all the social conditions of the world are undergoing change from day to day and month to month. To build a state and to form a society at such a time, or to establish university education for the betterment of this state and society, there must be a great ideal. Japan today stands at the point of contact between the civilizations of the East and the West. Our great ideal lies in effecting the harmony of these civilizations and in raising the civilization of the Orient to the high level of that of the Occident so that the two might co-exist in harmony. We must strive toward the realization of this ideal. In order to realize it we must, first of all, make our principal aim independence of study and the application thereof; we must strive to prosecute original research and then practically apply the results of such studies. Those who would engage in such a pursuit must respect their own individuality, strive for the welfare of their own families, work for the benefit of their state and society, and participate in world affairs. This, in effect, is the model citizen.

In general there are not many students who can go to college. They constitute a minority. It is this small minority of students who set the example for the nation at large. They are the leaders of the nation. They are the strength of the nation. They form the foundation for the steady progress of the nation. They are the ones who become the vanguards of civilizing enterprises. In order to become a model citizen, knowledge alone is not sufficient; the building of a moral personality is necessary. And he must aspire to make a contribution not only to himself, his family, and his nation, but also to the world. If I may explain this in terms of an ancient Chinese expression, it is "the cultivation of the personality, regulating of the family, ordering of the country, achieving of peace in the world."[1] To plan for the peace of the world we must stabilize our country first. According to present usage, the term "nation" has two parts. The one is the state, the other is society. If society does not develop in an orderly way, the nation cannot be stable. And at the very root of this relationship is the family. The family is the basis of the state. Morality and ethics find their source in family life. Customs of behavior also spring from the family. Thus, the fundamental principle of education must be the cultivation of character. Man becomes self-seeking if he strives only to acquire specialized knowledge and ignores what I have said above. Moreover, the spirit of self-sacrifice among men for their country and for the world will gradually decline. This would be deplorable. It will be the curse of civilization. To avoid this curse and to acquire the benefits of civilization is the responsibility of the model citizen. This is the essence of Waseda University's basic principles of education.

Conclusion to *Fifty Years of New Japan* 1907–8
[From Ōkuma, *Fifty Years of New Japan*, Vol. II, pp. 554–55, 571–72]

By comparing the Japan of fifty years ago with the Japan of today, it will be seen that she has gained considerably in the extent of her territory, as well as in her population, which now numbers nearly fifty million. Her government has become constitutional not only in name, but in fact, and her national education has attained to a high degree of excellence. In commerce and industry, the emblems of peace, she has also made rapid strides, until her import and export trades together amounted in 1907 to the enormous sum of 926,000,000 *yen* (£94,877,000), an increase of 84,000,000 *yen* (£8,606,000) on the previous year. Her general progress, during the short space of half a century, has been so sudden and swift

[1] From the Confucian classic, *Great Learning*.

that it presents a spectacle rare in the history of the world. This leap forward is the result of the stimulus which the country received on coming
into contact with the civilization of Europe and America, and may well,
in its broad sense, be regarded as a boon conferred by foreign intercourse.
Foreign intercourse it was that animated the national consciousness of
our people, who under the feudal system lived localized and disunited,
and foreign intercourse it is that has enabled Japan to stand up as a
world power. We possess today a powerful army and navy, but it was
after Western models that we laid their foundations by establishing a
system of conscription in pursuance of the principle "all our sons are
soldiers," by promoting military education, and by encouraging the manufacture of arms and the art of ship building. We have reorganized the
systems of central and local administration, and effected reforms in the
educational system of the empire. All this is nothing but the result of
adopting the superior features of Western institutions. That Japan has
been enabled to do so is a boon conferred on her by foreign intercourse,
and it may be said that the nation has succeeded in this grand metamor-
phosis through the promptings and the influence of foreign civilization. . . .

In the foregoing pages frequent references have been made to the
susceptibility of the Japanese to the influences of foreign civilization. If
Japan has been endowed from the earliest days with this peculiarly sensitive faculty, she is gifted also with a strong retentive power which enables her to preserve and retain all that is good in and about herself. For
twenty centuries the nation has drunk freely of the civilizations of Korea,
China, and India, being always open to the different influences impressed
on her in succession. Yet we remain today politically unaltered under
one Imperial House and sovereign, that has descended in an unbroken
line for a length of time absolutely unexampled in the world. This fact
furnishes at least an incontestable proof that the Japanese are not a race
of people who, inconstant and capricious, are given to loving all that is
new and curious, always running after passing fashions. They have welcomed Occidental civilization while preserving their old Oriental civilization. They have attached great importance to *bushidō,* and at the same
time held in the highest respect the spirit of charity and humanity. They
have ever made a point of choosing the middle course in everything, and
have aimed at being always well balanced. To keep exclusively in one

direction, or to run to extremes, or to look forward only without looking backward, or to remember one side of a thing, forgetting the other, is not a characteristic of our people. We are conservative simultaneously with being progressive; we are aristocratic and at the same time democratic; we are individualistic while being also socialistic. In these respects we may be said to somewhat resemble the Anglo-Saxon race.

YAMAGATA AND THE ARMY

Of the so-called Big Three of the Meiji Era, Itō was usually identified in the popular mind with the Constitution, Ōkuma with "public opinion," and Yamagata Aritomo (1838–1922) with the Army. Among them Yamagata also most conspicuously represented the forces of traditionalism. Yet just as the progressive Ōkuma stopped well short of a complete break with the past, so even Yamagata, stern and redoubtable samurai though he was, had one foot set squarely in the modern world. Like his fellow oligarchs, too, the soldier Yamagata shared in those eminently political virtues of moderation and conciliation, without which the collaboration of such divergent elements in the Meiji government would have quickly been disrupted. It is understandable, despite his reputation as an arch-reactionary and militarist, that some of the most hot-blooded nationalists and expansionists of the next generation should have written Yamagata off as just another compromising and conniving bureaucrat. But it was an ironic fate for one known in his youth as "The Wild One" and later by the pen-name "Pure Madness."

A Chōshū man, like Kido and Itō he had studied under Yoshida Shōin. As if Shōin's example of self-sacrifice were not inspiration enough, Yamagata also had that of his grandmother: after bringing the orphaned boy up from the age of five, she is said to have committed suicide lest he be more concerned for her welfare than for his patriotic duties. Having mastered the traditional military arts of Japan, Yamagata helped to organize some of the "grass-roots heroes" Shōin had spoken of into an auxiliary force, drawn from all classes, to aid in the defense of his fief against the expected Western attack. Later in the disastrous engagement at Shimonoseki with naval forces of the Western powers, Yamagata made two vital discoveries: first, that his peasant lads were at least the equals

of the samurai in combat; and second, that fighting spirit was no sub-
stitute for modern arms. These were lessons he did not forget when
later, by distinguishing himself in the field against the forces of the
shogunate, he rose high in the councils of the Restoration regime. At the
earliest opportunity Yamagata set off on a world tour to study the military organization of the most advanced powers, and on his return took
a leading part in the establishment of the new conscription system. The
value of this conscript army was fully demonstrated by its victory, under
Yamagata's command, over the samurai rebels of Satsuma's Saigō Takamori. Thereafter the triumphant warrior went on to achieve not only the
highest military honors—Army Minister, Chief of the General Staff, Field
Marshal—but the heights of political power as well. Twice Home Minister, twice Premier, three times President of the Privy Council, and
finally a Prince of the new titular aristocracy, Yamagata became, after
Itō's assassination, the senior elder statesman and adviser to the Throne.
Like Ōkuma, too, he had able protégés to perpetuate his influence well
after his death in 1922.

For the modern reader it may be difficult to appreciate how radical an
innovator Yamagata's introduction of conscription in 1872 made him.
What we take for granted as an almost inevitable part of national defense
was for Japan at that time not only a striking change in the military
establishment but a virtual social revolution. The samurai, who for centuries had guarded jealously their right to bear arms, found the sharing
of this privilege with the lower classes as hard a blow to their pride and
morale as the loss of their traditional pensions was to their livelihood.
Yamagata, however, saw it as a gain rather than a loss, even in samurai
terms. To him it was not a question of the old aristocracy being reduced
to the level of the peasantry, but of the peasant being raised to the dignity
of the samurai. Thenceforward every citizen would be expected to meet
the rigorous standards and fulfill the high ideals of the old warrior caste.

We may more readily understand, then, Yamagata's interest in other
aspects of Meiji policy than the strictly military. The samurai had been
distinguished both by his military functions and by his prerogatives as
a member of an elite ruling class. Justice required, then, that the new
citizen-conscript likewise enjoy a participation in government in return
for his military service. Just as the idea of a "social contract" in modern
Europe had echoed the feudal contract of medieval times, so in Yama-

gata's mind arose the notion that the granting of local self-rule, though on a limited scale, would be a fitting means of sharing power in return for service to the Throne. Accordingly he took an active part in planning and inaugurating a system of local self-government in 1888.

Also deriving from Yamagata's conception of the citizen-samurai was his deep interest in education. This was expressed in part by the issuance of the Imperial Rescript to Soldiers and Sailors in 1882, setting forth the traditional ethical precepts, essentially Confucian in character, that had governed the conduct of the samurai and should now guide their modern successors. Even wider application was given to this idea in the Imperial Rescript on Education (reproduced in an earlier section), which was promulgated while Yamagata was Premier in 1890 and served to establish traditional moral training as the basis of public school education.

Yamagata was a firm believer in constitutional government, but had his own understanding of it. To him it meant ruling in strict accordance with established law and precedent—consistent and well-ordered administration as contrasted to the arbitrary or capricious rule he associated with popular sovereignty. His opinion of parliamentary institutions was low, and party politics, marked by factional strife and corrupt dealings, seemed to him the very antithesis of impartial and stable government. (During his first ministry Yamagata seems to have agreed reluctantly to the buying of Diet votes by his lieutenants, but the bad aftertaste of such dealings only confirmed his detestation of party politics.) Above all, Yamagata was determined that the deleterious effects of the party system should not extend to the military establishment. In the framing of the Constitution and the promulgation of imperial ordinances which followed, his influence was exerted to keep the armed services under the direct command of the emperor and largely independent of the civil administration. Finally, recognizing the steady rise in power of the parties after the turn of the century, he gave his support to a kind of third party which he hoped would rise above politics and exert a steadying and restraining influence upon the Diet.

Thus, as the years passed restraint and the avoidance of ill-considered action became more and more the guiding principles of Yamagata. Indeed it is this very sense of realism and caution which distinguishes him sharply from the militarists of later decades, who had never experienced, as he did early in life, the sobering effects of overwhelming defeat at

Shimonoseki. In foreign policy his overriding concern was that Japan be able to maintain her independence and yet not be forced to stand alone against the world. The Anglo-Japanese Alliance of 1902 he supported vigorously. Fearful in his later years of an impending racial struggle between East and West, Yamagata also urged that the friendship of the United States and Russia be cultivated so as to prevent the coalescing of the Western powers against an isolated Japan. For the same reason the friendship and support of China seemed to him indispensable. Ironically, when the famous Twenty-One Demands were thrust at China by a party government under Ōkuma, it was Yamagata who argued that force would fail and a more conciliatory policy should be pursued.

Insight born of experience and the self-restraint of the samurai were manifested in another, perhaps unexpected, side of Yamagata's life and character—his love of poetry. From the early days of his travels through Europe to his last years as an elder statesman, this creative discipline revealed in Yamagata a depth of feeling and sensibility which did credit to the traditional Japanese ideal of the warrior who was a man of culture as well. In the classic 31-syllable form, which required the utmost in precision and restraint of expression, he recorded the experiences of a lifetime. One such poem recalls the tragic end of fiery Saigō Takamori and the powerful emotions his young antagonist must have held back when gazing at the heights on which the hero of the Restoration gave his life:

Kidomeyama shiramu toride no   Kidome heights looked white
Sutekagari kemuru to mireba   As if from the smoke of campfires.
Sakura narikeri.   But then I saw
                                   It was the cherry blossoms.[1]

YAMAGATA ARITOMO
Military Conscription Ordinance

Although there were several proponents of universal military conscription, among them Ōmura Masujirō, it was Yamagata who was chiefly instrumental in its establishment in 1872. The following is the Official Notice or Instructions issued together with the imperial decree promulgating the conscription system on November 28, 1872. Though issued in the name of the Council of State, it is believed to embody largely the views of Yamagata.

[From Tokutomi, *Kōshaku Yamagata Aritomo den,* II, 194–96]

[1] Symbols of the evanescence of life, as well as of Spring.

In the system in effect in our country in the ancient past everyone was a soldier. In an emergency the emperor became the Marshal, mobilizing the able-bodied youth for military service and thereby suppressing rebellion. When the campaign was over the men returned to their homes and their occupations, whether that of farmer, artisan, or merchant. They differed from the soldiers of a later period who carried two swords and called themselves warriors, living presumptuously without working, and in extreme instances cutting down people in cold blood while officials turned their faces.

Following the appointment of Uzuhiko as Governor of Katsuragi by Emperor Jimmu, military contingents were established as were the systems of imperial guards and coast guards. During the Jinki [724–28] and Tempyō [729–49] eras the system of Six Headquarters and Two Military Outposts was established for the first time. Following the Hōgen [1156–58] and Heiji [1159–60] eras, the court became lax, and military control passed into the hands of the warrior class. Feudal conditions spread throughout the country, and there appeared among the people a distinction between the farmer and the soldier. Still later, the distinction between the ruler and the ruled collapsed, giving rise to indescribable evils. Then came the great Restoration of the government. All feudatories returned their fiefs to the Throne, and in 1871 the old prefectural system was restored. On the one hand, warriors who lived without labor for generations have had their stipends reduced and have been stripped of their swords; on the other hand, the four classes of the people are about to receive their right to freedom. This is the way to restore the balance between the high and the low and to grant equal rights to all. It is, in short, the basis of uniting the farmer and the soldier into one. Thus, the soldier is not the soldier of former days. The people are not the people of former days. They are now equally the people of the empire, and there is no distinction between them in their obligations to the State.

No one in the world is exempt from taxation with which the state defrays its expenditures. In this way, everyone should endeavor to repay one's country. The Occidentals call military obligation "blood tax," for it is one's repayment in life-blood to one's country. When the State suffers disaster, the people cannot escape being affected. Thus, the people can ward off disaster to themselves by striving to ward off disaster to the State. And where there is a state, there is military defense;

and if there is military defense there must be military service. It follows, therefore, that the law providing for a militia is the law of nature and not an accidental, man-made law. As for the system itself, it should be made after a survey of the past and the present, and adapted to the time and circumstance. The Occidental countries established their military systems after several hundred years of study and experience. Thus, their regulations are exact and detailed. However, the difference in geography rules out their wholesale adoption here. We should now select only what is good in them, use them to supplement our traditional military system, establish an army and a navy, require all males who attain the age of twenty—irrespective of class—to register for military service, and have them in readiness for all emergencies. Heads of communities and chiefs of villages should keep this aim in mind and they should instruct the people so that they will understand the fundamental principle of national defense.

Imperial Precepts to Soldiers and Sailors, 1882

This rescript, formally accepted from the emperor by Yamagata in behalf of the army, expresses the latter's own views on moral guidance for the conscripts of the modernized armed forces. Note especially the cautious tone. It is not fanatic bravery so much as prudence, self-control, and disciplined loyalty that constitute the martial virtues.

After recalling the imperial ancestors' supreme command of a unified military organization, and the subsequent usurpation of this power in the feudal period, the rescript continues:

[From *Imperial Precepts*, pp. 3–14]

When in youth We succeeded to the Imperial Throne, the shōgun returned into Our hands the administrative power, and all the feudal lords their fiefs; thus, in a few years, Our entire realm was unified and the ancient regime restored. Due as this was to the meritorious services of Our loyal officers and wise councillors, civil and military, and to the abiding influence of Our Ancestors' benevolence towards the people, yet it must also be attributed to Our subjects' true sense of loyalty and their conviction of the importance of "Great Righteousness." [1] . . . Soldiers and Sailors, We are your supreme Commander-in-Chief. Our relations with you will be most intimate when We rely upon you as Our limbs and

[1] Or "the highest duty" (*taigi*) as earlier stressed by Yamaga Sokō.

you look up to Us as your head. Whether We are able to guard the Empire, and so prove Ourself worthy of Heaven's blessings and repay the benevolence of Our Ancestors, depends upon the faithful discharge of your duties as soldiers and sailors. If the majesty and power of Our Empire be impaired, do you share with Us the sorrow; if the glory of Our arms shine resplendent, We will share with you the honor. If you all do your duty, and being one with Us in spirit do your utmost for the protection of the state, Our people will long enjoy the blessings of peace, and the might and dignity of Our Empire will shine in the world. As We thus expect much of you, Soldiers and Sailors, We give you the following precepts:

1. The soldier and sailor should consider loyalty their essential duty. Who that is born in this land can be wanting in the spirit of grateful service to it? No soldier or sailor, especially, can be considered efficient unless this spirit be strong within him. A soldier or a sailor in whom this spirit is not strong, however skilled in art or proficient in science, is a mere puppet; and a body of soldiers or sailors wanting in loyalty, however well ordered and disciplined it may be, is in an emergency no better than a rabble. Remember that, as the protection of the state and the maintenance of its power depend upon the strength of its arms, the growth or decline of this strength must affect the nation's destiny for good or for evil; therefore neither be led astray by current opinions nor meddle in politics, but with single heart fulfil your essential duty of loyalty, and bear in mind that duty is weightier than a mountain, while death is lighter than a feather. Never by failing in moral principle fall into disgrace and bring dishonor upon your name.

The second article concerns the respect due to superiors and consideration to be shown inferiors.

3. The soldier and the sailor should esteem valor. . . . To be incited by mere impetuosity to violent action cannot be called true valor. The soldier and the sailor should have sound discrimination of right and wrong, cultivate self-possession, and form their plans with deliberation. Never to despise an inferior enemy or fear a superior, but to do one's duty as soldier or sailor—this is true valor. Those who thus appreciate true valor should in their daily intercourse set gentleness first and aim

to win the love and esteem of others. If you affect valor and act with violence, the world will in the end detest you and look upon you as wild beasts. Of this you should take heed.

4. The soldier and the sailor should highly value faithfulness and righteousness. . . . Faithfulness implies the keeping of one's word, and righteousness the fulfilment of one's duty. If then you wish to be faithful and righteous in any thing, you must carefully consider at the outset whether you can accomplish it or not. If you thoughtlessly agree to do something that is vague in its nature and bind yourself to unwise obligations, and then try to prove yourself faithful and righteous, you may find yourself in great straits from which there is no escape. . . . Ever since ancient times there have been repeated instances of great men and heroes who, overwhelmed by misfortune, have perished and left a tarnished name to posterity, simply because in their effort to be faithful in small matters they failed to discern right and wrong with reference to fundamental principles, or because, losing sight of the true path of public duty, they kept faith in private relations. You should, then, take serious warning by these examples.

5. The soldier and sailor should make simplicity their aim. If you do not make simplicity your aim, you will become effeminate and frivolous and acquire fondness for luxurious and extravagant ways; you will finally grow selfish and sordid and sink to the last degree of baseness, so that neither loyalty nor valor will avail to save you from the contempt of the world.

These five articles should not be disregarded even for a moment by soldiers and sailors. Now for putting them into practice, the all important thing is sincerity. These five articles are the soul of Our soldiers and sailors, and sincerity is the soul of these articles. If the heart be not sincere, words and deeds, however good, are all mere outward show and can avail nothing. If only the heart be sincere, anything can be accomplished. Moreover these five articles are the "Grand Way" of Heaven and earth and the universal law of humanity, easy to observe and to practice. If you, Soldiers and Sailors, in obedience to Our instruction, will observe and practice these principles and fulfil your duty of grateful service to the country, it will be a source of joy, not to Ourself alone, but to all the people of Japan.

Local Self-Government

Yamagata, who is remembered chiefly for his contributions to Japan's military development, also had a large part in initiating local self-rule in 1887. For him it was not difficult to reconcile a strong military organization, established primarily for national defense, with a system of local autonomy; the latter was owed to the citizen by the government for the military service which the citizen owed to the state. He saw this as the primary training ground of the people in their new political responsibilities, and as a means of preserving the local echelons of administration from the divisive effects of party politics on the national level. Otherwise politics threatened to become a sort of tyranny, subordinating all other considerations in life to the drive for partisan advantage. This excerpt is from an address to a conference of local officials on February 13, 1890, when Yamagata was Home Minister.

[From Tokutomi, *Kōshaku Yamagata Aritomo den,* II, 1097–1103]

I sense, first of all, many evils in the actual administration of the system of city, town and village governments. In the organizational scheme of the nation, the city, town, and village constitute the lowest body; but being at the base of the administrative scheme, they constitute the very foundation of the state. The city, town and village regulations are intended to let these bodies administer their own affairs within the limits prescribed by law. Thus, if sound self-governing bodies are established, the spirit of self-rule developed, and the people of the cities, towns and villages given experience in public administration so that they might gradually acquire the ability to assume the nation's duties, then the fundamental basis of constitutional government will have been laid and the foundation of the nation will have been strengthened. A sound administrative system for the city, town and village—one which will steer a middle course and produce good results—will not be affected by the political upheavals of the central government. It will retain its middle course in the midst of party strife and avoid the evils of administrative practice. Thus, the nation can expect to return to a more prosperous state of affairs.

If, on the contrary, there are mistakes in the administration of local government, then the system of self-rule becomes the instrument for party rivalry, and the people of the city, town, and village will be thrown into confusion. If, actually, the situation should fall into such a state of affairs, it would be impossible to promote the well-being of the state and to reap the benefits of constitutional government. In this way, the results of the actual administration of the system of city, town, and village government is closely related to the lasting interests and fortunes of the nation. We must be conscientious in this regard. According to what I have heard, discord between political parties has gradually extended into every aspect of community life. Hardly a person in social, business, and economic relations, and in education, has remained untouched by this situation. . . . There are some people who abandon what they should be doing and expend both time and effort in unproductive political debate, and some who, losing their sense of purpose, even run afoul of the law. These evils are spreading their influence, morally, economically, and politically, throughout the country. They will impair the people's happiness and exert a harmful effect on the prosperity of the nation. In general, if a new government, in the course of its establishment, is abused for reasons of personal interests, the results could be extremely harmful. They could affect the strength and the cohesion of the entire people and become the cause of the decline of the nation. The history of our country and that of other countries provides many such examples in every age. The people, if they wish to prevent the growth of such evil influences, must regard at all times the unified endeavor of all as their highest aim. And the responsibility of those in a position to guide the people must be to apply themselves as administrators of the government to this ideal.

His Majesty the Emperor has granted the constitutional system to his ministers and subjects for the purpose of elevating their morals and of promoting their happiness. By virtue of this constitution ministers and subjects have been enabled to gain a higher degree of freedom and to improve their lot in life so that they can stand on an equal footing with peoples of other civilized nations. But if, unfortunately, we should err—however little—in putting this constitutional system into operation, we the people will have lost our position of honor. And thus, today, the duty of a loyal subject is to cultivate true constitutional liberty and to enjoy its benefits in peace.

If men lack self-respect and self-restraint, there cannot be freedom in its true sense. One who respects himself will of necessity respect others. One who wishes others to respect his own opinions must respect the views of others. There is no logic in the position that only one's own opinions are correct. Irrespective of place, diverse opinions are inevitable when the interests of people are not the same. Thus, we must make every effort to tolerate the views of others and to resolve differences mutually. If this is not done contention will not cease. The constitutional system is an instrument for the adjustment of diverse views: the use of force and violence will not only fail to eradicate differences in viewpoints but will also aggravate them.

Political problems do not encompass the entire field of human interests. The people who might entertain different political views very frequently hold mutually identical views in religious and moral matters, and in matters of personal and social relations. It is not the way of a loyal, trustworthy man to set aside his religious, moral, personal, and social relationships in the sole interest of politics. Thus, to promote party rivalry to extremes is a human misfortune. Nay, to resort to violence and to use obstructionist methods against an opponent to promote one's political position is to permit personal passions to enslave him. It is against the principle of the observance of the law. It is against the spirit of the constitutional system.

It is especially undesirable that one abandon his occupational pursuit for the sake of a political cause. It is against his own interest as well as that of society as a whole. The economic strength of a country is dependent mainly on productive labor. Thus, it is not the way of the good citizen to indulge in needless arguments to the neglect of his calling. Not only will he thus fail to add his bit to the national wealth but he will also fail to induce others to develop industrious habits of self-reliance.

On the Unity of the Cabinet

A strong sense of unity, joint responsibility, and loyalty to the Throne had enabled the early Meiji oligarchy to provide strong leadership in modernizing the country. Ōkuma's ouster from the government in 1881 had resulted from an alleged breach of the strict, unwritten code governing the conduct of its members. With the inauguration of constitutional government, however, the unity of the cabinet was seriously affected by party politics, as during the Kuroda ministry in 1888–89. The situation prompted Yamagata to present the following memorial to the Throne.

[From Tokutomi, *Kōshaku Yamagata Aritomo den,* II, 1093–95]

To have a sense of personal responsibility is a constitutional obligation of members of the cabinet. Constitutionally, a minister's opinion may be acceptable, but it is his obligation to the Throne not to publicize his personal views to the Diet or to the people without the express sanction of the sovereign. Once a minister disregards this rule, he has, legally and morally, forfeited his right to his office. It is fundamental in the organization of the cabinet to have unity and accord. The individual members of the cabinet, notwithstanding minor differences of opinion among themselves, must spare no effort to be united in their public announcements and enactments of the government. To maintain this unity of the cabinet, secrecy of cabinet activities must be strictly observed. Although a constitutional government should be open and above board, and the activities of the Diet should be open and public, the deliberations of the cabinet must be secret so that the individual views of its members will not leak to the public to become the cause of public debate. A member of the cabinet may tender his resignation over the refusal of the sovereign to approve his views or over his inability to obtain the support of the majority of his colleagues for his views. But even so, it is the obligation of men in politics to maintain silence for some time on matters and events which transpire during their tenure. This is a moral responsibility of cabinet ministers. Such a practice of constitutional ethics must be cultivated at the very outset. If it is not done, it will be a hundred years before the evil is eradicated. If we do not firmly establish this ethical practice of cabinet members now—which is essential to constitutional government—its consequences will affect the Diet and the public, and the government will become the scene of political opportunism and tactical maneuvering for power and advantage. The future will suffer the consequences of an incurable disease. Your ministers, conscious of this fact, and out of a deep concern for the future, have each pledged their conscience to work together for the unity of the cabinet. I implore Your Majesty's attention.

Yamagata's Political Faith

Yamagata's answer to the divisive effects of a two-party system was the creation of a kind of "third force" on the Right. It was not intended to operate as a vote-getting machine, but as an acknowledged minority of men of high integrity and unquestioned patriotism, who would serve as the conscience of the Diet and a counterweight to the rival parties. In effect Yamagata hoped by this means to perpetuate the same sort of highly motivated, self-sacrificing leadership which had successfully guided the Restoration. His views are contained in an essay dated February 18, 1917, found among the papers of a former secretary of the Privy Council. Earlier in June 1898, he had proposed the creation of a Loyalist Party for the same purpose.

[From Takahashi, *San-kō Iretsu,* pp. 139–41]

Recently the evils of party strife have become increasingly acute. Even the great and unprecedented World War has become, in relation to this struggle for political advantage, like a fire on the far side of the river. Hardly a thought is given to the question of the fate of our neighbor China which is fraught with danger so far as the Far East is concerned. The parties seem smugly unconcerned over the danger to our country of having to stand alone and without support in the future among the powers of the world. The evils of partisan politics are indeed deplorable. If this trend is permitted to develop unchecked, I fear that the spirit of the Meiji Restoration will die and the splendid achievements of the late emperor will soon come to naught. The actual situation with respect to political parties in our country today indicates that when one party is excessively strong in Parliament, that party becomes reckless and arbitrary. When two parties are evenly matched, the struggle between them becomes extremely violent. Thus, to eliminate arbitrary actions and violent political struggles, it would seem advisable to divide their strength and to have them restrain each other mutually. I have faith in a plan to establish a three-party system in the Diet which would eliminate excesses and help foster moderation. If the third party is organized by men who are impartial and moderate, and possessed of intelligence and a sincere concern for the well-being of the country, it is my belief that it can make a contribution to the state toward the achievement of constitutional government, and it will set an example to others. At present there are two parties—the Kensei-kai and the Seiyū-kai—which are evenly balanced. We must organize a group consisting of fair and intelligent men who will stand between the two existing parties and be partial to neither; who can check party excesses and irregularities; who can restrain the ambitions of those who seek to satisfy their avarice or their desire for political power through the instrument of the party; who can transcend the common run of politicians for whom politics is a means of livelihood; and who can go forward, resolutely and firmly, with but the one thought in mind of service to the state. Only by the conduct of a central core of such men who would not be corrupted by thoughts of personal gain or fame, and only by having as a nucleus in the Diet men who would not falter in their public devotion, can the secret of true constitutional government be achieved.

The greater the number of such representatives we can gather, the better it will be. However, the number of such men, both economically established and patriotically inclined, need not be numerous. Only a sufficient number capable of standing between the two large parties and of checking their excesses is necessary. The immediate need is to find someone who would take it upon himself to rally such people together. So long as he is a man of true devotion to the country, it matters not whether he is a farmer, craftsman, or merchant. There must be several million among our population of seventy million who have fixed property and are economically secure, and who therefore are above corruption. If such men come forward to organize a solid nucleus in the Diet, the empire will be on a firm and secure foundation, and there need be no anxiety in the country. The epoch-making task of establishing our sovereign and our country was accomplished by thousands of devoted and self-sacrificing patriots of the period prior to and after the Restoration. Today, fifty years since the Restoration, when our national fortunes continue to rise, are there no patriots who would step forward to save our country from the dangers which are imminent? It is my fervent hope that such men will brace themselves and rouse themselves to action.

Racial Conflict and Japan's Foreign Policy

Yamagata in his later years viewed world conflict as fundamentally racial in character, and lamented the fact that China was not strong enough to stand beside Japan in resisting the onslaught of the white races, which he predicted would be intensified after the First World War. To meet this danger, however, he urged neither a whipping-up of racial feeling among Orientals nor a heavy-handed self-assertion by Japan on the Continent. He sought rather to win the confidence of China in promoting their common defense, and to forestall the impending coalition of Western powers against the yellow peoples by seeking the friendship of both Russia and the United States.

These excerpts are taken from a letter to Premier Ōkuma in August, 1914.
[From Tokutomi, *Kōshaku Yamagata Aritomo den*, III, 920–28]

There are people in our country who rely excessively on the military prowess of our empire and who believe that against China the application of force alone will suffice to gain our objectives. But the problems of life are not so simple as to permit of their solution by the use of force alone. The principal aim of our plan today should be to improve Sino-Japanese relations and to instill in China a sense of abiding trust in us. . . .

The recent international situation points to an increasing intensity in racial rivalry from year to year. It is a striking fact that the Turkish and Balkan wars of former years and the Austro-Serbian and the Russo-German wars of today all had their inception in racial rivalry and hatred. The anti-Japanese movement in the state of California in the United States, and the discrimination against Hindus in British Africa are also manifestations of the same racial problem. Thus, the possibility of the rivalry between the white and colored races henceforth growing in intensity and leading eventually to a clash between them cannot be ruled out entirely. When the present great conflict in Europe is over and when the political and economic order are restored, the various countries will again focus their attention on the Far East and the benefits and rights they might derive from this region. When that day comes, the rivalry between the white and the non-white races will become violent, and who can say that the white races will not unite with one another to oppose the colored peoples?

Now among the colored peoples of the Orient, Japan and China are the only two countries that have the semblance of an independent state. True, India compares favorably with China in its expansive territory and teeming population, but she has long since lost her independence, and there seems to be no reason today to believe that she will recover it. Thus, if the colored races of the Orient hope to compete with the so-called culturally advanced white races and maintain friendly relations with them while retaining their own cultural identity and independence, China and Japan, which are culturally and racially alike, must become friendly and promote each other's interests. China in the past has been invaded by other races and even subjugated by them. Thus, it is not difficult to understand why China, in the rivalry with white races, is not as deeply sensitive as Japan is in this regard. But the Chinese ought to know that China in her four thousand years of history has never been under the yoke of the white man. And thus, if she is approached with reason it will not be entirely hopeless to make her change her attitude and to instill in her the feeling of trust and reliance in our empire.

In the formulation and execution of our Chinese policy, an indispensable consideration is our American policy. America is rich, and of late she is giving great attention to the commerce, industry, and trade of China. Moreover, the great European war has not deterred her in the least. On the contrary, America enjoys, because of the war, the full advantages of the proverbial fisherman [who makes off with the catch while the birds quarrel over it]. And the government of China, suspicious of the true motives of our empire, and as a means of restraining our activities in China, has been turning to America. If we fail to dissipate China's suspicion of us, she will rapidly turn against us and instead turn more and more to America. America herself will take advantage of such a situation and will increasingly extend her influence over China.

The immigration problem in California has made for an unhappy situation in the relations between the empire and America. It is regrettable that this problem still awaits settlement. But the empire has never regarded America as a foe. Therefore, it is advisable, for the realization of our China policy, not to aggravate America's feelings toward us nor needlessly to arouse her suspicions over our actions. For the maintenance of peace in the Orient in the future, and the promotion of China's independence, I deem it a matter of utmost importance to negotiate in a frank and open manner with America.

I have explained above the prevailing trend of racial problems and my premonitions of a bitter clash in the future between the white and colored peoples. However, I consider it more prudent, as far as China is concerned, not to raise the issue of a league of colored peoples. Our empire is now in alliance with England; it has agreements with Russia and France; and we are mutually striving to promote both the peace of the Orient and the independence of China. But we must also realize the need to negotiate with America. Our politicians must be sternly warned against raising the issue of racialism which would hurt the feelings of other countries and impair their friendship for us. The crux of the matter is that China must be won over by hints and suggestions, and only gradually, before we can realize our plans in the future.

China and the Twenty-One Demands

Yamagata believed that Japan's dominance in Manchuria was essential not only to her own growth and security but also to the protection of a weak China from Russia. Tactful diplomacy could make the Chinese government under Yuan Shih-k'ai recognize this, he thought, whereas the petty bullying represented by the Twenty-One Demands would only alienate the Chinese. In this case Yamagata's political outlook disposed him toward a conciliatory approach to the conservative Yuan, whereas the liberal government of Ōkuma, more sympathetic to Sun Yat-sen, did not hesitate to demand of Yuan the same concessions already promised by Sun if he came to power. The following is taken from the record of a private conversation in Yamagata's home on May 14, 1915.

[From Takahashi, San-kō Iretsu, pp. 95–100]

Last year, when an ultimatum was sent to Germany [demanding surrender of her interests in China] I offered a number of suggestions on the possible aftermath of such a move. Again, this year, I disclosed my frank thoughts to [Foreign Minister] Katō. I told him that if it became necessary to resort to arms in order to dispose of the present Manchurian problem, I would throw my support to the move immediately. Manchuria is for the Japanese the only region for expansion. Manchuria is Japan's life-line. Thus, we must secure for our people the guarantee that they can settle there and pursue their occupations in peace. If this problem cannot be disposed of by diplomatic means, then we have no other alternative but to resort to arms. However, while a nation must resort to arms when it is involved in a national peril, it would, on the other hand, disgrace the honor of Japan—which stands among the nations of the world on the principle of fair play and justice—to apply force on China for the disposition of such trifling matters as the acceptance of Japanese advisers, purchase of Japanese arms, and free access for Japanese missionaries, as stated in Article V of the current negotiations. Thus it is that I have been making every effort to halt the present negotiations. As certain as fate, when the ultimatum [to China] was about to be dispatched, a note was received from the British Foreign Minister Grey sharply stating that such demands on China as the employment of Japanese advisers and the purchase of arms which would give Japan predominant rights in China were contrary to the spirit of the Anglo-Japanese Alliance, and that he, Grey, would be unable to explain Japan's actions should he be interpellated upon them in the British Parliament. There was great confusion at the receipt of this note, but even without the Grey objections, I could not have given my approval to the mistaken proposal of dispatching an ultimatum with the threat of resorting to arms on the questions involved. Thus, Article V of the ultimatum was stricken out. However, I deem it foolish to leave the matter of Chinese diplomacy in the hands of Minister Hioki at the present juncture. The head of the Ministry of Foreign Affairs should go to China when the opportunity presents itself—and we have the examples of Ōkubo and Itō—and shake Yuan [Shih-k'ai]'s hand and frankly divulge Japan's true aims and explain Japan's position. So long as Yuan is not a log or a stone or an unreasonable fellow, I am sure that this would be a step toward ameliorating ill-feeling between the two countries.

In their essence Sino-Japanese relations are extremely simple and clear. What I should like to explain to Yuan is that the cause of war in various parts of the world today is, in general, racial in character. A recent example is the conflict between Turkey and Italy. The current European war is also basically a manifestation of the racial problem. The racial problem is likewise the key to the solution of the Asia problem. Now, are not Japan and China the only true states in Asia? Is it not true that other than these two countries there is no other which can control all of Asia? In short, we must attempt the solution of our myriad problems on the premise of "Asia for the Asians." However, Japan is an island country. She is a small, narrow island country which cannot hope to support within its island confines any further increase in population. Thus, she has no alternative but to expand into Manchuria or elsewhere. That is, as Asians the Japanese must of necessity live in Asia. China may object to the Japanese setting foot in Manchuria, but had not Japan fought and repelled Russia from Manchuria, even Peking might not be Chinese territory today. Thus, while the expansion of Japan into Manchuria may be a move for her own betterment and that of her people, it would also be a necessary move for the self-protection of Asians and for the co-existence and co-prosperity of China and Japan.

CHAPTER XXVI

THE HIGH TIDE OF PREWAR LIBERALISM

The prewar Japanese liberal movement reached its height in the 1920s when for a time it appeared that the principles espoused by that movement had become the guiding light of Japanese political life. These principles might roughly be stated as follows: 1) that the government be conducted by party cabinets responsible to the majority in the lower house of the Diet; 2) that the lower house be elected by universal manhood suffrage; 3) that the people be guaranteed the full exercise of their civil liberties; 4) that Japan abandon a policy of force and aggression in China and do no more than maintain the rights she already possessed in Manchuria; 5) that Japan follow a policy of international cooperation, particularly with regard to disarmament.

The movement drew its main support from five groups: party politicians, businessmen, journalists, educators, and certain diplomats. Of course, not all of the principles stated above received an equal amount of support from each of these groups. The party politicians insisted very strongly on the principle of party cabinets, but they were not so consistently enthusiastic about the other four principles. Indeed, when the opposition of the Privy Council and the Peers to universal manhood suffrage suddenly evaporated, the party politicians displayed a surprising reluctance to enact the measure into law. To them it merely meant further complications in the business of getting elected, a point which was not lost upon the Peers, who seem to have been reasoning much along the lines followed by Disraeli when he extended the vote to English labor.

The liberal businessmen were primarily concerned with the first, fourth, and fifth principles. They favored party cabinets for the simple reason that these seemed to offer them the best chance for influencing the government's economic and social policies. In addition, those businessmen who either traded with China or produced for the China trade felt they had suffered great losses from the boycotts which Japanese aggression had sparked. Consequently, they were very anxious for a more conciliatory policy to be adopted toward China. Japanese financiers also believed that Japan had to cooperate with the Western Powers if she wished to retain access to international short term credits and investment funds. For this reason they desired to have Japan give an earnest of its peaceful intentions by entering into disarmament agreements.

The business world in general as well as the agricultural interests also backed these agreements in the hope that there would be a reduction in the military budget and therefore in the tax burden. In their support of these international policies they were joined by diplomats such as Baron Shidehara Kijūrō, whose study of the international situation in general and of the China situation in particular had led them to conclude that these were the only feasible policies for Japan. It is to be noted that though Shidehara was well known for his liberal position on international affairs he never publicly expressed a correspondingly liberal view with regard to domestic politics.

The only persons who can be said to have given an unqualified support to the whole liberal creed were the liberal journalists and educators. The journalists were the shock troops of the movement and at several critical moments in its history they helped to carry the day by utilizing the news and editorial columns of their newspapers to arouse public opinion. The educators, particularly university professors such as Yoshino Sakuzō and Minobe Tatsukichi, provided the intellectual foundations for Japanese liberalism and in their writings showed how the democratic ideal could be adapted to the Japanese scene. They also implanted liberal ideas in the minds of the students who passed through their lecture halls, frequently taking the initiative in organizing student groups dedicated to the spread and implementation of these ideas. During and after the First World War a number of these students, mostly the younger sons of wealthy landlord or business class families, entered politics and contributed greatly to the attempt to establish responsible parliamentary government. They constituted the only group of politicians who were seriously concerned with the civil rights issue.

It will be noted that organized labor has not been included among the groups giving important support to the liberal movement. Organized labor accepted many of the principles of Japanese liberalism and was quite willing to cooperate with the liberals in the accomplishment of common objectives, e.g., in the universal manhood suffrage movement. However, Japanese liberalism did not manifest much solicitude for social and economic reforms, matters which were of great interest to the labor movement. In fact, in these areas the thinking of most liberals tended toward a kind of paternalism which differed very little from that of the conservatives and the reactionaries. Consequently, organized labor devoted most of its political energies to the left-wing political movement, particularly after the achievement of universal manhood suffrage. It must be added that because of their social programs many of the ultranationalist groups also had much greater appeal for the lower orders than did liberalism. This failure to win the backing of labor was a serious weakness of the liberal movement, which needed all the support it could muster in its struggle to reshape the political life of Japan.

There were many unfavorable circumstances against which Japanese liberalism had to struggle. For one, the men who had fashioned the Japanese Constitution had placed the Diet in a very weak position: it had neither the legal means of holding a cabinet responsible nor any effective financial controls over the cabinet. What little power the Diet did possess the elected lower house had to share equally with the non-elected House of Peers. The popularly elected house was confronted with other well-established centers of power: the bureaucracy, the Privy Council, the military services, the informal council of Elder Statesmen (*genrō*) and the Imperial Household officials. Since most of these other centers of power had a legal veto over any attempt to curtail their prerogatives by law or by constitutional amendment, liberals had to work to establish within the existing framework extralegal customs which would give Japan the substance if not the form of a parliamentary democracy. This could only be accomplished if they rallied behind their program the mass of the Japanese people. Yet the diffusion of liberal ideals among the people was trammeled by primary and secondary education systems which had been deliberately designed to foster a spirit adverse to the values usually associated with a democratic society. Moreover, the operations of most Japanese social groups were not such as would engender that sense of individualism, personal responsibility, and self-confidence so essential to the proper functioning of representative government.

[213]

The weaknesses which have so far been discussed might be regarded as due to environmental or external factors, but the liberal movement was also plagued by a number of internal failings. Of these flaws the more important were those which impaired the strength of the political parties, for it was they who had the responsibility of proving the worth and viability of parliamentary government.

The gravest defect of the party politicians was their opportunism. They were rarely ready to suspend their differences and unite to defend parliamentary principles. If a party cabinet became involved in jurisdictional or policy disputes with one of the other centers of power, the opposing political party was more than willing to side with the latter in the hope that the occasion might be used to drive its opponents from office. They never seemed to care that the ultimate result of these petty maneuvers would be to weaken the political party movement as a whole. In fact, there were only two instances in which united fronts were organized to defend the principle of party government (the third Katsura cabinet and the Kiyoura cabinet) and both times a substantial number of party men gave their allegiance to the antiparliamentarian forces. Undoubtedly it was this niggling concern for office which persuaded party politicians to welcome into positions of party leadership Itō Hirobumi, Katsura Tarō, Katō Takaaki, Tanaka Giichi and many other products of the civil or military bureaucracy. These men were able to assume party presidencies on virtually dictatorial terms, since the parties, convinced that the *genrō* would entrust office only to such leaders, believed this to be the one means by which even a modicum of political power might be achieved.

This type of leadership had a most unfortunate effect upon the character of Japanese political parties. Party administration was bureaucratized, and policies were handed down from above on a take-it-or-get-out basis. Each party came to be held together by a panting eagerness for the crumbs of office rather than by a firm foundation of common principle. As a result they had little to offer to the wider public and therefore never became mass parties but always remained primarily aggregations of legislators and their immediate backers. Even if the principles had been present, it is doubtful that the parties could have developed mass support, for the leaders were reserved men and seldom appeared before mass audiences. Moreover when they did speak, they seemed incapable of articulating liberal ideas and one searches vainly among their cold speeches for any stirring expressions of their credo. The most momentous occasions, e.g., the passage of the Universal Manhood Suffrage Law, a wonderful opportunity for publicizing parliamentary principles, brought forth only perfunctory and jejune phrases. Japan's party leaders must stand charged with neglecting to educate the Japanese masses in the principles of parliamentary government. It matters little if the failure arose from a distaste for mass movements or from a feeling that the best way of advancing the liberal cause was to go about one's business silently and thus avoid arousing the active opposition of the conservatives and reactionaries. The end result was the same: when the crisis came, the party politicians were generals without armies.

The public came to look on the politicians not only as men without principles but also as men without morals. It was a rare candidate for office who felt he could win on his own merits and did not need to spend thousands of yen buying up votes through professional "election brokers." The practice was so widespread that only the most obtuse voter could have been ignorant of it. Faced with the need for huge campaign funds, the Diet member was quite willing to sell whatever influence he had for whatever price he could get. Those who could not obtain enough through their own efforts badgered the party headquarters for money. The party headquarters in turn received donations from businessmen who hoped to receive favors when and if the party formed a cabinet. Great bribery scandals were continually coming to light and undermining the public's confidence in the parties, though it is only fair to note that there were just as many scandals involving civil and military bureaucrats. In fact, the first widespread appearance of corruption among Diet members had occurred when the political lieutenants of Yamagata, finding that they could not control the Diet through either violence or dissolution, turned to systematic bribery. The businessmen who gave bribes were usually smaller businessmen who were not powerful enough in themselves to command favorable treatment from the government. On the other hand the greatest source of political donations, as distinct from bribes, was popularly supposed to be the *zaibatsu*, the Mitsui supporting the *Seiyūkai* and the Mitsubishi the *Minseitō*. These ties have never really been documented, but this hardly matters. The important thing is that it would have been difficult to find a Japanese who did not believe they existec

[215]

and that government by party cabinets meant therefore government in the interests of one or another of the *zaibatsu*.

There was another respect in which party cabinets—when they did come to power—proved a great disappointment to Japanese liberals. In their disregard of civil liberties they were unsurpassed by any of the bureaucratic cabinets of the past. Under them books and other publications continued to be censored with great rigor. The Hara and Hamaguchi cabinets were formally charged by the newspaper profession with prohibiting the mention in the press of more news items than any of their predecessors had. The Higher Special Police were regularly used to spy upon the activities of political opponents. The home ministers of two party cabinets were forced to leave office as a result of their flagrant interference in general elections (1915, 1928). The greatest mass arrests of nonconformist thinkers in Japanese history were conducted under *Minseitō* and *Seiyūkai* cabinets. They also began the process of rooting "dangerous thought" out of the nation's school systems, and of course it was under a coalition party cabinet that the Peace Preservation Law of 1925 was enacted. This law made it a crime to advocate any change in either the national polity or the capitalist system. It was officially interpreted to mean that the public could not even discuss a constitutional amendment.

Perhaps this attitude toward civil rights was only to be expected of the party cabinets, for from its very beginning the political party movement had contained a strong dash of ultranationalism. Whether from conviction or from cunning, the founders of the early Meiji political societies (the *Aikokutō* and the *Risshisha*) had argued that a parliament would strengthen the State for its task of national defense and expansion abroad. They had exalted the emperor's sovereignty and asserted that a Diet would unify the nation and so facilitate the execution of the imperial will. In the 1890s the party politicians constantly berated the bureaucratic cabinets for not being aggressive enough in their foreign policy, and one of the shrillest voices was that of the liberal Ozaki Yukio. Nor should it be forgotten that it was the liberal Katō Takaaki, serving as foreign minister under the liberal Ōkuma who, against the objections of the conservative Yamagata, presented the infamous Twenty-One Demands to China. To all this must be added the prominent role played by politicians of every party in such ultranationalist organizations as the

Kokusuikai, the *Kokuhonsha,* the *Seinendan,* etc. In view of these facts it is not surprising that in the 1930s the political parties offered such ineffectual resistance to the militarists.

It is obvious, then, that the Japanese liberal movement was beset with great difficulties. And yet its failure was by no means a foregone conclusion. In the 1920s there appeared a new crop of younger politicians who had come to maturity during the great upsurge of liberalism that had characterized the war and postwar period. These younger men had wholeheartedly accepted the liberal principles and dedicated themselves to creating a true parliamentary government in Japan. They were not backward about asserting the supremacy of the lower house of the Diet and attacking as anachronisms the Peers, the Privy Council, and the independence of the military services. When the Peace Preservation Law was presented to the Diet, it was they who in defense of civil liberties spoke out against the proposals of their own cabinet. If the world envisaged by the idealists of 1919 had come into being and achieved a degree of permanence, these young Japanese liberals might in time have brought the majority of the nation around to their view; for the Japanese are a people given to searching out and adjusting themselves to what they conceive to be the trend of world developments. In the 1920s the signs had seemed to read "democracy-capitalism-peace," and this was of inestimable help to the liberal movement. Unfortunately, by the early 1930s world political and economic events had produced a situation which both objectively and psychologically was unfavorable to the further progress of Japanese liberalism.

DEMOCRACY AT HOME

YOSHINO SAKUZŌ

On the Meaning of Constitutional Government and the Methods by Which It Can Be Perfected

Yoshino Sakuzō (1878–1933) was for many years professor of political history and political theory at Tokyo Imperial University. Shortly after receiving his appointment he went abroad for three years of study in Germany, England, and the United States. On his return in 1913 he began to write articles analyzing the problems of democratic government. For a number of years these articles appeared periodically in *Chūō Kōron,* an important journal of opinion. "On the Meaning of Constitutional Government," one of the most significant of these articles, was published in January, 1916. It was a powerful reaffirmation of faith in the inevitable triumph of democracy and represented a reaction against the belief current in certain Japanese circles that Germany's successes had proven the superiority of the Prussian pattern. Yoshino sets forth what he conceives to be the most important characteristics of democracy. He carefully demonstrates that democracy is fully compatible with the concept of the emperor's sovereignty, a principle which had become so sacrosanct as to remain unchallengeable. Very detailed consideration is given to the special problems confronting democracy in Japan, and techniques are suggested for their elimination. All of the problems he touches on were extremely important at the time he wrote—political corruption, non-party cabinets, the rise of a plutocracy, universal suffrage, the need for popular education in the ways of democracy, etc.

[From Yoshino, *Mimpon shugi ron,* pp. 1–130]

PREFACE

Whether or not constitutional government will work well is partly a question of its structure and procedures, but it is also very much a question of the general level of the people's knowledge and virtue. Only where the level is rather mature can a constitutional government be set up. . . . . However, since the trend toward constitutional government is world wide and can no longer be resisted, advanced thinkers must make the attempt to establish it firmly. They should voluntarily assume the responsibility of instructing the people so as to train them in its workings without delay. If they do not, constitutional government can never function perfectly however complete it may be in form. Therefore, the fundamental prerequisite for perfecting constitutional government, especially in politically backward nations, is the cultivation of knowledge and virtue among the generality of the people. This is not a task which can be accomplished in a day. Think of the situation in our own country. We instituted constitutional government before the people were prepared for it. As a result there have been many failures, failures which have caused those with high aspirations for government to feel that we have accomplished very little. Still, it is impossible to reverse course and return to the old absolutism, so there is nothing for us to do but cheerfully take the road of reform and progress. Consequently, it is extremely important not to rely upon politicians alone, but to make use of the cooperative efforts of educators, religious leaders, and thinkers in all areas of society.

The United States and Mexico illustrate how two countries with equally well-developed forms of constitutional government may be at opposite ends of the scale in its operation as a result of the different levels of knowledge and virtue attained by their peoples. [pp. 4–6]

I. WHAT IS CONSTITUTIONAL GOVERNMENT?

The word "constitution" invariably means a nation's fundamental laws. However, when used as a modern political term it has certain additional connotations. . . .

First, one usually assigns to a constitution greater force than to ordinary laws. . . . Since a nation's fundamental laws are of great importance, the idea has persisted from antiquity that there should be a distinction between them and ordinary laws. However, there is another reason why modern nations give such special weight to constitutions. The intention is to prevent the reckless infringement, at some later time, of the rights which have been laid down in them with great care. Whatever they may ostensibly be, modern constitutions have in fact appeared as a result of the long struggle for popular rights which was waged against those who in the past monopolized political power—those rightly called the privileged classes. [pp. 13–15]

Second, a constitution must include as an important part of its contents the following three provisions: 1) guarantees of civil liberties; 2) the principle of the separation of the three branches of government; and 3) a popularly elected legislature. . . .

1. The fifteen articles comprising Chapter II of the Japanese Constitution concern "Rights and Duties of Subjects." As the title indicates, some of these articles prescribe duties, but most of them enumerate those rights and liberties which are indispensable to the people's material and spiritual happiness and progress. . . . It is clearly provided that these rights and liberties may not be arbitrarily restricted by the government, but can only be limited by law, in the enactment of which the Diet participates. [pp. 16–17]

2. If it is defined theoretically, the principle of separation of powers becomes a very troublesome problem. Generally speaking, it means that the executive, judicial, and legislative powers are exercised by separate organs of the government. . . . It is true for all countries without exception that the purport of the principle . . . is best shown in the area

of judicial independence. However, nowadays its application to relations between the executive and legislative branches differs substantially from country to country. Of course, the executive and the legislature ought to be independent of each other, but if there is no provision at all for negotiations between the two, constitutional government cannot be expected to function smoothly. [pp. 18–19]

3. More than any other factor [provision for a popularly elected legislature] . . . is regarded by the public as the most important characteristic of a constitution. Indeed, there are many who think of it as the only essential characteristic of a constitution. . . . Why is this provision of such great importance? Because the popularly elected legislature is the only branch of government in the composition of which the people have a direct voice. The personnel of the other two branches are experts appointed by the government. The people have almost no direct concern in naming them. With the legislature it is just the opposite. Its members are directly elected by the people. Naturally, the people can exert influence upon it and thereby cause it to express fully the popular will. . . .

These are the [three] indispensable elements of a modern constitution. . . . If they are present, then there is a constitution. When such a constitution exists and is the guiding principle of political life, we have constitutional government. [pp. 21–22]

II. WHAT IS MEANT BY THE PERFECTION OF CONSTITUTIONAL GOVERNMENT?

Living as we do under a constitutional government we must work all the harder for its perfection. However we must not work blindly. The task requires a strenuous effort based upon the same . . . ideology that originally brought about the establishment of the Constitution and upon the fundamental spirit that lies concealed in its innermost depths. . . .

What then is the spirit of a constitution? No generalization is possible, for it varies from one country to another. . . . In some countries the privileged classes survive as relics of a bygone age and still continue to exercise their influence. Where this is so, even though the pressure of world trends has forced the promulgation of a constitution, there are many who try to implement it so as to do no injury to their antiquated political ideology. These people stridently emphasize the principle that their nation's constitution has nothing in common with that of any other, but instead possesses its own peculiar coloration. We frequently see the like in our country, where there is a tendency in constitutional theory to assert as the basis for the political structure a peculiar national morality of our own, attempting in this way to avoid interpreting the Constitution in accordance with Western constitutional ideas. . . . Of course, each country's constitution is tinged with that country's peculiar coloration. It would be difficult to summarize the unique qualities of each country's constitution, but it is possible to infer from the history of modern world civilization the spiritual basis common to them all. . . . The common spiritual basis which I discover in all constitutions is democracy. [pp. 26-28]

III. THE SPIRITUAL BASIS OF CONSTITUTIONAL GOVERNMENT: DEMOCRACY

The Japanese word *mimpon shugi* (democracy) is of very recent use. Formerly *minshu shugi* seems to have been generally favored and even *minshū shugi* and *heimin shugi* have been used. However, *minshu shugi* is likely to be understood as referring to the theory held by the social democratic parties that "the sovereignty of the nation resides in the people." *Heimin shugi* implies an opposition between the common people (*heimin*) and the nobility, and there is the risk it will be misunderstood to mean that the nobility is the enemy and the common people are the friendly forces. By themselves the words *minshū shugi* are not liable to such a misinterpretation, but they smack of overemphasis on the masses (*minshū*). Since . . . the basis of constitutional government is a universally accepted principle which politically emphasizes the people at large but which does not differentiate between nobles and commoners nor distinguish between a monarchical and a republican national polity, I suspect that the comparatively new term *mimpon shugi* is the most suitable. [pp. 28-29]

I think [the Western word] "democracy," as used in the fields of law and political science, has at least two distinct meanings. In one sense it means that "in law the sovereignty of the nation resides in the people." In the other it is used to mean that "in politics the fundamental end of the exercise of the nation's sovereignty should be the people." . . . I should like to use *minshu shugi* and *mimpon shugi,* respectively, as the suitable translations for these two senses of "democracy." [pp. 30-31]

In our country many people are prevented by the "popular sovereignty" aspect of *minshu shugi* from having a proper understanding of democracy. There has therefore been an unavoidable prejudice which has appreciably retarded democracy's development. Consequently, I believe that in order to have the people strive for the advancement of constitutional government with a correct understanding of democracy, it is extremely important to make clear the distinction between the two meanings of the word.[1] [pp. 31–32]

IV. THE DISTINCTION BETWEEN POPULAR SOVEREIGNTY AND DEMOCRACY

Even "popular sovereignty," if we examine it closely, is seen to be of two kinds. . . .

The first has been set forth in the following form: In the corporate body known as the nation the original and natural locus of sovereignty must be the people as a whole. This I call absolute or philosophic popular sovereignty. . . .

The second kind is set forth in the following form: In a specific country it has been decided by interpretation of the constitution that the sovereignty resides in the people. This I call popular sovereignty by mutual consent or by interpretation. . . . Both types, however, concern the legal location of the nation's sovereignty. Consequently, there cannot be the slightest doubt that the word "popular sovereignty" is inappropriate to a country like ours, which from the beginning has been unmistakably monarchical. Therefore, I believe it is very clear that while "popular sovereignty" and "democracy" are verbally similar, they differ a great deal in substance, for "democracy" raises no question of republicanism or monarchism and constitutes the fundamental spirit common to the constitutions of all modern countries. [pp. 32–38]

V. MISINTERPRETATIONS OF DEMOCRACY

Democracy is not contingent upon where legal theory locates sovereignty. It merely implies that in the exercise of this sovereignty, the sovereign should always make it his policy to value the well-being and opinions of the people. . . . There is no doubt that even in a monarchy this principle can be honored without contravening the established system in the slightest degree. . . . Nevertheless there are many who think

[1] Hereafter *minshu shugi* will be rendered "popular sovereignty" to distinguish it from the term Yoshino prefers for "democracy"—*mimpon shugi*.

that democracy and the monarchical system are completely incompatible. This is a serious misconception. [pp. 38–39]

Most of the misconceptions about democracy arise from emotional arguments which have no theoretical basis. This is especially true of the small class that up to now has possessed special privileges and monopolized political power. . . . In the past the system made them rulers of the common people. In the new age they must yield this formal dominance to the people and be content with the substance of moral leadership. . . . As long as they alter neither their attitudes nor their motives to accord with the change in the times, no true progress can be expected in constitutional government. The public is prone to say that constitutional government has failed to develop as we had hoped because the thought of the people has not developed. Yet, whether or not the people's thought develops is really determined by whether or not advanced thinkers properly guide it. When the small class of leaders holds to its narrow-minded views, it is impossible to implant in the hearts of the common people sound constitutional ideas no matter how much the necessity of spreading constitutional thought is preached. In this connection I must turn to the small enlightened intellectual class in the upper ranks of society and express the hope that they themselves achieve a true understanding of constitutional ideas and become conscious of their duty to guide the common people. [pp. 39–41]

In addition to misinterpretations based on emotional arguments, there are also criticisms of democracy which have a somewhat theoretical basis, or what would outwardly appear to be such. First, there are persons who confuse democracy with popular sovereignty and see no clear difference between them. They therefore think that democracy is opposed in theory to the principle of the sovereignty of the emperor. . . . Second, there are some who look at the history of democracy's development, see that it has invariably gone hand-in-hand with popular sovereignty, and conclude from this that it is incompatible with the monarchical system. . . . Up to a point, this theory is true. Indeed, if we look at the history of the development of constitutional governments, we see that they have for the most part passed through a revolutionary stage. . . . But it is a mistake to conclude that because in its origins constitutional government came from revolutionary democratic thought it must always be dangerous. This is as illogical as to argue that since man is descended

[223]

from the monkeys he will always have the monkey's inferior characteristics. . . .

If we hesitate for fear of possible evil effects, progress and development will never be started. If something is necessary for the advancement of the nation and society, we must quickly search for a method to attain it. And we must strive greatly to prevent the abuses that we fear may result. We should not live in idleness, bound by our old established ways. Progress requires strenuous effort. As a people with constitutional government we must willingly throw open our doors to world trends and actively seek the greatest progress and development for our nation and society. Yet, at the same time, we must resolve to pause and fight to overcome whatever harm may attend on this. This is truly the glorious responsibility borne by the advanced thinkers in a constitutionally governed country. As long as they are determined not to shirk it, I believe we need have no fear whatever for the future of the nation under democracy. [pp. 41-44]

VI. THE SUBSTANCE OF DEMOCRACY: POLITICAL OBJECTIVES

Earlier I defined democracy as the policy in exercising political power of valuing the profit, happiness, and opinions of the people. On the face of it, this definition reveals two aspects of democracy. First, the object of the exercise of political power . . . must be the people's welfare. Second, the policies which determine how political power is exercised . . . are settled in accordance with the people's opinions. . . .

The first requirement of democracy, then, is that the ultimate end of the exercise of political power be the good of the people. . . . In ancient times the objective of government was the survival and prosperity of a small number of powerful persons or the preservation of their authority; it was never the well-being of the people as a whole. . . . To the feudal mind, the land and people of a country were no more than the personal property of the royal family. But in the feudal period it became quite clear that land and people were the foundation upon which the royal family stood, so the people gradually came to be valued. . . . In general, international competition further deepened the ruling classes' feeling of dependence upon the people. . . . Accordingly, the feudal state came to treat the people with a great deal of consideration. . . . From our point of view today, the people were in the final analysis like servants happy under a kind-hearted master. They were not permitted to claim consideration for themselves as a matter of right. . . . Our democracy is opposed to placing the people in such a position. It demands that the ultimate goal of government must change and become the welfare of the people. It further demands that . . . [their welfare] absolutely never be used as a means to some other end. In modern politics it is certainly not permissible to sacrifice the general welfare to the interests of a small number. [pp. 44–48]

There may still be some who denounce democracy as contravening the idea of loyalty to the emperor, a sentiment which dates from the founding of our country. . . . There may be those who ask whether democracy would oppose setting aside the people's welfare even if this were to be done in the interest of the Imperial Family. In my answer to these criticisms I would make the following two points. First, there is absolutely no contradiction nowadays between the "interest of the Imperial Family" and the interest of the nation, [an interest] which stands at the very top of the people's well-being. . . . Since the Imperial Family is the unique head of the national family, it is utterly unthinkable that it should become necessary "in the interest of the Imperial Family" to disregard the interest of the people. Consequently, I believe the interest of the Imperial Family and the interest of the people can never conflict with each other. Second, let us yield the point and suppose such a conflict to have arisen between the two. Since democracy relates to the sovereign's way of using his powers, there is nothing to prevent him from establishing the basic principle that he will not arbitrarily disregard the welfare of the people. . . . It is the determination of the Japanese people willingly to go through fire and water for the sake of the emperor. However, if the state systematically exploited this devotion to secure the people's acceptance of acts which disregarded the people's welfare, might not a certain cheerlessness come to characterize the subjects' spirit of loyalty? I would therefore like to make it a principle that whenever the State demands from the people sacrifices beyond a certain level the choice of whether or not they are to comply should be left entirely to their moral judgment. . . . Our loyal people will never for fear of their own safety hesitate to strive for emperor and country. Loyalty* to the emperor is a spirit which dates from the founding of our country; it is the essence of our national polity. Reinforcing it by erecting it into a system would, I believe, lead to many evils but yield no advantage. [pp. 48–50]

Democracy does not permit the welfare of the people to be sacrificed for any purpose whatsoever. However, if we ask whether this point has today been completely realized in every country, [the answer is] most assuredly no. . . .

In our own country, unhappily, the people do not yet comprehend this problem and have not progressed to the point of insisting upon [the principle]. On the other hand, though in general the privileged classes have little by little come to understand the demands of the people and thus may be considered to be aware of the way in which to meet them, there are still narrow-minded persons in these classes who value themselves highly and are condescending to the people. . . . In order that the place of these classes in a democracy may be peacefully settled and a trend toward a healthy development of society thereby created, it is necessary that on the one hand we work for the development of the people's knowledge and that on the other we urge the upper classes seriously to search their hearts. [pp. 51–53]

In recent times there has been a trend in our country and others toward the appearance of certain new privileged classes in addition to the historic ones. Chief among these is the plutocracy. . . . It is contrary to the objective of democracy for economically superior and inferior classes to develop and as a consequence for profits to become the monopoly of a single class. Therefore, without touching on the fundamental problem of whether or not the organization of society should be basically reconstructed, it has of late been considered necessary in government to resort temporarily to moderate measures directed against these economically privileged classes. . . . To consider now the situation in our own country, in recent times capitalists have gained strength and with their huge financial power are finally on the point of wrongfully trampling upon the public interest. It is true that this tendency is not so strong [in Japan] as it is in America and Europe, but recently the influence of the capitalists has increased markedly. After the Sino-Japanese War and the Russo-Japanese War their power grew with especial rapidity. Wealth has never lacked a certain degree of power, but before the Sino-Japanese War the money power was in fact completely under the control of political power. In the early years of the Meiji Period, wealth bent the knee at the door of political power and under the latter's shelter worked by degrees to increase financial power. . . . The Sino-Japanese War forced political power to beg aid from wealth for the first time. In this way wealth first achieved a position of equality with political power. With the Russo-Japanese War, the government of Prince Katsura kowtowed to the capitalists in all matters and sought their financial aid. Thereupon, wealth in one jump achieved strength sufficient to control political power. Bestowal of peerages on rich men dates from this time. . . . In this way the wealthy put pressure on political power and for the profit of their own class demanded the passage of various unfair laws. As a result there are in force today various kinds of financial legislation which are very disadvantageous to the general public and serve the interests of the capitalist class alone. Thus there has recently been produced in our country a new privileged class whose interests are unfairly protected by law. This kind of privileged class will in the future come into conflict with the demands of democracy; how the two will be harmonized is a matter which engages our most anxious attention. Since the moneyed class are concerned with things from a materialistic point of view, they do not readily listen to the voice of the ordinary people. Consequently, if there come to be great difficulties in solving problems in the area of [constitutional government], will they not in all likelihood arise from this problem of the financially privileged class? If the plutocracy were by some chance to make common cause with the traditional privileged classes in confronting democracy, there could be no greater misfortune for the nation. In this connection I must incessantly arouse the attention of the intellectuals and entreat the reflection of the nobility and the plutocrats who are flouting the affections of the nation. [pp. 53–55]

VII. THE SUBSTANCE OF DEMOCRACY: DETERMINATION OF POLICIES

Democracy not only implies that the end of government is the welfare of the people, but also demands that in the final determination of policies the people's opinions must be valued highly. This certainly does not mean that in each individual problem the opinions of each individual person be heard. It is an overall principle according to which nothing is done in opposition to the views of the people and no political action is undertaken without their general approval—expressed or tacit. [p. 56]

However, one encounters quite strong criticisms of this second essential of democracy. If one examines these criticisms closely, they are, I think, seen to be of three kinds.

The first is the idea that democracy is opposed constitutionally to the principle of imperial sovereignty. . . . Yet, democracy is a theory of politics, not of law. From the legal standpoint, sovereignty resides in the emperor. Democracy comes in when one asks what principle ought to guide the emperor in the exercise of his sovereignty. It is in no way inconsistent with monarchy. Of course, I too am agreed that in order to protect the imperial institution we should reject the dangerous theory of popular sovereignty. However, opposition on this account to the advance of democracy—so similar in name to popular sovereignty, but so different from it in substance—is a serious problem for the future of constitutional government. [pp. 57–58]

Another criticism is the notion that, even conceding democracy to be a political concept, if in the exercise of his power the sovereign must by custom always take into account the general will of the people, his sovereignty is thereby limited and free exercise of his authority is prevented. However, those who believe this ignore the fact that in a constitutional country the sovereignty of the ruler is always limited in some way. It is because the word "limitation" is used that the above impression is produced; how would it be if the word "Way" were used in its place? Assume that constitutional government is a system under which a sovereign rules not by arbitrary whim but in accordance with the "Way." Is not this "Way" a sort of limitation on the free exercise of sovereignty? Well, the "Way" manifests itself both legally and politically; in other words, constitutional countries make it a rule to limit the power of the sovereign both in legal theory and in political practice. . . . Practically speaking, there is no country in the world today in which the sovereign decides all the policies of state by himself. . . . [Thus] the real problem is: what *kind* of limitations should there be on the ruler's authority? Should he be limited by concern for the will of the people generally, or by the opinions of two or three of his intimates? Concern for the will of the people may or may not be a limitation of the ruler's sovereignty, but I find it a one-sided argument not to admit that other limitations exist even when there is no such concern. Let us assume, for example, that there has been a cabinet change, and that custom demands that responsibility for forming a successor cabinet must be left to the leader of the political party that commands a majority in the parliament. It is objected that this practice imposes limitations on the ruler's sovereignty. . . . The ruler's complete freedom of action, if applied literally on such an occasion, would imply that without consulting anyone else he alone must decide who was to be the prime minister. . . . Yet, whether or not such a method would be practical, in fact the usual practice is for him to consult with two or three of the experienced ministers of his court. . . . As I see it, appointment of ministers according to party majorities in parliament and appointment on the advice of elder statesmen are both alike limitations of the ruler's authority. . . . The question which arises here is *which* sort of limitation should the ruler accept? Should he consult a small number of people, or should he consult at large with great numbers of people? Consequently, it is improper to reject democracy on the grounds that it limits the emperor's sovereignty and is therefore bad. If one wishes validly to reject democracy, one must go a step further and clearly demonstrate that it is always bad to take counsel with many men and always good to take counsel with a few men. Yet, in Japan since early Meiji it has been the fundamental national policy to take counsel with large numbers of persons. H. M., the Meiji Emperor, decreed at the beginning of the Restoration that deliberative assemblies should be widely established and all matters decided by public discussion. Thus the spirit of democracy, which consists in the just and equitable conduct of government in consultation with the majority of the people, has been our national policy since early in Meiji. Those who today deny this and advocate the principle of minority advice are moving counter to the general trend of political evolution. [pp. 58–61]

It is said that the enlightened are always likely to be a minority; that therefore the best government must be government by the minority; and that majority rule, on the other hand, deteriorates into mob rule. This . . . is partly true. However, one must not forget that minority rule is always government in a dark chamber. However splendid a person's character may be, when others do not observe him he is likely to commit excesses. . . . Some point to the corruption of the Diet and its members and say that there are bound to be evils in majority rule. . . . Yet in general, since government by the minority is secret government, many of its evils never come to the attention of the country; while since majority government is open government, there is a tendency to magnify its minutest deficiencies. [pp. 65–66]

It may be mistakenly thought that in majority government no use at all is made of the enlightened minority, but this is absolutely not so. . . . [This minority] can most properly fulfill their function as truly enlightened people when they modestly identify themselves with the majority, ostensibly following the majority will and yet as the spiritual leaders of the majority quietly working for the public good. . . . In all formal respects, the majority form the basis for the exercise of governmental power and they must be the political rulers, but within their ranks they in fact have need of spiritual leaders. . . . If the enlightened minority are truly to serve the national society, they must resolve to use their wisdom to guide the masses spiritually. At the same time they must resolve to enlist themselves in the service of the masses and by making their own influence prevail work for the public good. . . . Only when these two groups work in cooperation can there be a perfect development of constitutional government. Seen politically, this cooperation means the country is ruled by the will of the majority, but seen spiritually, it means the country is guided by the enlightened minority. . . . It is government by the people, but in one sense it can also be called government by the best. Thus one can claim that constitutional government reaches its most splendid perfection when there is a harmonious reconciliation of political democracy with spiritual aristocracy. . . . In this respect, I am thoroughly disgusted with the attitude of Japan's elder statesmen and other bureaucratic statesmen. Though they enjoy the special favor of the Imperial House and the esteem of the nation, they sometimes use their exalted position to interfere irresponsibly in political affairs. They will not reach down from their eminent position to establish contact with the masses, but instead take a hostile attitude toward democratic influences. It is much to be regretted that they thus fail to understand the true meaning of modern political life, but one must say it is especially unfortunate for the nation that they neglect the social function of the enlightened minority by not assuming the responsibility of popular leadership. After all, the ordinary people, surprisingly enough, actually pay an excessive respect to honors and titles. When the aristocrats who inherit historical and social authority are at the same time highly capable in point of actual ability and will jointly undertake the leadership of the people, the people gladly submit to this leadership. For the sake of the healthy development of constitutional government, nay, say rather for the sake of the future success of our society and nation, I entreat the enlightened minority to reflect deeply on this. We must hope that the aristocrats and plutocrats will respond to the handsome treatment they have received from the nation not only by giving great thought to how they should conduct themselves but also by giving serious attention to the education of their children and younger brothers. [pp. 67–70]

VIII. REPRESENTATIVE GOVERNMENT

In this section Yoshino argues the merits of representative government against those who claim that it does not go far enough toward meeting the demands of true democracy. Syndicalism and the popular referendum, he says, have been the two methods most commonly advanced for achieving more direct popular government, but both of them he feels to be impractical and unnecessary.

IX. THE RELATION OF THE PEOPLE TO THE LEGISLATORS

The most important point regarding the relation between the people and the legislators is that the people always occupy the position of master of the house, while the legislators are of necessity transients. The proper maintenance of this relationship is absolutely essential to the functioning of constitutional government. The abuses of constitutional government generally stem from the inversion of this relationship. And it is not just a question of the relation between the people and the legislators. The same truth holds as between legislators and the government. Whenever the legislators, who should supervise the government, are puppets of the government, many evils arise. Likewise, whenever the people, who should supervise the legislators, are instead manipulated by the latter, then the operation of constitutional government is replete with innumerable scandalous corruptions. If the government seduces legislators with offers of gain, if legislators also lead the people astray with offers of gain, then the proper relationships are inverted and the structure of constitutional government is filled with abuses. If we wish to clean up political life and see a normal evolution of constitutional government, the first thing we must do is to pay strict attention to rectifying the relationship between the people and the legislators. There are at least three measures that must be adopted in order to accomplish this. [p. 87]

1. Inculcation of election ethics. . . . I do not think that the ethics of the Japanese are, broadly speaking, especially low. Yet, since elections are a new experience for them, they have, regrettably, greatly ignored morality in conducting them. I feel it is necessary for us to inculcate the principles of election ethics in the people of the nation.

This being the case, what points should the people be made especially to understand? One of them is that though a single vote seems to be of very little importance, it actually is of great consequence to the fate of the nation. It is too sacred to be subject to influence by bribes or intimidation. A second point is that one votes in the interest of the nation, not for the profit of a single locality. To vote with local interests alone in view is likely more often than not to result in sacrificing the interests of the whole nation. A third point is that voting is our prerogative, not something to be done at the solicitation of the candidates. It is up to us to recommend proper candidates to the nation. Nowadays it is extremely important to drive these three points deep into the minds of the people. [pp. 88–89]

2. The necessity of adopting and enforcing strict election regulations. When legislators manipulate the people, invariably corruption and bad government flourish. Only when the people control their legislators does the operation of constitutional government follow the proper course. Therefore, it is especially important to impose strict penalties on the corrupt practices which may be carried on between the legislators and the people. . . . In this respect, a rather strict election law has been adopted in Japan; the only thing to be regretted is that it has not been rigorously enough enforced, and that the government tends to be lax in dealing with the activities of its own party. [pp. 91–92]

3. The necessity of extending the suffrage as widely as possible. If the suffrage is limited, corrupt practices are carried on unreservedly. When the suffrage is extended to the limit, there can be absolutely no distribution of bribes and the like. Moreover, only when it has become absolutely impossible for candidates to fight one another with money and things of value will they compete by sincerely and frankly presenting their views and personal qualifications to the people. Consequently, the people will gain an opportunity of receiving a political education

through this means. When suffrage is limited, as it is today, there is a chance of winning a contest without presenting one's views and qualifications. Therefore the political parties pay little heed to the political education of the people. . . . There is no doubt that politically Diet members truly represent all the people of the country. Therefore, they should not be only the representatives of one class. It is logical then that the scope of the electorate should be as broad as possible. . . . Today as in the past the basic political consideration is to have elections which result essentially in the representation of the overall interests of the people generally. We think it proper on this ground that the suffrage should be extended as widely as possible. Naturally this is not to say that suffrage should be unlimited. We must admit that from the standpoint of necessity and convenience there are several kinds of limitations to be set if the objectives of elections are to be achieved. To begin with we must probably exclude infants, the insane, criminals, persons on public relief, bankrupts, etc. . . . Whether or not women should be excluded is, in the final analysis, a problem for the future. Today, suffrage is generally the exclusive possession of men. Of course there are some countries that do extend political rights to women. [pp. 93–95]

Nowadays the two ways that have actually been adopted to weed out those unsuited [to exercise voting rights] are educational qualifications and property qualifications. . . . However, these days formal education alone is not the thing which distinguishes between those who have and those who have not the training proper to humanistic [moral] cultivation. In a time like today when formal education is extremely widespread, I suspect that this standard is of little practical value. Making educational requirements an absolute qualification is behind the times. . . . Furthermore . . . limitation [on the basis of taxation or property] has become meaningless in the present age. Practically, it is impossible to use a fixed amount of property as a criterion for mechanically distinguishing between those who have and those who do not have steadiness of character. . . .

Most of the civilized countries of the world have seen fit to adopt universal [manhood] suffrage. The only civilized countries . . . that impose comparatively great limitations on suffrage are Russia and Japan. In all other civilized countries universal suffrage is already a settled issue and no longer comes up for political discussion. In Japan the

[233]

agitation for extending the suffrage has recently increased, but it will apparently take a long time before the idea becomes generally accepted. Recently when the Ōkuma cabinet introduced a temporizing bill which would have reduced the present ten-yen tax voting qualification to five-yen, there was violent opposition in certain political quarters. Hence, I cannot help feeling that the establishment of universal suffrage is a long way off. Among many Japanese intellectuals there is an incredible misunderstanding of and violent antipathy to universal suffrage. Of course, in the beginning it was mainly the Socialists who advocated the system. This is by and large the probable reason for the misunderstanding. It is not strange that the upper classes are not pleased with the system, but it is a very peculiar phenomenon that the ordinary people do not welcome it wholeheartedly. A bill for the adoption of universal suffrage passed the House of Representatives at the 27th Diet in 1911, but at the time it was said that it was passed in the firm belief that it would never be approved by the House of Peers. As had been expected, the House of Peers rejected it by a huge majority. If we do not dispel this misunderstanding of universal suffrage and instill in the people the deep, heartfelt conviction that constitutional government cannot possibly develop properly unless universal suffrage is adopted, then the prospects for constitutional government are indeed gloomy. As a consequence of our present suffrage limitations, no more than three per cent of all Japanese are enfranchised. In the general elections of March last year [1915] only 1,544,725 persons had the right to vote. [pp. 102–3]

Thus, the extension of the suffrage and the strict enforcement of electoral laws are the most pressing matters facing Japan. The history of other countries shows that these two actions have often effected a clean-up in political life. If they are neglected, the ideal of constitutional government cannot be realized no matter how much one preaches about election ethics and prods the conscience of the people. The argument for extending suffrage is a subject that we must study most earnestly and we must henceforth advocate it most fervently. In so far as there are misconceptions among the public, we must on the one hand appeal to the intellectuals to reconsider the issue and on the other dispel the confusions of the political world. We must work diligently at these two things so that in the near future universal suffrage may become a reality. [p. 104]

X. THE RELATION OF PARLIAMENT TO THE GOVERNMENT

It is the government that takes direct charge of state affairs. Only when parliament oversees the government can there be just and equitable administration. But since the government wields real power, it is likely to use its position to control and manipulate the legislators, thereby reversing matters and ordering about as it pleases the very persons by whom, properly speaking, it should be supervised. Many hidden evils spring from such a situation. . . . Therefore, it is quite essential to the healthy functioning of constitutional government that the government be kept in a state of strict subordination to the parliament. [pp. 107–8]

Hence we consider it essential to sharpen the moral conscience of officeholders as much as possible. . . . Fidelity to conscience and regard for integrity are the very life and soul of a politician. For a politician there is no greater crime than to change his opinion for the sake of dishonest gain. It is strange that such affairs should be problems in a constitutional country. It is more than strange; it is shameful. Under constitutional government, worthless individuals should not become legislators in the first place. Government is fundamentally a very exalted calling, one that can only be undertaken well by persons of high cultivation. Therefore is it not an insult to a politician merely to investigate his character? It is the practice in Western countries that men about whose character there is some doubt are never accepted as politicians in the first place. . . . The frequent occurrence of corrupt behavior among legislators is probably a peculiarity of Japan. With such a state of affairs it is absolutely impossible for constitutional government to progress in Japan. To prevent [corruption], as I have said again and again, it is necessary to keep the people from committing errors at the very start in the elections. Moreover, it is extremely necessary that the people inflict the severest punishments upon representatives who defile their offices. We must not only by means of law sternly punish any representatives who defile their offices; we must also resolve to employ the power of public opinion to bury them in political oblivion.

In this regard, one point I wish to emphasize most sharply is that the offense of one who tempts [an official] is far more serious than that of the one who is tempted. [pp. 109–10]

Making the legislators morally independent of the government is only

[235]

the first step. If we are to get the legislators fully to discharge their supervisory responsibility and thoroughly inquire into transgressions of the government, it is also essential that the government be made to fulfill its political responsibility to the parliament. . . . If the principle of responsible cabinets has not been firmly established in political institutions or usage, it is impossible to achieve the proper relationship between the government and the parliament. Consequently the requisites for democracy cannot be fully met.

In contrast to the responsible cabinet system there is also the principle of the nonparty cabinet. According to this idea, the cabinet should rise above the wishes of parliament and occupy a position of absolute independence. Under this system, no matter how much the government is opposed by parliament, no matter even if on occasion there are votes of nonconfidence [in parliament], the government unconcernedly continues in office. To put the theory in its worst light, it is a pretext which enables the government freely to perpetrate any kind of arbitrary misrule. Thus it is inconsistent with the principle that final decisions on policy should depend upon the views of the people generally. Therefore, the nonparty cabinet system is decidedly not the normal rule in constitutional government. Of course, under our Constitution theoretically the ministers of state are responsible to the sovereign alone, so it is not absolutely necessary for them immediately and as a matter of course to resign their posts when the Diet opposes them. That is to say, it cannot be called unconstitutional. However, it is clear from the foregoing that it is contrary to the spirit of constitutional government. [p. 112]

The usual method used nowadays for calling the responsibility [of the government] into account is the parliamentary cabinet system. In most countries it has recently become the practice for the government to be formed by the leader of the political party that has a majority in parliament. In this sense most governments are today party cabinets. . . . In countries where there are just two major parties, this system works well, but in those with many small parties, it does not. . . . In order that the wisdom of the party cabinet system may be demonstrated, it is absolutely necessary to encourage the establishment of two major parties. However, the coming into being of two major parties is a matter which is determined by the course of events, and cannot very well be controlled by a constitution's theory. As a result, the workability of the party cabinet system always varies from one country to another. Hence the problem arises as to whether party government can really work smoothly in Japan. . . . Since I am interested in the progress of constitutional government in Japan, I should like to present to the nation the reasons why the natural trend toward a two-party system should be promoted and why the factors that stand in its way should be removed with the utmost vigor. Unfortunately there are a number of politicians who are in the grip of petty feelings and deliberately build up differences. These men are too narrow-minded to discard petty differences and form a union based upon greater common interests. They are sulky political malcontents who hide behind beautiful phrases such as "remaining loyal through ten years of adversity." The great misfortune of Japan today is the narrow-mindedness of politicians. . . .

I have explained why a fully responsible cabinet system must be adopted if constitutional government is to reach its most perfect development. However, in the West this matter was settled long ago and is hardly an issue any more. If there were a place where this became an issue today, that place would be unexpectedly showing itself to be way behind the times in the development of constitutional government. [pp. 113–20]

As I see it, Japan is, in general, on the right track in this respect. Though the responsible cabinet system has not been fully attained, today everyone seems to hold the firm belief that a vote of nonconfidence in the Diet should inevitably result in the resignation of the cabinet. Consequently it has become the practice for the government always to dissolve the Diet as soon as it sees that a nonconfidence motion is definitely about to be passed. Since December, 1885, when Count Itō . . . first instituted the present cabinet system, there have been about twenty cabinet changes. The great majority of them resulted from clashes with the Diet. Even in the beginning when the principle of nonparty cabinets was asserted, no cabinet could maintain its position in the face of parliamentary opposition. . . . At that time a nonparty cabinet seems to have meant a cabinet which stood aloof from the political parties in the Diet; it does not seem to have meant a cabinet uninfluenced by Diet decisions. Half-way through this thirty year period, Katsura and Saionji inaugurated the custom of alternating with each other as prime minister. Since that time, though the principle of party cabinets has not yet been fully implemented, it has become impossible for anyone to enter the cabinet without allying himself in some fashion or other with the majority forces in the Diet. We should endeavor to promote this tendency and attain a more thorough enforcement of party government. From this point of view, I believe that even though good results might temporarily be achieved with a national unity cabinet, such as has been advocated from time to time, or with the cabinet of "talents" that some schemers have occasionally dreamed of, we must firmly reject these for the sake of the progress of constitutional government. Therefore in this area we must today struggle and contend on an even larger scale. If we are to have the Diet adequately supervise the government and thereby make the Diet in fact the central force in government, I believe it is absolutely essential that we should eradicate the bigoted views [that prevail about party cabinets].

It is essential to the operation of constitutional government that parliament should be the central force in government. This is why we have preached the principle of responsible cabinets. Yet, the West has gone ahead to a still further stage of development. Namely, in one or two countries it is no longer the government that is the powerful obstruction to making parliament, especially the popularly elected house, the central political force. If there is anything today that still somewhat stands in the way of the political supremacy of the popularly elected house, it is the upper house. Hence it has come to be advocated that the lower house should be made supreme over the upper house. . . . Originally the upper house [was established as a body whose] duty it was to give further consideration to the decisions of the lower house because it was felt that the people, whom the lower house represents, were not yet sufficiently well informed. Yet there are some among the masses today who are extremely highly advanced. Accordingly, from the practical point of view, no great harm would come if the restraining powers of the upper house were eliminated and the supremacy of the lower house recognized. [pp. 122–24]

The advanced nations of the West believe the popularly elected house is extremely important to the functioning of constitutional government They believe this because the essence of constitutional government is after all, democracy; and the complete realization of democracy, presupposing as it does the various reforms I have mentioned above, ultimately consists in making the lower house the central political force. Thus intellectuals in all countries are extremely anxious to give the lower house both in form and in fact a position of supremacy over the upper house and the government. In Japan the meaning of a responsible cabinet is only now becoming clear. Though this is cause for rejoicing, we must at the same time regret very much that the authority of the lower house, which directly represents the power of the people, is not very important. This is partly because the legislators that comprise it are not as yet endowed with knowledge and dignity. No matter how important the lower house ought to be in the governmental system, the authority of the nation will never be vested in it if those who actually make up its membership consist solely of mediocre, unprincipled fools. Because able men are not attracted into it, it lacks the authority to deal with the upper house; and when a cabinet is formed the unseemly truth is that at the very least the prime minister must be sought outside of the lower house. As long as the lower house lacks able men, it will lack power; as long as it lacks power, men of promise will seek careers elsewhere. In this vicious circle the wisdom of the responsible cabinet system cannot be fully demonstrated. Under the present circumstances it is useless for the lower house to assume an air of importance. Screaming that the lower house should be respected will not endow it with any actual power. In this matter, we must on the one hand earnestly seek self-respect and strenuous effort from the legislators; on the other, we must ardently hope that the people will not go astray in elections, and that they will not neglect to spur on, indirectly and directly, the legislators whom they have chosen. As regards the Elder Statesmen and other upper class politicians, we must earnestly hope that they do not assume an attitude of detached loftiness, of useless disparagement of the lower house and of disdain for the power of the people's representatives. We must earnestly hope that as Japanese they too will, like us, cooperate for the sake of the nation in the task of strengthening the lower house. [pp. 128–30]

MINOBE TATSUKICHI
Defense of the "Organ" Theory
("Clearing up a Misinterpretation of a Constitutional Theory")

Minobe Tatsukichi (1873–1948) was professor of constitutional law at Tokyo Imperial University from 1900 to 1934. As early as 1911 he had expounded his famous theory that the emperor was an organ of the State. At that time conservative scholars attacked his theory, but as a result of Minobe's vigorous

[239]

and effective defense, it became generally accepted among legal scholars. With the growing ultranationalism of the 1930s, however, the attack on Minobe was renewed. In February, 1934, General Baron Kikuchi Takeo denounced Minobe's theory in the House of Peers. The selection below is the refutation Minobe published a few days later in the *Imperial University News*. This answer shows very clearly what Minobe meant when he called the emperor an organ of the State. It also illustrates the principles of constitutional interpretation employed by him in his lifelong endeavor to give a liberal content to the forms of government devised by the Meiji oligarchs. Moreover, we have here a demonstration of the clever way in which Minobe was able to bring to the support of his arguments the hallowed symbols of the past. In addition, one sees with what devastating logic Minobe could hoist the enemy on his own petard.

Unfortunately, logic was not enough in the Japan of the 1930s. In February, 1935, Baron Kikuchi resumed his attack in the House of Peers. The following month both houses of the Diet passed resolutions demanding that the government "clarify the national polity." In April the Home Ministry banned all of Minobe's writings which had any reference to the organ theory, including the present selection. Minobe resigned his seat in the House of Peers and just barely escaped trial for lese majesty. (One might add just barely escaped with his life, for in February, 1936, an extremist assaulted and wounded him.) On October 1, 1935, the cabinet announced its determination to eradicate the organ theory and initiated measures which culminated in the publication of *Fundamentals of Our National Polity* (*Kokutai no Hongi*).

[From Minobe, *Gikai seiji no kentō*, pp. 337–47]

In a speech . . . delivered on February 7 at a session of the House of Peers Baron Kikuchi Takeo touched upon the theories of constitutional law taught at the Imperial University. He did not mention me by name but he cited one of my works and quoted a passage from it which he made out to be contrary to our national polity. He thundered that if such theories were not stamped out the future of the nation would be endangered. For a person with the slightest knowledge of constitutional law this attack does not require any refutation. However, a work of mine has been publicly cited at a session of the House of Peers and the whole Imperial University slandered. For the honor of the University, if for no other reason, I think it necessary to say a word about these irresponsible utterances.

As extracted from the minutes of the House of Peers the exact wording of that part of the Baron's speech which was concerned with my book is as follows:

"Nevertheless, there are books which today advocate this; among them one called something like *Kempō Satsuyō,* which is used at the Imperial University. . . . When you take a look at this book, you find that edition after edition has been published without there being eliminated from it the theory that the emperor is an organ of the State and other doctrines which are in contradiction to our national polity. Merely to think of our emperor as the same as the Chinese emperor or . . . any Western sovereign is, I believe, to forfeit the spirit of our national polity. If we do not stamp out the thought of scholars and politicians who think in that way, the future of the nation is threatened.

"This textbook emphasizes the influence of actual circumstances and vigorously expounds logic and the law of reason. It says that even though the words of the Constitution remain the same, the interpretation of these words may gradually come to be changed. . . . If possible, it would be preferable to change the problems on the Higher Civil Service Examination. The chairman or any other member of the Higher Civil Service Examination Committee who believes in this kind of idea should be thrown out. That is what I think."

These are his comments on my theory of the Constitution. He cited three points which he claimed were subversive of the national polity: 1) the theory that the emperor is an organ of the State; 2) the theory that the nation's law changes under the influence of actual circumstances; 3) the theory that even though the words of the nation's law are not altered there may be changes in its official interpretation.

I am second to none in my deeply rooted conviction that our unique national polity is our people's greatest glory and that therein partly lies the strength of the nation. The greatest duty of the people is to clarify the concept of our national polity and to support and uphold it.

However, I do not think the national polity is at all being upheld when a person who obviously has no understanding of scholarship arbitrarily rejects the theories of others, uselessly maintains narrow-minded opinions, and in the name of "national polity" tries to impede the development of serious learning. On the contrary, it is to be feared that such behavior will have an unfavorable effect upon the national polity.

As for the three points which, in a very fragmentary way, he cited from my book, it is simply his failure to understand my theories that makes him think them contrary to our national polity.

[241]

The scholarly validity of the theory that the sovereign is an organ of the State is an old chestnut which has already been under discussion for many years. Since the settled opinion of the academic world has already arrived at its foreordained conclusion, it does not seem at all necessary to discuss it again now. The idea that the theory is contrary to our national polity is a fallacy which arises, in the first place, from a misunderstanding of the term "organ" as it is used in jurisprudence.

To say that the sovereign is an organ of the nation merely expresses the idea that the sovereign governs not for his own private ends but for the ends of the whole nation. Article IV of the Constitution clearly states that the emperor is the "head of state." This means that if the nation is likened to the human body, the emperor occupies the position of its head. Prince Itō in his *Commentaries on the Constitution* says in this connection: ". . . just as the brain in the human body is the primitive source of all mental activity manifested through the four limbs and the different parts of the body." Needless to say, the brain is just one of man's organs, but it is the pivotal and paramount organ. In other words, the emperor-organ theory is identical in meaning with the Constitution's statement that the emperor is the head of state. It has no other meaning than that.

If it is denied that the ruler is an organ of the nation, how is the relationship between the ruler and the nation to be interpreted? There are only two interpretations possible: either the ruler is regarded as identical with the nation and therefore *is* the nation; or the nation is the passive object of the ruler's governing.

It is plain that the idea the ruler *is* the nation cannot be accepted in its literal sense. Since the foundation of the Japanese state there has been only one Japan; the one and the same nation has been in continuous existence. Yet from the Emperor Jimmu to the present emperor there have been 124 rulers. How then can one say that the ruler and the nation are identical? The nation is a community of the ruler and the people; both the ruler and the people are together the main elements which constitute the nation. If the people were all eliminated, how would it be possible for the ruler alone to constitute the nation? To come now to the idea that the nation is the passive object of the ruler's governing, this makes the nation something inanimate and devoid of energies and therefore is contrary to a completely sound national spirit. How is it possible to arouse a sense of patriotism if the nation is regarded as a dead object without energies? The Imperial Rescript granted on the promulgation of the Constitution says: "We consider both the prosperity of the nation and the welfare of Our subjects to be Our foremost joy and glory."

Also in the Preamble to the Constitution there are the words: ". . . hoping to maintain the progress of the nation in concert with our subjects . . ."

How would it be possible for a lifeless object to prosper, to maintain progress? The idea of a nation prospering or progressing assumes as its basic premise that the nation is a vital, dynamic entity comparable to a living body. The emperor is its head and occupies the position of its paramount organ.

Baron Kikuchi says that those who advocate the emperor-organ theory regard our emperor as on a par with monarchs in foreign countries. How naively he argues! He seems completely incapable of differentiating between the assertion that two things belong to the same conceptual category and the assertion that two things are regarded as identical. This manner of thinking would lead to a person believing that because Japan is a nation and Russia is a nation, Japan and Russia are identical; or that because red is a kind of color and white is a kind of color, there is no difference between red and white. A person who does not accept this way of thinking will not be able to approve the Baron's argument.

As for his second point, one does not have to go to the length of studying foreign countries in order to see that a nation's law is transformed and changed by the influence of actual circumstances. A mere glance at a few pages of Japanese history shows it to be a fact no one can dispute.

To give just one example, it would be well to consider why the Taihō Code, the most complete set of laws in our medieval period, became invalid. To this very day it has not been formally repealed. That code gradually ceased to be enforced and finally completely died out simply as a result of changes in circumstances. In other words, the force of actual circumstances resulted in one of the nation's written laws crumbling of itself into decay.

If a second instance is required, the interpellation which the Baron himself made proves in itself the point. The Baron is probably aware of the reason for this. Section 48 of the Law of the Houses provides that in order to ask a question of the government a member of the Diet has to secure the backing of thirty or more members of his House, prepare a statement embodying the substance of his question, have this statement signed by his backers, and then submit this document to the president of his House. However, the Baron made his interpellation of the Minister of Commerce and Industry individually and orally: he was seconded by no one, and he prepared no document embodying the substance of his inquiry. This clearly contravened the provisions of the Law of the Houses. The Baron might say that his speech was not an inquiry within the meaning of the Law of the Houses but rather a question directed to a minister's speech. However, his question was occasioned by no matter that appeared in any speech by any minister, and particularly not by the Minister of Commerce and Industry, who did not speak at all. It was nominally a question directed at a minister's speech, but in substance it was purely an inquiry to the government. And yet it did not meet the requirements for an inquiry laid down in the Law of the Houses. Thus, from the standpoint of the express provisions of the Law of the Houses, the Baron's speech was clearly irregular. On what grounds does the Baron think such a speech is permissible? It is only because among parliamentary precedents there has been established the tradition that under the guise of a question directed toward a minister's speech a Diet member may ask questions about any aspect of administration, even those not touched upon by the minister. In other words, under the influence of a precedent, i.e., actual circumstances, the provisions of the Law of the Houses have to this extent been changed. If it were not admitted that the nation's law changes under the influence of actual circumstances, the Baron would not have been allowed to make such an interpellation. In view of this, I wonder if he has the temerity to deny that the nation's law alters under the influence of actual circumstances?

The Baron also says that "the influence of actual circumstances is stressed to the utmost," but if he has reference to my text this is a falsehood entirely without foundation. I merely take into account that as an objective legal phenomenon there is the fact that a nation's law changes under the influence of actual circumstances. It is obvious to any one who reads my books that I am not one who emphasizes "to the utmost" actual circumstances.

In contrast, consider the following words which the Baron spewed forth in his speech: "Since they are soldiers, they may do something reckless; for those who believe they are acting out of patriotism may do anything." Ought not such a remark be regarded as an incitement to use force to destroy the nation's law?

When it comes to the Baron's third point, there are abundant examples showing that even though there may be no alteration in its phraseology, the nation's law may change because the official interpretation has changed. For those who have some knowledge of jurisprudence and have investigated juridical precedents, this is axiomatic and needs no explanation.

I will give a few familiar examples. 1) Take the case where an emergency ordinance issued under Article VIII of the Constitution has been submitted to the Diet but when the Diet ends it has as yet been neither approved nor disapproved. Originally the government's interpretation was that the emergency ordinance continued to be fully effective. However, since the Ōkuma cabinet the official interpretation has been altered and in [such] . . . circumstances the cabinet is obliged immediately to proclaim that for the future the ordinance has ceased to be valid. [Example 2 omitted] 3) During the period of the Satsuma and Chōshū cabinets the purpose of a Diet dissolution was interpreted to be an alteration in the composition of a House of Representatives which was not properly discharging its functions. It resembled a kind of chastisement. Consequently, it was thought that there was no objection to the same cabinet's dissolving the Diet as many times as it wished. However, since the Ōkuma cabinet the official interpretation has been changed, and it is now held that a Diet dissolution is effected in order to ask the people for a vote of confidence. 4) . . . . This is another example of how in connection with the same constitutional text there have been changes in interpretation.

Many more instances of this kind could be cited. After all, words are imperfect means of expressing thought. Frequently a given text is susceptible of a variety of interpretations. It is quite natural that through changes in interpretation alterations should be made in the nation's law even though the text remains the same.

The Baron denounced the fact that I expound the law of reason. This merely demonstrates his failure to reflect on the matter sufficiently. I hear that after his speech he discussed with his friends the possibility of offering a resolution to censure the Minister of Commerce and Industry. Since the Minister resigned, the matter ended without the resolution being introduced. However, several years ago the House of Peers did pass a resolution which censured an action of the then prime minister, Tanaka, as being thoughtless and imprudent. I wonder what the Baron thinks are the legal grounds upon which such a resolution of censure is permitted? Nowhere in the Law of the Houses, nor, of course, in the Constitution, is there any provision which accords such a right to the House of Peers. It can be explained only through the law of reason. If the Baron does not recognize the law of reason, how can he defend himself against the criticism that such a resolution is not permitted by the Constitution?

To sum up, the Baron delivered in a public forum a speech which cited my book, criticized my theories, and even defamed the honor of my university and the Higher Civil Service Examination Committee. I think we can conclude that it was a thoughtless speech with absolutely no foundation in fact. It is all right to expound the dignity of our national polity. The advocacy of the Japanese spirit is also to be warmly welcomed. However, great harm will be done our nation and society if a person with bigoted views based upon a smattering of knowledge, thinking himself alone to be a defender of the national polity and a supporter of the Japanese spirit, makes out those who have opinions differing from his own to be traitorous rebels subversive of the national polity and lacking in respect for the Japanese spirit, and then proceeds under the shelter of the "national polity" to shackle their freedom of speech. One of the greatest merits of the Japanese spirit is the virtue of tolerance. One does not have to go far back into history to seek examples of a bountiful imperial clemency which, once peace had been restored, pardoned even those who had taken up arms against the Throne and thus been stigmatized as rebels. In the reign of the Meiji Emperor we find signal instances of this. Indeed, this act of the emperor in not hating even rebels against the Throne must be considered the very essence of the Japanese spirit. Even though they style themselves believers in Japanese principles, that gang which wantonly prides itself upon attacking and entrapping others is at great variance with the true Japanese spirit.

PEACEFUL COOPERATION ABROAD

Baron Shidehara Kijūrō (1872–1951) is so closely identified with the peaceful and cooperative policies usually followed by Japan in the 1920s that they have come to be designated as "Shidehara diplomacy." From

1915 to 1919 he was vice-minister of foreign affairs. In 1921–22 he was a chief delegate to the Washington Conference, a gathering whose outcome typifies his diplomacy since it provided for naval disarmament, for security in the Pacific through international agreement, and for conciliation of China by a settlement of the Shantung Question. In 1924–1927 and again in 1929–1931 he held the post of foreign minister in the *Kenseikai* and *Minseitō* cabinets. Largely as a result of the high regard in which he was held by foreign opinion, Shidehara came to play a prominent role in the political life of Japan after the Second World War, serving as prime minister in 1945–1946.

SHIDEHARA KIJŪRŌ
A Rapprochement with China

This is an extract from a policy statement which Shidehara made to the Diet on January 21, 1930. It is a good illustration of his conciliatory attitude toward China and his sympathetic regard for the problems created by the Nationalist Revolution.

[From *Documents on International Affairs,* 1930, pp. 180–82]

In China endless scenes of internal commotion and strife have in the past from year to year presented themselves. They have not only caused untold misery and hardships to the Chinese people themselves, but have also exercised a most harmful influence upon our political and economic relations with China. Nothing was more gratifying to us than to witness the measure of success which the Nationalist Government, through tremendous efforts, was able to attain in 1928 in the great enterprise of effecting a national unification. Having regard, however, to the historical and geographical background of China, and other conditions surrounding her, we are not blind to the many difficulties with which any attempt at the establishment of peace and unity in all parts of that vast country will necessarily have to grapple. As a matter of fact, the political situation in China began once more to show signs of unrest in the spring of last year. Recent indications are more reassuring, but the future alone can tell if the crisis has been averted once and for all.

We in Japan have only to look forward with sympathy and patience to the achievement of their task by those who have been devoting their attention and energy to composing China's existing difficulties. We cannot, however, dismiss from our mind an apprehension born out by various instances in history that, in any country faced with similar troubles, the temptation may grow strong for men in power to resort to an adventurous foreign policy with a view to diverting the minds of the people from internal to external affairs. It would be needless to point out that, in our modern world, a policy repugnant to all sense of reason and moderation can scarcely tend to enhance the prestige of a nation, or to serve the purpose for which it is intended. I sincerely trust that the responsible statesmen of China will avoid all such temptations, and will proceed to work out their own country's destiny by steady and measured steps.

The future of Sino-Japanese relations is variously viewed in this country. There are pessimists who maintain that, however fair and liberal a course Japan may steer, China will never meet us half-way, but will be swayed by considerations of domestic politics and assume towards us an attitude more wanton than ever, which would only be calculated to aggravate the situation. Others entertain a more optimistic view. They hold that all the suspicion and mistrust which the Chinese people have hitherto harbored toward Japan rest on no substantial grounds, and that, with better understanding on China's part of our real motives, there must come a better relationship between the two peoples. They further anticipate that the stabilization of the internal political status of the Chinese government will be followed by a reorientation of China's foreign policies upon more moderate and normal lines.

I am not here to pass judgment either way upon these conflicting views. In any case, whatever response we may receive at the hands of the Chinese, we are determined to exert our best efforts to regulate our relations with China on a basis which we believe to be just and fair. Our peculiarly close relations with China, and more especially the complexity and variety of their ramifications, are naturally bound to give rise to questions from time to time calling for diplomatic treatment, and tending to excite the feelings either of the Japanese or of the Chinese people.

If, however, one takes a broader view of the future well-being of both China and Japan, one will be satisfied that there is no other course open to the two nations than to pursue the path of mutual accord and cooperation in all their relations, political and economic. Their real and lasting interests, which in no way conflict but have much in common with each other, ought to be a significant assurance of their growing *rapprochement*. If the Chinese people awaken to these facts and show themselves responsive to the policy so outlined, nothing will more conduce to the mutual welfare of both nations. Should they, on the contrary, fail to understand us, and seek trouble with us, we can at least rest assured of our strong position in the public opinion of the world.

International Cooperation and Arms Reduction

This extract from the ten-point policy statement issued by the *Minseitō* cabinet when it assumed office in July, 1929, further elucidates Shidehara's foreign policy and at the same time shows how his thinking influenced that of the political party cabinet with which he had become associated.

[From Amako, *Heimin Saishō Hamaguchi Yūkō*, pp. 13–19; *Tōkyō Asahi Shimbun,* July 10, 1929, p. 6]

IMPROVEMENT OF RELATIONS WITH CHINA

One of the most urgent needs of the day is the improvement of Sino-Japanese relations and the deepening of a neighborly friendship between the two countries. In connection with changes in the "unequal treaties," our policy of friendly cooperation with China has already been demonstrated in a practical way by the holding of the Special Customs Conference and the Extraterritoriality Conference. In view of the present developments in China this administration recognizes the necessity of increasingly carrying out this policy. In their relations each country must understand and give sympathetic consideration to the special viewpoint of the other, and thereby seek a fair and impartial point of balance. To chase about aimlessly after minor interests is not the way to preserve the main interest. To move troops about rashly is not the way to enhance the national prestige. What this administration desires is co-existence and co-prosperity. Especially in the economic relations between the two countries must there be free and untrammeled development. Our country is determined not only to reject an aggressive policy for any part of China but also to offer willingly our friendly cooperation in the attainment of the aspirations of the Chinese people. Nevertheless, it is the undoubted duty of this government to preserve those legitimate and important rights which are indispensable to our nation's prosperity and existence. We believe that the Chinese people also will fully understand this. This administration will emphasize the improvement of relations between the empire and the other powers, and the encouragement of mutual commerce and enterprise. We must be ever vigilant against being too partial to the political point of view and failing to give due consideration to economic relations. The improvement of our international financial position depends primarily upon the peaceful development of commerce and overseas enterprises. In view of our present position among the powers it is also the high destiny of our country to contribute to the peace of the world and the happiness of mankind by cooperating in the activities of the League of Nations. This administration attaches great importance to the League of Nations and will make every effort to help in the realization of its aims.

PROMOTION OF ARMS LIMITATION

At this time we must, in cooperation with the other powers, resolutely promote the establishment of an international agreement. The object of this agreement should not be restricted merely to the limitation of arms but should include substantial reductions in arms. The empire's sincere attitude in this matter has already often been demonstrated. Although plans for such an agreement have repeatedly met with difficulties in the past, public demand is more intense, and the time is becoming ripe for the accomplishment of this cherished desire. It is believed that the consummation of this great world undertaking will not be difficult if each power approaches this matter in a spirit of mutual conciliation and, taking into consideration the special situation of each country, provides equally for the security of all.

YAMAMURO SŌBUN
Call for a Peaceful Japan

The following is taken from a speech made in December, 1929, by Yamamuro Sōbun (1880–1950), an important Mitsubishi executive who was at that time president of the Mitsubishi Trust Company. It indicates one important source of support for Shidehara's policies and the reasons behind that support. Shidehara was married to a member of the family which owned the Mitsubishi enterprises, and the *Minseitō*, it will be remembered, was popularly believed to receive a substantial part of its funds from Mitsubishi.

[From Yamamuro Sōbun, *Waga kuni keizai oyobi kin'yū*, pp. 292–93]

When we consider [the state] of Japan's national economy, when we think of our scarcity of natural resources, when we reflect upon today's international situation, [the solution to our problems might seem to lie in] either the seizure of dependencies under a policy of aggression or the establishment of a Monroe Doctrine. Nevertheless, there is absolutely no place in Japan's future for [these policies]. Japan can keep itself a going concern only by means of international cooperation. Under this policy of international cooperation we can get along by producing goods of the highest possible quality at the lowest possible price, thereby expanding our foreign markets to the greatest [extent] possible. A country as deficient in natural resources as Japan buys raw materials from foreign countries at low prices and processes [these materials] at a low cost. Of course, circumstances peculiar to Japan have [modified] our development. For example, silk has been an important item. However, in addition to encouraging the expansion of this industry we must endeavor through a policy of international cooperation to establish our country as an international industrial producer of international commodities. To that end we must do our best to create an amicable atmosphere in international relations. If we have the reputation of liking war or of being militarists, [a policy of] international cooperation will be impossible. We must resolutely follow a policy of peace. It is essential to make all foreigners feel that the Japanese have been converted from their old religion and have become advocates of peace. For that reason we must as far as possible eliminate international barriers. In that sense, a commercial treaty with China is probably necessary. For this same purpose, the abolition of unnecessary tariffs is also required. I wonder if the best way to manage the post-resumption [1] financial world is not to eliminate the various international barriers, to adopt a viewpoint as similar as possible to that of the foreigner and to maintain close cooperation with foreigners.

[1] That is, after Japan returned to the Gold Standard, Jan. 1930.

CHAPTER XXVII

THE RISE OF REVOLUTIONARY NATIONALISM

The Meiji Period was marked by the rapid growth of Japanese national-ism. In the 1870s most Japanese, except for the literate samurai, were still unconscious of and indifferent to national affairs, but by the end of the century Japan demonstrated striking national unity and determination on matters of national and international concern.

This consciousness of belonging and of participation on the part of the Japanese people was the product of many things. Mass education, which made Japan the first literate Asian nation, made it possible to activate the populace by means of the press. Conscription broadened the horizons of peasant youths who served in various parts of the country they would not otherwise have seen. Industrial developments which unified the country through better communications brought foreign goods and ideas to all the coastal population centers. The centralization policies of the Meiji govern-ment standardized administration throughout the country and weakened the force of particularist customs and dialects. The growing scope of constitutional government increased the responsibilities and interests of community leaders. And Japan's successful wars were both the products and the causes of bursts of national self-confidence. The victory over China in 1895, followed hard by the refusal of Germany, France, and Russia to allow Japan to occupy the Kwantung peninsula in Manchuria, and the victory over Russia in 1905, followed by the annexation of Korea in 1910, provided proof of Japanese accomplishment together with evi-dence of further problems and responsibilities which would require still greater national determination and effort.

Together with the growth of Japanese nationalism—a growth which was not unlike the development of nationalism in the nineteenth-century West—came the growth of extremist ultranationalism. The ultranationalists feared that Japan was becoming too "Western," and they appealed to ancient and feudal traditions in fighting for their cause. The ultranationalists maintained consistent pressure on their government and countrymen for expansion abroad and orthodoxy at home.

The ultranationalists were indignant because of injustices, real and fancied, which the West had inflicted on Japan. In the Meiji Period they could complain about the unequal treaties. In later years Western criticism of Japanese imperial aspirations and Western restrictions on Japanese immigration and trade served to convince them of continued oppression and interference. The ultranationalists were also resentful of what they considered an excessive influx of Western ideas and institutions into modern Japan. They were at all times sharply critical of Japanese infatuated with Western ways of doing things, and they insisted on a priority for Japanese ideas and institutions—ideas and institutions which culminated in the person and symbol of the emperor. And, since Japanese ideas and institutions were superior to those of the West, and since the West was constantly threatening to envelop Japan and the rest of Asia into its economic and ideological sphere, the ultranationalists were convinced that it was Japan's mission to lead and protect Asia. They were critical of their government when it seemed to neglect opportunities for such leadership, and they were cooperative with it when it proved alive to its mission. Thus the main stream of the ultranationalist movement was vigorously xenophobic, emperor-centered, and Asia-conscious.

Yet it would be a dangerous oversimplification to imagine this main stream as a consistent and a distinct group at all times. There was a large area of agreement between the ultranationalists and others who were less willing to resort to extremist measures. And internally the ultranationalist movement represented a complicated picture of personal and regional cliques whose standards and objectives shifted frequently in response to the dictates of opportunism.

In terms of social thought and political influence at home the Japanese ultranationalists attained their true significance only in the twentieth century. Until the time of the First World War their chief efforts were expended on behalf of a vigorous foreign policy. But although the themes and emphases of agitation shifted, the make-up of the leadership group of twentieth-century extremist organizations was for long related to that of the patriotic societies formed early in the Meiji Period.

[253]

JAPAN AND ASIA

In 1881 a group of disgruntled ex-samurai of Fukuoka formed the *Genyōsha*. They took this name from the *Genkainada,* the body of water which lies between Fukuoka and the Asiatic mainland, and in so doing they signified their determination to work for a vigorous policy of expansion in Asia. Tōyama Mitsuru (1855–1944) and the other leaders of this organization were alarmed by the extent of social and ideological change that had followed the overthrow of the feudal regime, and they were indignant because of the treatment given the warrior class. They considered themselves highminded idealists like the samurai of Restoration days, and they were able to attract youthful activists prepared to show, by deeds of individual heroism and violence, their sincerity in opposing the "Western" policies of the Meiji government. One of their number, who very nearly succeeded in assassinating Foreign Minister Ōkuma in 1889, was thereafter honored by an annual ceremony of rededication. New deeds of valor, as when a Foreign Office official was murdered in 1913, drew new recruits for the cause of "Japanism."

The *Genyōsha* members at first cooperated with the liberal parliamentarians, but they soon saw that the interests of expansionist groups in the military and business worlds lay closer to their own. They harbored and helped revolutionaries and reformers from Korea and China who sought asylum in Japan, and they encouraged trips to the mainland for commerce and espionage by their friends. They did their best to speed the war with China which came in 1894, and thereafter they turned to the problem of Russia.

In 1901 the *Genyōsha* leaders formed the Amur Society (*Kokuryūkai,* literally, Black Dragon Society). Tōyama and his friends threatened government leaders who sought for agreement with Russia, they sponsored trips into Siberia and Korea and the study of Russian, and they helped to establish liaison with Manchurian bandit groups for the coming war.

Yet despite their idealism, their denunciation of the government, and opposition to the corrupting influence of money and big business on the national morality, the patriotic society leaders did not hesitate to accept financial help from interested individuals in the Westernized industrial world whose influence they professedly sought to curb. They received support from some sectors of the business world, from secret army funds, and at times from other government agencies. In addition they were involved in many questionable transactions on the borderline between legitimate business and labor racketeering. They were not "secret societies," for they made every attempt for full publicity to exaggerate their influence. Neither were they mass societies; they preferred to remain small elite groups clustered around charismatic leaders.

After the defeat of Russia most of Japan's overseas aspirations seemed satisfied. But the ultranationalists were not therefore lacking in material for indignation and agitation; domestic issues now came to the fore. After the First World War a larger and more restless proletariat worried some of them, and in the countryside resentful tenant farmers, unable to maintain the standard of living they had achieved during the war, grew mutinous. Patterns of familial obligation and imperial loyalty seemed endangered by social reformism, internationalism, democracy, and communism. Moreover, Japan's post-Meiji government, dominated by big business, showed a willingness to enter international agreements for naval limitation, and it also sought to ward off Chinese nationalist agitation by a milder policy on the mainland. In the meantime restrictions upon Japanese trade and immigration increased. By the end of the 1920s the world Depression and the resulting distress in Japan provided ultranationalists with persuasive arguments against the business leaders and their moderation in foreign policy.

The patriotic societies thus turned to fight subversion at home. At the same time they kept alive—and elaborated on—their exploits of the past in order to recreate the sense of urgency and of destiny which had been theirs in the Meiji Period.

An Anniversary Statement by the Amur Society

In 1930 the Amur Society (*Kokuryūkai*) prepared for its thirtieth anniversary a two-volume *Secret History of the Annexation of Korea* which stressed the prominent part which the Society had played in that achievement. To this history was added a history of the Society's past activities and an explanation of its future intentions. The document ends with a statement of rededication for the future. Although the Society has here shifted its emphases considerably, it will be seen that its principal program is little different from that which featured the activities of the early group of ultranationalists in Fukuoka.

[From *Nikkan gappō hishi,* I, Appendix, pp. 1-4]

Today our empire has entered a critical period in which great zeal is required on the part of the entire nation. From the first, we members of the Amur Society have worked in accordance with the imperial mission for overseas expansion to solve our overpopulation; at the same time, we have sought to give support and encouragement to the peoples of East Asia. Thus we have sought the spread of humanity and righteousness throughout the world by having the imperial purpose extend to neighboring nations.

Earlier, in order to achieve these principles, we organized the Heavenly Blessing Heroes in Korea in 1894 and helped the Tong Hak rebellion there in order to speed the settlement of the dispute between Japan and China. In 1899 we helped Aguinaldo in his struggle for independence for the Philippines. In 1900 we worked with other comrades in helping Sun Yat-sen start the fires of revolution in South China. In 1901 we organized this Society and became exponents of the punishment of Russia, and thereafter we devoted ourselves to the annexation of Korea while continuing to support the revolutionary movement in China. At all times we have consistently centered our efforts on the solution of problems of foreign relations, and we have not spared ourselves in this cause.

During this period we have seen the fulfillment of our national power in the decisive victories in the two major wars against China and Russia, in the annexation of Korea, the acquisition of Formosa and Sakhalin, and the expulsion of Germany from the Shantung peninsula. Japan's status among the empires of the world has risen until today she ranks as one of the three great powers, and from this eminence she can support other Asiatic nations. While these achievements were of course attributable to the august virtue of the great Meiji emperor, nevertheless we cannot but believe that our own efforts, however slight, also bore good fruit.

However, in viewing recent international affairs it would seem that the foundation established by the great Meiji emperor is undergoing rapid deterioration. The disposition of the gains of the war with Germany was left to foreign powers, and the government, disregarding the needs of national defense, submitted to unfair demands to limit our naval power.

Moreover, the failure of our China policy made the Chinese more and more contemptuous of us, so much so that they have been brought to demand the surrender of our essential defense lines in Manchuria and Mongolia. Furthermore, in countries like the United States and Australia our immigrants have been deprived of rights which were acquired only after long years of struggle, and we now face a highhanded anti-Japanese expulsion movement which knows no bounds. Men of purpose and of humanity who are at all concerned for their country cannot fail to be upset by the situation.

When we turn our attention to domestic affairs, we feel more than deep concern. There is a great slackening of discipline and order. Men's hearts are become corrupt. Look about you! Are not the various government measures and establishments a conglomeration of all sorts of evils and abuses? The laws are confusing, and evil grows apace. The people are overwhelmed by heavy taxes, the confusion in the business world complicates the livelihood of the people, the growth of dangerous thought threatens social order, and our national polity, which has endured for three thousand years, is in danger. This is a critical time for our national destiny; was there ever a more crucial day? What else can we call this time if it is not termed decisive?

And yet, in spite of this our government, instead of pursuing a farsighted policy, casts about for temporary measures. The opposition party simply struggles for political power without any notion of saving our country from this crisis. And even the press, which should devote itself to its duty of guiding and leading society, is the same. For the most part it swims with the current, bows to vulgar opinions, and is chiefly engrossed in money making. Alas! Our empire moves ever closer to rocks which lie before us. Yet the captains and navigators are men of this sort! Truly, is this not the moment for us to become aroused?

Our determination to rise to save the day is the inescapable consequence of this state of affairs. Previously our duty lay in the field of foreign affairs, but when we see internal affairs in disorder how can we succeed abroad? Therefore we of the Amur Society have determined to widen the scope of our activity. Hereafter, besides our interest in foreign affairs, we will give unselfish criticism of internal politics and of social problems, and we will seek to guide public opinion into proper channels. Thereby we will, through positive action, continue in the tradition of our past. We will establish a firm basis for our organization's policy and, through co-operation with other groups devoted to similar political, social, and ideological ideals, we are resolved to reform the moral corruption of the people, restore social discipline, and ease the insecurity of the people's livelihood by relieving the crises in the financial world, restore national confidence, and increase the national strength, in order to carry out the imperial mission to awaken the countries of Asia. In order to clarify these principles, we here set forth our platform to all our fellow patriots:

PRINCIPLES

We stand for Divine Rulership (*tennō shugi*). Basing ourselves on the fundamental teachings of the foundation of the empire, we seek the extension of the imperial influence to all peoples and places and the fulfillment of the glory of our national polity.

PLATFORM

1. Developing the great plan of the founders of the country, we will widen the great Way (*tao*) of Eastern culture, work out a harmony of Eastern and Western cultures, and take the lead among Asian peoples.

2. We will bring to an end many evils, such as formalistic legalism; it restricts the freedom of the people, hampers common sense solution, prevents efficiency in public and private affairs, and destroys the true meaning of constitutional government. Thereby we will show forth again the essence of the imperial principles.

3. We shall rebuild the present administrative systems. We will develop overseas expansion through the activation of our diplomacy, further the prosperity of the people by reforms in internal government, and solve problems of labor and management by the establishment of new social policies. Thereby we will strengthen the foundations of the empire.

4. We shall carry out the spirit of the Imperial Rescript to Soldiers and Sailors and stimulate a martial spirit by working toward the goal of a nation in arms. Thereby we look toward the perfection of national defense.

5. We plan a fundamental reform of the present educational system, which is copied from those of Europe and America; we shall set up a

basic study of a national education originating in our national polity. Thereby we anticipate the further development and heightening of the wisdom and virtue of the Yamato race.

AGITATION BY ASSASSINATION

The displeasure with the business world shown by the Amur Society document above was shared by all groups of the Japanese ultranationalist movement. It was logical that leaders of the business world should have been early targets for extremists. Their tremendous wealth contrasted strikingly to the poverty of the masses, and it showed a success in personal ("selfish") aims which contrasted to the declared selflessness of the disinterested "idealists" who pursued them. The business leaders were chief agents of the cosmopolitanism which the ultranationalist feared. With the decline in number of the *genrō* and the decline in prestige of the army in the years after the First World War, the businessmen advanced to the center of the political stage. Their control of and contributions to the political parties which formed cabinets during the Taishō Period resulted in periodic disclosures of scandals and corruption. Since the extremists felt that existing laws had been framed to protect the wrongdoers, they had to resort to extralegal violence to achieve their end.

The manner of this violence provided some features which set the Japanese ultranationalist movement off from the fascist movements in Germany and Italy. While Hitler and Mussolini strove for large scale organizations and a mass following, the Japanese fanatics concentrated on individual heroics. They felt that a few spectacular acts of protest by idealists willing to sacrifice their lives would suffice to force major changes in the political and social order. In this belief they followed honored Japanese traditions, for the loyalist patriots of Restoration days also exploited fully the possibilities of self-sacrifice and of political and ideological assassination. But most of the Japanese fanatics were quite unprepared with a blueprint for action to be taken once they succeeded in breaking down the old order. As one of the assassins in a plot which cost Prime Minister Inukai's life in 1932 explained, "We thought about destruction first. We never considered taking on the duty of construction.

We foresaw, however, that the destruction once accomplished, somebody would take charge of construction." Thus the first step was to consist of individual, uncoordinated acts of violence against representative figures in society.

ASAHI HEIGO
Call for a New "Restoration"

The first important murder in the campaign against the capitalist leaders came a full decade before the ultranationalist terrorism of the 1930s. On September 3, 1921, Asahi Heigo, a leader of the *Shinshū Gidan,* or Righteousness Corps of the Divine Land, assassinated Yasuda Zenjirō, head of the Yasuda *zaibatsu* house, at Yasuda's home. Asahi left a statement explaining his reasons which illustrates his thorough contempt for the established political and social leaders. Like the young army officers of the 1930s who worked for a "Shōwa Restoration," Asahi called for a "Taishō Restoration" (*Taishō* being the reign name of the emperor ruling from 1912–1926, and *Shōwa* of his successor, known to the West as Hirohito).

[From Shinobu Seisaburō, *Taishō seiji shi,* III, 749–51]

The *genrō* set up the model, and today our political affairs are run by scoundrels. Fujita Densaburō became a baron by making counterfeit bills by order of Itō Hirobumi. Ōkura [another *zaibatsu* house] became a baron by contributing a part of the money he dishonestly made through selling canned goods containing pebbles. Yamamoto Gombei [a premier whose cabinet was overthrown in 1914 by the discovery of corruption in warship contracts] built an enormous fortune by his performance in the Siemens warship scandal. Ōkuma, Yamagata, and other old notables are wealthy now because of their corruption while in office. The *Kenseikai* is backed by Iwasaki [head of the Mitsubishi interests] and the *Seiyūkai* [the government party] raises its campaign funds from the South Manchurian Railroad and from opium. The other statesmen and dignitaries too are all skilled in evil-doing and they work with only self-interest in mind. And while the great individual fortunes have been built up by Mitsui, Iwasaki, Ōkura, Asano, Kondo, Yasuda, Furukawa, and Suzuki, the other plutocrats are no better. . . .

Alas, this is a time of danger. Foreign thought contrary to our national polity has moved in like a rushing torrent. The discontent of the needy masses who have been mistreated for long years by this privileged class but who have hitherto kept their bitter feelings deeply hidden is now being stirred up. The cold smiles and reproachful eyes of the poor show that they are close to brutality. There is a growing likelihood that the desperation of the people will take account of neither the nation nor the emperor.

Some of our countrymen are suffering from tuberculosis because of overwork, filth, and undernourishment. Others, bereaved, become street-walkers in order to feed their beloved children. And those who were once hailed as defenders of the country are now reduced to beggary simply because they were disabled in the wars. . . . Moreover, some of our countrymen suffer hardships in prison because they committed minor crimes under the pressure of starvation, while high officials who commit major crimes escape punishment because they can manipulate the laws.

The former feudal lords, who were responsible for the death of our ancestors by putting them in the line of fire, are now nobility and enjoy a life of indolence and debauchery. Men who became generals by sacrificing our brothers' lives in battle are arrogantly preaching loyalty and patriotism as though they had achieved the victory all by themselves.

Consider this seriously! These new nobles are our enemies because they drew a pool of our blood, and the former lords and nobles are also our foes, for they took our ancestors' lives.

My fellow young idealists! Your mission is to bring about a Taishō Restoration. These are the steps you must take:

1. Bury the traitorous millionaires.
2. Crush the present political parties.
3. Bury the high officials and nobility.
4. Bring about a universal suffrage.
5. Abolish provisions for inheritance of rank and wealth.
6. Nationalize the land and bring relief to tenant farmers.
7. Confiscate all fortunes above 100,000 yen.
8. Nationalize big business.
9. Reduce military service to one year.

These are initial steps. But the punishment of the traitorous millionaires is the most urgent of all these, and there is no way of doing this except to assassinate them resolutely.

Finally, I want to say a word to my colleagues. I hope that you will live up to my principles. Do not speak, do not get excited, and do not be conspicuous. You must be quiet and simply stab, stick, cut, and shoot. There is no need to meet or to organize. Just sacrifice your life. And work out your own way of doing this. In this way you will prepare the way for the revolution. The flames will start here and there, and our fellow idealists will band together instantly. So forget about self-interest, and do not think about your own name or fame. Just die, just sleep. Never seek wisdom, but take the road of ignorance and come to know the height of great folly.[1]

THE PLIGHT OF THE COUNTRYSIDE

In contrast to the cult of the all-powerful State which distinguished the ultranationalist movements in Europe, a great deal of Japanese ultranationalism was marked by a nostalgic longing for the values of primitive agrarian society. Several theorists turned from the evils of their society to envision a society with less government, more local autonomy, and more closely knit ties of familial solidarity. These ties would of course culminate in the person of the emperor as father of the nation, but the total structure they envisioned would necessarily remain very different from the highly centralized and industrialized society which Japan was developing.

The most influential exponents of this position were Tachibana Kosaburō (still alive) and Gondō Seikei (1866–1937). Both of them owed much to traditional Taoist-utopian ideals of social organization. Tachibana wrote that a state could exist forever only under agrarian communalism, and he warned that "Japan cannot be herself if separated from the earth." Gondō, for his part, felt that Japan had been founded on the principle of autonomous living, in which "the sovereign does not go far beyond setting examples, thereby giving his people a good standard." Gondō felt that the small-scale groupings of society in primitive times were the only natural and desirable ones, and his writings show a profound distrust of big government and big army.

Together with this praise of primitive society came laments for the distress of the villagers in modern Japan. Victimized by big government,

[1] A notion adapted from the Chinese Taoist classics, *Lao Tzu* and *Chuang Tzu*.

big business, and by the burden of the wasteful military. the villagers were being deprived of their autonomy and their livelihood. Instead of the equality of primitive communalism, Japanese society was showing a very unhealthy class differentiation. For Tachibana this was an evil of urbanization; "according to a common expression," he wrote, "Tokyo is the hub of the world. But I regret to say that Tokyo appears to me nothing but a branch shop of London." Gondō too lamented the decline of agrarian life, "the foundation of the country and the source of habits and customs," while "Tokyo and other cities have expanded out of all proportion to agrarian villages and are built up with great tall buildings." Inequalities of this sort presaged the doom of what he called the "bureaucratic administration patterned after the Prussian style of nationalism."

Thus the agrarian-conscious rightists found traditional grounds for a strong attack against their society. They did not entirely renounce industrialization and machinery, for it had its necessary role in livelihood and national defense. But the unjust social structure upon which Japan's modern society rested was, they thought, likely to make all plans for defense and reform go wrong.

Writings of this sort had a considerable appeal to the young officers in the army. By the Shōwa Period Japan's officer corps was no longer dominated by members of the samurai class, but it was increasingly drawn from the countryside and the peasantry. Discontented with what they saw in the urban sector of Japanese life, unable to understand why their senior commanders worked with the politicians and businessmen, the young officers were prepared to accept Gondō's explanation that the military clique was just another wing of the bureaucratic ruling class.

GONDŌ SEIKEI

The Gap between the Privileged Classes and the Commoners

Gondō's works, *Principles of Autonomous People* (*Jichi mimpan*) and *Essay on the Self Salvation of Farm Villages* (*Nōson jikyū ron*), were written during the years of the Great Depression when distress in the villages was most acute. His writings served in a measure as the ideology of the young officers who struck down Premier Inukai in May of 1932. Gondō himself, however, had little or no connection with the extremists who were moved to action by his writings.

[From Gondō, *Jichi mimpan*, pp. 185–88]

It was during this period [the late nineteenth century] that the criminal law was codified, civil law was codified, the system of cities, towns, and villages was put into effect, and the protection of private fortunes was really established on the principle of property rights. This made those who profit without working and the members of the privileged classes the pampered favorites of the state. The bureaucracy, the *zaibatsu,* and the military became the three supports of the state, the political parties attached themselves to them, and the scholars fawned upon them. These groups allied with each other through marriage and they all combined to form a single group. In a country so ordered, it is quite obvious that no matter how it may be kept up in the future, the nation's military affairs cannot be supported by means of the privileged class of military alone. I am not an advocate of disarmament nor am I a pacifist. I have a sincere desire for adequate national defense. For that very reason I have strong misgivings about the present system of military preparation. Leaving aside a detailed discussion for another time, I will say here only that even if we train millions of soldiers, unless we are able to produce the weapons and necessary supplies in quantity, the soldiers in the line will be no more than puppets. It is well known that our numbers of primary and secondary reserves and our capacity to train troops and supply material are military secrets, and there is no use in trying to be specific about them. But actually it is a deplorable state of affairs. The situation had its origin in the period after the Russo-Japanese War, when one faction rashly added to the number of people living on army appropriations in order to add to the prestige of the military clique.

The change in popular sentiment in all nations after the First World War, largely a result of economic theories, was also reflected in great changes in this country. Moreover, with the Russian Revolution, the disorders on the China mainland, the ebb and flow of Eastern and Western old and new thought, took place partly in response to economic pressures and partly to scientific advance. The idea of a militaristic, Prussian nationalism declined into such a foul state of decay that not even the dogs would eat it. If only Japan had, in accord with the spirit of the times, persevered in this course, might she not have been able to take her place at the world game-board? But there seems to be something more or less frightening in any sort of militaristic administration. Let me explain. The empty gesture of reducing strength by four divisions was carried out. Yet in spite of this military appropriations have not been reduced in the slightest. There is nothing very assuring about such slipshod management of affairs in this critical period of change, and in the wake of the earthquake and fire [of 1923].

In militaristic states, whether of early or recent times, the plutocracy never fails to come out on top. When the plutocrats conspire with those who hold political power, the resources of the people fall under their control almost before one is aware of what is happening. When this happens, the common people fall upon evil days; they are pursued by cold and hunger, and unless they work in the midst of their tears as tools of the plutocrats and those holding political power they cannot stay alive. When people are pursued by hunger and have to work tearfully in the face of death, what sort of human rights do you suppose remain? Already the country's basic resources—land, raw materials, the machinery of transport and finance, mines, fishing grounds—are, for the most part, becoming the private property of a small number of powerful capitalists. In this setting have come labor disputes and tenantry problems. In the beginning, the capitalists held themselves aloof from these, but as their base became stronger and as they furthermore established close contacts with various parts of European society, they were the ones who, when the European labor practices came to be stressed, set up various institutions to smooth adjustments. These then became a part of the general social policy, and the government too began step by step to set up similar bureaus; they talked about reforms. The government's new social bureaus, and the setting up of officials concerned with tenantry, are all precious items of this sort. But trying to reconcile capital and labor by such means in these times makes about as much sense as trying to find fish by climbing trees. In prosperous times, Bismarck's social policies might have secured a certain degree of tranquillity in Germany for a while. Now, however, not only do the laborers and tenants themselves see through the capitalists and politicians, but the amount of knowledge built up by scholarly research and pragmatic study which tends to support the laborers and tenants is actually coming to exceed that of the scholars who are hirelings of the capitalists or who comprise some of the trash in the bureaucracy. If only they could work with the backing of the law, some of the temporizing measures of those in power could probably be carried out, but actually it is totally unrealistic to expect cooperation or reforms.

[265]

Since the conditions under which the people live are in fact as I have indicated, the foundations of the military regime cannot be secure. To be sure, the military officers, men who hold office for life, are guaranteed an adequate living, and so they are usually conspicuously loyal, brave, and noble. And indeed they have to be. But the soldiers who dutifully have to shed their blood are all sons and brothers of the common people. The great majority of these soldiers were born in poverty and hardship; they entered the barracks, and then had to submit to the orders of their superior officers. As the sons and brothers of the common people, they will not under any circumstances forget that they are themselves common people. If, then, we infer what goes on in their minds, and take this problem of the commoners' plight and the privileged classes as proportionate, think of the changes that will take place in men's hearts; look back on the labor and tenant problems—from disturbance to struggle, and from struggle, what will come? Granted, it is the army's duty to maintain peace and order, but the good and obedient soldiers in the ranks whom you are leading are for the most part the sons and brothers of the impoverished common people. They are certainly not people who are serving to kill the common people. No, they are persons who offer their lives and bodies for the sake of the wider public morality.

KITA IKKI AND THE REFORM WING OF ULTRANATIONALISM

A group of revolutionaries headed by Kita Ikki stood out in sharp contrast to the primitive utopians like Gondō Seikei. These were men well-read in the radical literature of the West, and they owed more to Marx than they did to Lao Tzu. Their praise of imperial divinity and perfection was combined with some very sharp criticism of the Imperial Household and its works. They called for radical changes in Japanese society and institutions, and held out the promise that a revolutionary Japan would be able to take the lead in a union of resurgent Asiatic peoples.

Kita Ikki (1884–1937) was the most important spokesman for this group. Born the son of a struggling *sake* brewer on the island of Sado, he became interested in socialism at an early age. His desire to promote a revolutionary Asia led him to join the circle of adventurers and Amur Society members who cooperated with the nationalist revolution of Sun Yat-sen in China.

Kita was in China during the revolution of 1911, and his chagrin at the failure of that revolution to bring about a democratic China had a profound effect on his later thought. His *An Unofficial History of the Chinese Revolution* (*Shina kakumei gaishi*) criticized the Japanese activists in China for placing their reliance upon Sun Yat-sen, whom Kita now saw as a superficial user of Western slogans, instead of working for a better balance of Western and Oriental ideologies. Kita's early socialism was now becoming more "Oriental"; henceforth he would call for a blend of Western revolutionary thought and Oriental wisdom which he called Japanism. Kita also criticized the policy of the Japanese authorities in China. In particular he resented the maneuverings of the *zaibatsu* houses whose offers of loans had, it seemed to him, helped to drive the Chinese revolutionaries into their compromise with the conservative Yuan Shih-k'ai in order to avoid Japanese exploitation. Thus Kita, remaining convinced of the inevitability of a revolutionary Asia, now saw the need for profound changes in Japanese society to enable Japan to assume the leadership in the new Asia. Selfish *zaibatsu* would have to be curbed, corrupt politicians would be done away with, and the Imperial Household itself must undergo changes to free it from the crippling influence of the timid bureaucrats who were at the beck and call of their *zaibatsu*-political party colleagues.

There can be no mistaking the genuine radicalism of Kita's views. He advocated sweeping changes in all sectors of Japanese society—seizure and nationalization of major industries and fortunes, an eight-hour work day, and a land reform program. Nor is there much doubt of his proclivity to extremism. His 1926 preface hailed the murderer of Yasuda Zenjirō, Asahi Heigo, as a man whose ideology had been based on the spirit of his own writings. Kita himself had strong ties with the young officers whose concern over Japan's China policy played such an important role in the military *putsches* of the 1930s. He was involved with the *Kōdō ha* (Imperial Way faction), the radical group responsible for the mutiny which began with a wave of assassination attempts and ended with the seizure of central Tokyo on February 26, 1936. Arrested then, Kita was executed in 1937. His book, banned until the end of the Second World

War, was reprinted thereafter by men who held that Kita's gloomy forebodings about the need for a thorough reformation of Japanese society as a prerequisite to leadership of a revolutionary Asia had been amply borne out by the events which followed his death.

KITA IKKI

Plan for the Reorganization of Japan

An Outline Plan for the Reorganization of Japan (Nihon kaizō hōan taikō) contained Kita's suggestions for changes necessary in Japanese society. Written in 1919 while Kita was still in Shanghai, the book was printed secretly and passed from hand to hand by Kita's associates. In 1920 its distribution was forbidden by the police. In 1923, after major excisions, the book was published, only to be banned again shortly afterward. A third edition came in 1926, but it too was later banned.

The *Outline Plan,* of which the opening section is given below, consists of cryptic announcements of steps to be taken followed by notes which justify the steps and anticipate probable objections.

[From *Nihon kaizō hōan,* pp. 6–14]

At present the Japanese empire is faced with a national crisis unparalleled in its history; it faces dilemmas at home and abroad. The vast majority of the people feel insecure in their livelihood and they are on the point of taking a lesson from the collapse of European societies, while those who monopolize political, military, and economic power simply hide themselves and, quaking with fear, try to maintain their unjust position Abroad, neither England, America, Germany, nor Russia has kept its word, and even our neighbor China, which long benefited from the protection we provided through the Russo-Japanese War, not only has failed to repay us but instead despises us. Truly we are a small island, completely isolated in the Eastern Sea. One false step and our nation will again fall into the desperate state of crisis—dilemmas at home and abroad—that marked the period before and after the Meiji Restoration

The only thing that brightens the picture is the sixty million fellow countrymen with whom we are blessed. The Japanese people must develop a profound awareness of the great cause of national existence and of the people's equal rights, and they need an unerring, discriminating grasp of the complexities of domestic and foreign thought. The Great War in Europe was, like Noah's flood, Heaven's punishment on them for arrogant and rebellious ways. It is of course natural that we cannot look to the Europeans, who are out of their minds because of the great destruction, for a completely detailed set of plans. But in contrast Japan, during those five years of destruction, was blessed with five years of fulfillment. Europe needs to talk about reconstruction, while Japan must move on to reorganization. The entire Japanese people, thinking calmly from this perspective which is the result of Heaven's rewards and punishments, should, in planning how the great Japanese empire should be reorganized, petition for a manifestation of the imperial prerogative establishing "a national opinion in which no dissenting voice is heard, by the organization of a great union of the Japanese people." Thus, by homage to the emperor, a basis for national reorganization can be set up.

Truly, our seven hundred million brothers in China and India have no path to independence other than that offered by our guidance and protection. And for our Japan, whose population has doubled within the past fifty years, great areas adequate to support a population of at least two hundred and forty or fifty millions will be absolutely necessary a hundred years from now. For a nation, one hundred years are like a hundred days for an individual. How can those who are anxious about these inevitable developments, or who grieve over the desperate conditions of neighboring countries, find their solace in the effeminate pacifism of doctrinaire socialism? I do not necessarily rule out social progress by means of the class struggle. But still, just what kind of so-called science is it that can close its eyes to the competition between peoples and nations which has taken place throughout the entire history of mankind? At a time when the authorities in the European and American revolutionary creeds have found it completely impossible to arrive at an understanding of the "gospel of the sword" because of their superficial philosophy, the noble Greece of Asian culture must complete her national reorganization on the basis of her own national polity. At the same time, let her lift the virtuous banner of an Asian league and take the leadership in a world federation which must come. In so doing let her proclaim to the world the Way of Heaven in which all are children of Buddha, and let her set the example which the world must follow. So the ideas of people like those who oppose arming the nation are after all simply childish.

Suspension of the Constitution. In order for the emperor and the entire Japanese people to establish a secure base for the national reorganization, the emperor will, by a show of his imperial prerogative, suspend the Constitution for a period of three years, dissolve both houses of the Diet, and place the entire nation under martial law.

(Note 1: In extraordinary times the authorities should of course ignore harmful opinions and votes. To regard any sort of constitution or parliament as an absolute authority is to act in direct imitation of the English and American semisacred "democracy." Those who do so are the obstinate conservatives who hide the real meaning of "democracy"; they are as ridiculous as those who try to argue national polity on the basis of the [Shintō mythological] High Plain of Heaven. It cannot be held that in the discussion of plans for naval expansion Admiral Tōgō's vote was not worth more than the three cast by miserable members of the Diet, or that in voting on social programs a vote by Karl Marx is less just than seven cast by Ōkura Kihachirō. The effect of government by votes which has prevailed hitherto is really nothing more than a maintenance of the traditional order; its puts absolute emphasis on numbers and ignores those who would put a premium on quality.)

(Note 2: Those who look upon a *coup d'état* as an abuse of power on behalf of a conservative autocracy ignore history. Napoleon's *coup d'état* in refusing to cooperate with reactionary elements offered the only out for the Revolution at a time when the parliament and the press were alive with royalist elements. And even though one sees in the Russian Revolution an incident in which Lenin dissolved with machine guns a parliament filled with obstructionists, the popular view is still that a *coup d'état* is a reactionary act.)

(Note 3: A *coup d'état* should be looked upon as a direct manifestation of the authority of the nation; that is, of the will of society. The progressive leaders have all arisen from popular groups. They arise because of political leaders like Napoleon and Lenin. In the reorganization of Japan there must be a manifestation of the power inherent in a coalition of the people and sovereign.)

(Note 4: The reason why the Diet must be dissolved is that the nobility and the wealthy upon whom it depends are incapable of standing with the emperor and the people in the cause of reorganization. The necessity for suspension of the Constitution is that these people seek protection in the law codes enacted under it. The reason martial law must be proclaimed is that it is essential for the freedom of the nation that there be no restraint in suppressing the opposition which will come from the above groups.

However, it will also be necessary to suppress those who propagate a senseless and half-understood translation of outside revolutionary creeds as the agents of reorganization.)

The True Significance of the Emperor. The fundamental doctrine of the emperor as representative of the people and as pillar of the nation must be made clear.

In order to clarify this a sweeping reform of the imperial court in the spirit of the Emperor Jimmu in founding the state and in the spirit of the great Meiji emperor will be carried out. The present Privy Councillors and other officials will be dismissed from their posts, and in their place will come talent, sought throughout the realm, capable of assisting the emperor.

A Consultative Council (*Kōmonin*) will be established to assist the emperor. Its members, fifty in number, will be appointed by the emperor.

A member of the Consultative Council must tender his resignation to the emperor whenever the cabinet takes action against him or whenever the Diet passes a vote of nonconfidence against him. However, the Council members are by no means responsible to either the cabinet or to the Diet.

(Note 1: Japan's national polity has evolved through three stages, and the meaning of "emperor" has also evolved through three stages. The first stage, from the Fujiwara to the Taira, was one of absolute monarchy. During this stage the emperor possessed all land and people as his private property in theory, and he had the power of life and death over the people. The second stage, from the Minamoto to the Tokugawa, was one of aristocracy. During this period military leaders and nobility in each area brought land and people of their locality under their personal control; they fought wars and made alliances among themselves as rulers of small nations. Consequently the emperor's significance was different from what it had been. He now, like the Roman pope, conferred honor upon the *Bakufu*, the leader of the petty princes, and showed himself the traditional center of the national faith. Such a development can be compared with the role of the Roman pope in crowning the Holy Roman Emperor, leader of the various lords in the Middle Ages in Europe. The third stage, one of a democratic state, began with the Meiji Revolution, which emancipated the samurai and commoners, newly awakened, from their status as private property of their shōgun and feudal lords. Since then the emperor has a new significance as the true center of government and politics. Ever since, as the commanding figure in the national movement and as complete representative of the modern democratic country, he has become representative of the nation. In other words, since the Meiji Revolution Japan has become a modern democratic state with the emperor as political nucleus. Is there any need whatever for us to import a direct translation of the "democracy" of others as though we lacked something? The struggle between those who stubbornly talk about national polity and those who are infatuated with Europe and America, both without a grasp of the background of the present, is a very ominous portent which may cause an explosion between the emperor and the people. Both sides must be warned of their folly.)

(Note 2: There is no scientific basis whatever for the belief of the democracies that a state which is governed by representatives voted in by the electorate is superior to a state which has a system of government by a particular person. Every nation has its own national spirit and history. It cannot be maintained, as advocates of this theory would have it, that China during the first eight years of the republic was more rational than Belgium, which retained rule by a single person. The "democracy" of the Americans derives from the very unsophisticated theory of the time which held that society came into being through a voluntary contract based upon the free will of individuals; these people emigrating from each European country as individuals, established communities and built a country. But their theory of the divine right of voters is a half-witted philosophy which arose in opposition to the theory of the divine right of kings at that time. Now Japan certainly was not founded in this way, and there has never been a period in which Japan was dominated by a half-witted philosophy. Suffice it to say that the system whereby the head of state has to struggle for election by a long winded self-advertisement and by exposing himself to ridicule like a low-class actor seems a very strange custom to the Japanese people, who have been brought up in the belief that silence is golden and that modesty is a virtue.)

(Note 3: The imperial court today has restored corrupt customs of the Middle Ages and has moreover added others which survived in European courts; truly it has drifted far from the spirit of the founder of the nation —a supreme commander above an equal people. The revolution under the great Meiji emperor restored and modernized this spirit. Accordingly at that time a purification of the imperial court was carried out. The necessity for doing this a second time is that when the whole national structure is being reorganized fundamentally we cannot simply leave the structure of the Court in its present state of disrepair.)

(Note 4: The provision for censure of members of the Consultative Council by cabinet and Diet is required in view of the present situation in which many men do as they wish on the excuse that they are duty-bound to help the Emperor. The obstinacy and arrogance of the members of the Privy Council is not very different from that of the court officials in Russia before the revolution. The men who cause trouble for the emperor are men of this kind.)

The Abolition of the Peerage System. The peerage system will be abolished, and the spirit of the Meiji Restoration will be clarified by removal of this barrier which has come between the emperor and the people.

The House of Peers will be abolished and replaced by a Council of Deliberation (*Shingiin*), which shall consider action taken by the House of Representatives.

The Council of Deliberation will be empowered to reject decisions taken by the House of Representatives a single time. The members of the Council of Deliberation will consist of distinguished men in many fields of activity, elected by each other and appointed by the emperor.

(Note 1: The Restoration Revolution, which destroyed government by the aristocracy, was carried out determinedly, for it also confiscated the estates of the aristocracy. It went much farther than did European countries, for with the single exception of France they were unable to dispose of the medieval estates of earlier days. But with the death of men like the great Saigō, who embodied the revolutionary spirit, men like Itō Hirobumi, with no understanding of our advancement, and men who simply acted as attendants in the Revolution, imitated and transplanted

[273]

backward aristocratic and medieval privileges which had survived in Western countries. To abolish the peerage system is to abandon a system translated directly from Europe and to return to the earlier Meiji Revolution. Do not jump to the conclusion that this is a shortcoming we are seeking to correct. We have already advanced farther than some other countries as a democratic country.)

(Note 2: The reason a bicameral system is subject to fewer errors than a unicameral system is that in very many cases public opinion is emotional, uncritical and changeable. For this reason the upper house will be made up of distinguished persons in many fields of activity instead of medieval relics.)

Universal Suffrage. All men twenty-five years of age, by their right as people of Great Japan, will have the right, freely and equally, to stand for election to and to vote for the House of Representatives. The same will hold for local self-government assemblies.

Women will not have the right to participate in politics.

(Note 1: Although a tax qualification has determined suffrage in other countries and this system was first initiated in England, where the Parliament was originally set up to supervise the use of tax money collected by the Crown, in Japan we must establish it as a fundamental principle that suffrage is the innate right of the people. This universal suffrage must not be interpreted as a lowering of the tax qualification on grounds that all men pay at least indirect taxes. Rather, suffrage is a "duty of the people" in the same sense that military service is a "duty of the people.")

(Note 2: The duty of the people to defend the country cannot be separated from their duty to participate in its government. As this is a fundamental human right of the Japanese people, there is no reason why the Japanese should be like the slaves in the Roman Empire or like the menials driven from the imperial gate during the monarchical age—simply ruled, having to live and die under orders from a ruling class. Nothing can infringe upon the right and duty of suffrage under any circumstances. Therefore officers and soldiers on active service, even if they are overseas, should elect and be elected without any restrictions.)

(Note 3: The reason for the clear statement that "Women will not have the right to participate in politics" is not that Japanese women today have not yet awakened. Whereas the code of chivalry for knights in medieval Europe called for honoring women and gaining their favor, in medieval apan the samurai esteemed and valued the person of woman on approximately the same level as they did themselves, while it became the accepted ode for women to honor the men and gain their favor. This complete ontrast in developments has penetrated into all society and livelihood, nd continues into modern history—there has been agitation by women or suffrage abroad while here women have continued devoted to the ask of being good wives and wise mothers. Politics is a small part of uman activity. The question of the place of women in Japan will be atisfactorily solved if we make an institutional reorganization which vill guarantee the protection of woman's right to be "mother of the nation nd wife of the nation." To make women accustomed to verbal warfare s to do violence to their natural aptitude; it is more terrible than using hem in the line of battle. Anyone who has observed the stupid talkaiveness of Western women or the piercing quarrels among Chinese vomen will be thankful that Japanese women have continued on the ight path. Those who have developed good trends should let others vho have developed bad trends learn from them. For this reason, one peaks today of a time of fusion of Eastern and Western civilization. But he ugliness of direct and uncritical borrowing can be seen very well in the natter of woman suffrage.)

The Restoration of the People's Freedom. The various laws which ave restricted the freedom of the people and impaired the spirit of the onstitution in the past—the Civil Service Appointment Ordinance, the 'eace Preservation police law, the Press Act, the Publication Law, and imilar measures—will be abolished.

(Note: This is obviously right. These laws work only to maintain all orts of cliques.)

The National Reorganization Cabinet. A Reorganization Cabinet will e organized while martial law is in effect; in addition to the present ninistries, it will have ministries for industries and several Ministers of tate without Portfolio. Members of the Reorganization Cabinet will not e chosen from the present military, bureaucratic, financial, and party liques, but this task will be given to outstanding individuals selected hroughout the whole country.

All the present prefectural governors will be dismissed from their ffices, and National Reorganization Governors will be appointed by the ame method of selection as given above.

(Note: This is necessary for the same reasons that the Meiji Revolution could not have been carried out by the Tokugawa shogun and his vassals. But a revolution cannot necessarily be evaluated according to the amount of bloodshed. It is just as impossible to say of a surgical operation that it was not thorough because of the small amount of blood that was lost. It all depends on the skill of the surgeon and the constitution of the patient undergoing the operation. Japan today is like a man in his prime and in good health. Countries like Russia and China are like old patients whose bodies are in total decay. Therefore, if there is a technician who takes a far-sighted view of the past and present, and who draws judiciously on East and West, the reorganization of Japan can be accomplished during a pleasant talk.)

The National Reorganization Diet. The National Reorganization Diet elected in a general election and convened during the period of martial law, will deliberate on measures for reorganization.

The National Reorganization Diet will not have the right to deliberate on the basic policy of national reorganization proclaimed by the emperor.

(Note 1: Since in this way the people will become the main force and the emperor the commander, this *coup d'état* will not be an abuse of power but the expression of the national determination by the emperor and the people.)

(Note 2: This is not a problem of legal philosophy but a question of realism; it is not an academic argument as to whether or not the emperor of Russia and Germany were also empowered with such authority, but it is a divine confidence which the people place only in the Emperor of Japan.)

(Note 3: If a general election were to be held in our present society of omnipotent capital and absolutist bureaucracy the majority of the men elected to the Diet would either be opposed to the reorganization or would receive their election expenses from men opposed to the reorganization. But, since the general election will be held and the Diet convened under martial law, it will of course be possible to curb the rights of harmful candidates and representatives.)

(Note 4: It is only because there was such a divine emperor that despite the fact that the Restoration Revolution was carried out with greater thoroughness than the French Revolution, there was no misery and disorder. And thanks to the existence of such a godlike emperor

apan's national reorganization will be accomplished a second time in
an orderly manner, avoiding both the massacres and violence of the
Russian Revolution and the snail's pace of the German revolution.)

The Renunciation of the Imperial Estate.[1] The emperor will personally
show the way by granting the lands, forests, shares, and similar property
owned by the Imperial House to the nation.

The expenses of the Imperial Household will be limited to approximately thirty million yen per year, to be supplied by the national treasury.

However, this amount can be increased with consent of the Diet if the
situation warrants such action.

(Note: The present imperial estate began with holdings taken over
from the Tokugawa family, and however the true meaning of the emperor
might shine forth, it is inconsistent to operate such medieval finances.
It is self evident that every expense of the people's emperor should be
born by the nation.)

THE CONSERVATIVE REAFFIRMATION

During the years in which one branch of the ultranationalist movement
turned to suggestions for radical social reforms and produced sweeping
denunciations of existing Japanese society, there were many who were
not prepared to follow such a headlong course. By the 1930s a sharp
cleavage between social radicals and ideological conservatives was apparent.

The conservatives met the problems of social change and unrest by a
reaffirmation of the unique values of "Japanism." Since they furnished
a safe alternative to the radicalism of the extremists, the conservative
ultranationalists were able to get the financial backing of respected seg-
ments of the business and political world. The National Purity Society
(*Kokusuikai*) was founded in 1919 to ward off foreign ideologies, reaffirm
traditional values of manliness and chivalry, and reawaken loyalty to the
Imperial House. It had close contacts with the leading political party,
the *Seiyūkai*. In social issues like labor disputes it urged mediation or
marshalled force as seemed preferable, usually to the advantage of management. The League to Prevent Bolshevization (*Sekka bōshidan*) was

[1] This entire section was censored in pre-war editions.

formed in 1921 to fight socialism and communism, and it was unreservedly opposed to labor and radical movements of all kinds. And the National Foundation Society (*Kokuhonsha*) was founded in 1924 to guide the people's ideology, strengthen the foundations of the nation, advance wisdom and virtue, and make clear the essence of the national polity. It was sponsored by Baron Hiranuma Kiichirō, and enjoyed the favor of many highly placed in the bureaucracy, military, and financial worlds.

The conservative societies and spokesmen—among them Ōkawa Shūmei—appealed more to the established and respectable than they did to the young and discontented. Their backers were quite as convinced of international inequality from which Japan suffered as was Kita, but they were more likely to seek solutions through diplomatic and military measures than they were through social reformation.

The violence of the early 1930s, most of it carried out by young followers of the radical ideologists, culminated in the spectacular mutiny of February, 1936. Thereafter it was perfectly clear to all conservatives that strong measures were necessary to preserve social order and military discipline. It seemed a wise compromise to give the military leaders more of a free hand on the continent in return for promises to keep their young extremists under control. Kita Ikki and the leaders of the February Incident were executed after brief and secret trials. In China the army prepared for further measures, while at home its control over production, education, and politics was strengthened.

FUNDAMENTALS OF OUR NATIONAL POLITY

The movement for the enunciation of "national polity," Japan's unique structure of state and society which was based upon a divine emperor, reached its apogee with the publication by the Ministry of Education of *Fundamentals of Our National Polity* (*Kokutai no hongi*) in 1937. This short work, with an initial printing of 300,000 copies and an eventual sale of 2,000,000 or more, was designed to set the ideological course for the Japanese people. Study groups were formed to discuss its content, school teachers were given special commentaries, and a determined effort was made to reach ideological uniformity by guarding against deviation.

The introduction sets forth the underlying problems of contemporary Japanese thought which require a solution: how are Western influences to be absorbed without permitting them to destroy Japanese national traditions, and how may Japan resolve the dilemma created in the West itself by the inherent contradictions of individualism.

A recurrent theme throughout this work is the transcendent importance of the nation and state as manifested in history. In part this may reflect the sympathetic reception given to German philosophy, and particularly that of Hegel, among professional philosophers of Meiji Japan.

[Adapted from Hall and Gauntlett, *Kokutai no hongi*, pp. 52–183]

INTRODUCTION

The various ideological and social evils of present-day Japan are the result of ignoring the fundamental and running after the trivial, of lack of judgment, and a failure to digest things thoroughly; and this is due to the fact that since the days of Meiji so many aspects of European and American culture, systems, and learning, have been imported, and that, too rapidly. As a matter of fact, the foreign ideologies imported into our country are in the main ideologies of the Enlightenment that have come down from the eighteenth century, or extensions of them. The views of the world and of life that form the basis of these ideologies are a rationalism and a positivism, lacking in historical views, which on the one hand lay the highest value on, and assert the liberty and equality of, individuals, and on the other hand lay value on a world by nature abstract, transcending nations and races. Consequently, importance is laid upon human beings and their groupings, who have become isolated from historical entireties, abstract and independent of each other. It is political, social, moral, and pedagogical theories based on such views of the world and of life, that have on the one hand made contributions to the various reforms seen in our country, and on the other have had deep and wide influence on our nation's primary ideology and culture. . . .

Paradoxical and extreme conceptions, such as socialism, anarchism, and communism, are all based in the final analysis on individualism, which is the root of modern Occidental ideologies and of which they are no more than varied manifestations. Yet even in the Occident, where individualism has formed the basis of their ideas, when it has come to communism, they have found it unacceptable; so that now they are about to do away with their traditional individualism, and this has led to the rise of totalitarianism and nationalism and to the springing up of Fascism and Nazism. That is, it can be said that both in the Occident and in our

[279]

country the deadlock of individualism has led alike to a season of ideological and social confusion and crisis. . . . This means that the present conflict seen in our people's ideas, the unrest of their modes of life, the confused state of their civilization, can be put right only by a thorough investigation by us of the intrinsic nature of Occidental ideologies and by grasping the true meaning of our national polity. Then, too, this should be done not only for the sake of our nation but for the sake of the entire human race which is struggling to find a way out of the deadlock with which individualism is faced. [pp. 52, 54–55]

The body of this work presents a résumé of Japanese traditions concerning the founding of the country and of the Imperial House, the virtues of imperial rule and of loyal subjects, manifestations of the Japanese spirit in history, natural features of Japan, and the inherent character of the people, as well as manifestations of these in the social and cultural life of the nation. The following selections focus upon those attitudes of mind thought to represent the best in Japanese tradition, and their superiority over prevailing Western views.

LOYALTY AND PATRIOTISM

Our country is established with the emperor, who is a descendant of Amaterasu Ōmikami, as her center, and our ancestors as well as we ourselves constantly have beheld in the emperor the fountainhead of her life and activities. For this reason, to serve the emperor and to receive the emperor's great august Will as one's own is the rationale of making our historical "life" live in the present; and on this is based the morality of the people.

Loyalty means to reverence the emperor as [our] pivot and to follow him implicitly. By implicit obedience is meant casting ourselves aside and serving the emperor intently. To walk this Way of loyalty is the sole Way in which we subjects may "live," and the fountainhead of all energy. Hence, offering our lives for the sake of the emperor does not mean so-called self-sacrifice, but the casting aside of our little selves to live under his august grace and the enhancing of the genuine life of the people of a State. The relationship between the emperor and the subjects is not an artificial relationship [which means] bowing down to authority, nor a relationship such as [exists] between master and servant as is seen in feudal morals. . . . The ideology which interprets the relationship between the emperor and his subjects as being a reciprocal

[280]

relationship such as merely [involves] obedience to authority or rights and duties, rests on individualistic ideologies, and is a rationalistic way of thinking that looks on everything as being in equal personal relationships. An individual is an existence belonging to a State and her history which forms the basis of his origin, and is fundamentally one body with it. . . .

From the point of individualistic personal relationships, the relationship between sovereign and subject in our country may [perhaps] be looked upon as that between non-personalities. However, this is nothing but an error arising from treating the individual as supreme, from the notion that has individual thoughts for its nucleus, and from personal abstract consciousness. Our relationship between sovereign and subject is by no means a shallow, horizontal relationship such as implies a correlation between ruler and citizen, but is a relationship springing from a basis transcending this correlation, and is that of "dying to self and returning to [the] One," in which this basis is not lost. This is a thing that can never be understood from an individualistic way of thinking. In our country, this great Way has seen a natural development since the founding of the nation, and the most basic thing that has manifested itself as regards the subjects is in short this Way of loyalty. [pp. 80–82]

FILIAL PIETY

In our country filial piety is a Way of the highest importance. Filial piety originates with one's family as its basis, and in its larger sense has the nation for its foundation. Filial piety directly has for its object one's parents, but in its relationship toward the emperor finds a place within loyalty.

The basis of the nation's livelihood is, as in the Occident, neither the individual nor husband and wife. It is the home. . . . A family is not a body of people established for profit, nor is it anything founded on such a thing as individual or correlative love. Founded on a natural relationship of begetting and being begotten, it has reverence and affection as its kernel; and is a place where everybody, from the very moment of his birth, is entrusted with his destiny.

The life of a family in our country is not confined to the present life of a household of parents and children, but beginning with the distant ancestors, is carried on eternally by the descendants. The present life

[281]

of a family is a link between the past and the future, and while it carries over and develops the objectives of the ancestors, it hands them over to its descendants. . . .

Such things as [the carrying on of family traditions] show that the basis of the nation's life is in the family and that the family is the training ground for moral discipline based on natural sympathies. Thus, the life of a household is not a thing confined to the present, but is an unbroken chain that passes through from ancestor to offspring. . . .

The relationship between parent and child is a natural one, and therein springs the affection between parent and child. Parent and child are a continuation of one chain of life; and since parents are the source of the children, there spontaneously arises toward the children a tender feeling to foster them. Since children are extensions of parents, there springs a sense of respect, love for, and indebtedness toward, parents. [pp. 87–89]

LOYALTY AND FILIAL PIETY AS ONE

Filial piety in our country has its true characteristics in its perfect conformity with our national polity by heightening still further the relationship between morality and nature. Our country is a great family nation, and the Imperial Household is the head family of the subjects and the nucleus of national life. . . .

In China, too, importance is laid on filial duty, and they say that it is the source of a hundred deeds. In India, too, gratitude to parents is taught. But their filial piety is not of a kind related to or based on the nation. Filial piety is a characteristic of Oriental morals; and it is in its convergence with loyalty that we find a characteristic of our national morals, and this is a factor without parallel in the world. [pp. 89–91]

HARMONY

When we trace the marks of the facts of the founding of our country and the progress of our history, what we always find there is the spirit of harmony. Harmony is a product of the great achievements of the founding of the nation, and is the power behind our historical growth; it is also a humanitarian Way inseparable from our daily lives. The spirit of harmony is built on the concord of all things. When people determinedly count themselves as masters and assert their egos, there is nothing but contradictions and the setting of one against the other; and

harmony is not begotten. In individualism it is possible to have cooperation, compromise, sacrifice, etc., so as to regulate and mitigate this
contradiction and the setting of one against the other; but after all there
exists no true harmony. That is, a society of individualism is one of clashes
between [masses of] people . . . and all history may be looked upon as
one of class wars. Social structure and political systems in such a society,
and the theories of sociology, political science, statecraft, etc., which are
their logical manifestations, are essentially different from those of our
country which makes harmony its fundamental Way. . . .

Harmony as in our nation is a great harmony of individuals who, by
giving play to their individual differences, and through difficulties, toil
and labor, converge as one. Because of individual differences and difficulties, this harmony becomes all the greater and its substance rich.
Again, in this way individualities are developed, special traits become
beautiful, and at the same time they even enhance the development and
well-being of the whole. [pp. 93–94]

THE MARTIAL SPIRIT

And then, this harmony is clearly seen also in our nation's martial
spirit. Our nation is one that holds *bushidō* in high regard, and there are
shrines deifying warlike spirits. . . . But this martial spirit is not [a
thing that exists] for the sake of itself but for the sake of peace, and
is what may be called a sacred martial spirit. Our martial spirit does not
have for its objective the killing of men, but the giving of life to men.
This martial spirit is that which tries to give life to all things, and is not
that which destroys. That is to say, it is a strife which has peace at its
basis with a promise to raise and to develop; and it gives life to things
through its strife. Here lies the martial spirit of our nation. War, in this
sense, is not by any means intended for the destruction, overpowering, or
subjugation of others; and it should be a thing for the bringing about
of great harmony, that is, peace, doing the work of creation by following
the Way. [pp. 94–95]

SELF-EFFACEMENT AND ASSIMILATION

A pure, cloudless heart is a heart which, dying to one's ego and one's
own ends, finds life in fundamentals and the true Way. That means,
it is a heart that lives in the Way of unity between the Sovereign and

his subjects, a Way that has come down to us ever since the founding of the empire. It is herein that there springs up a frame of mind, unclouded and right, that bids farewell to unwholesome self-interest. The spirit that sacrifices self and seeks life at the very fountainhead of things manifests itself eventually as patriotism and as a heart that casts self aside in order to serve the State. . . .

In the inherent character of our people there is strongly manifested alongside this spirit of self-effacement and disinterestedness, a spirit of broadmindedness and assimilation. In the importation of culture from the Asian Continent, too, in the process of "dying to self" and adopting the ideographs used in Chinese classics, this spirit of ours has coordinated and assimilated these same ideographs. To have brought forth a culture uniquely our own, in spite of the fact that a culture essentially different was imported, is due entirely to a mighty influence peculiar to our nation. This is a matter that must be taken into serious consideration in the adaptation of modern Occidental culture.

The spirit of self-effacement is not a mere denial of oneself, but means living to the great, true self by denying one's small self. [pp. 132–34]

BUSHIDŌ

Bushidō may be cited as showing an outstanding characteristic of our national morality. In the world of warriors one sees inherited the totalitarian structure and spirit of the ancient clans peculiar to our nation. Hence, though the teachings of Confucianism and Buddhism have been followed, these have been transcended. That is to say, though a sense of obligation binds master and servant, this has developed into a spirit of self-effacement and of meeting death with a perfect calmness. In this, it was not that death was made light of so much as that man tempered himself to death and in a true sense regarded it with esteem. In effect, man tried to fulfill true life by way of death. . . .

The warrior's aim should be, in ordinary times, to foster a spirit of reverence for the deities and his own ancestors in keeping with his family tradition; to train himself to be ready to cope with emergencies at all times; to clothe himself with wisdom, benevolence, and valor; to understand the meaning of mercy; and to strive to be sensitive to the frailty of Nature. Yamaga Sokō (1622–1685), Matsumiya Kanzan (1686–1780), and Yoshida Shōin (1830–1859) were all men of the devoutest character, who exercised much influence in bringing *bushidō* to perfection. It is this same *bushidō* that shed itself of an outdated feudalism at the time of the Meiji Restoration, increased in splendor, became the Way of loyalty and patriotism, and has evolved before us as the spirit of the imperial forces. [pp. 144-46]

CONCLUSION

The conclusion to this work provides a general critique of current Western social philosophies, and shows how Japanese tradition offers the basis for a new synthesis of Eastern and Western thought. The emphasis upon Japan's historical mission as a creative force in unifying and transcending antithetical tendencies, suggests the expansive, rather than the purely defensive character, of Japanese traditionalism in the twentieth century.

Every type of foreign ideology that has been imported into our country may have been quite natural in China, India, Europe, or America, in that it has sprung from their racial or historical characteristics; but in our country, which has a unique national polity, it is necessary as a preliminary step to put these types to rigid judgment and scrutiny so as to see if they are suitable to our national traits. . . .

To put it in a nutshell, while the strong points of Occidental learning and concepts lie in their analytical and intellectual qualities, the characteristics of Oriental learning and concepts lie in their intuitive and aesthetic qualities. These are natural tendencies that arise through racial and historical differences; and when we compare them with our national spirit, concepts, or mode of living, we cannot help recognizing further great and fundamental differences. Our nation has in the past imported, assimilated, and sublimated Chinese and Indian ideologies, and has therewith supported the Imperial Way, making possible the establishment of an original culture based on her national polity. . . .

Now, when we consider how modern Occidental ideologies have given birth to democracy, socialism, communism, anarchism, etc., we note, as already stated, the existence of historical backgrounds that form the bases of all these concepts, and, besides, the existence of individualistic views of life that lie at their very roots. The basic characteristics of modern Occidental cultures lie in the fact that an individual is looked upon as an existence of an absolutely independent being, all cultures comprising the perfection of this individual being who in turn is the creator and determiner of all values. Hence, value is laid on the subjective thoughts of an individual; the conception of a State, the planning of all systems, and the constructing of theories being solely based on ideas conceived in the individual's mind. The greater part of Occidental theories of State and political concepts so evolved do not view the State as being a nuclear existence that gives birth to individual beings, which it transcends, but as an expedient for the benefit, protection, and enhancement of the welfare of individual persons; so that these theories have become expressions of the principles of subsistence which have at their center free, equal, and independent individuals. As a result, there have arisen types of mistaken liberalism and democracy that have solely sought untrammeled freedom and forgotten moral freedom, which is service. Hence, wherever this individualism and its accompanying abstract concepts developed, concrete and historical national life became lost in the shadow of abstract theories; all states and peoples were looked upon alike as nations in general and as individuals in general; such things as an international community comprising the entire world and universal theories common to the entire world were given importance rather than concrete nations and their characteristic qualities; so that in the end there even arose the mistaken idea that international law constituted a higher norm than national law, that it stood higher in value, and that national laws were, if anything, subordinate to it.

The beginnings of modern Western free economy are seen in the expectation of bringing about national prosperity as a result of free, individual, lucrative activities. In the case of the introduction into our country of modern industrial organizations that had developed in the West, as long as the spirit of striving for national profit and the people's welfare governed the people's minds, the lively and free individual activities went very far toward contributing to the nation's wealth; but later, with the dissemination of individualistic and liberal ideas, there gradually arose a tendency openly to justify egoism in economic management and operations. This tendency gave rise to the problem of a chasm between rich and poor, and finally became the cause of the rise of ideas of class warfare; while later the introduction of communism brought about the erroneous idea which looked upon economics as being the basis of politics, morality, and all other cultures, and which considered that by means of class warfare alone could an ideal society be realized.

The fact that egoism and class warfare are opposed to our national polity needs no explanation. Only where the people one and all put heart and soul into their respective occupations, and there is coherence or order in each of their activities, with their minds set on guarding and maintaining the prosperity of the Imperial Throne, is it possible to see a healthy development in the people's economic life.

The same thing holds true in the case of education. Since the Meiji Restoration our nation has adapted the good elements of the advanced education seen among European and American nations, and has exerted efforts to set up an educational system and materials for teaching. The nation has also assimilated on a wide scale the scholarship of the West, not only in the fields of natural science, but of the mental sciences, and has thus striven to see progress made in our scholastic pursuits and to make education more popular. . . . However, at the same time, through the infiltration of individualistic concepts, both scholastic pursuits and education have tended to be taken up with a world in which the intellect alone mattered, and which was isolated from historical and actual life; so that both intellectual and moral culture drifted into tendencies in which the goal was the freedom of man, who had become an abstract being, and the perfecting of the individual man. At the same time, these scholastic pursuits and education fell into separate parts, so that they gradually lost their synthetic coherence and concreteness. In order to correct these tendencies, the only course open to us is to clarify the true nature of our national polity, which is at the very source of our education, and to strive to clear up individualistic and abstract ideas. . . .

In the Occident, too, many movements are now being engaged in to revise individualism. Socialism and communism, which are types of class individualism and which are the opposites of so-called bourgeois individualism, belong to these movements, while recent ideological movements, such as that called Fascism, which are types of nationalism and racial consciousness, also belong to this category. If, however, we sought to correct the evils brought about by individualism in our country and find a way out of the deadlock which it has created, it would not do to adopt such ideas as Occidental socialism and their abstract totalitarianism wholesale, or copy their concepts and plans, or [on the other hand] mechanically to exclude Occidental cultures.

Our present mission as a people is to build up a new Japanese culture by adopting and sublimating Western cultures with our national polity as the basis, and to contribute spontaneously to the advancement of world culture. Our nation early saw the introduction of Chinese and Indian cultures, and even succeeded in evolving original creations and developments. This was made possible, indeed, by the profound and boundless nature of our national polity; so that the mission of the people to whom it is bequeathed is truly great in its historical significance. [pp. 175, 178, 180–83]

THE JUSTIFICATION FOR WAR

However wide the disagreements on matters of domestic policy within the ultranationalist movement, there was unanimity in the face of Western criticism of Japan's imperialistic policies. The two selections which follow illustrate typical lines of argument. Ōkawa Shūmei appeals to Japan's historic mission as the spokesman for and champion of Asia, while Hashimoto Kingorō, a prominent army leader of extremist groups, argues the necessity for expansion.

ŌKAWA SHŪMEI
The Way of Japan and the Japanese
[IMTFE, International Prosecution Section, Document 693A, Exhibit 2180A]

Asia's stubborn efforts to remain faithful to spiritual values, and Europe's honest and rigorous speculative thought, are both worthy of admiration, and both have made miraculous achievements. Yet today it is no longer possible for these two to exist apart from each other. The way of Asia and the way of Europe have both been traveled to the end. World history shows us that these two must be united; when we look at that history up to now we see that this unification is being achieved only through war. Mohammed said that "Heaven lies in the shadow of the sword," and I am afraid that a struggle between the great powers of the East and the

West which will decide their existence is at present, as in the past, absolutely inevitable if a new world is to come about. The words "East-West struggle," however, simply state a concept and it does not follow from this that a united Asia will be pitted against a united Europe. Actually there will be one country acting as the champion of Asia and one country acting as the champion of Europe, and it is these who must fight in order that a new world may be realized. It is my belief that Heaven has decided on Japan as its choice for the champion of the East. Has not this been the purpose of our three thousand long years of preparation? It must be said that this is a truly grand and magnificent mission. We must develop a strong spirit of morality in order to carry out this solemn mission, and realize that spirit in the life of the individual and of the nation.

HASHIMOTO KINGORŌ

The Need for Emigration and Expansion
[From Hashimoto, *Addresses to Young Men*, IMTFE, International Prosecution Section, Document 487B, Exhibit 1290]

We have already said that there are only three ways left to Japan to escape from the pressure of surplus population. We are like a great crowd of people packed into a small and narrow room, and there are only three doors through which we might escape, namely emigration, advance into world markets, and expansion of territory. The first door, emigration, has been barred to us by the anti-Japanese immigration policies of other countries. The second door, advance into world markets, is being pushed shut by tariff barriers and the abrogation of commercial treaties. What should Japan do when two of the three doors have been closed against her?

It is quite natural that Japan should rush upon the last remaining door.

It may sound dangerous when we speak of territorial expansion, but the territorial expansion of which we speak does not in any sense of the word involve the occupation of the possessions of other countries, the planting of the Japanese flag thereon, and the declaration of their annexation to Japan. It is just that since the Powers have suppressed the circulation of Japanese materials and merchandise abroad, we are looking for some place overseas where Japanese capital, Japanese skills and Japanese labor can have free play, free from the oppression of the white race.

We would be satisfied with just this much. What moral right do the world powers who have themselves closed to us the two doors of emigration and advance into world markets have to criticize Japan's attempt to rush out of the third and last door?

If they do not approve of this, they should open the doors which they have closed against us and permit the free movement overseas of Japanese emigrants and merchandise. . . .

At the time of the Manchurian incident, the entire world joined in criticism of Japan. They said that Japan was an untrustworthy nation. They said that she had recklessly brought cannon and machine guns into Manchuria, which was the territory of another country, flown airplanes over it, and finally occupied it. But the military action taken by Japan was not in the least a selfish one. Moreover, we do not recall ever having taken so much as an inch of territory belonging to another nation. The result of this incident was the establishment of the splendid new nation of Manchuria. The Powers are still discussing whether or not to recognize this new nation, but regardless of whether or not other nations recognize her, the Manchurian empire has already been established, and now, seven years after its creation, the empire is further consolidating its foundations with the aid of its friend, Japan.

And if it is still protested that our actions in Manchuria were excessively violent, we may wish to ask the white race just which country it was that sent warships and troops to India, South Africa, and Australia and slaughtered innocent natives, bound their hands and feet with iron chains, lashed their backs with iron whips, proclaimed these territories as their own, and still continues to hold them to this very day?

They will invariably reply, these were all lands inhabited by untamed savages. These people did not know how to develop the abundant resources of their land for the benefit of mankind. Therefore it was the wish of God, who created heaven and earth for mankind, for us to develop these undeveloped lands and to promote the happiness of mankind in their stead. God wills it.

This is quite a convenient argument for them. Let us take it at face value. Then there is another question that we must ask them.

Suppose that there is still on this earth land endowed with abundant natural resources that have not been developed at all by the white race. Would it not then be God's will and the will of Providence that Japan go there and develop those resources for the benefit of mankind?

And there still remain many such lands on this earth.

THE DECLARATION OF WAR

The Emperor's Rescript declaring war on the United States and Great Britain summed up Japan's grievances against the Western democracies and explained that Japan had had no real alternative to going to war.

Shortly afterwards a commentary on the Rescript was issued by Tokutomi Iichirō, the dean of Japan's nationalist writers. Tokutomi, who in early life went through phases of tremendous enthusiasm for Christianity and liberalism, gradually became a firm defender of his civilization and government against the West. In his autobiography he writes that during the Sino-Japanese War in 1894 he first thought of the government leaders as his own and not as a group to be opposed. Thenceforth his writings and work were increasingly closely connected with the nationalist cause, and by the 1930s he was one of the leading spokesmen for the nationalist point of view.

TOKUTOMI IICHIRŌ
Commentary on the Imperial Declaration of War

Tokutomi's commentary analyzes the Rescript point by point, restates Japanese grievances, and, in the spirit of war-time exhortation, discusses the steps needed for Japan to become the Leader and the Light of Asia.

[From Tokutomi Iichirō, *The Imperial Rescript Declaring War on the United States and British Empire*, pp. 9–11, 20–22, 123–24.]

CHAPTER IV: THE BASIS OF THE IMPERIAL WAY

The virtue of sincerity is represented by the Mirror, the virtue of love is represented by the Jewels, and the virtue of intelligence is represented by the Sword. . . . The interpretation given by Kitabatake Chikafusa [1]

---

[1] The interpretation of the Three Imperial Regalia: Mirror, Jewel, and Sword. See Volume I, Chapter XIII.

has, indeed, grasped the true meaning. Then, it is not wrong to liken the Three Sacred Treasures to the three virtues of intelligence, love, and courage by saying that the Mirror represents the intelligence which reflects everything, the Jewels, the love which embraces everything, and the Sword, the courage which judges between justice and injustice, honesty and dishonesty.

In any case, the basis of the Imperial Way lies in truth, in sincerity, and in justice. Its range is wide and there is nothing it does not embrace. It expels evil, subjugates injustice, absolutely maintains the tenets of justice, and itself occupies a position which can never be violated. The august virtue of the divine imperial lineage has not a single instance when it did not arise from these three virtues. In other words, they form the national character of Nippon, and, at the same time, the national trait of the people of Nippon. Combining them all, we call it the Imperial Way.

The phrase "The three virtues of intelligence, love, and courage" may sound very much like a common ethical teaching, but when considered realistically, it gives us the reason why our country, under whatever circumstances, has never resorted to arms for the sake of arms alone. . . .

CHAPTER VIII: THE UNIQUE FEATURES OF THE NATION OF NIPPON

What we should note first of all is that Nippon is not a country built upon that Western individualism patterned after the insistence on rights, nor a country built with the family as the basis as in China . . . our Nippon is neither a country of individualism nor a country of the family system. In Nippon, the family is valued and good lineage is highly regarded the same as in China. However, in Nippon there is that which goes farther and which is greater than these. There is the Imperial Household. In China, there are families, but there is not the Imperial Household. In Nippon, there are families, but still, above them, there is the Imperial Household. In China, families gather to form a nation, but in Nippon the Imperial Household deigns to rule the land, and on the land the families, the members of which are subjects of the Imperial Household, flourish.

That is why, in China, one speaks first of the family and then next of the nation, but, in Nippon, the nation comes first and next the family. In China, if it is to be asked which is valued higher, the nation or the family, it must be answered that, under whatever circumstances, the family is valued first and next the nation. In the West, the individual is valued first, and next the family, and last the nation. In Nippon, the nation is valued first, then next the family, and last the individual. The order of the West is absolutely reversed in Nippon. . . .

CHAPTER XLVIII: THREE QUALIFICATIONS OF THE LEADER OF
GREATER EAST ASIA

Now that we have risen up in arms, we must accomplish our aim to the last. Herein lies the core of our theory. In Nippon resides a destiny to become the Light of Greater East Asia and to become ultimately the Light of the World. However, in order to become the Light of Greater East Asia, we must have three qualifications. The first is, as mentioned previously, strength. In other words, we must expel Anglo-Saxon influence from East Asia with our strength.

To speak the truth, the various races of East Asia look upon the British and Americans as superior to the Nippon race. They look upon Britain and the United States as more powerful nations than Nippon. Therefore, we must show our real strength before all our fellow-races of East Asia. We must show them an object lesson. It is not a lesson in words. It should be a lesson in facts.

In other words, before we can expel the Anglo-Saxons and make them remove all their traces from East Asia, we must annihilate them. In this way only will the various fellow races of Greater East Asia look upon us as their leader. I believe that the lesson which we must first show to our fellow-races in Greater East Asia is this lesson of cold reality.

The second qualification is benevolence. Nippon must develop the various resources of East Asia and distribute them fairly to all the races within the East Asia Co-Prosperity Sphere to make them share in the benefits. In other words, Nippon should not monopolize the benefits, but should distribute them for the mutual prosperity of Greater East Asia.

We must show to the races of East Asia that the order, tranquillity, peace, happiness, and contentment of East Asia can be gained only by eradicating the evil precedent of the encroachment and extortion of the Anglo-Saxons in East Asia, by effecting the real aim of the co-prosperity of East Asia, and by making Nippon the leader of East Asia.

[293]

The third qualification is virtue. East Asia embraces various races. Its religions are different. Moreover, there has practically been no occasion when these have mutually united to work for a combined aim. It was the favorite policy of the Anglo-Saxons to make the various races of East Asia compete and fight each other and make them mutually small and powerless. We must, therefore, console them, bring friendship among them, and make them all live in peace with a boundlessly embracing virtue.

In short, the first is the Grace of the Sacred Sword, the second, the Grace of the Sacred Mirror, and the third, the Grace of the Sacred Jewels. If we should express it in other words, we must have courage, knowledge, and benevolence. If Nippon should lack even one of the above three, it will not be able to become the Light of Asia.

THE WAR GOAL

Japan's war planners envisioned a long struggle, in several stages, to achieve their new Asia. The new Asia was to be known as the Greater East Asia Co-Prosperity Sphere. The Southern region would supply raw materials and surplus food, while Manchuria and North China provided the materials and basis for a heavy industry complex. The rest of Asia would become a vast market, defended and integrated by Japanese planning, tools, skills, and arms.

DRAFT OF BASIC PLAN FOR ESTABLISHMENT OF
GREATER EAST ASIA CO-PROSPERITY SPHERE
[From *Draft of Basic Plan,* IMTFE, International Prosecution Section, Document 2402B, Exhibit 1336]

Part I. Outline of Construction

This document, produced as a secret planning paper by the Total War Research Institute, a body responsible to army and cabinet, in January of 1942, reveals the nature of long-range planning during the early war years before defeats began to take their toll of optimism and confidence.

The Plan. The Japanese empire is a manifestation of morality and its special characteristic is the propagation of the Imperial Way. It strives

but for the achievement of *Hakkō Ichiu,* the spirit of its founding. . . .
It is necessary to foster the increased power of the empire, to cause East
Asia to return to its original form of independence and co-prosperity by
shaking off the yoke of Europe and America, and to let its countries and
peoples develop their respective abilities in peaceful cooperation and
secure livelihood.

The Form of East Asiatic Independence and Co-Prosperity. The states,
their citizens, and resources, comprised in those areas pertaining to the
Pacific, Central Asia, and the Indian Oceans formed into one general
union are to be established as an autonomous zone of peaceful living
and common prosperity on behalf of the peoples of the nations of East
Asia. The area including Japan, Manchuria, North China, lower Yangtze
River, and the Russian Maritime Province, forms the nucleus of the
East Asiatic Union. The Japanese empire possesses a duty as the leader
of the East Asiatic Union.

The above purpose presupposes the inevitable emancipation or independence of Eastern Siberia, China, Indo-China, the South Seas,
Australia, and India.

*Regional Division in the East Asiatic Union and the National Defense
Sphere for the Japanese Empire.* In the Union of East Asia, the Japanese
empire is at once the stabilizing power and the leading influence. To
enable the empire actually to become the central influence in East Asia,
the first necessity is the consolidation of the inner belt of East Asia;
and the East Asiatic Sphere shall be divided as follows for this purpose:

The Inner Sphere—the vital sphere for the empire—includes Japan,
Manchuria, North China, the lower Yangtze Area and the Russian
Maritime area.

The Smaller Co-Prosperity Sphere—the smaller self-supplying sphere of
East Asia—includes the inner sphere plus Eastern Siberia, China, Indo-
China and the South Seas.

The Greater Co-Prosperity Sphere—the larger self-supplying sphere of
East Asia—includes the smaller co-prosperity sphere, plus Australia, India,
and island groups in the Pacific. . . .

For the present, the smaller co-prosperity sphere shall be the zone in
which the construction of East Asia and the stabilization of national
defense are to be aimed at. After their completion there shall be a gradual
expansion toward the construction of the Greater Co-Prosperity Sphere.

Outline of East Asiatic Administration. It is intended that the unification of Japan, Manchoukuo, and China in neighborly friendship be realized by the settlement of the Sino-Japanese problems through the crushing of hostile influences in the Chinese interior, and through the construction of a new China in tune with the rapid construction of the Inner Sphere. Aggressive American and British influences in East Asia shall be driven out of the area of Indo-China and the South Seas, and this area shall be brought into our defense sphere. The war with Britain and America shall be prosecuted for that purpose.

The Russian aggressive influence in East Asia will be driven out. Eastern Siberia shall be cut off from the Soviet regime and included in our defense sphere. For this purpose, a war with the Soviets is expected. It is considered possible that this Northern problem may break out before the general settlement of the present Sino-Japanese and the Southern problems if the situation renders this unavoidable. Next the independence of Australia, India, etc. shall gradually be brought about. For this purpose, a recurrence of war with Britain and her allies is expected. The construction of a Greater Mongolian State is expected during the above phase. The construction of the Smaller Co-Prosperity Sphere is expected to require at least twenty years from the present time.

The Building of the National Strength. Since the Japanese empire is the center and pioneer of Oriental moral and cultural reconstruction, the officials and people of this country must return to the spirit of the Orient and acquire a thorough understanding of the spirit of the national moral character.

In the economic construction of the country, Japanese and Manchurian national power shall first be consolidated, then the unification of Japan, Manchoukuo and China, shall be effected. . . . Thus a central industry will be constructed in East Asia, and the necessary relations established with the Southern Seas.

The standard for the construction of the national power and its military force, so as to meet the various situations that might affect the stages of East Asiatic administration and the national defense sphere, shall be so set as to be capable of driving off any British, American, Soviet or Chinese counter-influences in the future. . . .

CHAPTER 3. POLITICAL CONSTRUCTION

Basic Plan. The realization of the great ideal of constructing Greater East Asia Co-Prosperity requires not only the complete prosecution of the current Greater East Asia War but also presupposes another great war in the future. Therefore, the following two points must be made the primary starting points for the political construction of East Asia during the course of the next twenty years: 1) Preparation for war with the other spheres of the world; and 2) Unification and construction of the East Asia Smaller Co-Prosperity Sphere.

The following are the basic principles for the political construction of East Asia, when the above two points are taken into consideration:

a. The politically dominant influence of European and American countries in the Smaller Co-Prosperity Sphere shall be gradually driven out and the area shall enjoy its liberation from the shackles hitherto forced upon it.

b. The desires of the peoples in the sphere for their independence shall be respected and endeavors shall be made for their fulfillment, but proper and suitable forms of government shall be decided for them in consideration of military and economic requirements and of the historical, political and cultural elements peculiar to each area.

It must also be noted that the independence of various peoples of East Asia should be based upon the idea of constructing East Asia as "independent countries existing within the New Order of East Asia" and that this conception differs from an independence based on the idea of liberalism and national self-determination.

c. During the course of construction, military unification is deemed particularly important, and the military zones and key points necessary for defense shall be directly or indirectly under the control of our country. . . .

d. The peoples of the sphere shall obtain their proper positions, the unity of the people's minds shall be effected and the unification of the sphere shall be realized with the empire as its center. . . .

CHAPTER 4. THOUGHT AND CULTURAL CONSTRUCTION

General Aim in Thought. The ultimate aim in thought construction in East Asia is to make East Asiatic peoples revere the imperial influence by propagating the Imperial Way based on the spirit of construction, and to establish the belief that uniting solely under this influence is the one and only way to the eternal growth and development of East Asia.

And during the next twenty years (the period during which the above ideal is to be reached) it is necessary to make the nations and peoples of East Asia realize the historical significance of the establishment of the New Order in East Asia, and in the common consciousness of East Asiatic unity, to liberate East Asia from the shackles of Europe and America and to establish the common conviction of constructing a New Order based on East Asiatic morality.

Occidental individualism and materialism shall be rejected and a moral world view, the basic principle of whose morality shall be the Imperial Way, shall be established. The ultimate object to be achieved is not exploitation but co-prosperity and mutual help, not competitive conflict but mutual assistance and mild peace, not a formal view of equality but a view of order based on righteous classification, not an idea of rights but an idea of service, and not several world views but one unified world view.

General Aim in Culture. The essence of the traditional culture of the Orient shall be developed and manifested. And, casting off the negative and conservative cultural characteristics of the continents (India and China) on the one hand, and taking in the good points of Western culture on the other, an Oriental culture and morality, on a grand scale and subtly refined, shall be created.

CHAPTER XXVIII

THE JAPANESE SOCIAL MOVEMENT

The "social movement" is a term applied generally to efforts in modern Japan to reform society and help the workingman, but especially to the trend toward socialism. Since the Meiji Restoration this movement has been stimulated by many factors, including concern over social distress and inequality, the dissatisfactions and frustrations of many intellectuals, and the tradition of direct, forceful action inherited from Tokugawa times and the Restoration movement itself. But the preponderant influence of Western social thought is apparent both in the intellectual origins of such movements, and in the fact that Japanese radicals, attempting to assess the effects of Japan's rapid modernization, have drawn heavily upon Western doctrines for the type of analysis and solution offered to the problems of the day. Thus to a very large degree Japanese radical thought has been imitative and adaptive, making little pretense at even such originality as the more moderate and indigenously rooted movements displayed. It was assumed that the "trend" in the modern West was toward the "left," and that progressive Japanese need only catch up with the most advanced social thinking of Europe and America. To be abreast of the times was to have absorbed the latest theories and terminology from abroad, not necessarily to have studied the actual facts of recent Japanese history with a view to re-examining outworn concepts. Nevertheless, even in this process it is possible to discern certain prevalent Japanese attitudes at work.

The bête noire of Japanese radicals was from the outset "capitalism," this extremely complex and varied pattern of Western economic organization being interpreted simplistically in terms of its nineteenth-century manifestations and, of course, in terms of Western imperialism. In the decade or so after the First World War, when industrialization and monopolistic capitalism made rapid advances, this type of thinking gained wider currency. With the rise of militaristic nationalism, however, leftists found that they too suffered from the bridling of capitalism and the suppression of bourgeois democracy. Throughout these years, moreover, and into the postwar era, there has been an almost continuous cleavage within the social movement between those who looked for reform through democratic processes and trade-unionism and those who put their main hope in world revolution.

The philosophy, if it may be called such, of "trade-unionism, pure and simple," is deeply rooted in the labor history of Japan. Its first systematic expression may be observed in the years immediately after the close of the Sino-Japanese War when several Japanese workers, who had lived for many years in the United States, attempted to apply their lessons in American trade-unionism. Their pamphlet, "A Summons to the Workers," was widely distributed in Tokyo in April, 1897, and presented to Japanese readers the labor outlook of the American Federation of Labor. This document is of interest not only because it lays the foundations for a moderate trade-union view in Japan and rejects revolutionary tactics, but also because it reveals overtones of nationalism. The problem of appealing to the masses both as "Japanese" and as "workers" was to cause many a radical leader considerable distress in later years.

A Summons to the Workers

Note how this summons appeals less to the workers as members of a class-conscious proletariat with a revolutionary mission than it does to traditional Japanese attitudes among them: fear of foreign domination and exploitation, the desire for self-improvement and the preservation of family life, their generally law-abiding character, and finally to their sense of social cohesion and responsibility.

[From Katayama and Nishikawa, *Nihon no rōdō undō*, pp. 18–22]

The year 1899 will see Japan really opened to foreign intercourse. It will be a time when foreign capitalists will enter our country and attempt to amass millions in profits by exploiting our cheap labor and our clever workers. In such a situation, these foreign capitalists, who are not only different in character, manners, and customs, but who are also notorious for their cruel treatment of workers, will try to become your masters within the next three years. In the light of this situation, you workers must soon start to prepare yourselves or you cannot help suffering the same abuses as the workers of Europe and America. Considering recent developments, moreover, the relations between the workers and employers of our country will in the same way as in Europe and America undergo daily change as factories and plants increase in number.

Considerations of profit alone will prevail. The strong will be triumphant and the weak will be destroyed. Since the superior are heading for days of prosperity and the inferior for times of ruin, it will be no easy task to conquer and to flourish in the days that lie ahead. When, moreover, the foreigners do enter our country, it will be vitally necessary for you to double your resolution and to devise moderate means to protect your position on the field of struggle, without getting yourselves involved in scrapes on their behalf.

You workers, like others before you, are people without capital who provide a living for others than yourselves. One of your arms and one of your legs are, so to speak, devoted to the support of society. When you meet with some misfortune and are disabled or when you become infirm with age and can no longer work, you are immediately deprived of the means of earning a living and are turned out into the street. Should death overtake you, your wives and your children are hard put to stay alive. In this state of affairs you are really as helpless as a candle in the wind. Unless you workers heed the precept of the ancients and prepare for adversity while you are able, and make it your practice to provide for ways to cope with future difficulties while you are strong and sound of body, it will be hard for you to avoid transgressing the fundamental obligations of a human being, a husband, or a parent. This matter demands sober consideration.

In this day and age our country is still not enlightened. In the olden days, when there were no machines, your wives and children stayed at home and worked and helped to earn a living. But with the rise of factories and mills your wives, who should be looking after the home, take themselves off to work in the factories. And since even innocent children work at the machines, the life of the home is thrown into confusion. At times the lives of children are endangered, as machines, which should be of benefit to man, function improperly and present the astounding spectacle of doing him harm. In some factories children with delicate bodies are made to work hours which would be too long even for adults. The life-blood of those who are little more than infants is squeezed out with impartiality, and for their parents this is indeed unbearable. It should be evident that you must first and foremost take vigorous action and devise ways and means of coping with the situation. You must put your homes in order and protect the lives of your women and children. Do not forget, you workers, that those who take the lives of men do not do so only with the lethal instruments of murderers and criminals.

It is evident that when wives who should be caring for the home and children who should be in school are working in factories, an extremely unnatural state of affairs exists. If we seek the reason for this, we find that because of the cheapness of labor a man with only one pair of hands cannot support a wife and children. This is truly a most deplorable situation. If you are husbands, you cannot but want to give your wives a comfortable life. If you are parents, you cannot but want to see your children educated. These must of course be your feelings, and if you would only once rouse yourselves you would in the end find a way to correct this unnatural state of affairs and, by so doing, preserve your dignity.

One more matter which should be mentioned concerns your behavior. If you are an honest man earning a living by selling your labor power and if you make no mistakes in your work and conduct, you need not fear anything under the sun. But if you once do something dishonest or improper, your reputation as an upright man is thereby destroyed and your life itself is ruined. The saying that honesty prevails in the end is known to all of us. The way to protect yourselves lies in this. Furthermore, men who are in the unfortunate position that you are in find it difficult to obtain completely satisfactory results if, in attempting to improve their position, they are the least bit indiscreet in their behavior. Accordingly, it is necessary for you to strive to advance and extend your position and interests and, at the same time, to be courageous enough to follow a righteous course. Why should you workers not try to improve yourselves and mend your ways and pursue your ends in an open and above-board fashion? Know that the most heartless person will not prevail before your righteousness.

How you workers are to undertake the necessary acts of resolution and preparation, which have been indicated previously, will understandably raise questions in your minds. Some of you will say: "Matters have by now gone beyond the stage of talking. The rich are becoming richer and the poor are becoming poorer. The injustices and ruined circumstances which are the workers' lot are indeed cause for bitterness. Only by a revolution correcting this situation may the differences in wealth be equalized." This argument is truly attractive, and it would be splendid if you were able to achieve complete reform by the revolution advocated by its proponents. But the affairs of the world are not so simple as these men believe. Unexpected developments occur, making it completely impossible to realize original objectives, while great disorders are not infrequent.

You workers should think twice before accepting these arguments. The advances of society have always been at a leisurely and orderly pace. Revolutionists are opposed to the supporters of order and, when the former make haste and recklessness a prime factor, the actions of the two groups become diametrically opposed. As far as equalization of economic differences is concerned, since all men are not equally wise, inequalities in the amount of property individually possessed are inevitable. Proposals for the elimination of differences between rich and poor are more easily stated than achieved.

In view of this, you workers should firmly and resolutely reject ideas of revolution and acts of radicalism. To advance a mile one must go forward by steps. You should thus spurn the counsels of the economic levelers.

We would recommend, consequently, that you workers establish trade unions based upon the feelings common to men engaged in the same work and possessed of kindred sentiments. These trade unions, moreover, should be organized on a nation-wide cooperative basis. In viewing carefully your past actions, it is evident that you have refrained from combining, that you have struggled with one another, and that you have achieved no unity. Thus, if there are some of you who have with laborious effort and after countless appeals finally secured an increase in wages, there are others who remain satisfied with their outrageously low wages. There are some who want to reprove your unworthy fellow workers but there are also those who want to protect them. The spectacle of some men building and other men destroying, of kindred people engaged in mutual strife, is really cause for regret.

Your internecine strife, the contempt in which the foreigners hold you, and the position in which you find yourselves today, all may to a large extent be attributed to the failure of you workers to act unitedly.

As has been indicated previously, attack by the foreign enemy may be expected. Today, when deplorable evils exist among you, you must stop your fratricidal struggles and see the necessity for engaging in a vast combined effort. You workers must not remain apart but should wisely combine and keep pace with the advances of society. Inwardly you should nourish wholesome thoughts and outwardly comport yourselves in sober and steady ways. Shouldn't you seek to remedy the evil practices of your heartless employers and of the foreigners? Remember that there will be others who will think as you do.

Labor is holy. Combination is strength. It is for you who are engaged in holy labor to achieve the union that is strength.

KŌTOKU SHŪSUI
Renunciation of Parliamentary Tactics

The trade-union movement and an equally young socialist movement, which emerged during the last years of the nineteenth century, were short-lived. In 1900 the Japanese government, fearful of social unrest, passed the Public Peace Preservation Law which legally hamstrung radical social movements for two decades and more. One of the principal effects of this legislation was the constriction of radical expression, which tended to become increasingly theoretical, intellectual, and polemical. On the other hand, with the gradual strengthening of parliamentary government and the extension of suffrage, many radicals were encouraged to think that their objectives could be achieved through the ballot-box.

It was in this atmosphere that Kōtoku Denjirō, better known by his pen name Shūsui (1871–1911), and his anarchist philosophy made their appearance. Few, if any, intellectuals in modern Japanese history have wielded a more trenchant pen than Kōtoku. A fearless and outspoken foe of established institutions, he was still a young man when he was executed in 1911 for allegedly having plotted against the emperor's life. Just four years before, at a meeting of the Socialist Party in Tokyo, Kōtoku had proclaimed his break with parliamentarianism and his new-found conviction in direct action. With the passage of the years the fame of the man, rather than of his ideas, has continued to grow. To all radicals he has been a symbol of opposition to oppression.

[From Tanaka, *Shiryō Nihon shakai undō shi*, pp. 154–56]

Advocates of universal suffrage and proponents of parliamentarianism are both necessary for the awakening and organization of the voiceless laborers. But even if universal suffrage were put into effect, nothing at all would be done in the Diet if the laborers were not awakened and organized. However, if the workers were really awakened and united, is there anything they could not do by their direct action? Matters have by now come to such a pass that there is no need to elect representatives and to depend upon parliaments.

If a member of the Diet becomes corrupt, that is all there is to it. If the Diet is dissolved, that is the end of the matter. The social revolution, that is, the revolution of the workers, must in the final analysis rest upon the strength of the workers themselves. Rather than serve as stepping-stones for parliamentary candidates, who are the ambitious ones in the gentlemen's set, the workers should immediately move ahead by themselves and look to the security of their livelihood. It is up to them to satisfy their elemental material needs.

Universal suffrage, campaigns, and the election of parliamentary representatives are all doubtless forms of propaganda. If, however, there is to be propaganda, why not direct propaganda? Why take such indirect steps? Are we to place our faith in the futile casting of ballots and not devote ourselves to effective organizational training? In Japan today the expenses of one candidate in a political campaign are no less than two thousand yen. If even that small an outlay were to be spent purely for propagandizing and organizing the workers, what tremendous results might we not see.

Recently many of the European socialist parties have become disgusted with the meager results obtained through parliamentary power. A tendency has arisen in continental Europe for socialist parties and the working class to be at constant loggerheads. In the trade unions of England, where frantic attempts are being made to elect representatives to Parliament, reserve funds and membership are gradually being depleted. Are these not points which we of the Japanese Socialist Party should particularly note?

What the working class wants is not the seizure of political power, but the "seizure of bread." They do not want laws; they want a livelihood. The working class can, accordingly, have but scant use for parliaments. If we are to rest content with the insertion of a clause in this law before the Diet, we might as well leave our work to the social reformers and to the state socialists. But if, on the contrary, we really want to improve and guarantee the living conditions of the working class by carrying out a social revolution, we must devote our utmost effort to organizational training of the workers rather than to the acquisition of parliamentary power. The workers themselves must be resolved to attain their objective by their own strength, by their own direct action, and not by relying upon the likes of the parliamentary politicians of the gentlemen's set. I repeat, it is not for us to rely upon members of parliament and upon literary contributions.

Even so, I never held that acquiring the right to vote was wrong. I am not unreasonably opposed to the movement to revise the electoral laws. If universal suffrage is introduced, the Diet will to a greater or less extent take into account the views of the workers when it enacts or revises laws. These benefits alone are certain. But these benefits are no different from the institution of workmen's insurance, factory regulation, and tenancy laws, no different from legislation to revise or abolish the Peace Preservation Laws and the newspaper ordinances, no different from all the other social reform work and legislation for the protection of the worker and for the relief of the poor. It is not wrong to carry on these campaigns; I have no doubt that it is good to do so. But I also believe that being a socialist does not require a person to do so.

I would never deem it wrong for you, my comrades, to stand for parliament and to engage in election contests. I would never oppose your campaigns in the Diet. I rejoice to see our comrades increase in the government and in business society, in the army and in the navy, in the world of education, among the workers and peasants, and in all the classes of society. For the same reason, I would be delighted by an increase in the number of our comrades among the members of the Diet. If, accordingly, an election campaign could be carried out, it would be good to do so. But I cannot see that it would be a vital matter that had to be undertaken by the Socialist Party in particular.

I, who am at the least a socialist and a member of the Socialist Party, believe that, in order to attain our goal, which is a fundamental revolution in the economic system, that is to say, the abolition of the wage system, it is far more important to awaken ten workers than to obtain a thousand signatures on petitions for universal suffrage. Rather than spend two thousand yen in an election campaign, I believe it is much more urgent to use ten yen for the organization of the workers. I believe it is infinitely more promising to have one talk with the workers than to deliver ten speeches in the Diet.

Comrades, I hope that for the above reasons the Japanese socialist movement will henceforth cease its policy of parliamentarianism and adopt primarily the tactics and line of direct action by the workers who are to be organized.

Resolution of the Japan General Federation of Labor, February, 1924, on Labor and Political Action

Before 1920 radical political movements were sponsored chiefly by intellectuals and attracted little mass support. As a result of industrial expansion during and after the First World War, however, the working class increased greatly in size, labor unions blossomed forth, and there were frequent strikes during the period of economic readjustment in the early '20s. At the same time the political consciousness of the workers was stimulated by the rise of political parties and the extension of the electorate which culminated in the enactment of universal manhood suffrage in 1925. In such circumstances radicals inspired by European socialism or the revolutionary success of Bolshevism in Russia were eager to direct the labor movement toward the achievement of political objectives as well as of economic gains. The influence of Marxism-Leninism is quite evident in this resolution of the Japan General Federation of Labor (*Nihon Rōdō Sōdōmei*), calling for political action on a wide scale. Both the general tone of the document and its stress on a correct analysis of the historical situation in Marxist-Leninist terms indicate that the basic draft was Communist-inspired. Moderate elements, however, tended to emphasize those aspects of the resolution involving democratic agitation and the use of parliamentary processes, while extremists saw these as only a preparation for the eventual class struggle. The resolution thus signalizes the joining together of labor and radical politics to produce the "mass" movements of the '20s, and the precarious unity they achieved among different shades of left-wing opinion.

[From *Rōdō*, No. 150 (March, 1924), 3]

The labor movement in Japan has now reached a most important turning point. We firmly believe that the resolution proclaimed here at our Convention for the year 1924 is especially significant not only for the movement embraced by the Japan General Federation of Labor but also for the broader history of the labor movement of our country.

The labor and proletarian movements must constantly undertake to revise their strategy in keeping with changes in the stages of development of their antagonist—capitalism—with the conditions revealed by these stages, and with their own strength.

The dark shadows of social insecurity cast by the Great European War have added increasingly to the internal contradictions of capitalist society and have brought closer the moment of its destruction. Simultaneously, one can observe the rapid development of the proletarian movement. The ruling class, with a courage born of desperation, is bending every effort to maintain the existing system and holds the blade of pitiless oppression over the heads of the proletarian class.

When we take another look at the labor movement in our country after the Great European War, we note that the Japanese labor movement, stimulated by the rise of proletarian movements throughout the world, has joined in the class struggle with an unanticipated spirit and fervor. The militant elements in our country's laboring class have become conscious of their mission and objective of emancipating the working class and, after being subjected to numerous tests, have finally been able to lay the foundation of a militant labor union.

From the first, capitalism in Japan did not develop along normal lines and after being subjected to the severe pressures of world imperialism, prematurely assumed the form of imperialism, the highest stage in the development of capitalism. Capitalism in our country, accordingly, did not experience liberalism but immediately became militaristic, with strong tinges of absolutism. Numerous obstacles were thus raised restricting the freedom of the proletarian movement.

In addition, the world-wide class struggles which were then reaching their height caused, on the one hand, a few elements of our proletarian class who had been awakened after the Great European War to raise sharply their ideological levels. On the other hand, however, these elements did not acquire sufficient understanding of the mission and duty of labor unions in the movement to emancipate the proletarian class. Such a situation necessarily made the democratization of the proletarian movement difficult and resulted in the movement's being carried on by a small number of men burning with idealism and prone to fastidiousness and immaturity.

We believe that the course of our labor movement in the past has inevitably been in accordance with the anomalous development of capitalism in Japan. And if we continue in the future to maintain the attitude we have held in the past, this alone would be a major error and blunder.

Out of sheer necessity we must devise realistic and positive policies to replace those of the past. This necessity is evident to us who have been able to observe correctly the increase in the strength of the working class as well as the tendencies which have been recently revealed in the capitalism of our country. The labor movement in Japan has shifted from a movement of a small minority and has become a virtual mass movement. The attitude toward social reform policy, which has hitherto been negative, must be changed and made positive.

Thus, although our expectations for the fundamental emancipation of the working class as a result of action taken by the bourgeois Diet are not very sanguine, we hope when the franchise is extended to acquire some political benefits by exercising the suffrage effectively. At the same time, we plan to hasten the political awakening of the proletarian class and to consider with due deliberation our policy towards the International Labor Organization. All this we plan to do in behalf of our nation's labor unions.

We must work for the merging of the independent labor unions by uniting their class interests as well as for the organization of the unorganized working class. And, while securing practical benefits [for labor itself], we must exhibit the true character of a labor union movement advancing toward its ultimate goal. We militant labor union members of today, who are possessed of clear critical ability and who have awakened to our class consciousness, are firmly resolved not to be led astray, even though we turn to good account the reform policies of the ruling class which are designed to blunt the revolutionary spirit of the working class.

We who participate in the movement to liberate the proletarian class must in the future change our strategy in keeping with shifts in our strength and in the condition of the enemy. But no matter how practical necessity may lead us to alter our policies, we vow to remain constant in our basic spirit of liberating the proletarian class.

ABE ISOO

The Second Restoration

Abe Isoo (1865–1949), titular head of the Socialist Masses Party (*Shakai Taishū tō*) from 1932 to 1940, was associated with the Japanese social democratic movement from its inception. In 1879 Abe had entered Dōshisha University where he was deeply influenced by Dr. Joseph H. Neesima (Niishima

Jō, 1845–1890) of Amherst who later helped him enter Hartford Theological Seminary. There, upon reading Edward Bellamy's *Looking Backward,* he was converted to socialism. For twenty-five years he taught at Waseda University, and after entering politics, was elected to the Diet four times in the period from 1928 to 1940. Of a moderate temperament, Abe expended great effort in attempting to convince the authorities that socialism was not subversive and to persuade the working class not to resort to violent methods. In addressing the common people, he used simple, homely speech, if a bit old-fashioned, and sought to identify the proletarian movement with the Japanese historical and cultural context. For example, he likened the proletarian leaders of his day with the *rōnin* or masterless warriors who were considered the heroes of the Meiji Restoration. In the selection which follows, originally a speech delivered around 1929–30, he calls for "a Second (or Shōwa) Restoration," employing terminology similar to that of the ultranationalists but with the notable difference of an emphasis on peaceful means.

[From Abe, *Jidai no Kakusei,* pp. 229–47]

Man's primary concern is livelihood. Let us think of this in terms of building a house. Economics is the groundwork and foundation of the house. Man's livelihood makes up the economic sphere. I believe we can look at politics as the superstructure that can be erected on this sphere when it is completed.

However, in looking at contemporary conditions, we see that the superstructure of politics is approaching comparative completion. Man's desires are now eight or nine tenths realizable in the political sphere, but the economic sphere is very backward. It is from here that the unrest and instability in society at present come. Because the foundation is shaky, the superstructure is in a state of instability. In order to explain this, I have to say something about political change.

How have politics progressed up to the present?

Formerly in all countries a minority controlled political rights under despotic government, ruling the majority of the people in an oppressive manner. The people who were ruled could not interfere in politics. There was absolutely no right of political participation. That was the situation in former days. Now things have advanced to the point where all the people in every country of the world have completely attained the right of political participation.

In the particular case of Japan, since the achievement of constitutional government, all sovereignty, constitutionally speaking, rests with His Majesty the Emperor. Despite the fact that His Majesty the Emperor can

do anything He wills, in reality it is otherwise, and He orders the formation of a cabinet by a party when it has become the strongest party in
accordance with an election which demonstrates the will of the people.
This is the established rule. [pp. 229–31]

Conversely, what about the condition in the economic sphere? Even
today it has not changed the slightest from Tokugawa times. If we take
a factory, and if the factory has three to five hundred men employed, still
the right of management is held by the stockholders, if it is a stock company, or held by a single owner, if it is an individually owned concern,
but the workers in the factory have not the slightest management rights.
It is the typical situation today that the workers have no voice in the
operation of the factory any more than political participation existed under
despotic government, and the workers remain under the authority of the
employer like the people under the feudal lord of yore. [p. 232]

In sum, the present question is: cannot we do something about the fact
that although politics is going well, in economics we are still copying the
Tokugawa Period?

This something we think of as the Second Restoration.

The Meiji Restoration completely did away with forty thousand samurai and three hundred daimyo [feudal barons]. Because of this, we have
become enabled to take part in politics.

However, at present, one Tokyo magazine writes that there are a hundred and fifteen daimyo of the economic world comparable to the daimyo
of the Meiji Restoration, classifying them as people who own more than
ten million yen worth of property. If you add the owners of down to seven
to eight hundred thousand yen, you have three hundred men like the
daimyo of old. They are dominating the economic world of Japan today
like feudal lords. . . .

How was the great work of the Restoration accomplished? Thanks to
the fact that here and there great men such as Saigō Takamori, Kido
Kōin, and Ōkubo Toshimichi came forward, the *Bakufu* [shogunate]
finally came to an end, and here the reforms of the Restoration were accomplished without difficulty. Indeed, in the case of Japan, no great
war was necessary, and looking back, it seems the whole thing happened
like a dream.

In Fukuoka on Kyūshū where I was born, my father was in service to the Kuroda fief and received a stipend of three hundred *koku* of rice [one *koku* equals 5.12 bushels], but at the time of the Restoration the way in which he surrendered his rights as a samurai was to receive a section of the territory of the former fief which yielded three hundred *koku* of rice each year. Thus, he was no different from a landlord of today. Now if the Second Restoration comes, just as the samurai gave up their rights, the landlord can be given a monetary compensation and the whole thing can be accomplished without much ado.

To explain this in simple terms, in the case of a landlord, give him four years' worth of tenant farmers' rent and have him return all his land rights as they are to His Majesty. This would certainly not be difficult. [Also] the monetary compensation need not be exactly four years' rent. However, if we are to do what our forebears did in the Meiji Restoration, it will certainly not be difficult to do away with the three hundred financial barons [*zaibatsu daimyō*] and gain a voice in the economic sphere. . . .

If we do this, we will not need to use force at all. There will be ever less need for any blood to flow. The reform of the Restoration did not involve cutting off the head of a single of the three hundred daimyo. Even the number one leading figure, Tokugawa Shogun, himself, was not bodily harmed in the slightest. What happened to the Honorable Tokugawa who turned in his right to be shogun? For a long time he served as President of the House of Peers and accumulated great honor. In comparing the period when he was shogun and the present period, which was better for Tokugawa-san? Only Tokugawa-san himself knows.

Similarly . . . if we once again deal decisively with the present Japanese economic world in the same way as was done in the Meiji Restoration, then the unrest and instability in Japan arising from the cause and effect relationship between politics and economics can be solved peacefully.

However, all of you may say that without capital probably no work can be made available at all, and is it not on account of capital that the industry of Japan prospers? I would reply that, yes, capital is necessary but capitalists are not necessary. If capital is needed for industry, all of us can chip in a little money and so create capital, and also the state can levy taxes and create capital. It is a great mistake to think that work will not be available without such financial barons [*zaibctsu*] as Mitsui and Mitsubishi. There are many actual examples of the availability of work without the existence of capitalists.

In preparing to bring about the Second Restoration, we will have not the slightest need for the sword, in contrast to the situation in the past. If we arm ourselves with the ballot instead of the sword, it will certainly not be hard to create a Second Restoration.

KAWAKAMI HAJIME

Kawakami Hajime (1879–1946), a gifted journalist, poet, and university professor, was one of the most effective intellectual spokesmen for Marxism between the two World Wars. His eventful life was marked by three major climaxes, each summed up in a poem. The first was written at the age of twenty-seven when Kawakami, deeply influenced by his reading of the New Testament and Tolstoi's *My Religion,* joined the Unselfish Love Movement, a communalist, social service organization founded by a former priest of the True Pure Land Sect of Buddhism. In so doing Kawakami gave up his teaching position at Tokyo University, stopped writing for newspapers, left his wife and child, and sold everything he owned except a copy of the Bible and the poems of Shimazaki Tōson. The "thoroughgoingness" which he later identified as perhaps his most characteristic trait, led him in this case to renounce everything that did not benefit others, including sleep. The natural consequence of this— death—he determined to prepare himself for. It was in the midst of this spiritual crisis that he wrote:

> To Unselfish Love I have resolved to give my life
> And yet each day bestows new life on me.

Within a few months Kawakami abandoned both this experiment and the Unselfish Love Movement, but took up briefly the study and practice of Zen Buddhism. Eventually he returned to journalism and teaching, advancing rapidly in his academic career at Kyoto University and becoming a leading writer on economic questions. In the course of his study of Western economic theories he encountered Marxism, of which he quickly made himself one of the earliest and most authoritative interpreters. After the Russian Revolution, however, younger men newly returned from the headquarters of world communism subjected him to severe censure for his views. In spite of the fact that one of these critics was a former student of his, Kawakami humbly accepted correction and resolved to start anew in his study of Marxism. At this point he wrote:

> Without shaking off
> The dust of the last journey,
> I must set out again on a new road.

This further study led him fully to embrace Communism. At that time, however, the government was taking stronger measures against the Communists and his position as professor at an imperial university became untenable. After his resignation in 1928 he found himself drawn more and more into what was called the "actual movement" (i.e., mass political action). This would have been difficult enough for an intellectual quite unused to the hurly-burly of mass movements, but to make it worse the hazards of open political activity were increasing. Nonetheless, Kawakami felt keenly the need to prove that he was no mere "academician." Like Yoshida Shōin, who had come from the same province of Yamaguchi and had been Kawakami's hero and guiding star in his youth, he set out on the road to possible martyrdom, leaving his protesting wife in tears. After a period of open activity within the Communist-backed New Labor-Farmer Party, for which he ran as a candidate in one election, he was eventually forced underground. Shortly thereafter he finally gained formal admission to the Communist Party, an event which moved him deeply.

> Here, standing at my destination and looking backward—
> How far I have traveled across the rivers and mountains!

After his imprisonment in 1933, Kawakami's Marxist views did not change but his estimation of his own capacities for the political struggle did. When finally released he was a broken man, who died in 1946 after years of deprivation and malnutrition. Yet during the Second World War he voiced his faith in the future of Communism in characteristically religious terms: "Now, as I spend my remaining years in the midst of the Second World War, and watch things develop, I firmly believe in and eagerly await the advent of the communist society, in which everyone's daily conduct will accord with [the teaching]: 'Give to him that asketh thee, and from him that would borrow of thee turn thou not away.'" [1]

[1] *Jijoden* V, 157, October 28, 1942.

A Letter from Prison
[From Kawakami, *Jijoden*, V, 36–38]

I went to Tokyo to study at the age of twenty, after graduating from Yamaguchi High School. I had read the *Analects* of Confucius and Mencius, but had never laid hands on either the Buddhist scriptures or the Bible. The latter I read for the first time after going to Tokyo. But the moment I came across the passage "whoever shall smite thee on thy right cheek, turn to him the other also. And whosoever shall compel thee to go a mile, go with him twain. Give to him that asketh thee, and from him that would borrow of thee turn not thou away" [Matthew 5:39–42], it had a most decisive effect upon my life. This was something beyond all reasoning. My soul cried out from within itself, "That's right. It must be so." Of course, I was unable truly to put this teaching into practice, but every time something came up these words stimulated me, encouraged me, and drove me on to "extraordinary" actions. Thus the direction of my life was set toward a concern for others as well as for myself.

Two incidents took place before I moved from Tokyo to Kyoto. One was that I went and heard some speeches appealing for aid to the victims of copper poisoning at the Ashio Mine,[1] and donated the scarf and overcoat I was wearing. Furthermore, after going home, I packed up everything but what I had on and turned it over to them. Hearing that many people were on the verge of death from cold and disease in the affected area, and being urged to give anything I could spare, even old stockings, I was deeply moved and felt as if I were going to the rescue of somebody on the point of drowning. I thought I had done something good. But later I was scolded severely by my mother and suffered from a tremendous mental dilemma. It was quite natural that she should become angry, because she was supporting me without even having enough for herself to wear. And I freely gave away to others the things she had sent me at such great sacrifice to herself. This happened a little before I graduated from college.

The second incident was my joining up with the Unselfish Love Movement. This was two years after my graduation and while Kishiko[2] was

[1] Pollution from the Ashio copper mine affected farms nearby and became a big social and political issue at the time (1907).
[2] Refers to his first daughter.

still in her mother's womb. Unselfish Love was a movement propagated at that time by Mr. Itō Shōshin. (He is still engaged in a movement bearing the same name, but over the years it seems to have undergone a change in its content.) I joined the movement, giving up my teaching position and everything. After joining, I found out that the movement was a little different from what I had imagined it to be from the words "unselfish love," but I followed his theory and engaged in a sort of religious movement for a while. It was about this time that I made up my mind not to sleep at all, and consequently prepared myself for imminent death. It was an occasion when "death had to be faced squarely." Ever since, I believe, thanks to that ordeal I attained a great flexibility in life.

Looking back I realize that almost thirty years have passed since then. You might as well say that my being here in prison at the age of sixty stems from those passages in the Bible. I was given Bibles by some people at Toyotama Prison, Ichigaya Prison, and here. But I personally feel that I may be closer to the spirit of the Bible than those people who gave them to me.

Concerning Marxism

These excerpts are from Kawakami's *Prison Ramblings,* written shortly before and emended just after his release from prison in 1937. More of a personal testament than a theoretical discourse, it sets forth his basic faith in Marxism as the scientific solution to the problems of world depression and world war. Though Kawakami deprecated the value of anything written under the conditions of his confinement, prison memoirs like these were very popular reading after the Second World War and moved many people who would have been untouched by theoretical works to sympathize with Kawakami's cause.

[From Kawakami, *Gokuchū zeigo,* pp. 26–60]

The ruling classes in the various capitalist countries of today feel that Communism, which is trying to take the place of capitalism, is their greatest menace, and they fear and hate it more than anything else. As a consequence, in capitalistic countries at the present time such a thing as the free study of Communism is unthinkable. Night and day, the spurs are applied to conscious and unconscious counterpropaganda designed to slander Communism and Marxism, while refutations, arguments, and propaganda from the Marxist side that might oppose it are all prohibited. Even now, therefore, it is extremely difficult for ordinary people in society—those who are said to enjoy "liberty"—to obtain the books and materials with which to understand Marxism adequately, and they can hardly hope to do so without resorting to illegal methods (such as obtaining secretly books the importation or publication of which is prohibited).

Since this is true even in society, where there is "freedom," in an institution like a prison, whose function is precisely to restrict a man's freedom, it is more difficult to know the truth than to see a crow on a dark night. Common sense tells us that prisons nowadays are equipped with as many instruments as possible for causing men to think that Marxism (Communism) is mistaken. There sentiments such as might draw one to Marxism are as far as possible done away with. At least in the case of thought-criminals all the equipment and rules seem to have been consciously devised for the purpose of separating them from Marxism. Locked up in such a place, one can expect to have no true understanding of Marxism. In the last analysis, the second thoughts about Marxism one has in prison have nothing to do with true Marxism. It is natural, therefore, that though I was in prison for five years, there was no change in my academic beliefs. [pp. 26–28]

In our country, thought-criminals—and not only a small number of leaders but those of all degrees—have come to express a change in their thinking while imprisoned. It seems to me this may have become a sort of trend. In my view, this phenomenon has two meanings.

In one sense, it is proof of the fact that—as I have pointed out before—present-day Japanese prisons provide as many instruments as possible to make people think Marxism is mistaken.

In another sense, it is powerful evidence as to how many among the elements that have come to devote themselves to the Communist movement go no deeper than the superficial aspects of it and only echo the views of others. [The reasons for this are:] 1) The development of capitalism in Japan has been slower than in Western European countries; 2) On the occasion of the Meiji Restoration the bourgeois democratic revolution was not thoroughgoing and left feudal remnants in varying degrees; police restrictions on freedom of discussion and the like persisted throughout and were very cruel; 3) Beside the fact that the movement for Communist organization in Japan is young (capitalism entered a period of general crisis only after the World War), its growth has been ceaselessly trampled on from the beginning. Hampered by these circumstances, Communist education in Japan has been woefully incomplete. Also as a consequence, the majority of those who have come to devote themselves to the movement as "Communists" have not passed through the ideological discipline of Communists. Their basic training is very shallow, and they have not been Communists at all in the strict sense. The fact that thought-criminals—who are sometimes called "criminals by conviction"—necessarily lack firm convictions in Japan is certainly rooted in peculiarly Japanese conditions, but these peculiarities are not of the sort spoken of as the "Japanese spirit," or as a "national polity without parallel in the world," but are only peculiarities due to the development of Japanese capitalism and hence of the Japanese Communist movement. [pp. 30–32]

Again and again Communists are arrested and accused of being "disloyal to the nation." That this is a simple misconception, however, is made perfectly clear if we take just one glance at actual conditions in the Soviet Union. . . . Detailed figures on economic conditions in the Soviet Union are published annually. If studied carefully, they indicate the following: 1) there is no longer a single unemployed person in the Soviet Union; 2) national income and the wage fund are increasing by a certain percentage each year; 3) this lies in part in the annual increase of treasury expenditures for educational, health, and recreational facilities for the masses; 4) as a consequence the standard of living of the masses is very rapidly improving; 5) in order to make all this possible the productivity of labor (amount of production per worker), which is the "basic motive force of history," is truly developing rapidly; and 6) in this respect Japan, whose stagnation ranks with that of Hungary, Poland, and Rumania, is in a diametrically opposite condition. All this proves beyond doubt that my conjectures while in prison were in no way mistaken.

Reconsidering the question, then, we may well ask: Do such great advances in the fortunes of the Soviet Union and the unusual rise in the standard of living of its people indicate that the Russian Communists have been disloyal to their nation or betrayers of their country?

All they have destroyed is Russia's old ruling class. This class lived on the labor of all the people, but in number they were as one hair on nine oxen compared with the total population. Now that great socialist country, which in addition to destroying the old class society has incorporated one hundred some million people into a single "classless society," keeps the objective of a Communist society in view and has taken a huge step forward from a country of coercion to a country of freedom. The old Russia, which existed for the sake of the few, has fallen, and the new Russia, which exists for the sake of the masses, has risen. Such is the work of the Communists in Russia. The ruling class in Japan is said to be building a paradise in Manchuria. However, let us leave Manchuria aside for the moment. There is no doubt that Japan itself—particularly the farming villages in the Northeast—does not even come within ten thousand miles of paradise.

Since leaving prison, every time I have heard of political conditions in Japan—particularly when I heard of the outbreak of the Feb. 26 [1936] incident—I have realized that the contradictions inherent in Japanese capitalism are becoming progressively more and more violent. Everything has happened just as we scientifically predicted it would; nothing domestic or foreign has gone contrary to our expectations. How can one say that our thinking is mistaken? [pp. 47, 53-55]

One thing I must say is that the danger of a world war is increasing day by day. The prelude to a world war has already begun; the smell of gunpowder permeates both East and West, and the fire is waiting for some opportunity to break out suddenly and spread over the whole world. Even the most ignorant person must be aware of all this. (This spring—the sixth since the outbreak of the Manchurian Incident—there was a special ceremony at the Yasukuni Shrine. I heard on that occasion that from January to December last year [1936] the number of dead commemorated in the Yasukuni Shrine increased by one thousand several hundred. We must realize that it is not only in Spain that war is going on.)

Yet who is it that has proved scientifically that a world war is inevitable? Who has a scientific grasp of the basic causes of it? Who has a scientific faith that they can be eradicated?

It is none other than the Marxists—the Communists. This is my unalterable belief. For this reason, whenever during my imprisonment my spirits flagged, I spurred my will by reminding myself of the recent World War.

Thirty-four nations participated in it; 67,000,000 men volunteered or were conscripted; 70,000,000,000 yen were spent; some 7,000,000 men were killed; the wounded (outside of France, Rumania, and Russia) numbered 10,670,000; the misery entailed was truly indescribable. Since Japan was far removed from the center of the fighting, it suffered the least loss, so most of its citizens have no clear idea of how fearful a thing modern war is. If anything, they harbor feelings of bellicosity and are inclined to resort to war to settle things. However, if we reflect on the extraordinary advancement in weapons since the last World War—especially of air forces—the coming Second World War, with the misery it will bring to humanity, is truly a cause for alarm. In point of war dead alone, it will probably exceed by thousands upon thousands the dead of the first world war. Every time I think of it, while it engraves on my heart the chaos of the world, I also feel painfully that the responsibility Marxism has taught us to bear is indeed heavy.

Why is this?

Because only the Marxists know the real reasons why world war is inevitable; only the Marxists have the real method that the world offers us for eradicating it and, seeing their duty in regard to this method, fight for it.

Those who have foretold from the start on the basis of science that the international wars which have broken out since the beginning of the twentieth century would become world-wide are in truth none other than the Marxists. Those who have warned repeatedly that as long as capitalism is maintained, such periodic wars—together with world economic panics—are unavoidable, are in truth none other than the Marxists.

Whenever I think of this, even though confined in my study-room as a scientist, my blood becomes inflamed. Even when I was confined in prison, I saw no reason to drink the poison that would cause my heart to freeze. Fortunately my blood is still warm.

Our faith is such that, even though we should be imprisoned for a number of years, it would be possible to direct anew the attention of some dedicated men—themselves ready to undergo the same hardships—to the truth of Marxism. If we think of this, we can discover the full meaning of daily life, and there will be no real hardship. Since it is to save the hundreds of thousands and millions of lives that would be sacrificed in world wars breaking out among the nations every twenty or thirty years, the jeopardizing of one's own life need hardly be considered. [pp. 56–60]

A Change of Direction?

The most successful effort to gain left-wing representation in the Japanese Diet was made by the Socialist Masses Party (*Shakai taishū tō*), organized in 1932 to unite the forces of socialism. It had no sooner won a substantial bloc of seats in the 1936–37 elections, however, when the outbreak of war in China and the upsurge of nationalism confronted the party with a difficult choice: whether to support or oppose the war effort. At a party congress held in November, 1937, it was decided, in effect, that as a "mass" party the *Shakai taishū tō* had to identify itself with the whole Japanese people rather than with the proletariat as a separate class, and hope that it might thereby exert an influence in reshaping the new Japan. Its only left-wing rival, the Japan Proletarian Party (*Nihon musan tō*), which had proposed an "anti-fascist popular front," was suppressed that same year.

The significance of the new party platform and of the policy statements defending it in the party newspaper, as given below, should be seen in the light of the basic principles adopted at the founding of the party five years before. These were: 1) "Our party fights to protect the livelihood of the workers, farmers and laboring masses in general"; and 2) "Our party aims at the overthrow of capitalism and the liberation of the proletarian class."

[From *Shakai taishū shimbun*, Nos. 102 and 103]

BASIC PRINCIPLES OF THE SOCIALIST MASSES PARTY, NOVEMBER 30, 1937

1. Our party, on the basis of the fundamental principles of our national polity, plans for the advancement and development of the Japanese people, and in this way aims at the uplift of human culture.

2. Our party, representing the laboring masses, aims by reforming capitalism to achieve the planning of industry and the stabilization of the people's livelihood.

POLICY STATEMENT: THE MEANING OF THE REVISED PLATFORM

In the cooperative campaign policy statement, adopted at the second national convention in 1933, our party declared as follows: "Our class movement is not a narrow class movement. It does not imply a selfish kind of class interest, which gives no thought to the continued existence of the Japanese people or which would cause a rift between [the proletarian] class and [the Japanese] nation. Our movement denies that the Japanese people are conservative by nature. Through our movement we accept complete responsibility for the destiny and continued existence of the Japanese people." Again, in the autumn of 1934, when the War Ministry published its Army Pamphlet, "The Fundamentals of a Proposal on National Defense and How It Can Be Strengthened," our party immediately backed the theory of "national defense in the broad sense," as [the pamphlet] propounded it, and advocated relating national defense to the people's livelihood.

As long as our party was no more than a minor force in politics, even though we claimed to accept complete responsibility for the future of the Japanese people, no great importance was attached to that claim. Even party members themselves were unable to grasp with real feeling its great significance. Now, however, the rapid progress of our party has caused a change in the situation. In particular, the outbreak of the China Incident has prompted the party to take a clear stand in regard to the national polity and the Japanese people as a nation.

There are still some people who cannot understand how a proletarian party can be anything more than a political group for class conflict. When the party's responsibility toward the nation and the people is shown to them, they either become confused, or criticize it from a lofty point of view, or say that the party craves power. Such people conceive of our party simply as a party of perpetual critics or a perpetual opposition, "seasoning" parliamentary government. Or they expect it to be a mere cathartic in bourgeois politics, in a word, to have an Ozaki Yukio-like existence. That is, they are completely opposed to our party's wielding any political power.

Much as we regret saying it, our party has no reason to meet the wishes or expectations of these gentlemen. In fact, the party is rapidly advancing toward its goal of political power, and cherishes the hope that the Japan of the future will be built by our party. A political party is not a study group, let alone an association of critics.

To put it bluntly, in a wartime situation, these people are nothing but cowardly, negative pacifists, who shrivel up, folding their arms and lamenting that the times are against them.

In outward form, the present war is an incident between China and Japan, but in truth, it is a struggle against British capitalism in the Orient. Hence, it will not be easy to bring it to a conclusion. The success or failure of our national development probably hinges upon this profound international conflict.

At the same time, modern wars are not fought by soldiers alone, but require the mobilization of all of a nation's resources. Hence, they do not stop short of bringing about profound changes throughout society. While the laboring masses serve the nation by expending themselves on the battle field, they are also spending their strength on the home front to achieve increased productivity. If the internal organization of the nation which embraces all of them continues to be capitalistic as it has been in the past, basically dedicated to the principle of making profits for the capitalists, then there can be only temporary palliatives for the pressing problem of giving our servicemen full support on the home front by supplying them with, weapons and ammunition, much less for those problems of exchange, prices, and currency which have increasingly suffered the ravages of the piercing gale of international economic forces; and it will be impossible to construct any far-sighted program for the nation.

With a new platform and a new spirit of leadership, our party is advancing, not retreating. In the spirit of renovation, and with a conviction that the coming age belongs to us, we will fight with all our might to build a new Japan. [No. 102, November 30, 1937]

SUPPLEMENTARY STATEMENT, DECEMBER 15, 1937
Why Was the Platform Revised? . . . Why has the party revised its platform? In a word, it is because the party has progressed. To some the revision of the platform represents a change in direction for the party, but it is definitely not a change of direction; it is a step forward.

The pervading spirit of the previous platform was the class solidarity and class advancement of the proletariat, and further through these, the [drastic] reform [1] of capitalism. The goal of the party has been the reform of capitalism. However, the central problem of the proletarian party movement in its early stages has been the consolidation of the forces of reform—that is, the substantive [2] forces which should carry out reform. How can these substantive forces be organized?

The True Meaning of the Class Movement. Our party has taken as its

[1] The Japanese term *kaikaku* is ambiguous in that it is stronger than mere reformism yet does not necessarily imply violent revolution. The term "renovation" used elsewhere is meant to suggest the same kind of change.
[2] *Shutaiteki,* sometimes translated "subjective," here indicates the active core by whom, and in whose primary interest, other more passive elements are mobilized and led.

primary goal in the renovation movement to impart consciousness to the masses who have no [class] consciousness, to organize the masses who are ignorant of organization, and to give the capacity to fight to the masses who lack the capacity to fight. The renovation movement cannot exist where the substantive forces are not organized. In order to organize these key forces, we must clearly identify the special characteristics of this newly risen political force and aid its growth and development. Up to now we have to a greater degree than necessary stimulated a consciousness of the conflict between the working class and the capitalist class. Moreover, we have become sharply opposed to the established parties as political forces antagonistic to reform. This was an essential step in organizing the rising political forces for renovation. It was also natural that our former platform should indicate with special clarity the above-mentioned goal at that stage in the development of the toiling masses of the whole nation. However, though our movement has up to now emphasized class interest and striven hard for it, class interest was not its be-all and end-all, but only one policy in the process by which we hoped to advance the development and growth of all the toiling masses of the entire nation. . . .

Shouldering the People's Mission. In the past ten years through our movement we have developed from a minor force, a mere handful of reformers, to establish our present splendid position as the third party in the Diet, and have succeeded in building a substantive force of more than one million persons throughout the country. Now, as the present China Incident is reaching a crisis, the Japanese people are risking the survival of their race and are advancing into the very center of profound international conflicts. Now is the time for consolidating our gains of more than a decade. The inexorable mission which we must take upon ourselves is to shoulder full responsibility for the destiny and continued existence of the Japanese people, in accordance with the great Way for the renovation of Japan.

The first article of the new platform points out: "Our party, on the basis of the fundamental principles of our national polity, plans for the advancement and development of the Japanese people, and in this way aims at the uplift of human culture." This shows how we shall accomplish the racial mission of the Japanese race which we have taken upon ourselves. All the members of the party must be deeply moved by the

glorious achievement of having arrived at the point where the crystalliza-
tion of twenty years of toil and struggle has enabled us to shoulder the
mission of our race.

Push Forward Toward Renovation. Our party must not remain forever the "seasoning of parliamentary government." Some defeatist critics
may cherish the idea of its being a party of perpetual criticism, a party of
perpetual opposition, but this was never the mission of our party or the
reason for its existence. Our party does not exist for the sake of professional critics. It must exist for the sake of all the people of the whole
country. Guided by our new platform and following in the direction of
our new campaign policy, we must take our place triumphantly at the
head of the Japanese people, and thus move forward on the great path
of renovation. [No. 103, December 15, 1937]

KAWAI EIJIRŌ
Defense of Liberal Socialism

Kawai Eijirō (1891–1944), a professor in the Faculty of Economics at Tokyo
Imperial University, was probably the most brilliant of the non-Marxist
socialists in prewar Japan. Though he wrote about political and economic
questions of the day, such as capitalism, Communism, and Fascism, perhaps
his greatest contribution lay in developing a philosophical basis for humanitarian individualism in the Japanese context. This he derived in large measure
from his study of the works of Thomas Hill Green (1836–1882), the English
radical idealist of Oxford, where Kawai himself studied on one of his several
visits to Europe and America. Unlike most other prewar Japanese socialists,
either of the extreme or moderate variety, Kawai did not compromise himself
or "recant." He was put to the test in 1939 when he was investigated for an
alleged violation of the Press Code and was discharged from his post at the
University. The following selection is from a statement he submitted to the
court during his trial the following year which resulted in a verdict of innocent. In 1942, however, he was again brought to trial and convicted for an
"antiwar" article, after which he was forbidden to publish anything anymore.
What may seem a very moderate kind of socialistic liberalism (especially when
one notices Kawai's support of the "national polity") nevertheless took courage
and conviction in the context of wartime Japan.
[From Kawai, *Watakushi no shakai-shugi*, pp. 15–45]

In determining my position on social questions, I was confronted with
three factors. The first was the existing capitalist system enveloping my

environment, the next was liberalism, which was on the decline, and the third was Marxism, which was enjoying its greatest popularity. I could not accept capitalism in its present condition. The question was how to renovate it. The first thing I did was to study liberalism in order to put in order what should be retained and what might be let go. Next I turned to Marxism and decided to find out where its weaknesses lay. In this manner I constructed my position of what I called "third-stage liberalism" or idealistic social democracy. Taking this position, I opposed Marxism and was able to lend a hand in refuting its theoretical constructs. But one thing I would like to call attention to here is that, while opposing Marxism, along with emphasizing my differences with it, I unconsciously had to make certain concessions to it. This would have been unavoidable for anybody, I believe. It is both natural and effective to recognize what is correct in an opposing system of thought and accept that in order to refute the opposing system of thought as a whole. Accordingly, when you examine my socialism, I would like you to take into consideration the ideological background at the time I constructed my position, especially the popularity of Marxism. The important thing is the period when my writings were published and my theses made public. [pp. 15–16]

My concept of socialism was influenced by that of the British Labor Party, but no more than influenced, for I did not take over that concept of socialism as it was. My socialism is unique, and thus it is necessary for one first to discard any mental associations with socialism as it has existed in the past.

What I call socialist society is the *ideal* society which should succeed contemporary capitalism. According to my system of thought, it is the task of social philosophy to discuss the ideal of society. Since it tells us, "The society which is able to develop the personality of every member of society is the ideal society," this is the ultimate social ideal. With this social ideal as a norm we are enabled to perceive the various defects of contemporary capitalism. It is the task of social science to tell us what causes these defects and how we can correct them. Guided by both this social ideal and social science, we can conceive of the kind of society that should succeed contemporary capitalism. The socialist ideology which posits socialist society as the ideal is my type of socialism. [pp. 16–17]

I have been talking about socialism. But my brand of socialism does not rest on the philosophy of dialectical materialism like Marxism, and therefore, I do not say that, in analyzing capitalism scientifically, it will *necessarily* disintegrate or that socialism will *necessarily* arise. Idealists do not see society as progressing of necessity but rather as progressing in line with the wills of human beings guided by ideals. Thus, if socialism is an evil we must defend ourselves from it to the death; but if it is good, we must make its realization our goal. Here is the difference between deterministic socialism and teleological socialism. Because my philosophy is idealism, I do not explain things in terms of *necessity* as the Marxists do. I explain my aims in terms of my ideal. That is why when I talk about socialism my sentences have a strongly propagandistic flavor about them. This does not come from my "socialism" but from my "idealism." Anybody who explains socialism in terms of idealism, as I do, will necessarily become the same as I. Although I talk about socialism, as I shall explain subsequently, I reject illegal and espouse legal methods, abhor violent revolution, and prefer parliamentary means. Consequently, I do not address myself to the lowly plebs. I have never discussed socialism at a meeting of workers. I address my discussion of socialism to readers of a high class. I believe that actually only junior college graduates or above are able to read my writings. [pp. 24–25]

I have opposed the Marxist methods of violent revolution and dictatorship of the proletariat by substituting the means of formalistic liberty, namely, freedom of speech and freedom of political action. There are two methods of resisting violent revolution. One is to make clear the reasons why it is wrong. The other is to propose alternative policies. In my writings I have made clear the reasons why violent revolution, whether of the left or of the right, is wrong. I have proposed formalistic liberty as an alternative policy. But such an alternative policy must be logical all the way through and allow the enemy no opening for a thrust of logic. These are the terms in which I explain what I mean by formalistic liberty. That is, to the extent that it is speech and does not become action, I would give Marxism freedom of expression. And furthermore I would even give freedom of political activity to a Marxist party, as a legal political party, as long as it does not become the basis for carrying out revolution. As this point has led to a misunderstanding, I would like to try to explain it a little further here.

The first point to consider is whether, if the formalistic liberty I advocate is carried into effect, it will give rise to subversion. It is self-evident that, no matter what I advocate as an individual, it will not be carried into effect just as it is, since unfortunately I do not possess that much power or influence. Therefore, what I advocate will not be carried out until a majority in the Diet agrees with what I advocate. Even if what I advocate is a crime, it would not go into effect until a majority of the representatives in the Diet are my sympathizers. Furthermore, if the Diet is about to make a decision contrary to the beliefs of the governmental authorities, they can always take the step of dissolving the Diet. Therefore, in the case where the majority of the representatives have become my sympathizers, then the government itself agrees with me. Consequently the governmental authorities have become my sympathizers. Can advocating something that requires that the majority be its sympathizers before it can come into existence be a crime? Must someone who advocates something that can give rise to such conditions in the distant future through the process of cause and effect be a criminal? That he cannot seems to me clear, if one talks in terms of the conditions for the occurrence of a crime.

Up until now we have been supposing that the result would be subversive, if what I advocate were realized, but would the result really be subversive? 1) Since I have advocated freedom confined to speech and because I sanction regulation over₂ action, this is certainly not subversive action. 2) Also since I have placed speech directly causing action outside of the pale of freedom, as preparation for action, here again this is not subversive. 3) Since even in the category of speech, it is my opinion that freedom should not be allowed for speech that opposes the national polity (*kokutai*), this is not subversive in this respect either. 4) Even if the Communist Party, if not acting as an instrument to carry out revolution, were recognized as a legal party, there would be no danger. If the Communist Party were not practicing revolution it would be like a hound whose fangs had been extracted and it would not differ from other parties. Since speech or action directly preparatory to action, not to speak of immediately revolutionary action, are included in my definition of action, the party would be Communist in name only. Therefore, to be surprised by my saying that the Communist Party should be legal is to be made a prisoner of words.

Thus the result of allowing formalistic liberty would not be subversive at all. [pp. 36–39]

If any question still remains, it might be to say that advocating so cialism as such is detrimental. That is to say that, even if it remains only speech, it is detrimental and is disruptive to public peace and order. Earlier I made a statement to the court on "Is Socialist Propaganda Detrimental or Not?", but here I would like to add a supplemental statement from another angle. First of all, perhaps some people might maintain that socialism conflicts with the intent of the Constitution which guarantees the security of private property and that this causes unrest in the public mind. Certainly Article XXVII of the Constitution of the Empire of Japan says, "The right of property . . . shall remain inviolate . . ." and in the Preamble to the Constitution it is stated, "We now declare to respect and protect the security of . . . property." Nevertheless, the second paragraph of Article XXVII of the Constitution stipulates that private property can be limited by law. And based on this stipulation ownership has been greatly restricted by the Land Expropriation Law, the Requisition Order, the City Planning Law, the Forestry Law, the Rivers Law, the Mining Law, and so forth. Since socialism calls for the common ownership of the means of production in accordance with this stipulation, it does not conflict with the Constitution in the least. . . . Furthermore, the provisions of the Constitution clearly intend to provide protection from the incursions of dictatorship not based on law, and bearing in mind that second paragraph, it is not difficult to surmise that this protection would not be extended to limitations based on the agreement of the majority of the people. If it is said that socialistic speech gives rise to a feeling of insecurity concerning property it must be remembered that in the past and at present the state and municipalities have held and do hold such things as the postal, telegraph, and telephone systems, roads, water, gas, electricity, railroads, trolleys, and busses in common ownership. If common ownership of something is not detrimental, where is the logic for concluding that common ownership of all things is harmful? Besides, the present system of economic controls restricts everything from management to profits, and although ownership exists in name, so many restrictions have been placed on it in actuality it is almost as if it does not exist at all. Now finally a ration card system is being put into effect. This may be called a temporary set-up for the war emergency, but since the general tendency of capitalism has reached this development, it is only accidental that it is connected with war. Even after the war is over, it cannot be thought that all these controls will disappear entirely. If it be said that socialism brings about uneasiness in the popular mind, it must be remembered that the present system which is not yet socialism is already causing uneasiness in the public mind, but if this is not the case, then it cannot be said that socialism either gives rise to feelings of uneasiness. [pp. 40–45]

AKAMATSU KATSUMARO
The Japanese Social Movement in Retrospect

We have already seen in the preceding selections how the "unnatural" development of Japanese capitalism was believed to have a crucial effect on the labor and socialist movements. In this preface to a history of the Japanese social movement, written in 1951 by a veteran right-wing socialist, the conclusion is drawn that the prewar proletarian struggle, being inevitably linked with the development of capitalism and political democracy, was seriously hampered by the weakness of the bourgeoisie itself. It was in some such terms that most Japanese "intellectuals" in the post-Second World War decade explained the course of recent Japanese history.

[From Akamatsu, *Nihon shakai undō-shi,* i–iv]

Generally speaking, what we call the social movement is a movement for the emancipation of the working masses which arose in opposition to the abuses of capitalism, so it is a social phenomenon which has unfailingly emerged in every capitalist state. It is worthy of note, however, that the character of the social movement differs significantly in different countries. The most important point in this respect is that, though several states may all be called capitalistic, the nature of the social movement is extremely different in those states where democracy has been developed from those in which it has not. The states where democracy has developed are the advanced capitalist states and the states where there are still strong vestiges of feudalism are the backward capitalist states.

Now, according to the history of the advanced capitalist states, those who overthrew the feudal system were the bourgeoisie. This was not achieved by the power of the bourgeoisie alone, but their social power made the bourgeoisie the leading force. They seized political power, replacing the feudal lords, and developed the capitalism which had already been growing within feudal society to a high point. Their theory of revolution was democracy, it being necessary for capitalist society to take on a democratic character. Thus, capitalist society had to recognize freedom of speech, of assembly, and of association, which had not been recognized in feudal society. Thereupon, the social movement grew with these freedoms as a base. The social movement in the advanced countries was at first subjected to some oppression, but, because there existed this social base of democracy, it was able to follow a relatively normal course of development.

It goes without saying that Japan is a backward capitalist state. The Meiji Restoration struck the final note of the feudal period but it was not the bourgeoisie who overthrew the Tokugawa regime; it was anti-Tokugawa feudal power centered about the Satsuma and Chōshū clans. The Meiji government, which had newly seized political power, was subjected to the pressures of the tides of world capitalism and embarked upon the construction of a capitalist state. The policies which were adopted were modeled upon those of the advanced capitalist states. Beginning with government, finance, and economics, and extending to military and intellectual affairs, Europeanization was adopted in the name of civilization. The Meiji government, which attempted to resist the pressures of world capitalism and to maintain the independence of the state, pursued an inevitable course in adopting this hasty policy of Europeanization.

Capitalism in Japan was gradually built up but it was fostered by the state itself and not by the bourgeoisie. In order to achieve the state aim of a "rich country and strong army" the government, following a state policy of industrialization, transplanted capitalism from the West and protected and fostered its development. There was a step backward in the industrial policy of the government in about 1881 when a change was made from protectionism to liberalism. From the principle of model state-owned factories there was a shift to the principle of protection and encouragement of private enterprise. This was only a retreat by the government from the front line of industrial economics and no change at all from the original policy of protection. There was no history in Japan, as in the advanced countries, of the bourgeoisie, which had seized real economic power, taking its stand on laissez faire and struggling against state protectionism.

As has been indicated, nationalism and capitalism in Japan were linked together from the outset. Since capitalism developed under the wing of nationalism, there was no room for the growth of democracy. Consequently, the social conditions for the development of a social movement did not exist. Until recently there existed many legal regulations restricting the social movement and, despite the self-sacrificing efforts of pioneers, this was one of the basic reasons why the social movement had to carry on its struggles at a great disadvantage.

The social movement in Japan finally acquired a mass base after 1919. Taking advantage of the First World War, capitalism in Japan achieved a high point of development, and at the same time it was influenced by world-wide currents of democracy. On a political level, universal manhood suffrage was established, party government was brought into being, and a long step was taken toward creating a democratic system. As a consequence of this, the social movement was freed from the harsh oppression which had continued from the Meiji Period, and it became possible for it to grow in a democratic atmosphere.

With the First World War as a high point, capitalism in Japan gradually came to a standstill. At home and abroad the development of capitalism had all but reached the point of saturation. In addition, the world-wide depression after the war drew our economy into the torrent. The rapid increase in population and the poverty of our resources, which were the peculiar economic weaknesses of our country, cast a cloud of gloom over the outlook for capitalism.

The Manchurian Incident of 1931 was an attempt to break the deadlock by imperialistic methods. Next came the China Incident, and then the Pacific War. In the political arena the political parties made their exit and, with the rise of the military bureaucrats, the economic system was brought under rigid control. Thereupon, democracy was again driven into an unfortunate position, and the social movement was weakened and destroyed.

In short, the growth of a backward capitalism since Meiji times was abnormal, and as a consequence democracy did not develop properly. As a result, the social movement in its development in Japan was not able, as in advanced countries, to take on a proper character.

ŌYAMA IKUO
Japan's Future Course

Ōyama Ikuo (1880–1956), a professor of political science at Waseda University, first won fame as a "brilliant leader" of the left-wing when he assumed the chairmanship of the Labor-Farmer Party in 1927. With the increasing repression of radical movements after the Manchurian occupation, Ōyama took refuge in the United States, where he had studied earlier, and taught at Northwestern through the war years. It is a striking fact that Japan has had few political exiles in modern times (the only other noteworthy exception being Nosaka Sanzō, a refugee among the Chinese Communists). Despite the comfortable circumstances in which he found himself, Ōyama could not resign himself to the life of an expatriate, but felt increasingly a sense of identification with the Japanese people, of failure and shame over Japan's misconduct, and of responsibility for helping her rise from the ashes of defeat. When he finally returned to Japan in 1947, Ōyama soon became the "grand old man" of the left wing. Active in socialist and pacifist movements, but not associated with a particular party, he was elected to the upper house of parliament, and after visits to Communist China and the Soviet Union, was awarded a Stalin Peace Prize. The following excerpt, the conclusion to a book written shortly after his return to Japan, expresses attitudes and ideals shared by many Japanese, but especially by "progressives," in the postwar period.

[From Ōyama, *Nihon no shinro,* pp. 153–63]

Since the Meiji Restoration, the ruling class in Japan has built up a system of nationalistic ethics called "the essence of national polity" and based on the ideology of the family state inherited from the feudal age. It has indoctrinated the nation with this type of thought through universal conscription and uniform national education. By this method, the ruling class has tried, on the one hand, to check the trend toward the awakening of individuals that was engendered by the modernization of society, and, on the other, to expel the democratic and socialistic ideas that were rushing in from the outside world. However, this attempt was not entirely successful. For, despite the fact that it was backed by many suppressive laws and the threat of brutal oppression by the military and the police, there were widespread movements of resistance of various kinds, which it succeeded in eliminating only immediately before and during the Second World War. Unfortunately these resistance movements came too late. They were smashed before they could develop into nation-wide insurrection by the suppressive policy of the ruling class—a policy that hardened greatly in anticipation of the war. Nevertheless these movements clearly disproved the idea that the Japanese were an essentially authoritarian people.

Still, the policy of ideological seclusion inherited from the Meiji era was continued to the end. There was a short break during the decade after the First World War, a period of rising liberalism in Japan. But after the outbreak of the Manchurian Incident, it was increasingly strengthened until it reached its peak during the Second World War. During this war, the militarists established complete control over national public opinion. Thereby the intelligence and conscience of the people were completely benumbed. Thus, world-disturbing actions by Japan, which reached their climax in the attack on Pearl Harbor, had nation-wide support. At home, furthermore, even a number of former leaders of movements for the emancipation of the proletariat joined the camp of the ruling class and became supporters and propagators of the imperialistic policy; abroad, soldiers left the worst stains on our history by their atrocities. Truly, in this period, the intellectual and moral standard of the Japanese was at its worst. A sample of the propaganda used by the militarists was "War is the father of creation and the mother of culture." But the contrary has proved to be the case.

At this point, the Japanese have to criticize themselves thoroughly. They must re-examine every nook and corner of their souls. The most important thing for a new Japan is moral reflection. Without it, a new Japan is impossible and her return to international society is out of the question.

The Potsdam Declaration not only gave a ray of hope for the national existence of Japan but also suggested a future direction for Japan and provided a foundation for her democratization. It allowed Japan to have industry, to import raw materials, and to participate in international trade, in order to enable her to support her economy and to meet the demands for "just reparation" by the allies. The Japanese people know that the reparations problem is of the greatest consequence to the future of the nation. They are also aware that conclusion of a peace treaty is the first step in Japan's return to international society, which they look forward to. They also realize that it is high time to start preparing for her return.

As a result of defeat, the wall that secluded the Japanese mind from the outside world broke down. The Japanese people could see the world as it was for the first time. There they saw the great structure of the United Nations. This is the only existing organ for international cooperation for the maintenance of world peace. It embodies the ideals of international democracy and international ethics, which are based upon the concept of human solidarity, and which have gradually developed among the allied powers since the time of the League of Nations. Its present form may not be perfect. But the fact that such a thing has been realized is of the greatest historical significance.

When the Japanese people began to realize that democratization and international cooperation were a single historical necessity for Japan, the new Constitution was established in the full view of the public. Formally, it has some of the marks of a constitution granted by the sovereign, but in its content it contains a number of principles for which we fought in our struggles for political freedom. By and large, it is a democratic constitution. It may not be perfect, but it leaves the way open to correct its deficiencies. Even as it is, it is quite useful as an instrument for our present task: the establishment of democracy.

The new Constitution of Japan has two major principles: a proclamation that sovereignty lies in the people and a declaration to renounce war. Naturally, it corresponds to the United Nations Charter in many respects. In the process of establishing a democratic social order, we must try to make use of this Constitution so that it may not remain a mere piece of paper. But first we have to start by getting rid of the traditional nationalistic doctrine based upon the ideology of the family state and try to acquire an international political ethics corresponding to the concept of human solidarity.

We also have to realize fully the significance of the declaration renouncing war. This declaration is not a mere accessory, but a guiding principle to regulate our future national life. With this ideal, Japan is going to enter the international stage as an unarmed nation. This is a new role for the Japan that until yesterday was armed from top to toe as one of the imperialistic powers. A nation without arms is a nation without power. The political science of the past taught that a nation consists of land, people, and power. From Niccolò Machiavelli, who wrote *The Prince* at the beginning of modern times, to Lenin, who, at the beginning of this century, was the central figure of the Russian Revolution and was the author of *The State and Revolution,* there has been nobody who neglected the factor of power in the concept of the nation. The eminent Treitschke's favorite phrase, *"Der Staat ist Macht,"* from his history of political theory, is the essence of several centuries of theories on the concept of the nation. Power means mainly military forces and the police. According to section eight[1] of the new constitution, Japan is not to possess an army, navy, air force, or other military forces (except for police forces). From the point of view of a cynic, a state without power cannot be a nation. But for a student who earnestly accepts the new concept of sovereignty expressed in the United Nations Charter, it is undoubtedly a new type of nation. As such a new type of nation, Japan will live and develop in the new political surroundings of a world that has acquired the United Nations. If she succeeds in the experiment of existing as such a nation, her contribution to the world will be immensely great. For it will set a concrete example of the ideal of universal disarmament that mankind has been dreaming of for centuries.

In order for Japan to exist as a nation without arms, everlasting world peace is a necessary premise. Therefore, the efforts of the Japanese should be concentrated upon the establishment of such peace. It is for this purpose that Japan has to prepare as soon as possible for participation in the United Nations. She should not be more partial to some nations than to others in her international relationship. As soon as she re-establishes a normal national life, she should try to form most friendly relationships with all nations through the United Nations. This should be the only basic principle of her future international policy.

If Japan holds to absolute pacifism, she must ultimately rely upon science in order to build the material foundations for her national existence. In the past, the ruling class of Japan has tried to justify her thoughtless expansionist policy on the grounds of her so-called "over-population." We have to make it our central industrial policy to promote production through the utilization of science, discarding the idea of territorial expansion. Only by this policy can Japan make her "over-population" an asset instead of a liability. Especially if the peaceful use of atomic energy should start in the next few years, as nuclear scientists confidently predict, the establishment of the material foundations of Japan's existence may be hopefully expected. In this respect, it is reassuring to know that the past contribution of Japanese science to the progress of nuclear science has gained international recognition, and that the names of some Japanese nuclear scientists are commonly men-

[1] Actually section nine. [Ed.]

tioned by their American colleagues. Furthermore, from this point of view, I find a special significance in the movement to cooperate with UNESCO.

Lastly we have to study and do something about the problem of preventing a third world war, which is a continuous threat to the people of the world. I believe it of the utmost importance to start a powerful peace movement throughout the entire nation, in order to inform progressive people in the world of the fact that the Japanese people too have a fervent desire to establish world peace. I will do my best to contribute to this movement.

Let me repeat again. Establishment of a democratic Japan cannot be separated from establishment of a pacifistic Japan. Today the development of the democratic ideal has reached its peak in the concept of international democracy.

CHAPTER XXIX

THE JAPANESE TRADITION
IN THE MODERN WORLD

In this introduction to Japanese thought in modern times our attention has so far been focused upon political and social movements which had the most immediate effect on Japanese life or Japanese relations with the rest of the world. It has not been possible to examine in all their variety and complexity other currents of thought—intellectual, aesthetic, and religious—which ran in deeper channels beneath the surface of events and yet which may eventually prove of more lasting significance. Postwar Japan, however, presents us with a situation in which it is still more difficult to discern any clear trend of thought, even in the political sphere. It is true that since the occupation Japanese politics have been relatively stable. For a decade the government has been largely in the hands of those who are the direct heirs of the type of liberalism dominant in the '20s. Nevertheless their ascendancy in the '50s has not as yet been attended by an upsurge of liberal and democratic thought such as that which burst forth from a more self-confident and optimistic Japan in earlier decades. Nor does it seem today that the perennial Socialist opposition, which received much impetus and strength under the American occupation, has, for all its support among intellectuals and students, found spokesmen of commanding stature or bold originality of thought. This has been a period of intellectual readjustment and spiritual groping, as the Japanese have tried to find some solid ground upon which to rebuild after a shattering defeat.

But if, at such close range, the past ten years seem to have been a period of transition, we should remember that it is only the latest phase in a much larger process which has been continuing since Japan's opening to the West. Those today who seek a direction for Japan to take are looking to the past as well as to the future, to the West as much as to the East. They are re-examining those beliefs which seem to have failed them; they are listening again to men who could hardly be heard earlier. They are wondering what "East" and "West" represent, and what it means to be a Japanese in the modern world.

Questions of this sort have been in the minds of Japanese since the mid-nineteenth century, and the reconciliation of modern Western thought with Oriental traditions has been a central problem of Japanese thinkers ever since the days of Sakuma Shōzan. Shōzan's formula, "The ethics of the East, the science of the West," acknowledged the technological superiority of the West while reaffirming the traditional spiritual values of Japan. It sought the best of both worlds without seriously considering the question of their compatibility. In the early twentieth century, however, the effects of technological and social change were ever more strongly felt in the ethical and intellectual spheres, where the direct influence of Western thought in education and mass communication also challenged traditional attitudes. We have already examined one type of traditionalist reaction to this challenge, as expressed in the official *Fundamentals of Japan's National Polity*. Here Japanese culture was hailed as a successful synthesis of Eastern and Western civilization, based upon a distinctively Japanese "spirit" which was the key also to the unresolved dilemmas of Western society. Implicit in this ostensible synthesis of East and West, however, was a violent attack on some of those attitudes often considered basic to modern Western civilization—most notably its rationalism and individualism—together with an insistence upon a system of ethics justified mainly in terms of nationalism.

In postwar Japan the collapse of this system of ethics, in the artificial form in which it had been propagated by the State, has produced probably the most intense re-examination of its basic values by any nation in modern times. We have seen that in the prewar world ethical and spiritual attitudes were already considered to underlie basic political problems by exponents of democracy and liberalism as well as of Japanese tradition. More recently, as Ōyama Ikuo emphasizes in *Japan's Future Course,* the need for an ethical outlook which is "international" in character, which establishes a common bond between the Japanese and other peoples of the world, has been widely acknowledged, again, by persons of differing political views.

The purpose of this concluding chapter is to present a variety of significant opinions on such central issues as those raised above. It is meant to serve as a symposium, suggesting some of the alternatives which face Japan today and the diversity of opinion which exists in regard to basic issues. The readings therefore represent points of view which are seriously held and listened to with some respect today; they are not meant to represent definite trends or organized movements in recent Japanese thought.[1] The influence of some of these writers has been greater than that of others (this is especially true of the dead as compared to those still living). The level at which they approach these questions also varies according to the diverse roles of the writers in Japanese life: Uchimura Kanzō as a religious leader and social reformer whose influence has been felt among leading figures in contemporary Japanese education and journalism; Nishida Kitarō as a professional philosopher whose writings became best-sellers just after the Second World War; Kawakami Hajime as a Marxist (See Chapter XXVII) who had a wide audience among students and intellectuals; Tanaka Kōtarō as a jurist, and so on. Through their eyes the reader may gain a better idea of the range and variety of recent Japanese thought than the preceding chapters could suggest, and also obtain a better perspective on traditional Japanese thought and culture as seen today from the different vantage points these writers offer.

UCHIMURA KANZŌ, A CHRISTIAN AND A JAPANESE

Uchimura Kanzō (1861–1930) stands as a striking example of the attempt by a deeply dedicated man to integrate his new-found Christian faith into his personal and public life as a true Japanese. Born of a former samurai family, he was first drawn to Christianity at a new government agricultural school in Hokkaido and was later fully confirmed in it while studying at Amherst. Back in Japan he immediately became a storm center when, as a teacher, he refused to conform to the practice of bowing before the Imperial Rescript on Education, an act of loyalty assiduously promoted by the government but offensive to Uchi-

[1] Here, for example, the influence of Zen Buddhist thought is reflected in a professional philosopher (Nishida) and a Marxist theoretician (Kawakami). If we were dealing with religious movements as such, the name of D. T. Suzuki, whose writings are already well-known in the West, would have to be given a prominent place as one who gained for Zen the same recognition in the West that Vivekananda won for Hinduism.

mura's total devotion to Christ. Similarly, when he turned to journalism as a contributing editor to one of the most influential newspapers of the time, he came into conflict with the government as a social reformer and pacifist. Finally he shifted to a life of writing and teaching on his own, and gathered around him a group of able young men who have since established themselves as leaders in the fields of education and journalism.

As a Christian Uchimura developed no systematic philosophy or theology of his own, but propagated a new form of religion reflecting his fierce independence of mind and his determination to accept no foreign support. This was the non-church movement, completely devoid of a professional clergy or ecclesiastical organization, which depended solely on the contributions of native Japanese and had no ties with Western mission societies. Though widely known as a writer on social questions, Uchimura is most effective when his writing is of an intensely personal kind, dealing with his religious experiences and convictions.

UCHIMURA KANZŌ
How I Became a Christian

Uchimura's most famous work, this spiritual autobiography was first written in English and published in Japan in 1895. It was later republished in Japanese (and four European languages) and is still widely read. The selections included here represent the three stages of his religious development.

[From Uchimura, Zenshū, XV, 14–15, 96–97, 113–14, 120–21]

One Sunday morning a schoolmate of mine asked me whether I would not go with him to "a certain place in foreigners [sic] quarter, where we can hear pretty women sing, and a tall big man with long beard shout and howl upon an elevated place, flinging his arms and twisting his body in all fantastic manners, to all which admittance is entirely free." Such was his description of a Christian house of worship conducted in the language which was new to me then. I followed my friend, and I was not displeased with the place. Sunday after Sunday I resorted to this place, not knowing the awful consequence that was to follow such a practice. An old English lady from whom I learned my first lessons in English took a great delight in my church-going, unaware of the fact that sight-seeing, and not truth-seeking, was the only view I had. . . .

Christianity was an enjoyable thing to me so long as I was not asked to accept it. Its music, its stories, the kindness shown me by its followers, pleased me immensely. But five years after, when it was formally presented to me to accept it, with certain stringent laws to keep and much sacrifice to make, my whole nature revolted against submitting myself to such a course. That I must set aside one day out of seven specially for religious purpose, wherein I must keep myself from all my other studies and enjoyments, was a sacrifice which I thought next to impossible to make. And it was not flesh alone which revolted against accepting the new faith. I early learned to honor my nation above all others, and to worship my nation's gods and no others. I thought I could not be forced even by death itself to vow my allegiance to any other gods than my country's. I should be a traitor to my country, and an apostate from my national faith by accepting a faith which is exotic in its origin. All my noble ambitions which had been built upon my former conceptions of duty and patriotism were to be demolished by such an overture. I was then a Freshman in a new Government College, where by an effort of a New England Christian scientist, the whole of the upper class (there were but two classes then in the whole college) had already been converted to Christianity. The imperious attitude of the Sophomores toward the "baby Freshmen" is the same the world over, and when to it was added a new religious enthusiasm and spirit of propagandism, their impressions upon the poor "Freshies" can easily be imagined. They tried to convert the Freshies by storm; but there was one among the latter who thought himself capable of not only withstanding the combined assault of the "Sophomoric rushes" (in this case, religion-rush, not cane-rush), but even of reconverting them to their old faith. But alas! mighty men around me were falling and surrendering to the enemy. I alone was left a "heathen," the much detested idolator, the incorrigible worshiper of wood and stones. I well remember the extremity and loneliness to which I was reduced then. One afternoon I resorted to a heathen temple in the vicinity, said to have been *authorized by the Government* to be the guardian-god of the district. At some distance from the sacred mirror which represented the invisible presence of the deity, I prostrated myself upon coarse dried grass, and there burst into a prayer as sincere and genuine as any I have ever offered to my Christian God since then. I beseeched that guardian-god to speedily extinguish the new enthusiasm in my college, to punish such as those who obstinately refused to disown the strange god, and to help me in my humble endeavor in the patriotic cause I was upholding then. After the devotion, I returned to my dormitory, again to be tormented with the most unwelcome persuasion to accept the new faith.

Uchimura himself became a Christian shortly thereafter. A few years later he went to the United States and there tried to find salvation in service to those less fortunate than himself.

Soon after my arrival in America, I was "picked up" by a Pennsylvania doctor, himself a philanthropist of the most practical type. After probing a little into my inner nature, he agreed to take me into his custody, and placed me among his "attendants" with a prospect that I might taste all the ways up from the very lowest of practical charity. The change was quite a sudden one for me from an officer in an imperial government to an attendant in an Asylum for Idiots; but I did not feel it, as the Carpenter-Son of Nazareth taught me now an entirely new view of life.

Let me here note that I entered a hospital service with somewhat the same aim as that which drove Martin Luther into his Erfurt convent. I took this step, not because I thought the world needed my service in that line, much less did I seek it as an occupation (poor though I was), but because I thought it to be the only refuge from "the wrath to come," there to put my flesh in subjection, and to so discipline myself as to reach the state of inward purity, and thus inherit the Kingdom of Heaven. At the bottom, therefore, I was egoistic, and I was to learn through many a painful experience that egoism in whatever form it appears is of devils, and is sin. In my efforts to conform myself to the requirements of philanthropy, which are perfect self-sacrifice and total self-forgetfulness, my innate selfishness was revealed to me in all its fearful enormities; and overpowered with the darkness I descried in myself, I sunk, and writhed in unspeakable agonies. Hence the dreary records of this part of my existence. The present-day reader, more accustomed to the sunny side of human existence, may not be disposed to take them in with any degree of seriousness; but to the sufferer himself, they are the accounts of veritable Actualities out of which came the long-sought Peace, and all the blessed fruits resulting therefrom. . . .

[343]

As a result of thinking done while recuperating from an illness, Uchimura decided to enter Amherst College.

I was given a room in the college dormitory free of charge; and as I had neither a table, nor a chair, nor a bed, nor even a wash-tub, the kind president ordered the janitor to provide me with a few such necessities. There in a room in the uppermost story I settled myself, firmly making up my mind never to move from the place till the Almighty should show Himself unto me. With an aim like this in view, I was entirely insensible to the lack of my personal comforts. The former occupant of my room had the carpet removed from the floor, and the new occupant was not able to re-carpet it. There I found however a table crippled of its drawers, but as its four feet were stiff and strong, I made a very good use of it. There was also an old easy chair with one of its corners broken off, so that it stood readily upon tripods; but with a slight equiposing of my body, I could sit and work upon it quite comfortably. The bedstead was of wooden frame and a good one, but it squeaked, and the bed-cover harbored some living specimens of *Cimex lectualis,* commonly called the bed-bug. I provided myself with a Yankee lamp of the simplest construction, and this with a small wash-vase besides constituted the whole of my furnitures. I had my pen and ink and paper, and a praying heart to fill up all the rest. . . .

March 8 [1886]—*Very important day in my life. Never was the atoning power of Christ more clearly revealed to me than it is today. In the crucifixion of the Son of God lies the solution of all the difficulties that buffeted my mind thus far. Christ paying all my debts can bring me back to the purity and innocence of the first man before the Fall. Now I am God's child, and my duty is to believe Jesus. For* His *sake, God will give me all I want. He will use me for His Glory, and will save me in Heaven at last.* . . .

Those of you who are "philosophically" inclined may read the above passage with a sort of pity, if not with disdain. You say, by the advent of new science into this world, the religion of Luther, Cromwell, and Bunyan, has now passed into a "tradition." You say that "it stands against reason" that faith in a dead Saviour should give a man life. I do not argue with you then. Perhaps a thing like "the responsible soul before the Almighty God" has never troubled you much. Your ambition may not extend beyond this short span of existence called Life, and *your* Almighty

Judge may be that conventional thing called Society, whose "good enough" may give you all the peace you need. Yes, the crucified Saviour is necessary only to him or her who has eternity to hope for, and the Spirit of the Universe to judge his or her inmost heart. To such the religion of Luther and Cromwell and Bunyan is *not* a tradition, but the verity of all verities.

With all the ups and downs that followed the final grasping of the Crucified Son of God, I will not trouble my reader. Downs there were; but they were less than ups. The One Thing riveted my attention, and my whole soul was possessed by It. I thought of it day and night. Even while bringing up scuttles of coal from the basement floor to the topmost story where my lodging was, I meditated upon Christ, the Bible, the Trinity, the Resurrection, and other kindred subjects. Once I laid down my two scuttles (I carried two to balance myself) when I reached the middle floor, and then and there burst into a thanksgiving prayer for a new explanation of the Trinity that was revealed to me on my way from the "coal-hill." . . . Whenever Satan left me free to myself, I pictured to myself the dear and blessed homeland away beyond the seas, and spotted it with churches and Christian colleges, which of course had their existence in my imagination only. No inspiring thought ever came to my mind but I reserved it as a message to my countrymen. Indeed, an empire and its people swallowed up all my leizure [*sic*] hours.

The Case of Lese Majesty

This letter, written by Uchimura to an American friend two months after he had refused to bow before the Education Rescript, graphically portrays the personal consequences of his decision to become a Christian.
[From Uchimura, *Zenshū*, XX, 206–9]

March 6, 1891

Dear Mr. Bell,

Since I wrote you last, my life has been a very eventful one. On the 9th of Jan. there was in the High Middle School where I taught, a ceremony to acknowledge the Imperial Precept on Education. After the address of the President and reading of the said Precept, the professors and students were asked to go up to the platform one by one, and *bow* to the Imperial signature affixed to the Precept, *in the manner as we used to bow before our ancestral relics as prescribed in Buddhist and Shinto ceremonies.* I was not at all prepared to meet such a strange ceremony, for the thing was the new invention of the president of the school. As I was the third in turn to go up and bow, I had scarcely time to think upon the matter. So, hesitating in doubt, I took a safer course for my Christian conscience, in the august presence of sixty professors (all non-Christians, the two other Xtian prof.'s beside myself having absented themselves) and over one thousand students, I took my stand and did *not* bow! It was an awful moment for me, for I instantly apprehended the result of my conduct. The anti-Christian sentiment which was and still is strong in the school, and which it was a very delicate affair to soothe down by meekness and kindliness on our part, found a just cause (as they suppose) for bringing forth against me accusations of insult against the nation and its Head, and through me against the Christians in general. . . .

For a week after the ceremony, I received several students and prof.'s who came to me, and with all the meekness I can master I asked them if they found anything in me which was contrary to the Imperial Precept, in my daily conduct in the school, in my conversations among the students, and in my past history as a loyal subject of Mikado. I told them also that the good Emperor must have given the precepts to his subject *not* to be bowed unto, but to be obeyed in our daily walks in life. My logic and demonstrations were enough to silence them individually, but as a body, their anger and prejudice were unquenchable. Meanwhile, a severe form of influenza took hold of me. Within a week, it changed to a dangerous form of pneumonia. My poor wife and mother stood by my bed night and day, while the merciless world raged outside. They called up the principal of the school out of his sickbed to have satisfaction for my case. He, the principal, had been my good friend ever since my first connection with the school; so he tried his best to retain me in the school without compelling me to go through the humiliation of *bowing* before the precept. But the cry of my enemies was that of the Jews to Pilate, "If thou let this man go, thou art not Caesar's friend." He wrote me a very kind letter, approving and applauding my conscientious act and almost imploring me *to conform to the custom* of the nation, assuring me that the *bow* does *not* mean *worship,* but merely respect to the Emperor. Then he described the real state of the school, that to appease the students who could not understand me, the only course will be to bear humiliation on my part. The latter touched me, especially as I was in great physical weakness. That the *bow* does *not* mean *worship,* I myself have granted for many years. Here in Japan, it often means no more than taking of [*sic*] hat in America. It was not *refusal* but *hesitation* and *conscientious scruples* which caused me to deny the bow at that moment; and now that the Principal *assured* me that it was *not worship,* my scruples were removed, and though I believed the ceremony to be a rather foolish one, for the sake of the school, the principal, and *my* students, I consented to bow.

The Non-Church Movement [1]
[From Uchimura, *Zenshū,* IX, 210-13]

Mukyōkai does not have the negative meaning one sees in anarchism or nihilism; it does not attempt to overthrow anything. "Non-church" is the church for those who have no church. It is the dormitory for those who have no home, the orphanage or foundling home for the spirit. The negative character in the word *mukyōkai* should be read *nai*—without— rather than *mu ni suru*—destroy—or *mushi suru*—despise. Are not those without money, without parents, without houses to be pitied? We believe there to be many sheep without shepherds, many Christians without churches. It is for them that we are writing this small magazine. . . .

The true form of the church is *Mukyōkai.* There is no organized church in heaven. The Revelation of John says, "I saw no temple (church) within the city (heaven)." Bishops, deacons, preachers, and teachers exist only here on earth. In heaven, there is neither baptism nor communion; neither teachers nor students: "Then I saw a new heaven and a new earth, for the first heaven and the first earth had passed away, and there was no longer any sea. And I saw the new Jerusalem, the holy city, come down out of heaven from God, like a bride dressed and ready to meet her husband" (Rev. 21: 1-2, Goodspeed Translation). *Mukyōkai* hopes to introduce this sort of church to the world.

Naturally, however, as long as we remain on this earth, we need churches. Some people will join churches constructed by the hands of men: there they will praise God, and there they will hear his word.

[1] Translated from the Japanese original.

Some churches will be made of stone, others of brick, and still others of wood. But not all of us need churches of this sort. That there are many Christians who do not belong to organized Christianity is similar to the fact that there are many homeless children. But even those of us who do not belong to organized Christianity need some sort of church while we exist on this earth. Where is our church and what is it like?

It is God's universe—nature. Its ceiling is the blue sky, with stars bejeweling its boards; its floor is the green fields, and its carpets the multicolored flowers; its musical instruments are pine twigs and its musicians the small birds of the forest; its pulpit is the mountain peaks and its preacher is God himself. This is our church. No church, whether in Rome or in London, can approximate it. In this sense, *Mukyōkai* has a church. Only those who have no church as conceived in conventional terms have the true church.

Japanese Christianity
[From Uchimura, *Zenshū*, XV, 578–79]

I am blamed by missionaries for upholding Japanese Christianity. They say that Christianity is a universal religion, and to uphold Japanese Christianity is to make a universal religion a national religion. Very true. But do not these very missionaries uphold sectional or denominational forms of Christianity which are not very different from national Christianity? Are they sure that their Methodism, Presbyterianism, Episcopalianism, Congregationalism, Lutheranism, and hundred other Christian isms—they say that in Christendom there are above six hundred different kinds of Christianity—are they sure that all these myriad kinds of Christianity are each of them a universal religion? Why blame me for upholding Japanese Christianity while every one of them upholds his or her own Christianity? If it is not a mistake to uphold any one of these six-hundred different forms of Christianity, why is it wrong for me to uphold my Japanese Christianity? Please explain.

Then, too, are these missionary-critics sure that there is no national Christianity in Europe and America? Is not Episcopalianism essentially an English Christianity, Presbyterianism a Scotch Christianity, Lutheranism a German Christianity, and so forth? Why, for instance, call a universal religion "Cumberland Presbyterianism"? If it is not wrong to apply the name of a district in the state of Kentucky to Christianity, why is it wrong for me to apply the name of my country to the same? I think I have as much right to call my Christianity Japanese as thousands of Christians in Cumberland Valley have a right to call their Christianity by the name of the valley they live in.

When a Japanese truly and independently believes in Christ, he is a Japanese Christian, and his Christianity is Japanese Christianity. It is all very simple. A Japanese Christian does not arrogate the whole Christianity to himself, neither does he create a new Christianity by becoming a Christian. He is a Japanese, and he is a Christian; therefore he is a Japanese Christian. A Japanese by becoming a Christian does not cease to be a Japanese. On the contrary, he becomes more Japanese by becoming a Christian. A Japanese who becomes an American or an Englishman, or an amorphous universal man, is neither a true Japanese nor a true Christian. Paul, a Christian apostle, remained an Hebrew of the Hebrews till the end of his life. Savonarola was an Italian Christian, Luther was a German Christian, and Knox was a Scotch Christian. They were not characterless universal men, but distinctly national, therefore distinctly human, and distinctly Christian. . . .

I have seen no more sorrowful figures than Japanese who imitate their American or European missionary-teachers by being converted to the faith of the latter. Closely examined, these converted "universal Christians" may turn out to be no more than denationalized Japanese, whose universality is no more than Americanism or Anglicanism adopted to cover up their lost nationality.

"Two J's"

"Two J's" was composed in parallel English-Japanese five years before Uchimura's death. The tombstone inscription was composed in English while he was working in the home for mentally retarded children.

[From Uchimura, *Zenshū*, XV, 599–600; XX, frontispiece]

I love two J's and no third; one is Jesus, and the other is Japan.

I do not know which I love more, Jesus or Japan.

I am hated by my countrymen for Jesus' sake as *yaso*, and I am disliked by foreign missionaries for Japan's sake as national and narrow.

No matter; I may lose all my friends, but I cannot lose Jesus and Japan.

For Jesus' sake, I cannot own any other God than His Father as my God and Father; and for Japan's sake, I cannot accept any faith which comes in the name of foreigners. Come starvation; come death; I cannot disown Jesus and Japan; I am emphatically a Japanese Christian, though I know missionaries in general do not like that name.

Jesus and Japan; my faith is not a circle with one center; it is an ellipse with two centers. My heart and mind revolve around the two dear names. And I know that one strengthens the other; Jesus strengthens and purifies my love for Japan; and Japan clarifies and objectivises my love for Jesus. Were it not for the two, I would become a mere dreamer, a fanatic, an amorphous universal man.

Jesus makes me a world-man, a friend of humanity; Japan makes me a lover of my country, and through it binds me firmly to the terrestrial globe. I am neither too narrow nor too broad by loving the two at the same time.

O Jesus, thou art the Sun of my soul, the saviour dear; I have given my all to thee!

O Japan,

> Land of lands, for thee we give,
> > Our hearts, our pray'rs, our service free;
> For thee thy sons shall nobly live,
> > And at thy need shall die for thee."

—J. G. WHITTIER

> *To Be Inscribed Upon My Tomb*
> I for Japan;
> Japan for the World;
> The World for Christ;
> And All for God.

NISHIDA KITARŌ

THE PROBLEM OF JAPANESE CULTURE

The *Problem of Japanese Culture* (*Nihon bunka no mondai*) by Nishida Kitarō (1870–1945), from which these excerpts are taken, was originally delivered as a series of lectures at Kyoto University in 1938. This was just after the appearance of the official text of *Fundamentals of Japan's National*

Polity, which tended to glorify a kind of emotional nationalism at the expense of Western rationalism and individualism. Concerned over the rise of such tendencies, Kyoto Imperial University sponsored a series of lectures for the general public, which might check the growing anti-intellectualism of the times and give people a sounder understanding of Japan and the world. Nishida, the leading professor of philosophy at the time, was asked to give the first lectures. A follower of Zen Buddhism, Nishida had devoted his life to the study and assimilation of Western philosophy, being influenced by James, Bergson, Fichte, Hegel, and in his later years especially by Leibnitz and Aristotle. These lectures reflect the later stages of Nishida's philosophical development, marked by the strong historicism which prevailed in Japan during this period. What Nishida sees as best in the Japanese tradition is something which unites it to the West, rather than setting it apart. To him the Japanese spirit is not merely emotional and illogical, as the nationalists declared, but has the basic character of "going to the truth of things" beyond mere subjectivity.

A year later, in 1939, a book entitled *The Sense of Reason (Dōri no kankaku)* by one of Nishida's colleagues, Amano Teiyu, was attacked by nationalists and aroused a storm of debate. In spite of the dangers to which it exposed him, and against the advice of some of his colleagues, Nishida decided to publish his lectures in order that the true meaning of the Japanese spirit might be understood and the Japanese people not be misled in coming to crucial decisions at that moment in history. It was mainly on the basis of this book that he was attacked as pro-Western during the war, and also as a reactionary by many "progressives" after the war.

[From Nishida, *Nihon bunka no mondai,* pp. 1–107]

What I am going to discuss today under the subject "The Problem of Japanese Culture" is not intended as an interpretation of the characteristics of our own culture based upon historical research. There are others capable of doing that, I am sure. Needless to say, that kind of study is important; no one appreciates this more than I do. However, scholarly inquiry ought to hide nothing and withhold nothing; both the strong points and weaknesses of our culture should be openly and honestly pointed out; and the result should be such as to establish a basic connection with the core of world history. As the expression, "cherry blossoms fragrant in the rising sun" suggests, the Japanese spirit that has nurtured us has something fair, open, and honest about it, and the academic spirit must have its source in such an attitude.

The saying that "Oriental culture is doctrinal in character, occidental culture scientific" would seem to apply quite well to Chinese culture [but not to Japanese]. Japan, it is true, has been called a country where people

" 'following the way of the gods implicitly' are not argumentative."[1] But this means only that argument is not indulged in for argument's sake and concepts are not bandied about for their own sake. As Motoori Norinaga explained in *Naobi no mitama*, "It [the Way of the Gods] is nothing but the way of going to things," which should be taken in the sense of going straight to the true facts of things. Going to the true facts, however, does not mean following tradition out of the mere force of custom or acting in direct response to subjective emotions. To go to the true facts of things must also involve what we call a scientific spirit. It should mean following the true facts of things at the expense of self. "Not to be argumentative" should be understood as not to be self-assertive, but to bend one's head low before the true facts. It ought not to be a mere cessation of thinking or readiness to compromise; to penetrate to the very source of fact is to exhaust one's own self [and become objective].

I believe that underlying the Oriental view of the world and of humanity there has been something equal, if not superior, to Occidental conceptions. Underlying both Chinese and Indian cultures there was something truly great, but they lacked a spirit of resolutely seeking out the true facts and therefore became rigid and fossilized. That the Japanese alone in the Orient, though sharing in these cultural influences, have gone forward to absorb Occidental culture and have also been considered the creators of a new Oriental culture, is due, is it not, mainly to that same Japanese spirit, free and unfettered, which "goes straight to things"? [pp. 1–3]

In order to explain what Japanese culture is like, we must look back on its history, study its institutions and civilization. I have stated at the outset of this lecture that I appreciate such studies very highly. At the same time, I believe that we must examine in what sense Japanese culture today may be considered [to be becoming] a world culture and how it may develop as such. The question also arises, now that the Orient and Occident form one world, in what sense can Oriental culture con-

---

[1] A Shinto characterization commonly understood at this time as "following the will of the emperor without asserting one's own will." On the theory that actions speak louder than words, it was considered that the comparative inarticulateness of the early Japanese (i.e., their failure to develop a body of written literature or doctrine prior to contact with the Chinese) was a virtue rather than a weakness. See Holtom, *National Faith of Japan*, pp. 14–15, 192–95. [Ed.]

tribute as a world culture to future world history? They say those who are ignorant of foreign languages know nothing about their own language and, indeed, only through comparison with other things can we achieve a true understanding of a given thing. We can know ourselves by projecting ourselves into the mirror of objectivity and by knowing ourselves objectively we can act objectively; otherwise we cannot escape the charge of being boastful and conceited. It is not enough just to explain the distinctive features of Japanese culture. In the Japan of today, which is attempting to establish itself as Japan, a nation of the world, this point requires special attention. [pp. 3-4]

What in Japan have thus far passed for comparisons of Eastern and Western cultures have tended to be made by lining up two cultures and comparing their external characteristics. For example, people say that in the West there is such-and-such a theory; in the East there is a similar one. Or, alternatively, in the East there is such-and-such a thing, but in the West it is lacking. Needless to say, men as members of the same species, *homo sapiens,* have thought the same things often enough. However, even doctrines of a purely theoretical character are not independent of their historical backgrounds; discussion of them must therefore start with their historical bases and treat them as living things. To compare these ideas in such abstract terms as "isms" is bound to be superficial. For example, Fa-tsang's "free interaction of event with event" and Hegel's dialectics, at first glance, seem much alike, but one is Buddhistic while the other is Christian, which means that they are essentially different in spirit. Again, though we may speak of possessing something in Oriental thought which is lacking in Occidental thought, the difference may be merely extrinsic like the long-necked giraffe and the short-necked whale [which are nonetheless both mammals]. Such characterizations may be acceptable if it is merely a matter of description, but in discussing the relative merits of both cultures, we must re-examine things in terms of the intrinsic character of our historical life. That is why I think that we must first consider this intrinsic character of our historical life.

We cannot take any one culture and call it *the* culture. If we borrowed the term "archetype" which Goethe used in the morphology of living being and spoke of an "archetype of culture," what sort of thing would it be? Historical life, like biological life, may be said to assume various forms in different environments. But . . . in so far as it is human culture

[353]

it must have what is called an archetype, in relation to which different cultures are to be understood and compared. The archetype of course does not mean a stereotyped morphological state of culture, but something which forms itself ad infinitum, which is formative-functional. On this basis the varying directions of cultural formation and development can be interpreted. Oriental and Occidental cultures, like their opposition and their mutual relationship, have to be comprehended from such a standpoint.

This is the reason why I insist that today we have the utmost need for theoretical study; or in other words, for science. European culture, deriving from a Greek culture which was intellectual and theoretical in character and dedicated to an inquiry into true fact, has a great theoretical structure behind it, on the basis of which European scholars criticize different cultures and interpret the direction of their development. As a result of conflict and frictions among the various cultures for several thousand years, a certain theoretical archetype has been developed, which Europeans consider the one and only cultural archetype. On this basis they conceive of stages of cultural development, in terms of which Oriental culture is seen as still lingering in an undeveloped stage. Oriental culture must, if developed, become identical with the Occidental one, they believe. Even such a great thinker as Hegel shared this view. But I think a problem arises here.

Ranke declared that all cultures before Rome flowed into the lake called Rome, and all cultures after Rome flowed out of the lake called Rome. Since Roman times European countries can be said to have constituted one world. Each of them possesses its own peculiar culture, it is true, but they can also be considered different aspects of a single system of culture. By contrast the Orient, though it is spoken of as one, cannot be regarded as one in the sense that the European countries constitute one world. Needless to say, the Oriental cultures possess certain characteristics in common; but I wonder if that oneness is not of a rather general sort, and far from a systematic oneness. To achieve a true oneness in the Orient seems to be a matter for the future. Somewhere underlying Oriental culture we must find a principle that reaches the true reality of things. Instead of merely saying that such it was and such it is, the principle must be established which enables us to say such it ought to be. Something like the archetype of our humanity must be found. . . . Oriental cultures developed in isolation, separated from one another by mountains and seas, and have not experienced the vehement mutual negation found in Occidental culture. This explains, I think, why they lack the logical character which compels them to penetrate reality through a sweeping negation of themselves. Today, however, the nations of the East cannot simply rest content with having their own peculiarities, because the world is becoming truly one. [pp. 5–9]

Let us ask whether there is not any sort of logic underlying Oriental culture—the culture that has nurtured us for several thousand years. Does not our conception of human life and the world possess its own original way of looking at and thinking of things, or in short, its own logic? Is it, as many people think, simply emotional? I do not deny that Japanese culture is a culture of emotion; I made a remark myself elsewhere to the effect that Japanese culture is *rhythmical*. Nevertheless it is only through the attainment of reality that we can be creative, can live in truth. We must, therefore, obtain a logical grasp of our way of life at its very foundations. . . .

Leaving aside those who are studying the special character of Oriental culture from the historical point of view, do not the majority of those who treat Oriental culture from the philosophical point of view deal with it in Occidental terms? And, on the other hand, do not the remainder take something particular [i.e., specifically Oriental] for the universal; in other words, regard subjective hope or desire as the basic principle? Is "logic" in general nothing more than [Occidental logic, i.e.] the mode of thought and way of looking at things which underlies Western culture today? Must we assume Occidental logic to be the only logic, and must the Oriental way of thinking be considered simply a less-developed form [of the same way of thinking]? In order to decide these problems we shall first have to go back and re-examine the underlying sources from which logic emerged into the historical world and the part logic played in history.

Thinking in the last analysis is nothing but an historical event, which acts as the self-formative function [2] of our historical life. Willing as I am to recognize Occidental logic as a magnificent systematic development, and intent as I am on studying it first as one type of world logic, I wonder if even Western logic is anything more than a special feature of the

[2] A concept of Nishida's discussed in the next section of this excerpt.

historical life, an aspect of the self-formation of the historical life. Such a thing as formal, abstract logic will remain the same anywhere, but concrete logic as the form of concrete knowledge cannot be independent of the specific features of historical life. [pp. 10–12]

I am not saying that logic is of two kinds, Occidental logic and Oriental logic. Logic must be one; it is only as the form of the self-formative function of the historical world that it has taken different directions in the course of its development. Roughly speaking, we might say that Occidental logic is the logic that takes things as its object, while Oriental logic is the logic that takes mind as its object. Some may say that a logic with mind as its object is an impossibility, for logic must always be the logic of the objective object. [On the one hand] what we call this self of ours, however, is also a fact or event in the historical world. As such only is it something thinkable, something we can discuss. [On the other hand] what we call a "thing" really only exists as a fact in the historical world; and nothing exists in the historical world as mere object entirely apart from what we call "self." All [i.e., things and selves], therefore, should come under the logic of historical fact. Now in the logic of Buddhism, I think, there are the germs of a logic that takes the self as its object—a logic of the mind—though it has remained a sort of personal experience and developed no further. It has not developed into what could be called a logic of fact. We need first to study the Occidental logic thoroughly, but at the same time we must have a critical attitude toward it. What we call the study of the Orient today has meant only taking the Orient as an *object* of study. As yet a profound reflection about the Oriental way of thinking, in order to evolve a new *method* of thinking, has not been undertaken. [pp. 14–15]

At this point Nishida presents a brief statement of the theoretical position upon which he bases the evaluation of Oriental and Occidental culture given in the concluding selections (pp. 868–872).

The world is usually thought of as an aggregation of innumerable things or something which takes definite form through a combination of things. But the world of actuality is also a world in which things interact with other things. The form of the actual world, in its unique particularity, must be determined by the mutual determination, that is, by the reciprocal interaction, of innumerable things through ages past.

These things all operate in the actuality of the world. Thus, we—as historical beings—are born here, work here, and go to our death here in the world of historical actuality.

When we say that the interaction of many things produces one result, it necessarily means that the manyness becomes oneness. When we say things interact, those things must be in complete opposition. But between things merely in opposition, having no relationship with each other at all, even action is impossible. To act involves entering into a certain relationship and to enter into a certain relationship must presuppose something common to both, in which both are one. Take the case of a body interacting with another body in space; it means that both are spatial in nature.

When we say that the manyness becomes oneness, however, it means the negation of plurality, the extinction of opposition, the termination of mutual action. [This is because] the mutual action of things means complete opposition and thus mutual negation: A transforming B and B transforming A. But as already stated the establishment of a relationship between things must presuppose something common to both. So when we say A negates B, or transforms it, it can only mean that A has made a field common to B its own, that is, A has made itself into a universal field and by doing so A makes B its own; A itself becomes the world [which comprehends B]. Thus it also means that manyness becomes oneness, and necessarily implies that A negates itself. Thus what we call the opposition, the mutual negation, the reciprocal transformation of things means the self-negation of both things through which they become one. In that sense, both things must be thought of as the transformation of one thing or the self-determination of one world. Thus [in modern physics] the transformation of material things is considered a modification of [one] space. However, just one thing undergoing change by itself is unthinkable, as it would necessarily mean that there could be no interaction. Oneness must therefore be oneness-of-manyness and manyness be manyness-of-oneness. That is why I say that the actual world should be thought of as the contradictory self-identity of manyness and oneness.

We consider this world spatial as well as temporal. By spatial we mean the complete opposition of things in parallel, and by temporal we mean that these opposing things go on to become one, because time is the form of unity of these opposing things. Ordinarily time is thought of as rectilinear. There is no such thing as opposition in time. Time is usually taken as moving "from moment to moment." But if it simply moved from moment to moment with absolutely no relation to before and after, even time could not come into existence. In the present instant of time the past must be thought of as having already passed but not yet entirely passed away, and the future must be thought of as not yet having arrived but to some degree already manifest. Otherwise time is unthinkable. What is usually spoken of as "from moment to moment" can only be conceived of by minimizing the present in the form just mentioned [i.e., as comprising past and future]. In the sense that time comprises past and future, it must be taken as spatial. But being comprised in time everything becomes fused into oneness. However much we may take it as spatial, if everything were thought of as comprised in a single time, the true opposition of one thing to another would be out of the question. Therefore action would be impossible. So the world of the interaction of things, or the dynamic world, must be a world which is spatial at the same time that it is absolutely temporal, and temporal while at the same time absolutely spatial. It must be a world characterized by the contradictory self-identity of time and space. [pp. 16–19]

The world in which thing interacts with thing, and which moves on by itself as a contradictory self-identity, must be a world in which there is mutual determination of particulars. This is because we cannot think of the world as at its base a simple manyness or a simple oneness, nor can we consider it simply spatial or temporal. "Thing" and "thing" interacting as the reciprocal negation of things in complete mutual opposition necessarily means, as I have said before, that that one thing becomes the world, and that by "itself becoming the world" it completely negates the other. By "itself becoming the world" means that by unifying things which are in complete opposition, it itself becomes time. (That which acts operates as an antecedent in time; it fulfills the function of time in the world.) The particulars in nature must be temporal. However, that one thing becomes the world must mean, as I have said before, that it goes on negating itself. That time as the combination of opposing things is unifying things in complete opposition therefore means that time goes on negating itself and disappearing, but at the same time it becomes spatial. Therefore, the complete mutual determination of individual things, the interaction of individual thing with individual thing, must represent new birth through disappearance. To die is necessarily to live, as to live is to die. Manyness as ultimately the manyness-of-oneness [and thus as self-negating] is Nothingness; oneness as ultimately the oneness-of-manyness must also be Nothingness. That is why I call it determination without determinants, or the self-determination of absolute Nothingness. Being is at the same time nothingness, nothingness is at the same time being.

All that exists has the character of the absolutely contradictory self-identity of this manyness and oneness. Considered in its oneness [or totality] it is completely determined through the self-determination of absolute oneness. Beings must be beings through and through. The world determined as actuality has a definite and unalterable form, for it has been determined by causal necessity from ages past. Your own selves are also produced from the self-formation of such a world [and are consequently determined and unalterable]. However, being at the same time the oneness of absolute manyness, it must be a world of the complete mutual determination of individuals, the world of individuated manyness. The determined world of actuality, being determined as the complete contradictory self-identity of manyness and oneness, is necessarily something which ever goes on being negated and which is ever changing. Therefore I say "from that which has been formed to that which forms," and also that "form determines form itself." The world is not merely a mechanistic world as a world of individuated manyness or a world of the oneness-of-manyness. Again it is not merely teleological as a world of totalistic oneness, or as a world of the manyness-of-oneness. The [historical] world wherein manyness always remains manyness and oneness always remains oneness and yet which determines itself in the manner of an absolutely contradictory self-identity is necessarily a creative world which goes on forming itself. We all are, as individuations of such a world, creative elements of a creative world.[3]

[3] The foregoing passage beginning with, "However, being at the same time . . ." has been paraphrased and amplified as follows, in accordance with the suggestions of Dr. Kōsaka Masaaki of Kyoto University:

However, considered under the aspect of manyness, the world of actuality is ever-changing and self-negating, because it is a world of absolute manyness, a world of the complete mutual determination and negation of individuals; that is, a world of individuated manyness. Thus the determined world of actuality, being the world of the contradictory self-identity of manyness and oneness, is on the one hand completely determined and on the other ever self-negating and changing. Therefore I say "from that which has been formed to that

The world of historical actuality in which we are is not merely a world thought of mechanistically as proceeding from manyness to oneness, nor merely a world which is thought of teleologically as proceeding from oneness to manyness. If this were merely a world of mechanical causation, life itself could not be accounted for. Again even when we think of it teleologically as the manyness-of-oneness, the fact of our working with individuality cannot be accommodated. [And if so considered from the purely teleological standpoint], as the self-formation of totalistic oneness, only biological life and nothing else can be accounted for. In such a world there is no freedom, there is no productivity or *poesis*. This world of historical actuality must be not only a world out of which we go on being born and to which we go on returning at death, but one in which we make things and, through making, continue to be made. Even though I say we make things, it does not mean to move or to change the world from outside the world. We are born under the conditions of history and society, and we make things technically, and by making things we continue to form ourselves. While the thing made is something made by myself, being completely objective it is something which stands in opposition to me, and which in its own expression acts in turn upon me—and not only upon me but upon others as well. In this historical world, even things made by the people of ancient India and Greece are manifest to us and we are moved by them. They are still in the historical present.

The instinctive ability of living things may possibly be derived from the teleological formation of the world as totalistic oneness, but the behavior of man as *homo faber* ever alternating from that which is formed to that which forms necessarily emerges as the self-formation of a world of the contradictory self-identity of manyness and oneness. Each of us humans as the individuated manyness of such a world is *productive,*

---

which forms," and also that "form determines form itself." The world is not merely a mechanistic world, as a world of the oneness-out-of-manyness [that is, a world which consists of many individuals]. Again it is not merely a teleological world, as a world of the manyness-out-of-oneness [that is, a world of totality which differentiates itself into many individuals]. So I can define the world of actuality as the world of an absolutely contradictory self-identity, wherein manyness remains manyness and oneness remains oneness, and yet manyness is oneness and oneness manyness. And the result of such a dialectical process is a formation or creation of the world itself. The world of actuality is the world of self-creation, a creative world which goes on forming itself. We are all, as individuations of such a world, creative elements of a creative world.

forming and being formed, and in so far as we fulfill this to the highest degree we are free. Each of us, as the individuated manyness of a world of absolutely contradictory self-identity, lives with free will.

The world of historical actuality which I have analyzed above must be like this, otherwise it cannot be accounted for. However, people usually try to explain the world of actuality either mechanistically or teleologically, from both of which standpoints actuality is denied. They try to explain the one who thinks [the subject] in terms of that which has been thought [the object]. I am not one to reject such explanations. On the contrary, I believe that the world of the contradictory self-identity of manyness and oneness is necessarily, on the one hand, a world which can be thought of throughout as mechanistic, and on the other hand, a world which can be thought of throughout as teleological. However, such views [i.e., the mechanistic or teleological which try to explain actuality from a standpoint which negates actuality] are views which, in fact, we always hold outside the world of historical actuality. Absurb though it may seem, from the world of actuality, we conceive of a world which passes beyond actuality, and from the world in which we do exist, we entertain the thought of a world in which we do not exist. To speak in this way is not to think of the world subjectivistically. The so-called objective world which is conceived by simply negating man, is, in fact, always conceived in opposition to man, and so is rather itself something which does not get rid of subjectivism. The true objective world must be that which goes beyond ourselves, and which conversely embraces these selves. It must be a world which makes of our selves its individuated manyness. In this sense I am a thoroughgoing objectivist. [pp. 21–26]

The world of historical actuality, being a contradictory self-identity of totalistic unity and individuated plurality, is a world which, with subject shaping environment and environment shaping subject, is ever moving self-contradictorily from that which is formed to that which forms; that is to say it is a world which itself shapes itself. [p. 47]

In this shaping, the ethological or speciological activity of us human beings is cultural. Therein, however, it can be said further that in our human activity there are always two directions standing opposed to each other, that is, the opposition between the direction from subject to environment and the direction from environment to subject. Culture always consists in the contradictory self-identity of these two directions. Thus although culture always consists in the contradictory identity of these two directions, Occidental culture, on the whole, may perhaps be thought to move from environment to subject; Oriental culture, in contrast to this, may perhaps be thought to move from subject to environment. These two cultures can be said to have their centers of gravity respectively in one and the other of the two mutually opposing directions of the self-contradictorily identified world. However, thoroughgoing movement from environment to subject must make the environment self-contradictorily negate itself and become subjective. [This is because] the more the world becomes concrete, the more it must become dialectical. And opposed to this, thoroughgoing movement from subject to environment must make the subject self-contradictorily negate itself and become environment; that is, become things themselves. The two directions in becoming concrete conjoin in things of the world which itself determines itself, and become one in the actualized reality. The opposition of the two directions, fundamentally speaking, derives from that reality, and the conjoining also ends in that reality.

As for the characteristic feature of Japanese culture, it seems to me to lie in moving in the direction from subject to object [environment], ever thoroughly negating the self and becoming the thing itself; becoming the thing itself to see; becoming the thing itself to act. To empty the self and see things, for the self to be immersed in things, "no-mindedness" [in Zen Buddhism] or effortless acceptance of the grace of Amida (*jinen-hōni*) [in True Pure Land teaching]—these, I believe, are the states we Japanese strongly yearn for. Even what we call harmony, thinking of the phrase "In the observance of rites it is harmony that is prized" [*Analects*, I, 12], still cannot be thought of as penetrating into the essence of the Japanese spirit. The essence of the Japanese spirit must be to become one in things and in events. It is to become one at that primal point in which there is neither self nor others. [pp. 87–88]

Our country [Japan], while it is said to be quick to take in and clever in understanding and adapting the cultures of various foreign countries, anciently the cultures of China and India, and after Meiji, Western culture, is yet spoken of as not original. However, I think that in Japan, the Japanese have a way of seeing things and a way of thinking peculiar to themselves, and even while absorbing from Chinese and Indian cultures, the Japanese have come to create their own culture. However, as for it [Japanese culture] being an identity between subject and world and being what I call a vertical [or subjective] world,[4] it cannot but be

---

[4] That is, in contrast to the "horizontal" world of Europe. According to Nishida, Europe has developed through opposition and conflict between man and nature, man and man. In

regretted that it has been lacking in such qualities as incisiveness and grandeur. Though people often think, to the contrary, of the Japanese spirit as being mystical or illogical, I am opposed to this view. Logic in its most fundamental sense, properly speaking, must synthesize and unify the demands of all things given into one world, and must give or rather must find an objective expression sufficient to that world in its oneness (just as [the German architectural theorist Bruno] Taut said about Ise Shrine).[5] That is true concrete intelligence. Formal logic is no more than an abstract form of this intelligence. Even what we call science cannot come into being without such concrete intelligence. However, [natural] science is thoroughly external or environmental. Art, on the contrary, is subjective. Therefore it may be said that art and science stand at opposite poles of the self-expression of the contradictory self-identical world. . . . This is the reason why the Japanese spirit, identifying the subject and world, is thought to be artistic and unscientific. However, a spirit which goes to the truth of things must be one which has something in common with the scientific spirit. One who does not recognize a noetic aspect even in art does not understand art. I wonder if they are not far from understanding the true Japanese spirit, who think that the Japanese spirit, being only emotional, is illogical and mystical. [pp. 93–94]

It is needless to say that Japanese culture also, being subjective, belongs, generally speaking, to the form of Oriental culture. Our people, having developed almost in national isolation for several thousand years, has had no such thing as [contact with other] people in our environment. The attitude of the Japanese people was not negative toward them, but rather receptive. That is probably also because fundamentally our country's climate itself has not been negative toward man, but was so congenial

---

modern Europe various countries stood opposing each other respectively as subjects of history in the one world of Europe. This may be called a horizontal world. In Europe, however, various countries which stand side by side spatially are gradually becoming one unit. In contrast to this, Japan being located on a solitary island in the Orient and having developed peculiarly as an almost closed society for several thousands of years, may be said to have developed as a vertical world. To the Japanese people, Japan itself was a world. From this viewpoint Nishida says that Japan is a vertical world and has the character of an identity between subject (Japan) and world. Hereafter Japan must develop from the vertical to the horizontal, from time to space, just as Europe is developing from the horizontal to the vertical, from space to time. [Ed.]

[5] According to Taut beauty in a work of architecture consists in meeting most purely and powerfully the demands imposed upon it by the totality of factors (topography, climate, etc.) which constitute the womb out of which that art-work is born. Ise Shrine, with its simple logical structure, contains no capricious elements that offend the reason of man. [Ed.]

that man and nature have become one. In addition, being situated as a solitary island in the Eastern Sea, our country has never been menaced by other nations. However much we might have taken in foreign culture, we had not felt any danger to our national existence. It may be thought that probably this is the reason why until recently Japan has freely absorbed foreign culture. . . . Japan's historical world, being an identity between subject and environment, and between man and nature, may also be said to have developed self-identically. This may be the reason that Japan has vitally developed as a vertical world of the identity between subject and world.

A Japanese spirit which goes to the truth of things as an identity between actuality and reality, must be one which is based on this. Although I say "goes to things," that is not to say to go to matter. And although I say "nature," that is not to say objective or environmental nature. To go to things means starting from the subject, going beyond the subject, and going to the bottom of the subject. What I call the identity between actuality and reality [6] is the realization of this absolute at the bottom of our selves, instead of considering the absolute to be in an infinite exterior. However, that does not mean to see the world subjectively, but for the self to be absolutely negated, and for the self to become empty. And it must mean that we are always in accord with the expression of the world sufficient unto itself. That is one with the spirit of the Mahāyāna Buddhism of India. What is called nature in China is different from that in the Occident; it is nature as the unity of heaven and man. What is called the Way of the Gods (kannagara no michi), which "goes to things," may be said to be that which penetrates into nature so conceived. The Japanese spirit, while it is thus in its essence thoroughly Oriental, further has its characteristic in moving from the universal principle (ri) to the particular event (ji). The transformation of Genshin in the history of Tendai Buddhism . . . may be considered an example of this.[7] It also may be thought a result of this that Zen, a product of Chinese Buddhism in the early T'ang dynasty, which today has died out in China, nevertheless preserves its vitality in our country. It can be said that Zen does not merely preserve its vitality as a religion,

[6] According to Nishida what is actual in the historical world is not mere appearance but reality itself. [Ed.]

[7] That is, the redirection of Genshin's thought from the metaphysical truths of Tendai to the simple practice of the Nembutsu. See Volume I, Chapter X. [Ed.]

but has penetrated into and exerted a profound influence on the cultural life of our country. Confucianism too probably lived in our country, not as ritual formalism, but as something emotional which affected us directly. In the Japanese spirit, which goes to the truth of things proceeding from subject and going beyond subject to the bottom of subject, the spirit of Oriental culture is there made to live most fully, and at the same time it may possess something which can also combine directly with the spirit of environmentalistic Occidental culture. In this sense a point of union between Eastern and Western culture can be sought in Japan. Further therein perhaps we can foresee the future of history, which, as a contradictory self-identity of subject and environment, moves from being that which is formed to that which forms. [pp. 105-7]

KAWAKAMI HAJIME
Religious Truth and Scientific Truth

A colleague of Nishida at Kyoto University, the Marxist Kawakami was, as we have already seen in Chapter XXVII, a man of strong religious inclinations who had been deeply influenced by Zen and Pure Land Buddhism. That religious experience continued to be a subject of great importance to him even after he had become a Communist is indicated by his lengthy discussion of it in his *Prison Ramblings*. Because of his unusual personal background and what, for a Communist, was an exceptional knowledge of Buddhist teaching, Kawakami felt himself peculiarly qualified to judge the respective claims of Marxist and Buddhist truth. His conclusion that the two are not necessarily in conflict and that religious truth, properly understood, has a legitimate domain of its own, represents a striking modification of Marxist doctrine to accommodate the same Japanese religious insights which Nishida had sought to reconcile with modern science.

[From Kawakami, *Gokuchū zeigo*, pp. 75-160]

I am a materialist. I have no doubt that nature (existence, matter, things) is primary and that spirit (consciousness, thought, mind) is secondary. To our way of thinking, man too is a kind of organism with no previous existence and a form which could have no previous existence until the world existed. Afterwards, organic matter appeared on the earth, and after long continuous evolution the higher animals such as man appeared. Since the human body came to be equipped with specially developed brains, nerves, and retinas, by means of them it became capable of sensation, consciousness, and thought. Looked at in this way, sensation, consciousness, and thought are only functions of organic matter organized for specific and delicate work. We refer to such faculties (the spiritual functions) as mind.

I wish now to clarify five points. First I shall tell with what problems religious truth deals; next, how religious truth is apprehended; and then, what benefit people receive from having apprehended such truth. Having completed the explanation of religious truth in this fashion, I shall next go on to clarify the relation between religious truth and religion; and the relation between religious truth and scientific truth.

(I have no detailed knowledge of all the various religions. My first contact with religious books was as a college student, when I read the Christian Bible and was much moved by the Sermon on the Mount; but I have no special knowledge of Christianity. All I know comparatively well is the Jōdo and Zen sects of Buddhism. Consequently, in the following discussion of religious truth, I shall stress these two. Hence the discussion, if it had a title of its own, should be called "On Religious Truth in Buddhism.")

First, with what problem does religious truth deal? In answer, what it treats is consciousness of consciousness itself, or the mind reflecting on the mind. Here lies its fundamental peculiarity.

In us human beings, the faculty of consciousness is highly developed. This is how we know—for example—that there are desks, or houses, around us. We also know on the small scale of the existence of micro-organisms invisible to the naked eye, and on the large scale the characteristics of the sky, including the sun, moon, and stars. With scientific progress such consciousness becomes more and more exact and rich. Hence we are increasingly able to exercise a positive effect on our environment (the outside world), and can make endless improvements in it to obtain better living conditions. However, religious truth has nothing to do with this aspect of life, and hence serves no purpose here. When Kōbō Daishi [Kūkai] opened mountain land and built bridges, it was the work of a man of religion, but it was not religious work.

Religious truth is not knowledge of such external things, but is knowledge of consciousness itself. Conscious beings' consciousness of themselves—their consciousness of their own consciousness—is the mission of religious truth. In this case, the consciousness faces not outward, but inward. It does not act upon external things, but on itself. (The way such consciousness works is called "turning the light inward upon oneself." I shall say more about this later.)

This consciousness of one's own consciousness can be expressed in various other ways. For example, it can be called "knowledge of the self" (self-awareness). The concept of the "self" is only a creation of the faculty of consciousness. Since such things as the pebbles that fall by the roadside lack this faculty, they also lack the concept of the "self," but as men have the faculty developed to a high degree, the concept of "self" in them is strong. Yet, what is the substance of the "self"? To this question, Buddhism has from the beginning answered the "non-self" [non-ego]. (Here "non" is not "non-being" as opposed to "being," but that question does not really concern us at this point.) It is well known that the Zen Sect has made its central teaching the non-self, but it is also spoken of in the Jōdo-Shin Sect. [pp. 75–80]

However, when one speaks of the substance of the "self," one is also speaking of the substance of the "mind." Therefore, the consciousness of one's own consciousness can also be summed up as "knowledge of the mind." The Zen sect, which is a type of Buddhism emphasizing one's own effort, makes knowledge of the mind its special problem. . . . Furthermore, since "knowledge of the mind" is another way of saying "knowledge of the mind's nature," such words as "seeing one's nature" can also be used. Since "seeing" is a stronger way of saying "knowing," this means examining one's nature itself in its living state. This expression "seeing one's nature" is used most frequently in the Zen sect. . . . The problem can also be thought of in the following way. When we die, consciousness ceases. Rather, when consciousness ceases, we say that one is dead. In the end, consciousness is life; consciousness (mind, spirit) is the basis of life. Seen thus, the consciousness of consciousness, which thus becomes the question at issue, serves to make us aware of the basis of one's life, or to realize the true meaning of human life. Thus there is established an apprehension of human life different in meaning from knowledge of the world. [pp. 82–86]

Among the world's so-called religions are some primitive, childish ones which have almost no concern with religious truth in the above sense. However, there is no well-developed religion that does not include this sort of religious truth at least to some extent. Still they do not consist of such truths alone. As they have become current in the world—that is, in a class society—they have always absorbed various types of knowledge (philosophic or otherwise) and superstitions in addition to pure religious truth. They embrace in particular many arbitrary doctrines that serve as the "opiate of the masses" for the sake of putting to sleep the power of resistance of the oppressed and exploited and of paralyzing their will to struggle. [p. 88]

I move next to the second question: How can religious truth be apprehended?

As I have already said, since religious truth takes as its problem consciousness of consciousness, naturally it should consist in something other than the ordinary faculty of the consciousness, and this is its fundamental peculiarity.

We cannot see our eyes with our eyes. Of course, we can see our own eyes if they are reflected in a mirror, but in this case what we see is no longer the eyes themselves, but the eyes reflected in a mirror, that is, reflection of the eyes. Thus, whereas the eyes are organs for seeing things in general, they cannot see themselves.

The eye is invisible to the eye and the tongue cannot taste the tongue. In exactly the same way, the consciousness cannot by ordinary means (the means by which we are ordinarily aware of the outside world) be aware of itself. This is why knowledge of the mind is different from knowledge of things, and why religious truth is different from scientific truth. [pp. 89-90]

The phenomena of the external world reflected in consciousness by means of our sense organs can all be expressed in words (concepts); they can be explained, they can be comprehended by means of reason, and they are in no wise unnamable, inexplicable, or incomprehensible. However, the consciousness (mind-spirit-self) which apprehends such external phenomena cannot be reflected in the consciousness by the same means with which it apprehends those phenomena. In this sense it *is* unnamable, inexplicable, and incomprehensible. It is what the sūtra describes in the words: "Stop! Stop! Don't try to explain it. The Law of the Self is mysterious and difficult to comprehend." [p. 95]

Thus religious truth cannot be thoroughly apprehended by the same means as ordinary knowledge. This being the case, what should one do?

It is apprehended by a method called consciousness of one's own consciousness. I have said before that the eye is invisible to the eye, the tongue cannot taste the tongue, and in exactly the same way, the consciousness cannot by ordinary means be aware of itself. However, here the analogy stops. Of course, the eye cannot by any means see itself, nor the tongue taste itself, but by certain means the mind can reflect on itself and the consciousness can be aware of itself. Of course, the concrete methods adopted for this purpose (which comprise what is called religious practices) differ from one faith to another, but in so far as they are not fraudulent, their ultimate aim is to see with the mind the mind's own reflection. . . .

The reflecting by consciousness of consciousness itself is something which can be achieved in different ways, but in the Zen sect, one tries to induce it by means of "sitting in meditation" (*zazen*). [pp. 100–102]

When the conscious faculty, before it has reached out to external things even in the slightest, immediately turns to the direct reflection of consciousness itself, consciousness of one's own consciousness is accomplished and direct self-knowledge by consciousness arises. This is called "attaining Buddhahood by seeing one's own nature," or "great enlightenment," or "perception of the mind," or "seeing God," or "the apprehension of faith," and the brimming contents of consciousness then comprise religious truth.

One must not think of religion as thus far described simply as meaningless nonsense. In it lies the process which I have called the apprehension of religious truth. Our perception of this religious truth, just as in the case of scientific truth, grows progressively deeper and more intimate with each stage of our training. [pp. 105–6]

As I have said before, I recognize that there is a religious truth that is wholly different from scientific truth. So far so good, but past this point religion can encounter innumerable pitfalls and degenerate into superstition, error, priestcraft, and so forth.

Among my readers there may perhaps be some who will take it that, so speaking, I have already stumbled into such a pitfall, and they might wish to cross-examine me as follows:

"Hearing you talk like this, I wonder if you don't really have the same point of view as the philosophers of the Kantian school, who believe in the existence of a 'Thing in itself' as 'a thing that cannot be perceived,' 'a thing which differs as noumena from phenomena, and belonging to a

[369]

realm different in principle from phenomena,' and consequently 'a thing belonging to a transcendental realm, which cannot be apprehended by knowledge, but can only be understood by faith.' Doesn't this indicate that you have unexpectedly stumbled into the pitfall of metaphysics, which you yourself, as a Marxist, have come to repudiate?"

To this I would answer: "Of course I make a distinction between religious truth and scientific truth. However, it is no greater a distinction than I make within the sciences between social science and natural science. Since the objects of study of the social sciences differ from those of the natural sciences, the methods of study are also different. In the social sciences one cannot use a microscope, as one can in the natural sciences, and one cannot use chemical reaction materials either. Similarly, as the objects (the world) treated by scientific truth and religious truth differ, so must the means of apprehending these two kinds of truth differ. The important point is just that I do not believe in an absolute boundary between them that cannot be trespassed. The apprehension of scientific truth (i.e., the understanding of its nature by observation of external things) and the apprehension of religious truth (i.e., the understanding of the mind itself by means of self-reflection) are both knowledge by means of the human faculty of consciousness. The faculty of knowledge is only a highly developed function of the brain, contained in the organic system of the highly developed animal, man.

"Therefore, while I say that I acknowledge religious truth, I do not feel it necessary to escape to some other mysterious cloud-world. Apart from mankind, outside the material world reflected in man's consciousness (man's consciousness too is a material function), gods and Buddhas do not exist. Whether good or evil, gods and Buddhas are products of man's consciousness. The gods and Buddhas bear human qualities and display a human appearance not because they created man to resemble them, but because men created them. If tuberculosis germs had gods, they would doubtless be tuberculosis germs.

"In short, while I say that I acknowledge religious truth, I feel not the slightest obligation to sell myself to metaphysics. I remain as before a materialist, who takes the mind (consciousness, spirit) to be a material product. Religious truth is truth about consciousness. However, consciousness itself is only a function of the matter that makes up the human body."

I shall next devote a few words to the third question: Of what use is religious truth (what benefit can be derived from it)?

In general, ignorance (lack of understanding, inability to deduce things, unfamiliarity with things) breeds confusion and fear. On the other hand, since knowledge dispels confusion and fear, it brings peace of mind and happiness.

Now religious truth makes it its duty to clarify the substance of the self (the mind). Our apprehension of it enables us to understand our own nature. Therefore whenever someone catches it, the dark clouds immediately open and the light shines out limitlessly. Thereupon there appear great peace (what one calls peace of mind) and happiness (what one calls ecstatic joy). This is also stated in the form [of Confucius]: "If one hears the Way in the morning, one can gladly die in the evening." Since one understands the basis of life, one is no longer troubled by such problems as the existence and disappearance of one's own five feet of flesh [the body]. Herein lies the efficacy of apprehending religious truth. [pp. 113–18]

In regard to the fourth question, the relation of religious truth and religion, Kawakami deals at considerable length with the perversion of religious truth by organized religions in Japan to make it serve as an opiate for the people and an instrument of class domination.

As my fifth and last problem, I shall take up the relation between religious truth and scientific truth.

As is clear from what I have already said, religious truth belongs to the internal world, while scientific truth belongs to the external world. These two categorically different truths have different subject matters, different points of view, and different spheres. Yet the confusion between them is very great. In particular, I shall always think it strange, having studied Marxism as a scientist for many years, that public religious figures openly invade our sphere and rage away at will. I think that such confusion as practiced by religious leaders becomes a powerful conventional method for making religion the opiate of the masses, so that I must make clear in regard to the problems described above the definite spheres within which each of these two truths should stay.

Religious leaders today often meddle in social problems. Yet social problems are not problems of the mind, but quite literally problems of society. They cannot be solved at all by the method of folding the arms, facing the wall, and submerging into the interior of the mind, but can only be solved by the power of science (social science). These are not problems that can be solved by men of religion, just as the problems of curing sickness, improving crop cultivation, or the use of electricity are not.

As I have already said, the Zen sect which emphasizes the achievement of enlightenment by one's own effort naturally makes a major point of having no scriptures. But even in those sects that believe in the power of Another [the power of the Buddha alone to save], there is a saying that "men in the Pure Land sect attain the future life by becoming fools," and make a point of the fact that [to be saved] "one needn't know a single line of scripture." Here is the fundamental characteristic of the method for apprehending religious truth. However, in the sciences it is just the opposite. Apprehension of their truths makes it an indispensable condition that one possess detailed source materials. Consequently, before a scientist reaches a certain conclusion to a certain problem, he actually collects materials higher than the peak of Mont Blanc. Diametrically opposite to the idea that "one needn't know a single line of scripture," the scientist's necessary qualification is knowledge of all aspects of his field of study. The one kind of truth treats problems of the mind in the internal world, and the other treats those of things in the external world. Herein all kinds of things become reversed. Just as religious truth, which can seek truth through the gate marked "no need to know a single line of scripture," is helpless to solve social problems, so worldly knowledge is an encumbrance and useless in the apprehension of faith. Therefore, when men of religion intrude on the world of science and very freely offer their opinions, it is like a blind man's criticism of painting, or a deaf man's criticism of music. There is nothing worse than not knowing one's own limited function. It is not only a confession of ignorance of scientific truth, but it is proof that one lacks complete understanding even of religious truth. [pp. 152–55]

There are some who, knowing nothing whatever about what Marxism is or what sort of book *Das Kapital* is, think they can complain about Marxism, and rant on about it like some ridiculous joke. As I have said repeatedly, even though one has studied Zen deeply, there is no reason to believe that one understands the theory of capital. This is no different from saying that even if one practices Buddhism, one cannot understand the principle of electricity without training in the physical sciences, one cannot understand the construction of an airplane without mechanical knowledge, and one cannot understand the structure of the human body without medical knowledge. There is no way to know the structure of capitalistic society—its birth, maturation, and destruction—except from the detailed scientific explanation of it on all levels in Marxian economics. [pp. 159–60]

TANAKA KŌTARŌ

IN SEARCH OF TRUTH AND PEACE

A view of religious truth diametrically opposed to that of Kawakami is represented by Tanaka Kōtarō (b. 1888), whose book *In Search of Truth and Peace* asserts the inseparability of politics from its underlying ethical and religious bases. A graduate of Tokyo Imperial University, training ground of statesmen and jurists, Tanaka was a follower of Uchimura Kanzō before being converted to Catholicism in 1926. While Chief Justice of the Supreme Court in postwar Japan, he gained prominence as an interpreter of the new constitution and also as an outspoken critic of Marxism at a time when few writers dared oppose it on intellectual grounds. In these selections Tanaka discusses the main trends of thought in modern Japan as they affect the success of democratic institutions.

[From Tanaka, *Shinri to heiwa o motomete*, pp. 30–195]

ETHICS AND POLITICS

Surveying the general trend of political thought in the modern world, and particularly in Japan, we may observe that its most striking characteristic is its ethical indifference. This reflects the domination of humanistic studies in the nineteenth century by the dogmas of natural science. After the Meiji Restoration, with the introduction into Japan of European and American culture, we ignored the ethical and religious bases of that culture, and sought only to adopt its natural science, its material technology, and its external institutions. The subsequent trend of Japanese political thought has further intensified that tendency. The only thing that has lent any ethical character at all to our political life has been the consciousness of our "national polity" and a sense of reverence for the emperor; but in recent times not only did these attitudes lead to superstition and a loss of sanity, but they developed into a form of ultranationalism which recognized no ethical restraints upon the nation's conduct and justified immoral policies of imperialistic aggression.

The Japanese people cannot be considered traditionally unethical. The enlightened leaders of the early Meiji Period themselves had faith in Buddhism and were trained in Confucianism, but the generation which followed them was exposed neither to the discipline of Oriental moral codes nor to the influence of that Christian faith which underlies Western culture. As a result they lapsed into ethical indifference or lack of conviction. Even among those who held certain moral convictions, the majority were politically uneducated. Consequently they were unable to rise above the narrow limits of nationalism and radicalism, and accepted without question the irreconcilability of individual morality and political morality. Since the war, though nationalism and racialism have been overcome, the same kind of inconsistency prevails among political leaders.

One serious weakness in our political thinking which has not yet been corrected is the attitude of relativism. In the postwar period, with the adoption of the new constitution, democracy and pacifism have been loudly acclaimed; but do our people today really have faith in these fundamental principles? Do they, in the bottom of their hearts, realize how greatly they have erred in the past, or do they take the attitude that, having been beaten, there is nothing else they can do? Do they not subscribe to these principles because, from the practical standpoint, they find themselves incapable at the moment and for the indefinite future of competing militarily with the other powers? Are there not some who, so long as Japan herself was not involved or devastated by a catastrophic war, would perhaps hope for other countries to become engaged in a war from which Japan might profit, like the proverbial fisherman who watches the birds fighting over their prey and then seizes it for himself?

One form of relativism devoid of any genuine conviction is a naive and uncritical historicism. More than ten years ago, when the political party system began to lose the confidence of the people, one powerful party figure made the following comment: "The corruption of political parties is a natural outgrowth of their having reached a stage of maturity. As history spirals upward, the corruption of party politics inevitably develops as a natural phenomenon, and its very development contributes to our future political health." Those who view things historically often speak of history repeating itself, or moving in spirals or cycles, or progressing in dialectical fashion; or of "life inevitably ending in death," or of "disappointment being the rule of life," and so on. However, many people who argue thus fail to realize that each historical situation must also be judged in its own particularity. They do not recognize that history should be evaluated in terms of the true and false, the good and bad. This is because historicism does not admit the absoluteness of Truth.

From such a standpoint both individuals and peoples are absolved of any moral responsibility. The denial of moral responsibility ultimately means the denial of that freedom which constitutes the reverse side of responsibility. And by the denial of freedom man is completely deprived of his moral dignity.

The same sort of error that is found in historicism appears also in that attitude of thought which attributes all evil to society or the environment. Take the case of the recent debate in the Diet on the condemnation of adultery. Those opposing the condemnation of adultery contended that adultery was a phenomenon resulting from the old family system which forced marriage upon persons not in love with one another. To punish them would not be right, some say. Others declare that under present circumstances it would be premature. Considered in terms of causal relations, there is no crime which is not the product to some extent of defects in social life. Murder, robbery, stealing—of all these it is true. Particularly is it true of the sensational case of the juvenile criminal recently condemned to death, whose conduct seems to have been a result of the extreme hardship of life in the postwar period, of the general deterioration of morals and of deficiencies in education. All this notwithstanding, man is endowed with free will, and is capable of using his rational faculties to distinguish right from wrong and good from bad. To attribute all evil to the environment is to negate the law and negate morals. The excusing of crime would never stop with adultery and juvenile crime alone. Such reasoning makes man the slave of his instinctual nature and robs him of the dignity of moral character. In such questions, therefore, there is absolutely no room for sentimentalism.

Man creates and shapes his environment by the exercise of reason and free will. In this lies the lofty mission of mankind, and politics too contributes to the realization of this mission. Politics, through the free actions of people, creates and shapes both history and the environment; it is not, contrarily, controlled by them. In politics man must be steadfastly true to himself.

In the same way man must control the blind, instinctual, and animal forces within him, and not be himself controlled by them. Where there is emancipation from instinct there is the freedom spoken of by Kant which is the true source of personal dignity. We cannot, however, be satisfied with an emancipation from the instincts which is purely negative, but must seek the meaning of human life so that the instincts can be made positively to serve the final end of human life. Man, freed from the compulsions of instinct, is not free in relation to the final end of human life. As distinct from animals, man purges instinct by raising it to higher levels; he sublimates it. And this relationship of man to instinct also exists in the relationship of the individual to history and environment.

This same relationship may also be seen in man's relation to economics. In the economy the economic activity of every individual constituting it is a manifestation of free will—just as in the case of history and environment—and yet in relation to the individual it may be looked upon in a sense as a law of necessity, being a phenomenon which derives in the main from man's most primitive instinct—the desire for self-preservation. Thus on the one hand, man drifts in the stream of the economy, and on the other he possesses the freedom to direct that stream toward the ultimate end of human life. In this sense, the economy is not the master of man, but man the master of the economy. [Marxian] historical materialism, however, turns this relationship upside down. All ideologies, according to this view, are no more than superstructures on the substructure of economics, and any economic change in the substructure must bring a change in the ideological superstructure. Man can do nothing to modify such a law of necessity. . . . So strictly speaking, to cry "Workers of the World Unite!" is contradictory. A union must be predicated upon some kind of aim, but as long as man is governed by the laws of necessity his adoption of some aim and his striving to realize it are inconceivable. . . .

Out of indignation over the evils produced by the capitalistic system and in particular by capitalist exploitation, as well as out of sympathy for the pitiful conditions of the working class, men uncritically embrace Marxism as the only way of salvation. They feel a conscious attraction to the "scientific" character of Marxism, and unconsciously they are drawn by its apocalyptic vision of the society to come. But they fail to realize that it is only partially scientific, or to ask what possible connection with "science" there can be in this Utopia appearing as if from Heaven at the end of history. Most followers of Marxism, and particularly the young, having no fundamental knowledge of Marxism, and simply being dissatisfied with society as it is, do not stop to consider whether or not there may be some more rational and natural way to reform society in accordance with human nature. Rather they put blind faith in this as the only means of solution, or uncritically accept the dictates of a press which is drunken with the power it has to exploit the weaknesses of human passions. There is no difference, fundamentally, between this and the attitude which allowed great numbers of people to be dragged along by Nazism. . . .

We must not be led astray by the language of the historical materialists who deny all moral values. Indignation over "exploitation" cannot be explained in terms of historical materialism, but only when one has recognized that fundamental principle of natural law which comes down from Rome: "give each according to his due" (*suum cuique tribuere*). Indignation is an ethical sentiment aroused by the capitalist's seizure of what rightfully belongs to the worker, that is, to an act contrary to justice. If the development of capitalism follows from necessity, then, just as with natural disasters, an attitude of resignation is all that one can adopt. There is no reason to feel such emotions as hatred or indignation.

As long as one refuses to accept that human relations are subject to moral control, all talk of "love" is absurd. So the historical materialist's appeal to the "love of the people" is nothing but pretense. . . .

Politics has as its end the realization of the common good (*bonum commune*), which is inconceivable apart from the mission or destiny of man. What, then, is man's mission? Is man's mission to be found apart from his individuality, as, for instance, in an organization embracing the individual or in the service of culture existing apart from man? Or does it lie in the perfection of each individual self? If it lies in the perfection of self, is it a corporal and material thing, or a spiritual and moral thing? Which of these is considered correct will vary according to the view of the world one holds.

From the standpoint of collectivism, the supreme value lies in organization. The individuals that represent its parts are absorbed into the organization which stands for the whole, and, serving it, are considered mere means for the enhancement of its power and prosperity. The extreme example of this point of view is Nazism, the errors of which need not be elaborated upon here. From the standpoint of "culturism," which places a supreme value on culture, the meaning of human life is to be found in service to culture, in the creation of cultural value. Nevertheless, just as organization should exist for the sake of man, culture should exist for the sake of man and not man for the sake of culture. In the last analysis man's value as an individual comes first and the value of organization or culture has no more than a subordinate significance.

But in what does the value of the individual consist? If one views the significance of human life in terms of man's material existence or economic life, then man is hardly different from the animals. Man consists of flesh and soul. While, on the one hand, being possessed of a fleshly body, he shares the instincts common to all animals, on the other hand he is able through the exercise of reason to discriminate between right and wrong, good and bad, and thus differs from animals in that he can restrain and direct these instincts properly. Human life has an ultimate end, and all human actions may be directed to that end and ordered by it. There are many characteristics which distinguish man from animals, but the most essential of them is morality. Both the state and culture lose their own reason for existence when they disregard morality, but obtain life through serving it.

So to the common good which is the aim of government, though the material and economic life is by no means negligible, the most essential thing is morality and all else is at best secondary in significance. . . . Our new Constitution is permeated with the "lofty ideals which govern human relationships," based on the universal principle of humanity, the laws of universal political morality, equity, good faith, justice, peace, freedom and order. Thus the primacy of morality is recognized in the conduct of both our domestic and foreign affairs. Moreover, those who discuss politics today, almost without exception, acknowledge the necessity for a moral transformation of our political life. But to achieve this will require of our political analysts that their whole world-view be reintegrated in this direction. That is, they can no longer insist upon the importance of morality while permitting themselves the contradictory view that, in fact, economics and military power take precedence over morality. . . . To think that democracy and freedom can exist apart from morality is the greatest error of our times. In politics, in economics, in education, in culture—in every aspect of life, the firm establishment of moral authority must take precedence over all else. [pp. 30–43]

ON AUTHORITY

An utter denial of the idea of authority could well be called the characteristic of our present era of transition. It had been thought that authority was the most essential property of militarism and extreme nationalism. Now that they have been driven to the wall and face extinction, it is thought that authority too must be banished with them.

Authority, however, is not the special property of militarism or extreme nationalism. Like "rights" or "freedom," it is not intrinsically either good or bad but ethically neutral. It works for good or ill depending upon the end it is made to serve. If authority is put in the hands of those to whom it does not rightly belong or conferred on those whose authority should not be recognized, evil and injustices will arise. Furthermore, authority is both absolute and relative, constituting a hierarchical relationship. When one with relative authority usurps absolute authority, evils and injustices also arise.

Let us consider first the government. In the old Constitution the supreme authority in government was the emperor, but in the new Constitution it is what is called "the people as a whole." . . . The Meiji Constitution was adopted unilaterally by the will of the emperor; it was a so-called "constitution by imperial grant." The new Constitution, however, was adopted by the Diet, that is, by representatives of the people. The people's right to adopt the supreme law of the land, or constitution, derives from their possession of sovereignty.

Even assuming that the people possess absolute authority in the matter of government, can the Diet in fact decide anything and everything by majority vote? There are some things which not even the English Parliament, which is recognized as having absolute authority, can do, such as change males into females. The majority vote of the people is likewise limited by the laws of nature and the principles of things, which may take the form of natural laws or the ethical laws of human society. The

[379]

constitution adopted by majority vote may not be in conflict with such fundamental principles. . . . When an actual law does conflict with them, then whether it be an ordinance, an edict or even a constitution, it becomes invalid.

If this interpretation is correct, then while the Constitution is the supreme law in relation to other actual laws, still . . . as an actual law itself, there stands above it, behind it and under it as a base, the natural law which represents truth and order in the universe. This natural law is what defines the limits of actual laws. It demonstrates that even the will of the people, though having the supreme authority in the adoption of a constitution, nevertheless is not absolute but is relative to and governed by a higher principle. Whether sovereignty rests with the majority of the people or with the emperor makes no difference. The question was never raised under the Meiji Constitution, but it should be understood that even the supreme will of the emperor cannot be in conflict with the natural law.

The third article of the Preamble [to the new Constitution] states that "the laws of political morality are universal," and the eleventh article asserts that "the basic rights of man are enduring and inviolable." Such laws—such natural laws—are not confined to one nation or one period of time. They endure, and they do so because they are founded on the true nature of man.

Therefore, to say that the people possess sovereignty and supreme authority is true in a formal sense, but intrinsically the people are limited by what in a true sense is the supreme norm: the natural law. To put it another way, it is truth itself which governs social life. In truth itself rests true authority. . . .

In regard to the fundamental political, economic, and educational reforms brought about at the end of the war, a segment of our population can be heard murmuring, "We were beaten and could do nothing else." Even among the better-informed strata of our society one may find those who think that the new Constitution does not merit serious study because it will not outlast the occupation but will be replaced by the Meiji Constitution as soon as the occupation forces are withdrawn. Lately I attended a conference of school principals in a certain prefecture and one of them said: "During the last war we were re-educated to conform with the national policies of that time. Now we are being re-educated again in line with completely different policies. Who is to say policies will not change again in the future? I am completely at a loss to know which is correct." . . .

On the other hand, in direct contrast to this type of man who tends naively to accept the external authority of the world about him, there is another type, idealistic and egocentric, who contributes greatly to the intellectual anarchy of our time. This type attacks sharply, and with reason, those who put their whole trust in external authority; but they go to frenetic extremes in asserting the authority of freedom and personality. They are conscientious, reflective, and spiritual to the extent of being, in a sense, religious; but they are frightfully self-righteous and self-opinionated, and will accept nothing which lies beyond their own experience. Denying all external authority, the self becomes the absolute authority. . . . From such a standpoint, in judgments of the true, the good, and the beautiful, there is no external standard at all—neither society, nor historical tradition, nor the church—but only the self alone. . . .

But what is the self after all? His consciousness and experience ceaselessly ebbing and flowing; his conscience and sincerity now sharp and then benumbed; his devotion and faith wavering constantly; his judgment easily swayed by selfish considerations and passions—man by himself is utterly helpless. He may be "thinking" but he is as frail as the "reed." And yet he proclaims that, in the spiritual world, he sits in the seat of the Roman pope. Brazenly he challenges a historical tradition which is the treasury of human culture preserved for several thousand years, and the heritage of the Church which has been conserved and developed for two thousand years.

Such personal egocentrism has no right to sneer at the fantastic race-centrism—or "all-the-world-under-one-roof"-ism—which for more than a decade tried to force upon us the idea that the Japanese people were the sole possessors of the truth.

Men of this type may not deny fundamentally the existence of God or of objective truth. But they fail to realize that their "God," their "Truth," is simply the mirror of one's own self with all its inherent imperfections. Consequently, though they may attribute authority to Truth or to God, in fact they are making themselves the supreme authority. Before we talk about "Truth" and "God," we must, like Socrates, know ourselves.

We have discussed now two trends which contribute to our contemporary confusion and decadence of thought. One is blind conformity to an external authority unworthy of trust; the other is that egocentrism which denies any kind of external authority. The former drives us to a fatalistic determinism, which negates the dignity of human life, effort, freedom, and personality, and sinks into materialism and historical materialism, which deny morality and religion. The latter regards the self as the ultimate judge of the true, the good and the beautiful, and by deification of self makes it the victim of megalomania. Burdening the self with too great a responsibility, it leads to a spiritual breakdown, with anarchy in politics and "non-churchism" in religion as its final outcome. . . .

Many intellectuals, representative of a decadent urbanity, have lost the ethical conscience of the peasant, his simple sense of right and wrong. They are either too "sociological" or too "subjective." . . . They may speak of truth or they may not, but as they fail to recognize objective and universal truth, they cannot give a clear "yes" or "no" to anything.

In truth rests true authority, and only God, the true authority, can reveal truth to man. What struck the crowd in Jesus was that he spoke "not as a doctor of the law or as a pharisee, but as one having authority." With the authority of God, he taught about God.

Truth, which rests upon the authority of God, determines the limits and provides the norm for the free actions of man. It is what gives man true freedom. "The truth shall make you free" (*Veritas vos liberabit*) (John 8:32). [pp. 48–61]

JAPAN IN THE WORLD

Situated at the extreme eastern end of the known world, an isolated island with her back to the Pacific, Japan has never achieved a position, culturally speaking, as a cooperating member of the international community. It is true that Buddhist and Confucian culture were introduced by way of Korea and imported directly from China; and that four hundred years ago Catholicism was introduced and showed signs of spreading with striking rapidity before being suppressed for political reasons. But in return for what Japan received from other cultures, what had she to offer other peoples?

Since 1868 European and American culture and institutions have been introduced to Japan, but whereas the assimilation of Buddhism and Confucianism had extended even to their underlying ways of thought, the transplanting of Western culture and institutions was done in such a way that they could send down no deep roots here. Our society has been culturally no more than a colony of Europe. . . . Faced by the urgent need to fashion a centralized state, to develop the material prosperity of the nation, to revise the unequal treaties which had humiliated us internationally, Japan could not help but take a superficial and imitative approach to the adoption of Western culture. What we imported was, in a word, the individualism of the Enlightenment and the material technology—the natural science—of the West. Such tendencies were quite characteristic of the exponents of Europeanization in the Meiji Era [1868-1912], who believed that this type of culture actually represented Western civilization. Therefore it was not at all surprising that in reaction to this there should have appeared the exponents of Japan's "national polity." They mistook individualism and materialism for Western culture, and opposed to it a Japanese culture stressing collectivism and the national spirit. . . . The surprising thing is that the exponents of Japan's national polity, who started out by upholding our traditional "spirit" and condemning the materialism of Western culture, should have become in practical politics the spokesmen for militarism and state power. . . .

At the beginning of her history Japan kept her doors completely open to the world. Today Japan finds herself thrown completely into the maelstrom of world politics and world culture. Because of this, we should remember, we have acquired new responsibilities to the peoples of the world and to our times. To fulfill these responsibilities is the highest destiny of the Japanese people. . . . Japan must not only fulfill her own peculiarly creative mission among the peoples of the world, but realize her universal mission. Japan possesses her own characteristic moral convictions and fine social traditions which are a legacy from Buddhism and Confucianism. Of these she must preserve all that is good. The Oriental peoples, including the Japanese, have always recognized the natural [moral] law. This [recognition of] natural law is the common spiritual basis uniting the cultures of East and West. To raise this natural morality to the supernatural plane is the high mission of Catholicism. Faith in her own national moral virtues, as perfected in Christianity, could be for a reborn Japan her qualification as a member of the world community of peoples, giving us for the first time in our history a sense of Japan's place

[383]

and mission in the world, and providing a spiritual bond between East and West, as well as a firm basis for world peace. [pp. 191–95]

HASEGAWA NYOZEKAN
The Lost Japan and the New Japan

During the early decades of the twentieth century Hasegawa Nyozekan (b. 1875) was a leading figure among the radical journalists who spearheaded the movement for democratic and social reforms. In his later years, however, this intransigent radicalism mellowed into a genial liberalism. Hasegawa has also been known as a novelist and critic.

The following is the conclusion to his book *The Lost Japan,* published in 1952. Reviewing the changes Japan has undergone in his own lifetime, and re-examining the whole Japanese cultural tradition, he seeks to determine which of its characteristic features are conducive to a democratic society and which must be modified if Japan is to advance in the modern world.

[From Hasegawa, *Ushinawareta Nihon,* pp. 275–90]

The American decrees issued with respect to freedom and democratization in the internal administration of Japan resulted in five major changes: the enfranchisement of Japanese women (through granting of the vote); the encouragement given to the formation of labor unions; the liberalization of school instruction; the abolition of institutions which tended to cause the people to live in fear; and the democratization of the economic structure.

These five great changes in the government of the nation followed a course which the history of the modernization of Japan and of the Japanese themselves would have taken anyway if left to its natural tendency; they were, in fact, the direction towards which Japanese history was pointed. The history of Japan since the early '30s was distorted by the mistaken designs of the men in power, but the process of modernization itself was uncompromisingly carried out. We should not forget that its penetration into the very core of the Japanese nation and people made possible a political system which could serve as the external structure for Japan's emergence as a sound, strong, free, and democratic country. It became a basic condition of the culture of the race. We must, therefore, examine whether or not the culture of the Japanese people today is of a nature capable of turning Japan into a truly and completely modern nation. We must also make ourselves aware of those elements in both our strong points and our shortcomings which must be changed.

During the Meiji Era the nation and people advanced boldly in the historical process of modernization which permitted Japan to break out of her isolation and stand among the nations of the world. When we reached the '30s, however, Japan was carried away by the tide of an age of world reaction, and there ensued a revival of feudalistic Japanese institutions. That our nation should have been plunged into destruction by the coercive force of a union of the military and civil proves that there had been no break in the "feudalistic" nature of the forms of our characteristic racial, political and social activities. This factor lent a special quality to our national culture, a quality destined to determine Japanese national and racial characteristics and to lead Japan to its tragic fate. Thus, as a basic condition for the reconstruction of Japan as a free and democratic nation, a change in our cultural nature itself must be planned and executed. . . .

The first question is whether a change in the cultural nature is in fact possible. There are cultural characteristics born from established tendencies in the psychology and acts which form the general pattern of the life of the Japanese people; in order to change them the Japanese would have to be liberated from the element of blind subordination in their lives and given individual independence. The nature of the primitive Japanese political and social structures was centripetal in that it was organized around the belief in a racial-religious family with racial groups dependent on it. The cultural nature was therefore also obliged to possess a unity and a standardization derived from the guidance and instruction of the force at the center. As a result ordinary life came to be governed by the same kind of dependence as political life, and the tendency which may be found throughout the Orient for the lower classes to ape the upper classes in their preferences was all the more intensified.

If this was an inborn cultural characteristic of the Japanese from which they could not deliver themselves, Japan would already be past saving. But, as far as I am aware, this is by no means the case. The Japanese have always had the cultural feature of absorbing anything they consider worthwhile. They have, accordingly, been blessed with a comparatively balanced cultural history since the country was founded, and they have also developed their cultural sensitivity in a balanced manner. In contrast to the common phenomenon (found all over the world) of "cultural" things being perfected and brought to full maturity by the upper classes of society, the Japanese were constantly diffusing the upper-class culture among the broad masses of the people, creating a rich cultural universality. This is undoubtedly an excellence of the Japanese national cultural background, but this excellence before long developed into a fault. As a result of the imitativeness which came from an admiration for "worthwhile" things, there was a tendency on the part of the common people to follow the dictates of the upper classes in all things from literature and art down to language, customs, and habits. Even though the cultural level of the people as a whole rose, this tendency blocked individuality and independence of thought.

In point of fact, most forms of Japanese culture originated with the lower classes and only later penetrated the upper classes. The native Japanese folk songs made their way into the court music which had been transmitted from the continent. The rustic entertainments of the people developed into the Nō, which formed part of the upper-class culture of the country when it was under military rule. The bourgeois culture of the middle of the Tokugawa Period completely dominated the culture of that period, and its modernity prepared Japan to accept the modern world culture when it was introduced during the Meiji Era. Numerous such examples prove the importance of the culture of the Japanese lower classes. The refined culture perfected by the upper classes after it had been transmitted to them from below was based on a system of subordination along the political and social lines I have described. Once perfected, it usually was then imitated by the whole people. Thus, although the culture of most of the country had a history of originally independent development, it could not refrain from indulging in imitation of whatever was deemed "superior."

Since the Meiji Era this attitude has assumed the form of the widespread adulation paid the superior imported Western culture, particularly by the middle and lower classes. This is quite distinct from the Europeanization favored for political purposes by the upper classes. In the 1880s it gave rise to the ideological and intellectual quest for freedom and democracy which soared over the normal evolution of Japanese history. In the 1920s it took the form of the blind adherence to "democratic" theories by the intellectual class, theories which, as far as the roots of Japanese society were concerned, belonged to the future and were quite divorced from reality. In a similar way this same characteristic feature became in the 1930s the attraction for the nationalistic policies of those military men and officials who joined the wave of reaction that had swept the European continent; it also became the cooperation on a cultural level based on this relation. It was thanks to this same characteristic that the jingoism of the military clique and the officials was able to dominate the activities of the nation.

We may thus see that the discovery of a new means of freeing ourselves from this attitude of subordination and of developing cultural characteristics of independence which can be shared by the entire people is a prerequisite to the reconstruction of the nation.

The first essential to achieve is an educational and cultural program which will permit the free development of the feelings and intellect of the Japanese. We must restore the cultural attitude held by the Japan of ancient times with respect to all aspects of life: that is, to maintain a receptivity which is free, unbiased, and diverse.

Second, there must be a switch from imitativeness to creativity. Japanese culture, now as in former days, has been said to be imitative in character. This is because Japan during the period from the earliest days to the Middle Ages was always in the position of being obliged to take in the cultural nourishment of China. In modern times she has been in the same position with respect to the West. However, the Japanese have invariably digested and absorbed these cultural influences once they had passed the stage of imitation, and thereby succeeded in creating a new and purely Japanese culture. This fact may be recognized everywhere when one examines the new forms which Japanese culture assumed in each period, beginning with the Heian. The fact that Meiji Japan was unable to display prominently such creativity was because, like Nara Japan, it had not yet reached the historical stage of being able to free itself sufficiently from imitation.

However, even in such a period of transition as this, unless at the same time that Japan is importing the superior world culture it also struggles to create cultural forms proper to our present historical stage, we will stagnate forever in a period of imitation: instead of emphasizing creativity we will merely be copying the culture of other countries. The real reason why Japanese politics, philosophy, literature, and art from the Meiji

Period to the present have always been engaged in such a frantic pursuit of Western trends is that we have not been able to display sufficient creativity in the development of our own cultural nature.

This failing was not in the least compensated for by the pretended "discovery" or "creation" of "truly Japanese" things, stemming from the cultural commands of the military clique during the war. Such activities were no more than a kind of "cultural self-consolation." They prevented an interchange of world culture in any true sense and must be considered the workings of an evil policy which turned the course of cultural creativity into a false pursuit. The "truly Japanese" things are not things which can be "discovered" or "created" in this manner; they must be a natural product obtained from a nationwide ability and means to create. Education and research must be for the sake of fostering such an ability throughout the country and for the promotion of a structure, organization, form, and content which would permit such a process to take place throughout the country. Once this is accomplished, we must reflect humbly on what are said to be shortcomings in the cultural nature of the Japanese and devote our attention to the further development of those things which are said to be our excellences.

Third, there must be a switch from the intuitive to the intellectual. Of course this does not in the least imply the exclusion of the intuitive, but merely indicates that we must direct our efforts towards turning in the reverse direction the cultural nature of the Japanese, which hitherto has had a propensity for the intuitive, until it shows instead a propensity for the intellectual.

Japanese politics have been controlled by traditional feelings and emotions and have always been guided according to illogical reasons. They have been deficient in political sense, and, being left at the mercy of blind political ambitions, have never been able to achieve a development paralleling the lines of modern history. This situation has arisen because politics have been completely in the grip of intuitive action. The practice of politics has been governed by political ambitions derived from a blind mentality which lies outside the domain of the intellectual. This mentality in turn has undoubtedly resulted from the suppression of the intellectual caused by the gravitational relations of the intuitive.

This phenomenon too stems from the emphasis which Japanese culture in general places on the intuitive. The fact that national movements do not assume an intellectual direction is a reflection of the intuitive culture. Japanese religious and academic culture have similarly tended to be governed by primitive mysticism and illogicality. The war was started as the result of a mistaken intuitive "calculation" which transcended mathematics. We believed with a blind fervor that we could triumph over scientific weapons and tactics by means of our mystic will, and that we could in this way secure final victory. This resulted from the fact that the characteristic reliance on intuition by Japanese had blocked the objective cognition of the modern world.

There are undoubtedly elements in Western concepts of liberty and democracy based on intuitions derived from bitter experiences of modern life. The respect in which they differ most from the popular movements of ancient times and the Middle Ages is that these intuitions have been able to secure an objective validity through a cooperation with the intellect. The Meiji Restoration was achieved as a result of the stimulus given to the evolutionary process of the nation and people by a racial intuition. However, if it had not been accompanied to some degree at least by a scientific—that is, intellectual—cognition of the modern history of the world, this intuition, like the intuition of the "self-awakening of the people" preached by the Kogaku School before the Restoration, would have made the central Japanese view of the world a mere delusion, and the future of the nation could never have developed as it did.

That the new Japan would have to be free and democratic had been so widely recognized by the intuition of the whole Japanese people as to be simple common sense ever since the Meiji Era. This intuition, however, was frustrated by the ill-informed, fantastical intuitions of subsequent leaders, and the nation came to accept their mistaken intuitions. The paucity of intellect in the cultural nature of the Japanese of the time made them so weak as to be powerless to act on their own intuitions. The Japanese, who are realistic and seldom given to fancy, did not actually lack intellect even in their intuitions, but they came to reject the Meiji-type education as being excessively practical, and turned to a more conceptual kind of education. This in turn encouraged the statesmen of the '20s and later in their attempts to destroy the importance of the intellect in Japanese culture.

It is absolutely essential that the Japanese cultural nature be switched from an intuitive to an intellectual one. We must turn from the conceptual education of the continental European type—particularly the German—favored since the late Meiji Era and return to the English and American models of the early Meiji Era.

Fourth, the hedonism generally characteristic of Japanese culture must be changed. The character of Japanese culture is one of always being both perfectly adapted to life and capable of holding fast to the realities and practical aspects of life, but on the other hand it tends also to divorce all forms of culture from the practical aspects of life and to fritter itself away in pleasures.

Experts have pointed out that one reason why the development of mathematics in the early seventeenth century—a development which by coincidence enabled Japanese to arrive independently at the discoveries which Newton was making at the same time—was suddenly brought to a halt in the late seventeenth century was that the Japanese began to play with mathematics as if it were a kind of game.

Such a tendency sprang from what is actually one of the strong points of Japanese culture—the insistence that culture in general be geared to daily life. But it was responsible for lowering a science of which Japan had just become aware to the level of an amusement, and prevented its further development.

This kind of cultural habit manifests itself as a regular tendency to turn culture of a serious nature into a subjective and spiritual (or active) amusement, and especially to make of it an intellectual sport for the intelligentsia. It sometimes happens that even the operations of the government and the administration of public safety are victimized by this tendency. One may find examples of it in the political and social movements from about 1910 to 1925, when there was a considerable amount of intellectual activity in the various movements for democracy, socialism, and communism. Instead of acquiring a sufficiently objective grasp of the worldwide characteristics of modern history, the intelligentsia took up, most impulsively and intuitively, "the inevitability of the reduction to desperation of the people," and made of their imitative blueprint an intellectual sport. This was why oppressive measures taken against these movements succeeded and why the movements themselves soon dissolved.

Now, when Japan is beginning on a new footing as a free and democratic state (as the result of the directions and guidance imposed on us by America), it may be wondered whether instead of making intellectual judgments based on a strictly objective cognition of the realities facing Japan, there is not a tendency to indulge in a subjective, cerebral development of the abstract ideas of "freedom" and "democracy." We may also wonder what the practical results will be. This problem, we must recognize, has its roots in the tendency which exists in our culture to provide itself with a mental satisfaction akin to amusement. In order to change such a cultural habit we must liquidate the kind of playful quality existing in our lives and culture.

Fifth, there must be a change from the artistic to the scientific. The artistic element in Japanese cultural life has frequently caused Westerners to talk of Japan as if it were a kind of never-never land, and it may indeed be said to be a cultural asset if considered merely in emotional terms. However, such a tendency must be suppressed in so far as possible if we are to proceed with the development of our nation and people in a correct and consistent manner.

This is especially true now when the national existence and the lives of the Japanese people have fallen into a desperate plight. We must think and act in a way which will permit us to overcome this crisis in an objective and scientific manner. For a whole people to have fallen into the habit of patching up things for the moment with improvised, unscientific attitudes and, methods indicates the prevalence of—if not precisely an "artistic" nature—a kind of dodge, which in a manner to be found also in literature and art enables one to imagine that one has conquered subjectively and cerebrally realities which cannot be objectively surmounted. To deal with the problem of the nourishment of people in the most dire and desperate straits as if hunger were something which could be avoided by spiritual means rather than physiologically, or lightly to be solved in accordance with individual taste or whim by following ancient dietary methods, is to make sport of life and death themselves, and is but one step removed from turning the problem into a work of art.

This situation has much in common with the psychology and attitudes of the warriors of the Middle Ages who made vengeance and disembowelment "artistic." Artistic leanings may indeed be considered to be a cultural asset of the Japanese as a way of helping us to endure and beautify the conditions of a difficult life. When, however, it comes to attempting to overcome a national emergency, these leanings seem, rather, a decorative pose devoid of validity or use.

[391]

It is obvious how unlikely it is that such decorative attitudes and methods can help liberty and democracy to permeate the structure of the nation and the lives of the people. We must be on strictest guard lest any tendency should develop for dealing with our present crisis with such words and gestures.

In order to end this proclivity, the whole of the Japanese and in particular the intellectual class must acquire the ability and habit of criticism of the national temperament by means of a self-awareness based on logic and knowledge. To achieve this we must induce our nation to possess a strong interest in science and eventually to reach the state of experiencing pleasure from scientific knowledge. The extremely practical scientific knowledge, unattractive as it may first seem, must be made a vital part of the practice of life.

We must change the world of the daily life of the Japanese into an environment for living in which we, who up to now have led most unscientific lives, will be given a scientific purpose and form. We will thus be enabled to breathe in a scientific atmosphere, just as a newborn babe drinks its mother's milk. This may seem an empty dream, but to the extent that this dream is realized the lives and culture of the Japanese will be given a scientific nature both internal and external—that is, both in men's minds and their actions. The cradle of the modern science of the West was in the world of their daily life itself. The Japanese too must create in their country and their daily lives an environment capable of being the independent cradle of a similarly scientific culture.

Along with a consideration of the proposed changes in the cultural nature of the Japanese, there is also the question of how strong the will is to acquire a modern character.

It is impossible to deny that most of the better educated classes of Japanese society were unhappy over the blind acts of the military clique and sought to prevent them. That their strength was inadequate to the task was due not so much to a deficiency of intellect as to a weakness of the will.

This will power can be strengthened by cultural education or by means quite outside the realm of culture. It is claimed that a Spartan militaristic training is more effective towards this end than an Athenian one, and that the reason why the Japanese educated classes of today are lacking in will power is that their education was Athenian. It is also stated that the victory by blind will power of the military men over the educated classes before the war was attributable to their Spartan training.

However, we must not forget that the Spartan, purposefully militaristic training hampers the development of human knowledge and leads to instinctive, impulsive brute will power. It furnished the impetus for the atrocity cases of Japanese soldiers on enemy soil. True will power of a kind fit for human beings cannot be supplied by such a training. It must come from the environment in which each man lives. If the statesmen at the time of the Restoration showed much greater will power than those of the 1910s and 1920s, it was because it had been given them by an environment of hardships at the end of the shogunate.

Viewed in this light, the difficult conditions under which the Japanese have lived since the defeat may be said to contain hope if we think of them as the environment for strengthening our will power and for molding us.

What I have related above about how freedom and democracy can be established permanently in Japan may seem rather remote from present problems. It may not be able to escape criticism as being what is popularly called "eye-medicine administered from the second story." However, until these basic cultural characteristics are completely changed, freedom and democracy in Japan, no matter what their formal claims may be, will be no more than borrowed clothing.

KAMEI KATSUICHIRŌ
Return to the East

Kamei Katsuichirō (b. 1907) first came into prominence as a left-wing critic, the violence of whose views once caused him to be sent to prison. After some years of association with the extreme left, however, he began to turn towards the traditional Japanese values, particularly towards Pure Land Buddhism and the art of the Asuka and Nara periods. His book *An Ideal Portrait of Twentieth-Century Japan* (1954) expresses Kamei's doubts about Japan's long efforts to become "modernized," and advocates a return to what he calls Asian ideals, particularly those of Gandhi. He thus returns to a position earlier identified with Okakura Kakuzō (1862–1913), an authority on Oriental art who was for many years at the Museum of Fine Arts in Boston.

[From Kamei, *Nijisseiki Nihon no Risōzō*, pp. 191–201]

One of the problems with which Japanese have been burdened since the Meiji Era has been the necessity of examining Japan's place in Asia and our special fate as Asians. Japan, as everyone knows, was the first country in Asia to become "modernized," but it is not yet clear what meaning this modernization had for Asia. It is also a question whether Asian thought, which possesses strong traditions despite the repeated taste of defeat and a sense of inferiority before Western science, is doomed to perish without further struggle, or if it is capable of reviving in the twentieth century and contributing something which will enable us to surmount the present crisis. We must begin to consider these questions. In contrast with the fervor with which Europeanization has been pursued since the Meiji Era, this aspect of our lives has been extraordinarily neglected. I believe that the neglect—or perhaps one should say ingratitude—shown by Japanese towards Asia is the tragedy of modern Japan, and that to study it has become since the defeat the greatest responsibility incumbent on us.

It is true, of course, that "Asia" covers an immense area, and undoubtedly contains many "spiritual kingdoms" with which I am unfamiliar. I myself have never actually journeyed through Asia; I have not so much as glimpsed it with my own eyes. The best I have been able to do is to imagine what Asia is like by means of the books I have read. Nevertheless, looking back on Japanese history has revealed to me that in every age Asia has breathed in the minds of Japanese. We are all familiar with how Asian culture, transformed or more highly refined, became part of the flesh and blood of Japanese culture. However, like most young men of the past sixty or seventy years, I used not to consider Asia as being necessarily primary to us. My ignorance of and indifference to China and India did not trouble me in the least, and I was constantly fascinated by Europe. I thought that to learn from European knowledge was our first task, and I neglected the matter of learning from the wisdom of the East.

There was something even more seriously wrong with my attitude. My ignorance and indifference with respect to China and India might still have been pardoned if they had been no more than that, but to them in fact was joined a feeling of contempt for those countries. Since the defeat I have come to recognize the fact that it was a fatal error for us to have allowed such a feeling to attain the status of a deep-seated national prejudice. Japan, thanks to the fact that she was the first country in the Orient to become "modernized" (or perhaps on account of her modern military strength), began from about the time of the Russo-Japanese War to entertain attitudes of extreme superiority towards the peoples of Asia. This feeling, we must remember, was the reverse of the medal of our feeling of inferiority towards the Europeans, and it came to express itself in a kind of brutality towards the other Asian peoples. We cannot deny that we tended to look on them as our slaves. When and how the fate of Japanese as Asians went astray is the most significant problem of our modern history.

"Asia is one. The Himalayas divide, only to accentuate, two mighty civilizations, the Chinese with its communism of Confucius, and the Indian with its individualism of the Vedas. But not even the snowy barriers can interrupt for one moment that broad expanse of love for the Ultimate and Universal, which is the common thought-inheritance of every Asian race, enabling them to produce all the great religions of the world, and distinguishing them from those maritime peoples of the Mediterranean and the Baltic, who love to dwell on the Particular, and to search out the means, not the end, of life." [1]

"[The average Westerner] was wont to regard Japan as barbarous while she indulged in the gentle arts of peace: he calls her civilized since she began to commit wholesale slaughter on Manchurian battlefields. Much comment has been given lately to the Code of the Samurai—the Art of Death which makes our soldiers exult in self-sacrifice; but scarcely any attention has been paid to Teaism,[2] which represents so much of our Art of Life. Fain we would remain barbarians, if our claim to civilization were to be based on the gruesome glory of war. Fain would we await the time when due respect shall be paid to our art and ideals." [3]

"What mean these strange combinations which Europe displays—the hospital and the torpedo, the Christian missionary and imperialism, the maintenance of vast armaments as a guarantee of peace? Such contradictions did not exist in the ancient civilization of the East. Such were not the ideals of the Japanese Restoration, such is not the goal of her reformation. The night of the Orient, which had hidden us in its folds, has been lifted, but we find the world still in the dusk of humanity, Europe has taught us war; when shall she learn the blessings of peace?" [4]

These words were pronounced about the time of the Russo-Japanese War. They voice profound doubts and resistance on the part of one

[1] Okakura, *The Ideals of the East*, p. 1.   [2] The cult of the tea ceremony.
[3] Okakura, *The Book of Tea*, pp. 7–8.   [4] Okakura, *The Awakening of Japan*, p. 223.

Oriental to certain important aspects of the modern European civilization which was then penetrating eastwards. This situation was not confined to Japan. There should have been common outcries made by men in India, China, and Japan, as Orientals. There should at least have been outcries which would have linked Gandhi and Tagore, Sun Yat-sen and Lu Hsün, and Okakura—outcries of surprise and alarm, or of doubt, or of malediction, or of resistance to the European conquest of Asia.

It should certainly be a matter of the profoundest regret to the Orient that these outcries uttered in the nineteenth and twentieth centuries as Asians, in inflections which varied with the particular features of the different countries of Asia, should never have achieved full expression, but should have died out without reinforcing one another. To us Japanese the most important fact is that the responsibility for causing these voices to die out rests with us. The cause of the tragedy lies in our vigorous, precipitous modernization. We tried with desperate efforts to master European civilization, and in the act of acquiring it we lost something very precious—what I should like to call the characteristic "love" of Asia.

We cannot ignore the fact that this responsibility is connected with the singularity of our racial transformation. The period between the appearance of Perry's "black ships" at the end of the shogunate, and the completion of the battleship *Yamato* was a period when Japan was changing with extraordinary rapidity into "the West within the East." Indeed, if one were asked for what Japan poured out her strength most lavishly, and to what she devoted the finest flower of her scientific abilities during the years following the Meiji Restoration, one would have to answer that it was for warships. This emphasis on armaments must certainly have had its origins in the profound anxiety of our grandfathers who had seen before their eyes the nations of Asia being colonized, one after the other.

It undoubtedly represented an astonishing burst of energy displayed for the sake of national independence and self-defense, but, as fate would have it, the raw materials of the continent were necessary to it. One gets the feeling that in the matter of raw materials and the acquisition of markets Japan was hastily and sometimes crudely imitating the colonial policies of the European nations. We, first among the Asians, mastered the weapons which modern European civilization had employed to invade Asia in pursuit of its colonial policies, and we turned the points of these weapons on Asians. The modernization of Japan would have been impossible had we not victimized China and estranged ourselves from her. Japan has experienced this contradiction at least as a historical fact. The high development of the intellectual curiosity of the Japanese has often been mentioned, but this virtue has been accompanied on the Asian mainland by deadly vice.

This is not the only contradiction. There were during this same period quite a few men like Okakura Kakuzō who preached love for Asia. Indeed, one thing which surprises us when we read the history of Japan during the past half-century is how often the phrase "to secure the peace of Asia" was used by statesmen. The invasion of China, in fact, was carried out in the name of this principle. In the midst of the so-called Greater East Asia War, I myself believed in Okakura's words and approved of the war because of them. What can this mean?

Every war, inevitably, has its fine slogans which serve as its intellectual adornment. But in my case this was not the whole story. As I have already mentioned, there was in me a deep-seated contempt for the other Asian peoples, a contempt nourished in Japan from about the time of the Russo-Japanese War; one may say that I had become imbued with the conqueror mentality. I could as an overlord of Asia preach with equanimity the love of Asia. And yet it was of course true that Okakura's words were meaningful only so long as Japan did not invade any Asian country.

Japan carried out the European method of conquest: confronting other countries with weapons in one hand and a gospel of love in the other. Warships and Christianity were indivisible elements in the European conquest of Asia; Japan slaughtered people while preaching the love of Asia and the Way of the Gods.

What was the result? Japan became in the East the stepchild of the West, and as a consequence seems now to be fated to become this time the stepchild of the East. The intellectual energy which the Japanese showed when once they had received the baptism of modern Europe was undoubtedly the wonder of Asia, but it imposed strange contradictions on Japan.

One of these, it may be imagined, results from the fact that Japan is an island nation. Japan is assuredly a part of Asia, but it is a special area separated from the continent and, perhaps, though Asian should not really be called Asian at all. Sometimes I have found myself wondering along these lines. Of course Japan is not the West either. While on the one hand preserving in a uniquely assimilated form the various systems of thought and arts of the East, she has an insatiable intellectual curiosity which would make all of the West her own. Has ever a people harbored such frantic contradictions: impetuosity and caution, confusion and harmony, division and unity—and all of them changing at every instant? I have sometimes wondered whether Japan may not be the unique example in the world of a kind of "nation in the experimental stage." It was this island nation's knowledge which, in response to a ceaseless impulsion towards Europe, perpetrated the multi-sided betrayal of Asia.

At the same time—and one may also speak of this as a result—the defeat of Japan brought about the independence of the nations of Asia. The long European rule of Asia either collapsed or was shaken at its very roots. This, together with the revolution in China, represents the greatest event occasioned by the Second World War; one may indeed say that it effected an immense upheaval in world history. A further result, one can probably say, was the ironic one that European capitalism, after playing its part in Japan, should have met this fate in the other countries of Asia because of Japan. Japan, it needs hardly be mentioned, lost all the territory she had gained through aggression.

However, an important factor came into being at this juncture. Now, for the first time in modern Japanese history, Japan was furnished with the conditions of being able to deal with the nations of Asia on terms of equality—not as conquerors or as conquered, but on a genuinely equal footing. I should like to lay emphasis on this factor for which our defeat was responsible. The basis for Japanese independence is to be found here—by which I mean that it is the only ethical basis we have for independence.

The true meaning of what I am attempting to discuss under the theme of "return to the East" may be said in the final analysis to be the product of a sense of guilt towards the East. The only qualifications we have for a "return" is a sense of guilt, particularly towards China and Korea. This is not a question of who holds political power in these countries. A more fundamental question is the recognition of guilt for former aggression towards the peoples of Asia. We must abandon completely the consciousness of being "leaders" in Asia. I should like to consider the return to Asia as an ethical rather than as a political question.

As a basis for this return Japanese traditions must be scrutinized afresh: how has what Okakura called the "common inheritance of every Asiatic race" been transmitted from ancient times to the present, and should it be passed on in the future? A re-examination of Buddhism, Confucianism, and Taoism as they exist in Japan, together with a general re-examination of the characteristically Japanese types of learning and art as they have been influenced by these teachings, must be undertaken. I should like to call attention to the steady achievements of men in the fields of anthropology, Japanese literature, Chinese studies, and Buddhist studies. It is a question of the *roots* of the tree onto which European culture has been grafted, and this re-examination is essential if we are to discover the "individuality" of modern Japan which gives a native character to all our thought.

At the same time there has never been a greater need than today for intellectual interchange among the nations of Asia. Some interchange, however slight, has been begun with India, but Japan must seek out opportunities throughout the whole of Asia to discover what the possibilities are of "Eastern spirit." However long it may take, I believe that a deepening of intellectual interchange should be made a basic policy. And, may we not say, the primary goal should be the discovery of a possibility of common spiritual association in the East. This is the prerequisite for the establishment of a new image of the Asian.

There are in Asia Buddhism, Mohammedanism, Christianity, Communism. European influence also remains powerful. Various systems of thinking thus exist, but they are backed by a characteristically Asian quality, and there is unquestionably one way of thought in which they are all unified through a process of "Asianization." This is what we must look for. However, in so doing we must free ourselves from any infantile notions such as the simple schematization formerly in vogue here, according to which the East stood for the spirit and the West for material things. Indeed, the return to the East must not be accompanied by prejudices directed against the West or any form of xenophobia. In fact, it should result in the destruction of the very sense of opposition between East and West which figured so prominently in our former ideas.

INDEX

[401]

[403]

130088